F. Scott Fitzgerald

F. Scott Fitzgerald

New Perspectives

EDITED BY Jackson R. Bryer
Alan Margolies
Ruth Prigozy

The University of Georgia Press

ATHENS AND LONDON

Set in 10 on 13 Electra by G & S Typesetters, Inc.
Printed and bound by Maple–Vail
The paper in this book meets the guidelines for
permanence and durability of the Committee on
Production Guidelines for Book Longevity of the
Council on Library Resources.

Printed in the United States of America

04   03   02   01   00   C   5   4   3   2   1

Library of Congress Cataloging-in-Publication Data

F. Scott Fitzgerald : new perspectives /
edited by Jackson R. Bryer, Alan Margolies,
and Ruth Prigozy.
      p. cm.
   Collected essays of the First International
F. Scott Fitzgerald Conference, held at
Hofstra University in 1992.
   Includes bibliographical references and index.
   ISBN 0-8203-2187-7 (alk. paper)
      1. Fitzgerald, F. Scott (Francis Scott), 1896–1940
— Criticism and interpretation — Congresses.
I. Bryer, Jackson R.   II. Margolies, Alan.
III. Prigozy, Ruth.   IV. International F. Scott Fitzgerald
Conference (1st : 1992 : Hofstra University)

PS3511.I9 Z6139 2000
   813'.52 — dc21   99-088355

British Library Cataloging-in-Publication Data available

CONTENTS

INTRODUCTION

The essays collected in this volume are the outgrowth of the first International F. Scott Fitzgerald Conference, which was held at Hofstra University in 1992 and sponsored by both the university and the recently formed F. Scott Fitzgerald Society. The society was founded because it had become clear to many Fitzgerald scholars that the writer was losing ground among academics; the *Fitzgerald/Hemingway Annual,* an important source of scholarly and critical material for ten years, had been discontinued in 1979. There was thus no central publication for Fitzgerald essays, notes, commentary, reviews of contemporary scholarship, and queries about ongoing research. Many author societies had been established in the past two decades, and it seemed apparent to Fitzgerald scholars that such a central organization that would, on the one hand, serve as a clearinghouse for Fitzgerald studies and, on the other, serve as a stimulus to further research was badly needed. Thus, in 1990, the F. Scott Fitzgerald Society was founded, and its annual publication, the *F. Scott Fitzgerald Newsletter,* has since provided members with information about ongoing activities, scholarly as well as public events, connected with the author.

The 1992 conference was the most important early activity of the society, which is based at Hofstra University; it was held to create an academic forum for scholars and the general public interested in F. Scott Fitzgerald to come together to discuss their own work, to review recent scholarship, and, most important, to point to new directions for future scholarship. The conference was remarkably successful: more than two hundred people attended, and more than seventy scholarly papers were presented. This volume represents only a fraction of those papers; but, in our view, each essay published here fulfills a need in Fitzgerald scholarship that the conference itself attempted to meet. Each essay has been revised for publication. We believe that these essays represent the new direction that Fitzgerald scholarship is taking.

The interaction of scholars at the conference produced far-ranging results. The joint Fitzgerald-Hemingway Conference held in Paris in 1994 and the Centenary Conference at Princeton University in 1996 each featured many outstanding scholarly contributions. The *Fitzgerald Newsletter's* annual bibliography indicates that, since the society was formed and these scholarly conferences have been held, drawing participants from throughout the United States and abroad, interest in Fitzgerald has grown, major new books have been published, and the future of Fitzgerald studies in the academy is secure.

Because fully annotated bibliographical essays of Fitzgerald scholarship are readily available in the volumes edited by Jackson R. Bryer, *Sixteen Modern American Authors* (1973) and *Volume 2* (1989), as well as in the annual chapter on Fitzgerald and Hemingway in *American Literary Scholarship*, a brief survey of Fitzgerald scholarship will suffice here to place these new essays in an appropriate critical perspective. We believe that this collection will help to fill some of the gaps in Fitzgerald scholarship cited by Bryer and others in their earlier surveys.

The first significant date in the Fitzgerald revival is 1945, when *The Crack-up* and *The Portable F. Scott Fitzgerald* appeared. (Bryer's *Critical Reputation of F. Scott Fitzgerald* [1967] traces contemporary reviews and critical commentary on Fitzgerald from the 1920s through 1965.) Budd Schulberg's fictionalized tale of his relationship with Fitzgerald, *The Disenchanted*, appeared in 1950 and was later made into a play. In 1941, there had been a brief flurry of attention when Edmund Wilson's edition of *The Last Tycoon* appeared, but it was not until 1951, with the publication of Arthur Mizener's best-selling biography, *The Far Side of Paradise*, and Malcolm Cowley's selection of Fitzgerald's short stories, that scholarly interest in Fitzgerald began in earnest. Alfred Kazin's collection of essays, *F. Scott Fitzgerald: The Man and His Work*, published in the same year, reprinted the most important essays and reminiscences from 1920 to 1950 and reminded readers of the significance of this neglected writer. The years from 1951 through the early 1970s were a period of rediscovery, marked by publication of hitherto unavailable Fitzgerald works, as well as the quarterly *Fitzgerald Newsletter* (1958–68) and some important critical books, notably those by James E. Miller Jr. (1957), Sergio

Perosa (1965), Richard Lehan (1966), Milton R. Stern (1970), and John F. Callahan (1972).

Fitzgerald scholarship continued to prosper in the 1970s, with the publication of the *Fitzgerald/Hemingway Annuals*, edited by Matthew J. Bruccoli, who was largely responsible for the availability of so much new Fitzgerald material. John Kuehl and Jackson R. Bryer also edited the Perkins-Fitzgerald correspondence and *The Basil and Josephine Stories* in this period. As Bryer's bibliographical essays note, however, most of the attention focused on *The Great Gatsby, Tender Is the Night,* and a half-dozen of the short stories, with only scant attention paid to the three other novels and to the more than 130 other short stories and essays. Bryer also observes that from 1951 to 1967 relatively few new theses had been advanced and very few new approaches had been attempted. But the biographies and personal reminiscences had continued: Andrew Turnbull's memoir-biography (1962), Sheilah Graham's several accounts of her relationship with Fitzgerald, beginning with *Beloved Infidel* (1958), and later volumes by Tony Buttitta (1974) and Frances Ring (1985). In 1970, Nancy Milford's feminist biography of Zelda Fitzgerald caught the public's attention at the beginning of the women's liberation movement. In the 1980s, important new biographies of Fitzgerald appeared by Matthew J. Bruccoli (1981), André Le Vot (1983), Scott Donaldson (1983), and James R. Mellow (1984). Both Fitzgerald's granddaughter, Eleanor Lanahan, and Sheilah Graham's son, Robert Westbrook, published biographies of their mothers in 1995.

In the 1970s and 1980s, critical commentary on Fitzgerald's work continued to concentrate on the major works, but a variety of new approaches began to appear: motifs and metaphors that run through his fiction, the role of place, feminist criticism, stylistic studies, and the role of politics. Since 1972, with some 160 essays, notes, and book chapters on *The Great Gatsby*, one might well wonder if there is anything left to say about that masterpiece; but Ronald Berman has answered that question resoundingly with two seminal works, *"The Great Gatsby" and Modern Times* (1994) and *"The Great Gatsby" and Fitzgerald's World of Ideas* (1997). Although some approaches to *Tender Is the Night* have been similar to those that address *Gatsby, Tender* has also benefited from a number of psychoanalytic studies, which reflect the subject matter of the text.

The two most important scholarly contributions to the study of Fitzgerald's short stories appeared in 1982 and in 1996, both edited by Jackson R. Bryer. The first, *The Short Stories of F. Scott Fitzgerald: New Approaches in Criticism* (1982), contains ten general essays on Fitzgerald's stories, followed by twelve pieces on individual stories, four of them receiving critical attention for the first time. The second collection, *New Essays on F. Scott Fitzgerald's Neglected Stories* (1996), goes far to fill the void in criticism of all but a handful of the short stories. In this volume, which contains twenty-three essays, even the most neglected stories receive full attention, and hitherto forgotten gems are rediscovered. And finally, the story groups — the Josephine stories, the Philippe stories, and the Pat Hobby stories — receive careful scrutiny after only intermittent and cursory attention over a fifty-year period.

Other important contributions to the study of F. Scott Fitzgerald have been made in recent years: the Cambridge editions of *The Great Gatsby* (1991) and *The Love of the Last Tycoon* (1993), edited by Matthew J. Bruccoli, and *This Side of Paradise* (1995), edited by James L. W. West III; the *Reader's Companion to F. Scott Fitzgerald's "Tender Is the Night"* (1996), edited by Matthew J. Bruccoli and Judith S. Baughman; the Fall 1997 *Resources for American Literary Scholarship* essay, "Prospects for the Study of F. Scott Fitzgerald" by James L. W. West III; a collection of essays from the 1994 Fitzgerald/Hemingway Conference in Paris, *French Connections; Fitzgerald and Hemingway Abroad* (1998), edited by J. Gerald Kennedy and Jackson R. Bryer; and the forthcoming *Cambridge Companion to Fitzgerald*, edited by Ruth Prigozy.

Despite all of the critical material outlined above, we believe that the essays in this volume represent genuinely original and provocative approaches to works that have received wide critical attention as well as several that have never been discussed in a critical context. Each of these essays draws fruitfully on an awareness of previous scholarship while at the same time providing fresh avenues of critical inquiry. This is the first collection of original essays devoted to the full range of Fitzgerald's fiction issued by an American publisher. The only previous such book is A. Robert Lee's *Scott Fitzgerald: The Promises of Life* (1989), published in England.

The first four pieces are personal responses to F. Scott Fitzgerald either by those who knew him (Schulberg and Ring) or those whose lives he affected deeply (Scribner and Garrett), and were presented as informal talks. Budd Schulberg knew Fitzgerald during one of the most difficult periods of the latter's life. His account of their experience working for Walter Wanger on the film *Winter Carnival* is not the first he has given, but in many ways, it is the most moving. For Schulberg, the passage of half a century has served only to heighten his own response to Fitzgerald's torment, to feel once again a deep regret that this great writer would never know — except perhaps in his own heart — that he would one day achieve the recognition he craved. (Recently, screenwriter Maurice Rapf has offered a somewhat different account of Fitzgerald and Schulberg at Dartmouth in the collection of reminiscences of the Hollywood Blacklist, *Tender Comrades*, edited by Patrick McGilligan and Paul Buhle [New York: St. Martin's Press, 1997], 496–539.) Frances Kroll Ring worked for Fitzgerald as his secretary during the last eighteen months of his life. Her memories are as vivid as Schulberg's as she conveys the force of Fitzgerald's personality; working for this genuinely charming man, she says, was a "series of dramas."

Charles Scribner III brings the perspective of a publisher to his thoughts on Fitzgerald, indeed the firm associated with Fitzgerald throughout his career. Scribner did not know Fitzgerald, but the writer nevertheless has been part of his life as a Scribner and as a Princetonian. As an art historian, Scribner also adds a valuable appreciation of the Cugat painting on the original dust jacket of *The Great Gatsby*. This section concludes with noted writer George Garrett's sense of the impact of Fitzgerald's work on that of other American writers, like himself, of what Fitzgerald meant to Garrett's generation and to the younger generation of American writers. Garrett, also a Princetonian, offers a creative writer's appreciation of *Tender Is the Night* and of the slight but important tissue of connections between him and Fitzgerald.

The next group of essays concerns Fitzgerald's novels. All of the novels receive extended consideration, each essay bringing a fresh perspective to such relatively neglected works as *This Side of Paradise*, *The Beautiful and Damned*, and *The Last Tycoon*, as well as to the two novels that have received ample scholarly consideration over the years, *The Great Gatsby* and *Tender Is the Night*.

Nancy P. Van Arsdale offers a highly original reading of *This Side of Paradise*, rejecting the accepted view of the novel as bildungsroman in favor of the author's efforts to interpret what was for him the supreme symbol—Princeton University. Van Arsdale sees Princeton as the center of his universe, signifier of the divine, or paradise, "temporarily gained, inevitably lost, never forgotten," a modernist's redefinition of Eden through which Fitzgerald interpreted his world. Catherine B. Burroughs provides an equally new approach to *The Beautiful and Damned*. Even though feminist criticism has long been addressing Fitzgerald's fiction, this paper is unusual in that, first, it approaches the problem in this particular novel, and second, it argues that Fitzgerald evokes the inconstant narrative voice employed by Keats in "Lamia" to create an ambivalence that questions the desirability of idealizing erotic love. Keats has long been seen as a major influence on Fitzgerald; previous analyses have primarily found that influence in *Tender Is the Night*, and few have dealt with "Lamia." Burroughs's analysis is thus a genuine contribution to the study of that influence. Steven Frye offers another reading of *The Beautiful and Damned*, as he traces the effect of Fitzgerald's Catholic upbringing on this novel, in imagery and structure that reflect a specific and concrete aspect of Catholic theology, the Eucharist. Frye argues that Fitzgerald sees the material world as eucharistic in nature, a system of signs and signification processes whose referents are immaterial and mystical. Again, Fitzgerald's Catholic background has been addressed previously, but never with respect to *The Beautiful and Damned*; Frye's essay is detailed, specific, and, above all, original in its perspective.

The four essays on *The Great Gatsby* all approach this much-discussed novel from new vantages. *Gatsby* has generally been praised as a masterpiece of structure, but Richard Lehan examines its inconsistencies as a constructed text, a text that takes its being from what is dominant at a historical moment in narrative modes. Lehan notes that the novel takes its meaning from the play between romantic and naturalistic narrative modes, and then examines specific discrepancies in the text. André Le Vot offers an unusual comparison — Fitzgerald and Proust — but he demonstrates that an analysis of common technical approaches used by both writers deepens our understanding of *The Great Gatsby*, as if Proust, "in his fuller, more explicit treatment of the same theme, offers an enlightening commentary on what is merely suggested in Fitzgerald." Scott F. Stoddart looks at the 1974 film adaptation of *The Great Gatsby* primarily through its failure to replicate Nick Carraway's masculine perception, similar to the "gaze" identified by feminist critics. In his unusual analysis of the film, Stoddart finds that director Jack Clayton, by altering Nick's gaze, strips the character of his narrative power, and in so doing, weakens the film irreparably. The last essay on *The Great Gatsby* raises the problems faced by a translator of this prototypically American novel into French. Michel Viel, whose translation appeared in 1991, illustrates the choices he made throughout the process. One might assume that the rendering of proper names, titles, and allusions would be straightforward, but as Viel meticulously demonstrates, it is not. The title in French, *Gatsby le magnifique*, may be an over-translation, but if we consider that the formal distinctions in English for physical size and moral and intellectual greatness do not exist in French, we understand the translator's dilemma. Consideration of only one of the problems in translation, as Viel points out, illuminates the choices a translator must make throughout the process.

Dana Brand regards *Tender Is the Night* as a novel about tourism; he sees Fitzgerald using tourism in Europe as a metaphor for modernity. Brand describes consumerism as a primary symptom of the modern era and the tourist as the ultimate consumer. He carefully examines Fitzgerald's opening chapters, which establish the centrality of tourism, and considers the influence of Spengler (an influence previously noted primarily in discussions of *Gatsby*) on Fitzgerald's ideas about modernity.

The final essay in this section, Robert A. Martin's discussion of Fitzgerald's use of history in *The Last Tycoon*, notes that most historical studies of Fitzgerald have centered on *Gatsby* and *Tender Is the Night*. His reading suggests that Fitzgerald's use of history divides itself into two very distinct categories, mythical history and factual history. Martin believes that Fitzgerald's use of history is most complex and sophisticated in *The Last Tycoon*. He analyzes three primary and related levels of American history that Fitzgerald employs in the novel: heritage (Andrew Jackson allusions), symbolic associations (presidential names), and parodic and comic (contrast between the tycoons of the past and the shallow Hollywood illusionists of the present).

The third section of this collection is devoted to Fitzgerald's short stories and essays, which continue to demand serious critical attention. In his essay on "Winter Dreams," Quentin E. Martin observes that feminist criticism of Fitzgerald's fiction has tended to focus on the novels and to ignore the women in the short stories. He turns his attention to Judy Jones and offers a revisionist view of a young woman who has generally been regarded as a femme fatale. John Kuehl examines a truly neglected short story, "Outside the Cabinet-Maker's" (until now, only one critical essay has dealt with this story), linking it with "Babylon Revisited," where the father-daughter relationship conveys larger concerns of the author—here, the inevitability of human loneliness. Barbara Sylvester addresses textual problems in "Babylon Revisited," attempting to correct errors that offer contradictory details that confuse a crucial issue: the change in Charlie Wales resulting from his ability to identify a unifying purpose in his life. The essay focuses on one particular line, erroneously printed, that can affect the substance of the story, and then examines other emendations, demonstrating finally how even the smallest revision changes the artistry of Fitzgerald's story and at the same time illustrates how great a literary artist Fitzgerald was. Richard Allan Davison's approach to the same story is quite different: he sees the autobiographical elements in "Babylon Revisited" as crucial to understanding the work, concluding that Fitzgerald transmits some of his own guilt feelings, his need for self-justification, and his near despair through his protagonist, Charlie Wales.

The next three essays concern Fitzgerald's late writing: the "Crack-up" essays, the *Esquire* stories, and the Philippe, "Count of Darkness," group. Bruce L. Grenberg rebuts the commonly held assumption that the "Crack-up" essays are merely Fitzgerald's personal confession of a mental and psychological breakdown in the 1930s. He sees the form of the essays as anything but simple and suggests that some of the depths of Fitzgerald's imagination are reflected in these writings, depths deriving from Fitzgerald's notion of his own expanded self and from his identification with America and American history. They are, for Grenberg, sophisticated fictions written in the genre of "confession-anatomy." Edward J. Gleason explores the stories Fitzgerald wrote for *Esquire* in the last years of his life (some of which were published posthumously). He notes that the pieces create a subtext that deepens our understanding of Fitzgerald's artistic and personal troubles during his final years. Drawing on such critically neglected stories as "Design in Plaster," "On An Ocean Wave," "The Long Way Out," "An Author's Mother," "Author's House," and "I Didn't Get Over," he traces a pattern of loss, desperation, weariness, and guilt that sheds new light on Fitzgerald's problems in the months when he was also writing *The Last Tycoon*. The last essay in this section, by H. R. Stoneback, is only the second major discussion that focuses exclusively on the series of Philippe stories Fitzgerald wrote for *Redbook* in the mid-1930s. Stoneback reassesses the character of Philippe and opens a new line of inquiry through consideration of the Catholic elements in these stories. He also examines the Fitzgerald-Hemingway relationship and suggests that Hemingway's most direct response to Philippe-as-Hemingway may be found in Hemingway's play *The Fifth Column*.

The final essay in this collection points to further consideration of Fitzgerald's place in the American tradition. Edward J. Gillin comments on Fitzgerald's desire to be one of the greatest writers who ever lived, and on his wish to emulate some of these figures. One of them was Mark Twain; Gillin shows how Fitzgerald absorbed the Mark Twain legend from boyhood. He also examines the role of H. L. Mencken, who bridged the worlds of Twain and Fitzgerald. Gillin notes the similarities in the two writers' concerns and argues persuasively that Twain was in important ways a model of the American writer for F. Scott Fitzgerald.

We believe that this collection of essays marks a new phase in Fitzgerald criticism; Fitzgerald has now been securely established as one of the greatest writers of the twentieth century. As new readers and scholars discover him, new insights and perspectives develop. We trust this collection reflects those insights and perspectives and reaffirms the importance of F. Scott Fitzgerald in American literature as we enter the new century. We also hope it encourages further commentary on the hitherto largely neglected subjects it explores — *This Side of Paradise*, *The Beautiful and Damned*, the essays, and the less-studied stories. The volume also should stimulate others to use some of the new approaches it offers and apply them to the full range of the Fitzgerald canon.

For significant assistance in preparing the manuscript, we wish to thank Marc Singer and Tammy Oberhausen Rastoder. For their patience and their confidence in this project, we thank the University of Georgia Press, especially Karen Orchard.

PART ONE

Personal Responses

Remembering Scott

BUDD SCHULBERG

I felt a strange sense of unreality—as if I were in a dream—attending the first International F. Scott Fitzgerald Conference in 1992. But mainly it was Scott's dream that I was experiencing fifty-two years after (how vivid it still seems) being with him in his little apartment just off Sunset Boulevard and asking him to inscribe a book for me, a book I loved called *Tender Is the Night*.

Some memories dim, but not the ones I hold of him: talking to him about the work he was involved in then, *The Last Tycoon*, and seeing him in very modest surroundings compared to the glamorous Hollywood everyone read about—the great mansions in Beverly Hills, the stars, the glitter, and the big cars. His was a very modest place just around the corner from Schwab's Drugstore. Feeling the struggle that Scott was enduring, I couldn't help wondering if he'd make it—and what would happen to him if he didn't.

That was the miracle, for me to be standing at the conference delivering an account of my memories of Scott, flashing back, with the young me of my midtwenties standing beside me, leaning over Scott's shoulder to read something he had just written. To me it was miraculous that so many years later, after the kind of despair that Scott had expressed to me, we would gather for what I can only consider a Fitzgerald Festival. God knows, it was well earned—and hard-earned. It was a celebration of the remarkable gift that this man had and that too many overlooked at the time of his death.

This fate seems to be the cross that too many artists have had to carry. Of course Van Gogh comes to mind, but I think also of Melville's *Moby-Dick*. In an anthology of famous American writers published around 1900, there was no mention of Melville. Exactly the same thing happened to Scott. A number of studies of American novelists published in the early 1940s neglected even to mention the name of Scott Fitzgerald.

When you think about his work, even the imperfect works — the successful but somewhat sophomoric *This Side of Paradise*, the strangely prophetically titled *The Beautiful and Damned, Gatsby, Tender Is the Night*, and the unfinished symphony of *The Last Tycoon* — I think we all sense that the special quality that Scott Fitzgerald had was one we talk so much about, and hear a little too much about before every presidential election: the American Dream. We hear a lot of glib things about the American Dream, but in reading Scott Fitzgerald you do get a sense — and maybe that's why he's come back so strong and will survive — that he was the master of the American Dream. I guess he dreamt a lot back home in St. Paul. He dreamt about getting up in the world, dreamt a lot of material dreams. The American Dream was his subject: Where do we want to go in America? The wide open possibilities of life in America. What Gatsby was able to accomplish and the money he was able to accumulate regardless of how he accumulated it. But what does he want to do with it? What does he want it to mean? What does he want to do with that dream? And why does that dream often turn to nightmare, as it did in *Gatsby*, and as it did with Dick Diver in *Tender Is the Night*? And don't think it wasn't going to happen with Monroe, the "Stahr" in *The Last Tycoon*.

The tension between the ideal American Dream and the reality was what haunted Scott. I think it haunted him personally and tore him apart at the same time that it inspired and intensified his body of work. But I leave the analysis to the devoted scholars of his overall plan. As one of the few people left who had the privilege — by odd luck, really — to know him, to work with him, and also, incidentally, to like him, my job is to relate him to you.

I liked Scott enormously almost from the moment that we met, under not the best of circumstances. I was surprised when a mutual friend of ours, our fellow novelist John O'Hara, wrote somewhere that Scott Fitzgerald was not a very likable man. I found him quite the contrary. If you had not known he was a writer, if you had not known that he had written, if you didn't admire those books, I think you still would have found him, as I did, absolutely irresistibly appealing.

Here's exactly how I met him. I was a few years out of Dartmouth College and back in Hollywood where I had been raised. I had written a treatment for a movie based on our Dartmouth Winter Carnival called, with great originality, *Winter Carnival*. My producer was Walter Wanger, the man who had sponsored my going to Dartmouth. He had also gone there, and as Hollywood producers go he was fairly literate and was considered highly sophisticated. Sophisticated or not, he told me when I came into his large office on the Sam Goldwyn Studio lot that he thought my treatment was "lousy."

"Well," I said, "I actually wasn't crazy about the idea either. I didn't see a great story. I didn't see *War and Peace* in *Winter Carnival*. I'm just trying to make a living here."

Walter said, "So I think what we'll do is—"; I thought I was being fired. But instead he said, "What I think I'll do is put another writer on it with you." That was a common practice in those days, to get two writers, often two strangers, to work together as a team. That was more common than anybody writing his own work.

I sighed and said, "Okay, well who?"

"Scott Fitzgerald," he said.

I gulped and thought to myself, "Oh my God!" I had seen him briefly with Dorothy Parker about three years before, and he had looked ghostly white and frail and pale, so I said to Walter Wanger, "Scott Fitzgerald? Didn't he die?"

Walter said, "Scott's in the next room. And he's reading your treatment."

So I went in and there was our hero, there was Scott. There was Scott Fitzgerald indeed reading his way through all of my forty-eight or so pages of *Winter Carnival*. I sat there while he finished reading it. "Well, it's not very good," he said finally.

"I know it," I said. "I know it's not very good."

"Well," he said, "Walter wants us to work together."

I couldn't quite believe it, but I said, "Fine." We talked a little just about the practicalities—how we'd meet and how we'd work.

The next day we met about ten o'clock. I told him that in the honors program in my last year of college I was able to structure my own sociology course. I chose "Sociology and the American Novel." I had read a lot of his novels for the course—almost everything he had written, including the short stories. I told him how much I admired him and what I thought of *The Great Gatsby*, which I still think is one of the most perfect short novels I've ever read. I've read it backwards, forwards, taken it apart, read the holograph, and studied his editing. I still think it's one of the most incredible works of fiction that I've ever read. And there are passages in *Tender Is the Night* that—I said it then and I say it now—are unequaled in American writing. I don't think anyone in American fiction writing has ever matched some of its qualities, especially its feeling.

Anyway, I told him I knew these books and I liked them a lot, putting it mildly. Scott was amazed. He said, "I didn't think anybody your age read any of those books. You know they're practically out of print." I think he said he'd made thirteen bucks in the previous year; he said he had only sold three copies of one and five of the other. He kept saying, "I'm surprised that anybody your age reads me anymore." I said, "I have a lot of friends that do." That was only partly true. Most of my radical, communist-oriented peers looked on him as a relic. He complained that he was having a tough time, all those books out of print. He hadn't been able to make a living in a long time. The short story market had dried up, he had been dropped at MGM, and that's why he had taken this stinking job. He could get quite a lot of money for it. I was getting two hundred a week, and Scott was getting almost two thousand a week. That was an awful lot of money, but it could end very quickly. But I'm getting ahead of my story.

Anyway, we met and met, day after day, and we talked a lot about writers and writing. We compared "his" writers with "my" writers, you might say. We talked about Steinbeck and James T. Farrell. He talked about Hemingway — he seemed fairly obsessed with Hemingway — and we talked about just about everything but *Winter Carnival*. We were having a tough time even thinking about *Winter Carnival*. We would talk for hours, and, as I said, I found him just enormously likable. I was fascinated by him, and he talked very easily and openly. After about four or five days, it reminded me of sitting around a campus dormitory room in one of those bull sessions, talking about all the things we both shared and enjoyed. Every once in a while we would say to each other, "We've got to talk about *Winter Carnival*." But it was more like an afterthought. We'd say yes, and try to get on with it. But it was difficult.

Walter Wanger called us at the end of that week and asked us how we were getting along. Scott looked at me and said, "We're getting along fine. I like Budd. We're getting along. We seem to be very congenial." In Hollywood there's almost a course in the Screenwriters Guild on how to lie to your producer. If he asks you how you're doing, you say, "Oh, great. It's great. We feel very good about it!" But the trouble started when Wanger said, "Well, you'd better have an outline by the time you leave. We're going up to the Winter Carnival. We're flying out Monday." Scott said, "Walter, I really don't think that's necessary. Budd's only been out of there two or three years and he certainly knows what a Winter Carnival looks like. And I remember college parties from my Princeton days. I doubt they've changed that much. So I really don't see the need for making that trip." Walter came down on him hard: "Scott, I insist on it. You're going. You have to go." He wouldn't let him out of it. While I felt sorry for Scott, I have to admit that I was looking forward to going back to Dartmouth with Scott Fitzgerald, so I hoped he would give in. And the truth is, since he was only the hired writer and Wanger was the producer, Scott had no choice.

My father was at that time in charge of Paramount Studio. In spite of the fact that Scott had fallen on tough times and felt pretty much unread and neglected, there were still people around with enormous respect for him. My father was one of them. In fact, he was so excited that I was seeing and working with Scott Fitzgerald that when we were ready to take off on what would be an eighteen-hour flight, my father brought two bottles of champagne to the plane by way of celebration.

On the plane we went on talking and talking. Scott was telling me about Dos Passos and Edmund Wilson. And Hemingway. I don't think the whole story of Scott and Hemingway, even with everything that's been written, has ever been fully explored. Anyway, we opened the first bottle of champagne and talked on and on. After the plane stopped to refuel, we opened the second bottle of champagne. Scott was tired but excited. We seemed to stimulate each other, on every subject except the one we were being paid to write, *Winter Carnival*. Finally we landed at the old airport in New York and went to the Warwick Hotel. To this day, whenever I go by the Warwick, at Fifty-third, just off Sixth Avenue — it's amazing how time is like an accordion; it just moves in and out — I always stop to look up at our room on the tenth floor. It was a funny little suite with a small sitting room, and we each had a small bedroom. It had a little false balcony; you could just barely step out on to it. More than half a century later, I find myself still looking up at that room where we were "incarcerated."

We stayed there into the night, trying to work. Every once in a while we'd say, "We've got to work on this story, we've got to do it!" I would say, "Scott, you've written a hundred short stories, and I've written a few; between the two of us we should be able to knock out a damn outline for this story."

"Yes, we will, we will. Don't worry, pal, we will, we will."

A couple of friends I hadn't seen since I got out of Dartmouth called me. They were just two or three blocks away, they said, and asked if I'd come out just for a short time and see them. I welcomed getting out from under my writing obligations for a while, so I went. I was gone only about an hour and came back to find on my bed a note that I'd give anything to have today. (I have a feeling it may be in one of the cartons in my attic that haven't been opened in a long time.) The note had no punctuation in it. It just said, "Pal you shouldn't have left me Pal because I went down to the bar Pal and then I came back and looked for you Pal and then I went down to the bar again Pal and I'll be waiting for you there Pal when you get back Pal." I rushed down to the King Cole Bar at the Warwick and asked the bartender for him. I described him—nobody knew his name or anything—and the bartender said, "Oh, yeah, he was here for a while. He was getting pretty smashed. And then he went out somewhere." I asked which way he went and the customers told me east. I ran down that street and stopped in bar after bar after bar. About the third or fourth one down, I stopped at the Monkey Bar. Finally, there was Scott. I realized I had made a bad mistake, leaving him alone for an hour. Scott was pretty far gone.

We went back to the Warwick. We faced a meeting with Wanger early the next morning at nine o'clock at the Waldorf Towers. Back in our little suite in the Warwick, it was time for cold showers and trying to get that damn story together. We worked on it—ridiculous plots and more ridiculous plots. I won't go into them, but each tired plot sounded worse than the others. It's hard to write those kinds of stories, stories you don't believe in and have no interest in, just stories you try to make up—really hard. After a few hours of restless sleep, somehow we got up and went over to see Wanger.

Poor Scott! And I was in almost as bad shape by this time as he was. We'd stayed up all night. We sent down for more liquor. A dapper wide-awake Wanger asked me ever so casually, "Well, how was the trip? How was the flight?"

"Oh, fine," I said.

"Did you see anyone on the flight that you knew?" he asked.

I opened my big mouth and said, "In the back of the plane was someone I knew slightly, Sheilah Graham." She was a movie columnist I knew casually. Walter looked at Scott and said, "Scott, you son of a bitch!" There were a lot of things I didn't know, and one of them was that Sheilah was Scott's girl, and that Sheilah had, without letting Wanger know, come along on the trip.

When we got out of that fairly fruitless story conference, I said, "Scott, I'm really awfully sorry." And Scott, who, as I've said, was always nice, always human and very generous with me, said, "Well Budd, it's not your fault. I really should have told you. I should have told you about Sheilah. Sheilah was coming along on the trip, and she's staying at the Hotel Elysee which is just about a block and a half down."

We had only a few minutes to make the train. There was a Winter Carnival Special in those days, filled with the dates, eager seventeen- and eighteen-year-old children of the late 1930s, the dates of the Dartmouth boys or men panting for them up there in Hanover. There's nothing like it now. It's all past. The entire train was given over to Winter Carnival. Somehow, Scott and I got on the train. Walter wanted Scott and me to walk through the entire train to look at the girls, those beautiful young things, to get the spirit of it. Scott was not too enthusiastic about that.

Knowing a lot of writers, I've had experience with alcoholics, like Charlie Jackson whose novel *The Lost Weekend* describes their agonies and resourcefulness. They are like magicians in their ability to hide and then suddenly produce bottles. I thought about that and decided when I found Scott again that I was not going to let him out of my sight. But, by God, if he didn't have a little bottle of gin with him on the train. It was a half-pint or maybe a pint, a small bottle in his pocket. I don't know where he got it. I just don't have any idea. Maybe the bellboy slipped it to him. Walter Wanger took me aside and said, "Budd, tell me the truth. Has Scott been drinking?"

I swallowed hard and said, "Well, maybe a little bit. Not much."

Wanger said, "God damn it! His agent gave me his word of honor that if I hired Scott on this assignment that he wouldn't touch a drop. Not touch a drop." He went on: "You know Scott is an alcoholic. If he takes a drink, there will be no end to it." Nobody had told me, as they should have, that I was to take care of Scott on the trip; that should have been, I suppose, my main contribution. No one sat me down ahead of time and said, "This could happen, and it's your job to watch him."

We had a fatal weekend in Hanover. We finally made it to the Hanover Inn, which had no room for us. Someone had forgotten to make the reservation for the two of us, and Scott was muttering. (Scott may have sometimes looked as if he were falling-down drunk, but his mind never stopped. I'll never forget how amazed I was that he kept on saying very, very incisive brief things, observing an awful lot.) "We'll take the attic room, because that's where the screenwriters are usually put in Hollywood," he said. "In the system I guess that's where we belong. We'll take the attic room."

So there we were, in the attic in a bare room. It was not really a room for clients of the hotel. The furniture was a metal bed, a double-decker bed, and a small table. I don't remember a chair. We stayed there all the next day because Scott didn't want to go out and I didn't see any reason to.

The Dartmouth professor who had taught the "Sociology and the American Novel" course, Red Merrill, was a wonderful guy and a terrific fan of Scott's, so he couldn't wait to meet him. He also couldn't wait to bring a bottle of liquor along, which we then proceeded to drink. The thing went downhill. As Scott got worse and worse, Wanger was on us more and more.

There was a humorous side to our situation though. Wanger had a second unit director who was full of enthusiasm. He would come in and say, "We're ready. Goddamn it, we're ready! Just tell us where the next setup is and we'll get it for you. We'll knock the hell out of it!" He was like that. We would send him out on fool's errands, saying, "The next scene we have is in front of the Outing Club and we need . . ." "You got it!" he'd say, and out he'd run. We'd laugh, "That'll take care of Lovey" — Otto Lovering was his name — "for the next hour or so." Oddly enough, in *The Last Tycoon*, the unfinished novel Scott was working on when he died, he called him "Robinson." I called him something else, but he was the same character in my novel *The Disenchanted*.

We finally had a showdown. We had a meeting set up with the dean and the English department, with Wanger presenting us, not *us*, but Scott, wanting to show him off as the literary star telling the story of Winter Carnival. We tried hard to get out of it. But there was no way we could. We went through this fiasco; it was a disaster since it was pretty obvious not only that Scott was drunk but that we had no story.

That night, in a mood of dismal failure, we went down to the coffee shop; it was humorous in a way because there were all those kids enjoying Winter Carnival, everybody was so *up*, and we were so bedraggled, so down, so worried, in despair. Suddenly, Scott started to improvise a sort of brilliant, surrealist story of an ice carnival. He just went on in a kind of trance. It was fascinating to hear. I wish I had had a tape. So many times with Scott, as I look back, I'd give anything now to have been able to tape all those talks with him. The only substitute for a tape is my memory. I'm playing it back for you now. At the end of this monologue, he was very excited. He said, "Well, what do you think of it, Budd?" It was a fascinating piece. It could have been published somewhere as a prose poem on skiing, on a romantic mysterious meeting on the slopes. But, of course, it wasn't what Wanger was looking for. I said, "Well, you know, Scott, I guess we have to go back upstairs to our room and think some more."

Arm in arm, we staggered around the corner to the front of the inn, and there was Walter Wanger in a top hat. Saturday night it was, the gala Saturday night, and he looked at us and turned colors; I guess Dartmouth green was one of them. I still remember every word he said to us: "I don't know when the next train is out of here, but you two are going to be on it!" And, by God, they put us on the Montrealer that went down to New York. Without our baggage or anything, they put us on that train, and down we went.

Next morning at seven o'clock, we got into the station. We were sleeping in roomettes next to each other. The porter came into my roomette and said, "You'd better come in and try to wake up your friend. I can't get him up, and you've only got about ten or fifteen minutes and then you go into the barn." I jumped up and ran in. Scott was really out, really sick. With the porter's help, I got him up and out on the platform. Somehow we got a cab. We went back to the Warwick. We had no bags, and we had the same clothes on that we had left in. Somehow the days had run together and we hadn't changed.

The desk clerk said, "Oh, we didn't expect you back. Have they made a reservation for you?"

"No, we just came on ahead," I tried to explain.

"Well," he said, "I'm sorry. We don't have a single room."

We got another cab but couldn't get in any hotel. We tried five, six, seven, and the same thing happened every time. Nobody would let us in. No room at the inn. Then Scott finally said to me, "Well, Budd, I know where I can get in, at the Doctor's Hospital." And that's where we went, to the Doctor's Hospital. Finally, I told Sheilah and she took care of him. After about a week or so he was able to leave and go West again.

That's the end of the Winter Carnival story, almost. I got rehired because I was the only one who knew about Winter Carnival, I guess. I worked on it with Maurice Rapf, a Hollywood boyhood friend I had gone to Dartmouth with, and with a real hack writer who knew how to put the damn thing together, and did. It came out, unfortunately, and still shows up on the late-late shows. At Dartmouth now it's become a tradition at the Winter Carnival to show it at midnight on Saturday night. The kids absolutely flip out. I mean, it beats the Marx Brothers for comedy. They scream with laughter and fall out of their seats. I've sat there with them and thought, "Oh, if they only knew. If they only knew."

One of the things that would continue to impress me in the next year and a half that I knew Scott was that he kept sending me notes, ideas for the movie. It's true, it's really true. He sent me one that said, "Don't forget how the student waiters waiting on us were talking with the students they were serving, and asking them about tests or about games and so forth while they were serving them. I think that'll be a nice touch." He would send in little notes like that. I kept seeing him, realizing that he was having a very, very hard time. He was living out in the valley, as the tenant of a very successful film comedian, Edward Everett Horton. Horton had a big place in Encino and a small guest house over the garage with an outside stairway, which is quite common in Southern California. Scott rented that for about two hundred a month, and I used to go out and see him.

It was May of 1940, and he was struggling to make a living. He was writing those short stories for *Esquire* about a run-down hand-to-mouth screenwriter, the Pat Hobby stories. I believe he got $250 for each one. I honestly thought, even for those days, they underpaid him. But he got $250, and I think that's how he was paying Horton. He figured if he could write a story in one day, and if he was writing one a month, that was the way he could pay his rent. I found that heartbreaking and endearing about Scott. I remember a number of times sitting down with Sheilah in the back of the Horton place as Scott would come running down the stairs all excited; he'd just finished one of the short stories for *Esquire*, and he would read it out loud to us. They were not top drawer; they were not top-level Scott Fitzgerald. But they were funny and extremely observant, like everything he did. Many of the indignities that he suffered in Hollywood, and that almost every screenwriter except the very, very successful ones suffered and, to some extent, continue to suffer out there, were expressed in those hastily written tongue-in-cheek stories.

He had a quality that to me seemed sophomoric in the best sense. How many people have said of Scott Fitzgerald that he was not a serious thinker, although much of the work, his best work, rebuts that. Somehow he held on to his creative energy, despite all of the beating down that he suffered, trying to support his daughter Scottie and keep her in college and trying to pay for his wife, Zelda, in and out of the sanitarium. He still had this amazing enthusiasm. He was like a good student, a sophomore who had just read something interesting and was eager to learn. He responded to all kinds of ideas. Maybe that doesn't sound like the popular conception of Scott Fitzgerald.

I remember one evening—and I still feel a little uncomfortable about this—I was just about to go out for dinner. It was about six-thirty, and Scott burst in; he hadn't called or anything. He simply ran into my house and said, "Budd, I've just finished reading Spengler's *Decline of the West*, and I've got to talk to you about it."

I still feel guilty about this: I said, "Scott, *Decline of the West*! We'll be here for days, and I'm late for dinner. I've just got to go. I've got to." But he wanted to talk about it. He was so full of *The Decline of the West*. Finally, I walked out. As I look back, I really can't remember where I went to dinner that night or why it was so important, and I still feel bad that I told him I just couldn't stay and talk to him about Spengler and his ideas on the decline of the West. But that's the way he was, with incredible enthusiasm that he was somehow able to maintain in the midst of the enormous struggle to survive.

Another time I went out to see him at Horton's and he was reading another rather unlikely work. Of course, this was 1939 or 1940. The left wing and the Communist Party and the whole Marxist influence were very strong. It seemed like 90 percent of the writers were either members or fellow travelers. Scott was sitting outside and I asked him what he was reading. He held it up:

Karl Marx's "The 14th Brummiere." I'll never forget that either. Not only was he reading it, he was, again, all excited about it. He had this kind of adorable naivete about things that you would hardly expect from a man in his early forties. I thought of him as sixty, seventy. Of course, that's the arrogance of youth. Discounting that, he did look much older than forty-two or forty-three, which he was then. And he said, "I have to reexamine the economic relationships and the economic context of all my characters." Having left behind the Jazz Age of the 1920s, he had moved into the Marxist atmosphere of the 1930s. Since he identified me with the Marxist movement, he wanted to talk about it. He was so open, so eager, so curious.

When my daughter was born in May 1940, he had just sold his short story "Babylon Revisited" to an independent film producer, Lester Cowan. He actually sold it for nine hundred dollars and got a job writing the screenplay for five hundred a week, which was a cut in salary from what he had gotten from Wanger and from a few others, but since he barely had a screen credit his screenwriting stock was rather low. As he said at the time, he not only needed the money and felt he could write that screenplay in eight weeks, at least he had the pleasure of working on his own work and not, as he had had to do, adapt the work of other people.

The night my daughter was born he called me at the Cedars of Lebanon Hospital. When I told him she had just been born and that her name would be Victoria, he said, "Well then, in my screenplay 'Babylon Revisited' in her honor, I'm going to change the name from Honoria to Victoria." And so indeed in the "Babylon Revisited" screenplay, which I arranged to have published in 1993, the child is called Victoria. In my introduction I explain the circumstances of the screenplay; they were so typical of Scott's career in Hollywood. Cowan had paid Scott $5,000 for it. Then Cowan sold it to Metro-Goldwyn-Mayer for $100,000. They made the film and decided to change the title to "The Last Time I Saw Paris." Although that came after his premature death, once again I felt Scott had been cheated out of both money and any sort of artistic satisfaction in Hollywood.

A lot of eastern writers, famous novelists, went to Hollywood hoping to pick up the money — one can't blame them — and go back and do their own work. But Scott was different from them. I could see it, having been raised in Hollywood and having watched the many famous writers on my father's Paramount payroll at that time. Aside from the coveted paychecks, Scott had a truly serious interest in film. He went to films all the time and kept a card file of the plots. He'd go back and write out the plot of every film that he saw. He was seriously interested in the process of the motion picture and even in the art of the motion picture. He had moments when he thought it might even replace the novel as an art form.

Scott and I reacted to the *Winter Carnival* ordeal in different ways. I was fed up with Hollywood. I wanted to go away, away from screenwriting, so I went back to Dartmouth and started working on a novel, *What Makes Sammy Run?* As it turned out, Scott went to work on a novel also. In the course of our friendship, he had shown a very keen, extremely curious interest in Hollywood. He wanted to know how I grew up there, how I felt there, what it was like to be the son of a very prominent studio head, and how my father worked. He met my father, B.P., who admired him enormously.

At the end of November 1940, I went to see Scott at that little flat he had just rented—it was more convenient for him—on Laurel just off Sunset, and right around the corner from Sheilah's. Scott was in bed writing when I saw him the last time. I asked him about what he was working on, and, somewhat to my surprise, he showed me an opening chapter. I read it slowly, standing by the bed. I guess he noticed the look on my face. When I read the opening paragraph, although it was written more gracefully than I would have been able to write it, it said very much what I had said to Scott: being raised in Hollywood, you could never look at it as a glamorous town. It may look glamorous from the outside, but if you're from the inside, it's really just like any other factory town. It's very much a company town. The only difference is, instead of turning out steel or tires, you're turning out cans of film. The story of *The Last Tycoon* is narrated by a film executive's daughter, Cecelia, who goes to Bennington, which was at the time the women's equivalent of Dartmouth.

At that moment I was wondering, did Scott really like me as much as I thought he liked me, or was I just a convenient source, the son of a Hollywood mogul, you might say. B.P. and producer Irving Thalberg were often compared as Hollywood "intellectuals" and it hurt my feelings a little bit.

Scott saw the look on my face and said, "In Cecelia, I guess I did combine my daughter Scottie and you, and I hope you don't mind." Of everything I remember about him, this feeling of having been used may be the most negative, but I realize that's what all writers do. They can't help themselves. The only material they have is the material they draw from other people and the experiences they go through.

I was leaving to go East again to put the finishing touches on *Sammy* and would be back in a few months. He told me that when I came back he would show me more of the chapters that he had written.

Scott died a few weeks after that. Exactly twenty days later, Sheilah Graham called John O'Hara and me together and said that there was some thought from Scribners we might go over the outline and try to finish the book, which was not quite half finished and still a very rough draft. Well, John and I kicked it around for a few nights and decided that we'd be crazy to do it—that it could be worse than any tilting of any windmill by Don Quixote. Having read what Scott had written even in the first draft and having read the outline of where he planned to go with it, we felt that there was a tone and a voice that no one else could possibly capture. A perfectionist, Scott would have written it over and over again, as we know from his other work. O'Hara and I admired him too much. He was a hell of a writer. Nobody could touch what he was able to do at his best. *The Last Tycoon* had to stay the way it was. It was a tragedy that he couldn't finish that book. I admired him so much because for someone with failing health to mount that kind of creative energy, to put into it the remarkable work he did at the time of his heart attack, was an incredible act of heroism.

Finally, I want to turn my attention to Ernest Hemingway and his relationship to Scott. I'm sorry to say that Ernest was really mean-spirited toward Scott, putting him down at every opportunity. I wish I could have taped some examples of Scott's ambivalence toward Hemingway. It's been remarked over and over again how Scott could be inside of a subject and outside of it at the same time, able to observe it and somehow still be in the middle of it, writing basically about himself but somehow managing to shift from the subjective to the objective, and to observe so clearly what he was actually, personally suffering. I know that was very true of his attitude toward Hemingway. In some ways he was like a starstruck child looking up to a living legend. He idolized Hemingway. He was in awe of him. He was almost afraid of Hemingway. He wondered what Hemingway was going to think about this and think about that. Scott was obsessed with Hemingway, and at the same time Hemingway did not have the grace to return the favor.

Scott Fitzgerald showed great generosity toward me and Nathanael West but also toward Hemingway. When he first found Hemingway in Paris in the twenties, Hemingway was poor and unknown. He was writing those great early short stories but was not able to get them published. It should be better known that Scott was helping to support him with a check for a hundred dollars a month, pretty good money for France in those days. Scott also fought for him. When Hemingway wrote to ask him if "you can get me away from my Jew publishers" (Covici-Friede), Scott actually got him to Scribners. He helped him in every possible way. He became his sponsor, a rare and generous act for someone who might be considered a rival. When you read Hemingway's memoirs, like *A Moveable Feast,* you realize how Hemingway reciprocated that generosity by giving Scott the back of his hand, page after page of gratuitous put-downs. It was a heartless, mean-spirited, malicious thing that Ernest did to Scott. Scott didn't deserve it. Hemingway should have been bigger than that, although I know from many other experiences, my own as well as those of friends like the late Irwin Shaw, that it just wasn't in Ernest to be generous with people he considered his rivals or potential rivals.

I recall receiving an unexpected phone call from Scott about *For Whom the Bell Tolls. The Bell* was another big one for Ernest, a big moneymaker, a big critic-grabber, appearing in 1940 (when Hemingway had a large dollar sign on his forehead, an S for Success, while Scott bore the brand of Failure). Scott said, "You know, Budd, it's strange, but after all these years, from the time I first met him, Ernest hasn't learned a thing about women. He knows about me and he knows about those tests he's so crazy about, those tests of courage. But when it comes to women he still writes like a schoolboy. He's known interesting women, complicated women, but the way he writes women in *The Bell* is sophomoric. It made me uncomfortable to read it. He's really a child, a gifted child!"

His intelligence knew and understood his friend and rival's weaknesses and strengths, but his emotions left him to the very end the victim of Hemingway's emotions. He never stopped worrying what Hemingway would think of him. It was pathetic really, for Hemingway had had the gall to write to him that *Tender Is The Night* was not really a novel, since all the characters in the book were transparently Gerald and Sara Murphy and the famous people around them at Cap d'Antibes. As if readers in the know had not been able to fill in just as easily the real names for the characters Hemingway had limned in *The Sun Also Rises*!

But when Scott died, he left a lot of friends: Dorothy Parker, Donald Ogden Stewart, John O'Hara, Edmund Wilson. He had a lot of literary friends. To our consternation, the obituaries ran from condescending to downright vicious. They dismissed him as a spokesman for an age, the Jazz Age, an age that was dead, as if his own work and his own literary reputation had died with the trumpets and the saxophones of the twenties, almost like "good riddance!" To Westbrook Pegler, he was "just one of those crazy kids." It was mean and nasty. So a group of us, O'Hara and all, urged the *New Republic* to publish a special memorial issue dedicated to Scott Fitzgerald, not only in his memory but to his future. I wrote: "Despite the twin ironies that the best book that Scott wrote in the twenties had nothing to do with flaming youth, and his most profound if not most perfect work, *Tender Is the Night,* appeared toward the middle of the thirties, my generation thought of F. Scott Fitzgerald as an 'age,' not as a writer. And when the economic stroke of '29 began to turn 'sheiks' and 'flappers' into unemployed boys and underpaid girls, we consciously and a little belligerently turned our backs on Fitzgerald. We turned our backs on many things."

I'm talking now of "we" as a generation, my generation, but not of my own feeling for Scott. For in that memorial issue I'm quoting from, I noted, "Three weeks later I was up at Dartmouth, actually leaning, oddly enough, against an outside wall of the Hanover Inn where we had struggled together, when I heard that Scott was gone. The 'draft' he had promised to let me see when I returned was *The Last Tycoon*, which even in its sadly unfinished state reaffirmed Scott's high place as 'our best novelist.' 'He was writing a page a day now,' I had reported from his bedside. But it was a good page. Scott's comeback novel for the 40's was on its way."

From the final tribute in that memorial issue, I'd like to close with these words of Stephen Vincent Benét: "You can take off your hats now, Gentlemen. And I think perhaps you had better. This is not a legend. This is a reputation. Now seen in perspective, it may well be one of the most secure reputations of our century." That's the way a small group of us felt then, and that's the way I'm delighted to see that we all feel now.

Memories of Scott

FRANCES KROLL RING

Some memories play tricks. My memories of Scott Fitzgerald are still vivid after more than fifty years. The effect he had on my life is deep and ongoing not only because continuing interest in him from scholars and biographers have put questions to me about his last days but because I learned so much from him. I did not know him at the height of his fame but I did know him as a writer who had fallen on hard times and was embarked on a new work that would become *The Last Tycoon.*

As his secretary for the last twenty months of his life, I saw him almost daily. The time span was April 1939 through December 1940. His place in literature has been analyzed profusely; I will focus on his everyday life, his work method and habits.

When he hired me, he had finished a stint as a screenwriter at MGM. He was about to begin a novel about the motion picture industry, a novel he had been planning for some time fed by his experience inside the studio gates. He swore me to secrecy about the project because this was Hollywood, where gossip was a way of life, and he did not want anyone to know what he was up to. The secrecy created an aura of intrigue, and I was caught up in the drama.

I was soon to learn that working for Fitzgerald was a series of dramas — some dark with depression, others bright with devilment, and still others the scheming of a novelist to whom life itself was a plot to be developed and solved. So here I was with this faded blond, handsome, poetic-looking man waiting for the words to flow. It took a while.

What I didn't know was that he was recovering from an alcoholic bout and was not yet ready to take the plunge into a first draft. He busied himself with notes, fragments of ideas, personal letters. It seemed like procrastination until he produced a long treatment of the novel and sent it to *Collier's Magazine*. He wanted a promise from them to serialize it and advance funds. They turned him down.

Hell hath no fury like a Fitzgerald rejected when he needed acceptance. He believed this would be a definitive novel on the movie industry. He stormed and ranted at the gutless editor. He reported to Max Perkins at Scribners, who calmed him, encouraged him, and sent a check so that he could proceed.

I was quickly impressed by Scott's ability to pull himself out of his anguish. For a man whose life had been struck such shattering blows, the idea of a new work revitalized him. He was amazingly organized. He wrote brief biographies of his characters, divided the book into chapters, wrote episodes to be included in the chapters, drew from his ledgerlike books filled with notes, bits of description, a turn of phrase, a mood. He was a list-maker. Football plays and players, wars, reading lists, and this preparatory material for the novel—all of this brought a sense of order to his otherwise fragmented life. He had to know where he was going with this book—his first since *Tender Is the Night*. This had to be the book that would bring him back to the attention of new readers and reclaim old ones.

Another reason for his fastidious preparation was the reality of his financial demands. He was unable to hole up and write. He had constantly to put the novel aside to earn quick money for living—for Zelda's sanitarium bills, for Scottie's tuition at Vassar. He was the sole support system for this three-way family. They were his first consideration. His love for his daughter, Scottie, and his determination that she be an educated woman were his priorities. And Zelda: despite their separate lives, her well-being and treatment were his trust. She might never be well again, but he would never abandon her. For himself, he lived modestly, needing only books and records—a far cry from the extravagance of his youth.

So to offset the desperate economic pressure he interrupted the writing to take a week or two to repair screenplay dialogue that would net a couple of thousand. A series of Pat Hobby stories—unlike the novel, written spontaneously on a weekend—would pay the rent. Then back to the novel—always making a fresh start, changing, injecting new life, new concepts, name changes, a title change. There was never a first draft with him. Each sentence was scrutinized and edited or refined for his flawless standard. At last, he could get on with it. But no.

Film producer Lester Cowan asked him to do a screenplay based on his short story "Babylon Revisited." It was hard to turn away from the offer. It paid only $5,000, but the money would enable him to finish the book. Further, this was a chance to adapt his own story, one that he felt very close to. To those who say he was not a screenwriter, I disagree. He was fascinated by films. He understood them. He had a gift for dialogue. Isn't that what studios hired him to do? And he understood the power of this visual form. It was his alcoholic reputation many producers feared rather than his screenwriting ability.

Cowan gave him free rein, though they consulted frequently. Working in this medium was different from working on the novel. Instead of writing in longhand, Fitzgerald dictated, pacing back and forth, acting out scenes, speaking the dialogue. After Fitzgerald read one particularly emotional scene to Cowan over the phone, the producer wept. Fitzgerald's response to me was gleeful as he said, "At last I've made a son-of-a-bitch producer cry."

He finished his screenplay and went back to the novel. He worked steadily trying to make up for lost time. Then another interruption. A heart attack. The severity was unexpected though he had had previous warnings. The doctor ordered bed rest. Knowledge of treatment was very limited then. No one said stop smoking. No one said don't eat bacon and eggs. Cholesterol was not in the vocabulary.

Fitzgerald took to bed but not to rest. He turned out page after page in longhand, which I typed up in triple space. He corrected and edited. I then retyped in double space. He believed in his talent and in his ability to bring this novel off in style and substance. He was working against time. Was he aware of the limits? Perhaps. In an odd request, he had asked me to put aside some cash in case something should happen. What could happen? He smiled obliquely.

To answer a question: did he make changes because something he had written was untrue? No. Changes had nothing to do with truth. The research was done. Changes were made because upon rereading, he sought to improve his plan or because something he had written did not sufficiently capture the image verbally. He did not revise the fact but refined the language to meet his poetic satisfaction. For instance, the seduction scene at Malibu had to sing romantically. The back-lot description had to reflect the eerie wonder of a disaster in so unreal a background. The opening had immediately to attract young readers his daughter's age.

Fitzgerald was in his early forties and no longer the egocentric young man. He had honed his craft, had matured in his social and political views. When he was under contract to the studios, he had witnessed the efforts of writers and actors to unionize in order to gain power and recognition from studio "benevolent" employers. He wanted to reflect those actions in his novel, which would be a serious as well as romantic tale of this magical industry, and of his complicated hero-tycoon Stahr.

As for Hemingway, Scott was not in competition with him. They were at odds. Scott, who had admired and nurtured the earlier works of Hemingway, now felt that he was no longer looking inside himself in his writing. He had gone public and created a stage on which he could dramatize his own heroics and marriages.

So Fitzgerald wrote on, confident of his course, until the final interruption. Death concluded his story in its inimitable way. If, indeed, he had been contemplating death, I don't think he was expecting it so quickly. Certainly I was not expecting it on that dismal Saturday afternoon before Christmas. I lamented what I thought was a waste of his dream because at that time there was no indication that his pages would ever see print.

At the request of his executor, Judge Biggs, an old Princeton friend, I closed out his life in Hollywood with great pain. I had his body shipped back to Baltimore, stored his meager possessions, and was left with a vast void. There seemed no reason to remain in Hollywood. I had an extra copy of the manuscript and Scott's old briefcase. I went East, dropped off the manuscript and the case with Judge Biggs in Delaware, and went on to New York where I was born. There I met with Max Perkins, who might also be described as the last of the great editors. He, too, was shattered by the loss of his friend. He had not yet determined what he would do with the manuscript, though he knew he would find a way to publish it. Eventually, with Edmund Wilson's assistance, he brought out the unfinished novel. Wilson wrote a summary of how it might have ended based on Scott's outline, and supplemented with notes selected to reveal the serious craftsmanship of this now celebrated American writer.

Without seeming to eulogize him, for there were dark spots that dotted this day-to-day working schedule, I must say that he was to me a kind, gentle, and extraordinarily considerate man, as he was to his many friends. He was an enviable storyteller. A touch of blarney, yes, naturally. Catholic in his habits if no longer in his faith. And a writer always. Writing was his work and his lifeline.

His shadow has followed my life — even to now.

F. Scott Fitzgerald

A Publisher's Perspective

CHARLES SCRIBNER III

F. Scott Fitzgerald was born in 1896. Just as his life bridged two centuries, so his work has a Janus-like aspect, looking back to the romantic lyricism and expansive dreams of nineteenth-century America, and forward to the syncopated jazz strains of our own century. There is no generation gap among Fitzgerald lovers. It was not by chance. "My whole theory of writing," he said, "I can sum up in one sentence. An author ought to write for the youth of his own generation, the critics of the next, and the schoolmasters of ever afterward." How magnificently — if posthumously — he fulfilled that ideal. His fleeting literary fortunes — a dozen years of commercial and literary success followed by distractions and disappointments — ended in 1940 with a fatal heart attack at the age of forty-four. He was then hard at work on the Hollywood novel he hoped would restore his reputation. At the time of his death his books were not, as is so often claimed, out of print with Scribners, his publisher. The truth is even sadder: they were all in stock at our warehouse and listed in our catalog but no one was buying them.

A half century later, more copies of Fitzgerald's books are sold each year than the entire cumulative sale throughout his lifetime. His novels and stories are studied in virtually every high school and college across the country. I am only the fourth Charles Scribner to be involved in publishing his works since my great-grandfather first signed him up, at the prodding of Max Perkins, in 1919. But three generations and namesakes later (we are a repetitive family) I am struck by the realization that I am the first generation — of no doubt many to come — to have been introduced to this author's work in a classroom. My grandfather, Fitzgerald's contemporary and friend as well as publisher, died on the eve of the critical reappraisal and the ensuing revival of his works that gained momentum in the 1950s and has continued in full force down to the present time. It was my father who presided over a literary apotheosis unprecedented in modern American letters.

As a tyro publisher, I had the good fortune to work closely with Fitzgerald's talented and altogether wonderful daughter, Scottie, together with her dedicated collaborator and advisor Matthew J. Bruccoli, whose prolific scholarship and infectious enthusiasm have long fanned the flames of Fitzgerald studies. The day I met Professor Bruccoli, two decades and many books ago, I asked him what had prompted him to devote the lion's share of his scholarly life to Fitzgerald. He told me exactly how it happened.

One Sunday afternoon in 1949, Bruccoli, then a high school student, was driving with his family along the Merritt Parkway from Connecticut to New York City when he heard a dramatization of "The Diamond as Big as the Ritz" on the car radio. He later went to a library to find the story; the librarian had never heard of Scott Fitzgerald. But finally he managed to locate a copy — "and I never stopped reading Fitzgerald," he concluded with typical modesty. This story struck a familiar chord — for I too remember where I was when I first encountered that same literary jewel "as Big as the Ritz."

It was an evening train ride from Princeton to Philadelphia: a commute was converted into a fantastic voyage. Fitzgerald later converted my professional life just as profoundly, claiming more of me than any living author. There are worse fates in publishing than to be "curator of literary classics," especially if one's own scholarly training is in Baroque art. Placed beside my other specialties, Rubens and Bernini, Fitzgerald seems very young indeed: a newcomer in the pantheon of creative genius.

There is something magical about Fitzgerald. Much has been written — and dramatized — about the Jazz Age personas of Scott and Zelda. But the real magic lies embedded in his prose and reveals itself in his amazing range and versatility. Each novel or story partakes of its creator's poetic imagination, his dramatic vision, his painstaking (if virtuosic and seemingly effortless) craftsmanship. Each bears Fitzgerald's hallmark, the indelible stamp of grace. He is my literary candidate to stand beside the demigods Bernini, Rubens, and Mozart as artists of divine transfigurations. The key to Fitzgerald's enduring enchantment lies, I submit, in the power of his romantic imagination to transfigure his characters and settings — as well as the very shape and sound of his prose. There is a sacramental quality — one that did not wane along with the formal observance of his ancient Roman faith. I say "sacramental" because Fitzgerald's words transform their external geography as thoroughly as the realm within. The ultimate effect, once the initial reverberations of imagery and language have subsided, transcends the bounds of fiction. I can testify from firsthand experience.

When I arrived at Princeton as a freshman in the fall of 1969, I was following the footsteps of four generations of namesakes before me. Yet, surprisingly, I did not feel at home. It seemed a big impersonal place: more than ten times as big as my old boarding school, St. Paul's. At St. Paul's I had first been exposed to Fitzgerald in English class, where we studied *The Great Gatsby*. But my first encounter at Princeton was dramatically extracurricular. One day that fall, soon after the Vietnam Moratorium and the ensuing campus turmoil, I returned to my dormitory room to find that some anonymous wit had taped to my door that infamous paragraph from Fitzgerald's "The Rich Boy": "Let me tell you about the very rich. They are different from you and me." (My next-door neighbors in the dorm represented a cross section of campus radicals; and while I was hardly "very rich" by Fitzgerald's lights — closer to Nick Carraway than to the Buchanans — I was, as the son of a university trustee, *politically incorrect*.) Stung as I was by this welcome note, curiosity got the better of me. So off I went to the library, looked up the story, and read it.

Now hooked by Fitzgerald, I bought a copy of *This Side of Paradise*, his youthful ode to Princeton. Though university officials to this day bemoan its satirical depiction of their college as a country club (if there was any book they could ban, this would be it), they miss the point — the poetry, the sacramental effect of this early, flawed novel on their majestic campus. For me, this book infused the greenery and gothic spires with a spirit, with a soul, with life. Fitzgerald transfigured Princeton. I now saw it not as a stranger but through the wondering eyes of freshman Amory Blaine: "Princeton of the daytime filtered slowly into his consciousness—West and Reunion, redolent of the sixties, Seventy-nine Hall, brick-red and arrogant, Upper and Lower Pyne, aristocratic Elizabethan ladies not quite content to live among shop-keepers, and topping all, climbing with clear blue aspiration, the great dreaming spires of Holder and Cleveland towers. From the first he loved Princeton — its lazy beauty, its half-grasped significance, the wild moonlight revel of the rushes."

For me it was not love at first sight; but thanks to Fitzgerald, it was love at first reading. Oscar Wilde was right: life imitates art, not the other way around.

During my sojourn there, my friends and I would religiously recite Fitzgerald's sonnet of farewell to Princeton: "The last light fades and drifts across the land—the low, long land, the sunny land of spires."

I stayed on for two more graduations, leaving the university only when there were no more degrees to be had, but not before I had the pleasure of teaching undergraduates. Since my field was art history, the next transition—into the family publishing business—was abrupt, but once again facilitated by Fitzgerald. Ensconced at Max Perkins's old desk at Scribners, I dreamed up as my first book project in 1975, a revival of Fitzgerald's obscure and star-crossed play "The Vegetable," which featured a presidential impeachment too true to be good: can you believe the play had opened—and closed—in 1922 at *Nixon's* Apollo Theater in Atlantic City? My post-Watergate project not only justified repeated revisits to the Princeton University Library for research in the Scribner and Fitzgerald archives—the Mecca for Fitzgerald scholars—but, more important, brought me into a happy working relationship with Fitzgerald's daughter, Scottie.

By contrast, here is what Edmund Wilson wrote to me when I had first proposed that he reintroduce the play Fitzgerald had dedicated to him. Wilson had given its publication a rave newspaper review—a fact he now conveniently chose to forget: "I cannot write an introduction to the 'Vegetable.' The version I read and praised was something entirely different from the version he afterwards published, and I did not approve of this version. The trouble was he took too much advice and ruined the whole thing. I was not, by the way, as you say, closer to Fitzgerald than anybody else. I was not even in his class at college, though people still think and write as if I had been."

When I lamented this letter to my father, he said that for Wilson it wasn't so bad, jesting that "after God created the rattlesnake, he created Edmund Wilson." I am happy to report that Fitzgerald's *The Last Tycoon*, half a century after Wilson "polished" the unfinished novel, has finally been de-Wilsonized in a clean text prepared by Matthew Bruccoli. With less pride, I confess that I once allowed Wilson's first name to be misspelled "Edmond" in huge letters on the cover of our paperback edition of *Axel's Castle*. My Freudian slip is now a collector's item—which fortunately for me, Edmund did not live to see!

After approving my introduction to the play, Scottie wrote me a touching note about her parents' reburial service in the Catholic cemetery of Rockville, Maryland. I had been unable to attend and instead had arranged for a memorial mass to be said that day in the once exclusively Protestant Princeton chapel. No doubt Fitzgerald smiled at the delicious irony of both liturgies. "Surely it was the Princeton prayers," Scottie later wrote to me, "which made our little ceremony go so smoothly. The day was perfect; a mild breeze rustling the fallen leaves, and there were just the right number of people, about 25 friends and relatives, 25 press, 25 county and church 'officials,' and 25 admirers who just popped up from nowhere. As most of the guests had never before had bloody marys in a church basement, the party afterward was a jolly affair, too. I'm sorry you weren't there but loved knowing we were having a backup ceremony in his real spiritual home."

More Fitzgerald projects engaged me at Scribners. While writing an introduction to a new paperback edition of *Gatsby*, I happened to stumble upon two manuscript pages salvaged from the first draft of the novel. Fitzgerald had sent them to Willa Cather to prove that he had not plagiarized a passage from her novel, *A Lost Lady*. They are now preserved for posterity at the Princeton University Library. The more recent discovery by Matthew Bruccoli of Francis Cugat's preliminary sketches for the *Gatsby* dust jacket enabled me at last to merge art history and literature. I'm a Gemini. For this once, thanks to Fitzgerald, my dual career came into sync.

Francis Cugat's painting is the most celebrated — and widely disseminated — jacket art in twentieth-century American literature, and perhaps of all time. After decades of oblivion, I had revived it for our Scribner Library paperback edition in 1979; several million copies later, like the novel it embellishes, this Art Deco tour de force has established itself as a classic of graphic art. At the same time, it represents a unique form of "collaboration" between author and jacket artist. Under normal circumstances, the artist illustrates a scene or motif conceived by the author; he lifts, as it were, his image from a page of the book. In this instance, however, the artist's image *preceded* the finished manuscript and Fitzgerald actually maintained that he had "written it into" his book.

Cugat's small masterpiece is not illustrative but symbolic, even iconic: the sad, hypnotic, heavily outlined eyes of a woman beam like headlights through a cobalt night sky. Below, on earth, brightly colored lights blaze before a metropolitan skyline. Cugat's carnival imagery is especially intriguing in view of Fitzgerald's pervasive use of light motifs throughout his novel, specifically, in metaphors for the latter-day Trimalchio, whose parties were illuminated by "enough colored lights to make a Christmas tree of Gatsby's enormous garden." Nick sees "the whole corner of the peninsula . . . blazing with light" from Gatsby's house, "lit from tower to cellar." When he tells Gatsby that his place "looks like the World's Fair," Gatsby proposes that they "go to Coney Island." Fitzgerald had already introduced this symbolism in his story "Absolution," originally intended as a prologue to the novel. At the end of the story, a priest encourages the boy who eventually developed into Jay Gatsby to go

see an amusement park—"a thing like a fair only much more glittering"
with "a big wheel made of lights turning in the air." But "don't get too close,"
he cautions, "because if you do you'll only feel the heat and the sweat and
the life."

Daisy's face, says Nick, was "sad and lovely with bright things in it, bright
eyes and a bright passionate mouth." In Cugat's final painting, her celestial
eyes enclose reclining nudes and her streaming tear is green—like the light
"that burns all night" at the end of her dock, reflected in the water of the
Sound that separates her from Gatsby. What Fitzgerald drew directly from
Cugat's art and "wrote into" the novel must ultimately remain an open question. (For those interested, my own interpretation of the documents and art-
work was published in the *Princeton University Library Chronicle* 53 [Winter
1992]: 141–55.)

My family and I were transplanted to Gatsby's Island a decade ago after
several generations on the other side of the Hudson River. From our new van-
tage point, I cannot look out over the Sound, as I do each week, without smiling at Fitzgerald's description: "the most domesticated body of salt water in
the western hemisphere, the great wet barnyard of Long Island Sound." There
is no longer a dock at the beach in Lattingtown, and, as the crow flies, we are
several miles east of East Egg. But occasionally I catch a glimpse of a green
light reflected in the water, and each time I drive through the Valley of Ashes
and approach the twinkling Manhattan skyline, I feel very much at home. The
novel has made me a native.

One very wise teacher once said that the ultimate function of art is to
reconcile us to life. Fitzgerald's prose is life-enhancing; its evocative power
endures.

The Good Ghost of Scott Fitzgerald

GEORGE GARRETT

It is easy to forget that not all that long ago, at least measured in the spent years of my own lifetime, a gathering of friends, scholars, and critics to celebrate F. Scott Fitzgerald's work and name would have been almost unimaginable. Not that each and every serious and gifted writer (and even some not so serious or so gifted) is not perfectly capable of imagining a future so blessed with some vaguely similar honor. Certainly Fitzgerald had every reason to hope, perhaps at the end to pray too, that his life's work had earned something more than the genteel oblivion of the darkest and dustiest inches of library stacks. In his finest and happiest hours he, perhaps more than most of his peers, may well have been able to imagine and to consider that more than a half century after his death, there would be people who would love and support his art and would stand up for it in new, different, and, in many ways, unimaginable times. Fitzgerald was more acutely aware of his own times — the details, the flowering and the withering of the present — than most of our writers. He was more sensitive to change and decay than most, and for precisely that reason would be, I would guess, more startled and maybe delighted by the idea of a gathering of academics in his honor and, maybe just as much so, by the presence of living and working writers in the same company.

And so I would be surprised if I had not, in undeniable fact, lived in and through the half century since his death and been witness to and participant in much of the changing.

It is that changing that is my chief subject. I want to deal with it in a form that is odd enough to be misunderstood, though I hope that it will not be. Although I am speaking openly enough about myself, my true and proper subject is the powerful and continuing, though always changing, influence of the life and art of Scott Fitzgerald on American literature. I call myself to the witness stand not, by any means, claiming any special value or importance to myself as witness or to my work but because the example and influence of Fitzgerald have been strong, continuous, and constantly changing. In that sense I can claim to be typical of a great many American writers—poets as well as fiction writers—of roughly my age and generation and of the younger generation, too, who came on strongly as our bloody and brutal century staggered toward its bitter end.

Summer of 1948, a green, cool, pleasant summer in Princeton, New Jersey. It was the last summer school held at Princeton University, at least from then until now. Princeton, where the student body was still predominately made up of veterans home from World War II, eager to finish up their formal education and to resume their real lives. It was the first time that the Princeton English department offered a course in British and American literature published since 1900. This was English 251, for the record, and, to the best of my recollection, was taught by a young assistant professor named John Hite. The lectures took place in one of the big rooms, McCosh 10 or McCosh 30, I think, an eight o'clock class and always jam-packed. We read *The Waste Land*, *The Sun Also Rises*, and *The Sound and the Fury*, and, for F. Scott Fitzgerald, here being officially taught for the first time at his own school, we had *The Portable F. Scott Fitzgerald*. *Gatsby* was assigned for the course, together with some parts of *The Crack-up*, which was on reserve at the new Firestone Library. As late as that summer, first editions of Fitzgerald's books rested quietly and openly on the open stacks of the library. So did Faulkner's first editions at that same time. Not for long, to be sure. It is also a fact that as late as that same summer, almost halfway through our century, very, very few colleges yet offered any courses in twentieth-century literature.

And so it was more than discovery; it was vaguely illicit to be reading writers more or less of the same age as our parents and some of them still very much alive and writing. I had already read a lot of Hemingway. I had heard a little (from other readers in the family) about William Faulkner. But Fitzgerald was entirely new to me, though, for various reasons, I should have had a little knowledge and more interest. Also at that time there were very few American writers working at colleges and universities. There was always Frost, a regular visitor at Amherst; and there were a few others scattered here and there at one place and another, including Iowa, which was cranking up under the direction of Paul Engle. But the established connection between living and working writers and the Academy had not quite come to pass yet. It had never been a serious or valuable possibility for Fitzgerald's generation. When writers were brought into the groves of academe at all, they slipped in the back door and maintained a low profile. Thanks to Allen Tate and to R. P. Blackmur we had at Princeton several young writers acting as instructors—Randall Jarrell, John Berryman, Delmore Schwartz, and Saul Bellow among others. My preceptor in English 251 was the poet (and legitimate Ph.D.) Louis Coxe. But it was still a few years into the future before Dylan Thomas would show up, an hour or so late to be sure, and entertain an enthusiastic audience in McCosh 30.

We were assigned *The Great Gatsby*, and we read some pages of *The Crack-up*; and since the Viking Portable edition also had stories and the whole of *Tender Is the Night*, we read and talked about those too, though not as an assignment.

And where was I in those days? Well, Hemingway was writing about exciting and, it seemed, relevant things; and he had that style, more aptly and recently called, by Elmore Leonard, that "attitude." Faulkner was wild and woolly, throwing around great gobs of words the way, some years later, Jackson Pollock would be splashing paint. His subjects and places and people were familiar, down-home, close enough to be part of my own experience.

Fitzgerald seemed more of a straight arrow than the other two, at least in the writing. He was a college boy, too, an old-fashioned Princeton Charley. I loved all that I read, especially *Tender Is the Night*. Even as a young man, a green kid, I could admire *Gatsby*. But I loved *Tender Is the Night*. How could I not love it, when it took me directly to the Riviera, to the "bright tan prayer rug of a beach," and in less than a page was showing me a sun-glittering and wholly glamorous world as witnessed by Rosemary, "who had magic in her pink palms and her cheeks lit to a lovely flame, like the thrilling flush of children after their cold baths in the evening." Cowley's later revised edition aside, this is the only place and the only way to begin that particular story. It is illuminated by youthful witnessing and means so much more that way. It is so much more credible and moving because of the unforgettable impact of its powerful first impressions. It was only much later that I would come to recognize and to understand the technical skill of the author and the extraordinary capacity he possessed for evoking honestly and exactly the world of youth — of adolescence. It is something not at all easy to do without stumbling or pratfalls.

I loved *Tender Is the Night* and I admired *Gatsby*. I carried the Viking *Portable Fitzgerald* with me as I went to Texas, where I worked for a geophysical exploration crew, and into the Army to the Free Territory of Trieste, where I served for a time on the volatile, sometimes dangerous Yugoslav border. Then I carried it on up to Linz where an under-strength regiment of us faced forty thousand of Stalin's best on the other side of the Danube and where our tactical mission was to try to delay them for a short period of time, somewhere between fifteen minutes and a half hour, if and when they elected to come across the river, something I have now lately learned was entirely possible at that time.

If I carried the *Portable Fitzgerald* with me everywhere I went, I nevertheless had ambivalent, even contradictory, feelings about the author, about whom, of course, I knew next to nothing except the kind of glorified gossip that only serious and patient scholarship can and did eventually sweep away.

Meantime (as irony will have it) I could have done a lot better in getting to know him, to understand him better, anyway, if I had paid any attention to what was purely gossip. For it was all around me.

For example, for a couple of years, I shared first a room and later an apartment in New York City with Bruce Hotchkiss, nephew of Glenway Wescott; and we often spent weekends on the large, beautiful farm (now resting at the bottom of a reservoir) of the Wescott clan. Glenway Wescott knew a good deal about Fitzgerald, and in most ways his "The Moral of Scott Fitzgerald" (in the *New Republic* for February 1941 and reprinted in *The Crack-up*) is right on the money. At the time, of course, as an aspiring writer, I identified with some of the parts about Princeton, especially Wescott's criticism of the English department. Wescott wrote that although writers generally believed Fitzgerald "had the best narrative gift of the century," the English department did not help him to understand that or to enjoy his gifts. He learned chiefly to be an appreciative critic of the works of others. It seemed to me that the English department had not changed much, though it appeared to have some regard for the young W. S. Merwin and for Frederick Buechner and John Brooks, our official young novelists. And by then they even had some good things to say about Scott Fitzgerald.

On one hand I allowed myself to feel superior to him, because I made the cut on the freshman football team and he didn't. Like so many others, I was already haunted and challenged by the ghost of him. There is a mild and bitter irony about this feeling also. I have written about it elsewhere in another context:

Athletics occupied, at times, almost all my energy and desire. Beginning first with swimming—I learned to swim before I was two years old—and ending with college football where by the end of it I was wrapped in tape as any mummy from injuries of every kind. A David playing, without benefit of miracles, on a field of Goliaths. I ruined both knees, broke both feet, and covered my body with cloudy bruises. I recollect long afternoons spent in the steam and stink of the training room, then hobbling back to my dormitory, fresh tape binding me here and there, reeking from the scents of a medley of salves and liniments, groaning (quietly, quietly, a fixed smile on my face, lest anyone should suspect my pain) as I passed by the tennis courts where there were crowds of young white men all in white and all of them trim and handsome and graceful, not Goliaths, not a one, but every one of them a Scott Fitzgerald. (This was, after all, Princeton.) They flaunted what I had to admit was style. I can still hear, by an exercise of grim willpower, the crisp, tingy sounds of tennis balls and good rackets meeting each other in autumnal air. Can still summon up the slow fading of late-afternoon light, the scent of wood-smoke from somewhere not far; likewise the odor of leafsmoke—for they still innocently burned their leaf piles in those days. And in the midst of all this a boy-man mummy who would then and there cheerfully have leapt into a burning leaf pile if he could have vanished into the thick, pale grey smoke of it.

I did not know until many years later that Fitzgerald was short, also, small and compact. I might have liked him better at first if I had known that.

Another item. Directly behind our house in Orlando, Florida, lived a retired Marine officer, James Bettes, and his family. It turned out that he was in the same class as Fitzgerald at Princeton and even lived in the same entryway, and, together with many others, left Princeton to join the service in World War I. (For the record, Bettes, who always seemed a quiet and mild man, a gentle man, had served at one point as the commandant of the Portsmouth Naval Prison.) Bettes was not literary, but he thought that the Triangle shows that Fitzgerald and John Biggs and others had put together were quite wonderful.

Many years later I interviewed Judge John Biggs in Wilmington and had a fine day of it. One thing that came across clearly was another version of the honorable advice to trust the tale and not the teller. He described Fitzgerald as intellectually a kind of crank but also as intellectually precise and prescient as any seer or shaman.

Meantime, on my mother's side of the family, there was my Aunt Dorothy, whose life and whose world, in her youth, was very much like that, in general and some details, of Zelda Sayre of Alabama. They were astonishingly alike, really; and though they never met, Dorothy came to know a good deal about Zelda. Dorothy was engaged to a Princeton classmate of Fitzgerald named Henry Dunn. After the war, Dunn was in New York working at the same time as Fitzgerald, whom he greatly admired; and evidently they saw a good deal of each other for a while. He wrote letters to Dorothy every day full of stories about and sayings of his friend Scott Fitzgerald. Later Dorothy broke off her engagement to Henry Dunn — a fairly serious thing in the polite society of those days. She went on to marry a Texan and to move out there. Scholars will be relieved to learn that she burned all of her former fiancé's letters. She was not without good memory, though; and she told me a thing or two.

On the other side of the family there was my father's brother, my Uncle Oliver, Oliver H. P. Garrett, a celebrated young newspaperman for the old *New York Sun* (among others) in the 1920s. Beginning with the advent of sound pictures, he was a screenwriter until his death in the 1950s. He came out of a harder, tougher background. When Fitzgerald, John Biggs, Jim Bettes, and other Princeton students got around to answering the call to the colors, Oliver was already in infantry combat against the Germans. He was a rifleman in the trenches by the fall of 1917. He was wounded, won the (rare) Distinguished Service Cross, and was back home with the war over and behind him before he was old enough to vote. As a reporter he interviewed Adolph Hitler twice — once right after the failed Putsch of 1923 and once in the early 1930s. He covered the burning and sinking of the *Moro Castle* by rowing out to her and being on board until the last minute. He was the only newsman on board, but there were other people who were busy robbing the valuables, including the gold teeth of the dead and the dying. He wrote about them. He knew something of the American underworld, beginning with an exclusive interview with Al Capone and not quite ending when John Dillinger emerged from hiding to see Oliver's movie, *Manhattan Melodrama*, and was killed by the FBI when he came out of the theater. Oliver Garrett, it turned out, knew both Hemingway and Faulkner a little. He is credited with the adaptation of *Sanctuary* (*The Story of Temple Drake*) and with the Gary Cooper-Helen Hayes version of *A Farewell to Arms*, among maybe a hundred or more film scripts, both originals and adaptations. His path crossed that of Scott Fitzgerald when Selznick hired Oliver again (he had worked on an earlier version) to write what proved to be the final shooting script for *Gone with the Wind*. Oliver saw and used all the other scripts that Selznick had bought and paid for. He told me, when I asked about it, that Fitzgerald's versions were by far the best written of the lot and that the problem for Fitzgerald, as for others, had been Selznick's rigidity about time. He wanted a film of conventional length, and that was simply impossible. Oliver refused to sign on until he was given the freedom to write the film as long as he thought it ought to be.

I don't know, because I never asked, if Oliver Garrett ever actually talked to Scott Fitzgerald. I tend to doubt it. There was, however, one other odd connection between the two. Oliver was a close friend from early on and at one point a next-door neighbor to famed Hollywood producer Irving Thalberg, upon whom Fitzgerald based Monroe Stahr in *The Last Tycoon*. When Thalberg married movie star Norma Shearer, Oliver was an usher at the wedding.

Finally, I might add one more point of connection. My first three books were published by Scribners, where, years later, some of the legend remained, more a matter of haunting than of memory.

So there was always gossip from the beginning had I been willing and able to ask and to listen. There was also the sometimes acknowledged influence of Fitzgerald's work on many writers of my generation and after. Certainly *Gatsby* has been accorded, among the writers, an almost universal status, by consensus and acclamation, as a masterpiece. And the public image of Fitzgerald has haunted all of us. Conditioned by our expectations, our hopes and fears, we have looked to him for some kind of guidance, positive or negative.

Although a lot of my life has been spent in the Academy, it has seldom involved the teaching of modern and contemporary literature. Thus I was already in middle age, deep in my own career as a writer and teacher, before I had time and occasion to pause and to think about my own deeply mixed feelings about Fitzgerald. I knew that he was, line by line, move by move, one of the most gifted writers we Americans have ever known. Wescott was right, naming him as the possessor of "the best narrative gift of the century."

I also had come to learn, gradually, that Fitzgerald's great elegiac theme of change, change, change was more prophetic than he could have known or perhaps even wished. Tuned to change, fascinated by its nuances, he feared it as well. As well he might. Whether we recognize it or not, we are now so different in details that we are scarcely connected with his lost time and its ways and means. There is a natural tendency of American artists to imagine themselves as being part of a continuous progression, certainly including the previous generation or two. It is clear that Hemingway, Faulkner, Fitzgerald, and many others of their generation believed that they were more or less doing the same thing and that they belonged to the same grand tradition that included, for example, James and Conrad and Meredith. They were wrong about this, but not so much in error as are those of us who came afterwards and who may believe that we too are part of an ongoing progression and tradition including the great modern masters like Fitzgerald. Our calling, in keeping with the society where it is manifested, is radically different from that of our fathers and grandfathers. We cannot learn very many practical details from them and their examples. The world — even the shrinking world of literature — is too different to be justly compared. The same things will not likely happen again. All things are reduced to what Faulkner used to call "the old verities." It is there that Fitzgerald has instructed as well as delighted a whole generation of American writers. Proof of the century's changes is in his work, maybe more than anyone else's. It is from his work that we can most clearly discern where we have been and where we have come from. Ironically, then, his art, which so subtly records change and decay, transcends both.

What are some of the things that living writers are able to learn by calling up the example of Scott Fitzgerald? The great exemplary lessons of his impeccable and inimitable craft are subtle ones and run somewhat counter to the fashions and the forces of these times. His art is more admirable than directly influential. Mainly and more generally, his work teaches that it is possible to be original and innovative without embracing or asserting overt idiosyncrasy; that it is possible to cultivate a true and individual voice without calling unseemly, self-reflexive attention to the creator. But these are hard lessons, perhaps unavailable, maybe even undesirable to any but the mature artist. It seems to require maturity to be able to appreciate fully Fitzgerald's mature art.

It may be in the example of his vocational life (not his private life except insofar as it imposes upon the vocational) that he has most to show and tell other writers. I do not mean the easy and obvious lessons that are, in any case, more a matter of cliché than reality. For instance, Fitzgerald is often cited as a prime example of the catastrophe of early success, followed by a long, frustrated attempt to repeat that achievement. More to the point is the whole career, in the face of many formidable public and private troubles, during which he continued to grow and to develop as an artist and to produce work of the highest quality. He is not at all to be taken as an example of deflected talent and wasted gifts, though he, like anyone else, might well have done more and better work under better circumstances. The important, astonishing thing is how much and how well he performed under often very difficult conditions. One thing, then, that Fitzgerald represents for us who came along afterwards is enormous willpower, which, taken together with talent and courage and dedication, allowed him to keep working, creating for as long as he lived. He lives on, with honor, by that example.

PART TWO

The Novels

Princeton as Modernist's Hermeneutics

Rereading *This Side of Paradise*

NANCY P. VAN ARSDALE

Princeton, not Amory Blaine, is the center of *This Side of Paradise*. Although many critics tend to analyze the text as a bildungsroman, an episodic accounting of a young man's maturation, this first book is better understood as the author's effort to interpret what he had personally signified as the symbol of symbols, Princeton University. F. Scott Fitzgerald presented the institution as far more than a setting; indeed it became his center of the universe. Princeton must be analyzed as a modernist's paradise temporarily gained, inevitably lost, never forgotten. Readmission remains Amory's secret hope, as it was for Adam, Eve, and Scott. Contemplating the concept of a modernist's paradise within a hermeneutical framework that has evolved from traditional biblical study through American Puritanism, romanticisms, and realism leads us to the modernist's redefinition of Eden in this work: Princeton is the new religious, national, and social hermeneutics, an architectural and systematic text through which Fitzgerald interpreted his twentieth-century world.

How far should we stretch the idea of hermeneutical interpretation when examining the book of an atheist? In *Inventions: Writing, Textuality, and Understanding in Literary History*, Gerald L. Bruns argues that modern judicial, literary, and social concepts, in addition to traditional scriptural tenets, must be incorporated in a contemporary study of hermeneutics. Sacvan Bercovitch has studied how the hermeneutical interpretation of America as paradise has undergone ideological shifts through the centuries, yet remains fundamental to our national literature. In "The Image of America: From Hermeneutics to Symbolism," Bercovitch traces the hermeneutic tradition from Puritanism to the American Renaissance: "The American strategy undertakes to unite both of these developments, national and spiritual. In effect, it yokes together the internal and external Kingdom of God by asserting the simultaneity of a geographical locale, America, and a mode of vision." The poetry of Edward Taylor, for example, clearly reveals the minister's ambition to guide and steer his congregation, in effect *his* America, according to his imaginative application of scriptural tenets.[1]

More than a century after Puritanism had faded, American romantics continued to believe firmly in the idea of America as a reality, as a promised land, an earthly paradise provided by God. Bercovitch finds writers such as Hawthorne, Thoreau, Emerson, and Melville repeatedly re-creating in their work the *religious* experience of encountering a promised land. Such an experience leads to failure or expulsion, whether the setting is Melville's tumultuous and vast seas or Thoreau's Walden Pond. God is found in both the infinite and the infinitesimal, as these American allegories and parables explore the spiritual dimensions of nature in men's encounters with greater forces.

When we bring the Kingdom of God into Fitzgerald's modern world, the atheist dismisses the divine but nonetheless clings to a belief in the mythic Kingdom—Kingdom of *something*. Identifying that something becomes the challenge. America as an image of paradise is transmuted into the Ivy League campus in Fitzgerald's book, a place fraught with the symbolism of at least a higher culture even if the belief in a higher heaven has been relinquished. John Aldridge suggests that Amory Blaine is disappointed ultimately in Princeton's imperfection, but perhaps Fitzgerald was more disappointed in his own weakness, in his inability to be good enough to remain in paradise.[2]

In his later fiction, Fitzgerald distanced himself a little bit at least from his central characters by placing them at Yale and occasionally at Harvard, instead of Princeton, as Arthur Mizener has observed.[3] Nevertheless, Fitzgerald's earliest attempts to fictionalize the impact Princeton was having on him can be traced to his own undergraduate days there. In 1916, he published "The Spire and the Gargoyle" in the *Nassau Literary Magazine*, quite a bit of which, including the story's title as a chapter heading, was recycled in the final published version of *This Side of Paradise*. The features of the Gothic ornamentation on campus reveal the adolescent's first effort at adapting for literary purposes the architectural symbols of spiritual aspiration in the spire and human limitation in the gargoyle. Although the preliminary draft of the novel was titled "The Romantic Egotist," referring directly to his main character with his self-centered idealism, the final title returns to the evocation of place with a modernist's twist to the biblical reference; does the story take place outside of paradise from beginning to end, or does Amory find himself on "this side" after he leaves Princeton?

A close analysis of "The Spire and the Gargoyle" supports the latter idea, that Princeton is itself paradise and the world outside its gates is exile. Fitzgerald never even bothered to name his protagonist in the story, instead devoting his energies to signifying the architectural symbols that were, for the novice author, more important than the characters. In both the story and the novel, the architectural features can be symbolically interpreted as forces at odds with one another; this fact is essential to the story but is less effective in the novel. The spires represent academic achievement and ambition. The gargoyles are the narrow-minded preceptors and uninspiring instructors. The spires, like church steeples, point to the open sky, heaven, the divine; education can open up the human mind to infinite realms. In contrast, the gargoyles are small, frightening creatures—devils in stone. The two images thus juxtapose the concept of knowledge as liberation with the idea of institutional education as an evil, limiting process.

For the most part, both the story and the novel use poetic language to evoke Princeton as an intensely romantic setting. Its architecture is, in the eyes of the undergraduate, inspirational. Beautiful spring days transform the campus into a heavenly place, where the voices of singing seniors replace any need for choruses of angels on high. Scott Donaldson suggests that the "physical beauty of the place . . . helped to arouse the lyrical strain in Fitzgerald."[4] Fitzgerald apparently considered the spirit of the campus his own divine and personal muse.

The theme of "The Spire and the Gargoyle" focuses on personal responsibility. The main character, a student, has been under the delusion that acceptance to Princeton is a final goal. He has not been successful in terms of academic standards, cutting classes excessively. The tension of the first segment of the story revolves around a last-chance, make-up examination. If he fails, the student will be banned from Princeton, "his college days faded out with the last splendors of June."[5]

Before establishing the main character's character and predicament, Fitzgerald devotes much attention to presenting the campus and its effect on the student's imagination. The first sentences of the story depict the setting: "The night mist fell. From beyond the moon it rolled, clustered about the spires and towers, and then settled below them so that the dreaming peaks seemed still in lofty aspiration toward the stars" (105). Although the symbolic interpretations of the towers are clichés, they reveal Fitzgerald's attitude that a character cannot be separated from his environment. The student, now up in his room, reflects on his fate at the university:

> In view of his window a tower sprang upward, grew into a spire, yearning higher till its uppermost end was half invisible against the morning skies. The transiency and relative unimportance of the campus figures except as holders of a sort of apostolic succession had first impressed themselves on him in contrast with this spire. In a lecture or in an article or in conversation, he had learned that Gothic architecture with its upward trend was peculiarly adapted to colleges, and the symbolism of this idea had become personal to him. Once he had associated the beauty of the campus night with the parades and singing crowds that streamed through it, but in the last month the more silent stretches of sward and the quiet halls with an occasional late-burning scholastic light held his imagination with a stronger grasp — and this tower in full view of his window became the symbol of his perception. . . . To him the spire became an ideal. He had suddenly begun trying desperately to stay in college. (106–7)

Much of this architectural description reappears, virtually as is, in *This Side of Paradise*. Because considerably more effort has been put into Amory's characterization, the reader of the novel may miss the spire's significance to the student. To succeed at Princeton is to be admitted to the realm of higher spirituality pointed out by the spire. The temptation offered by the tree of knowledge of Eden is reinterpreted by Fitzgerald in both the story and the novel as a final examination. In the story, the role of the serpent is given to the preceptor who administers the exam; yet he is not represented in the novel. Ultimately, Fitzgerald must have decided that the preceptor was too obvious a depiction of the student's enemy; in *This Side of Paradise*, Amory's only enemy is Amory himself. Still, Fitzgerald handles the preceptor in "The Spire and the Gargoyle" once he, like the student, is forced to operate outside of paradise. The second part of the story takes place several years later when the student, who did fail the examination, meets the preceptor in New York at a museum. Again, the setting is used symbolically to identify the protagonist's current dilemma. The class and style of Fifth Avenue are juxtaposed with the masses and tackiness of Broadway. Although we are not informed of his current occupation, the protagonist obviously aspires to belong to the upper classes of the Avenue. He quests for a modernist's holy grail in a time when science has undermined religious faith: "Always a symbolist, and an idealist, . . . he sought around him in his common life for something to cling to, to stand for what religions and families and philosophies of life had stood for" (109).

The student has lost the one institution he did believe in: Princeton. He is surprised to learn, during tea conversation, that the preceptor has also left Princeton, at least for the moment. The preceptor explains that the needs of his growing family forced him to leave the college for a better-paying teaching position in Brooklyn. They both find a common bond in shared memories of the college's spires.

The third part of the story takes place months later, when the protagonist coincidentally meets the preceptor on a train to Princeton. The preceptor is visiting his brother, an instructor at Princeton, and he still hopes to return to his position there. The protagonist realizes that the preceptor, in spite of his financial difficulties, belongs to the place much more than he does: "The gargoyle, poor tired little hack, was bound up in the fabric of the whole system much more than he was." In contrast, the protagonist is struck by his own "complete overwhelming sense of failure" (114), his detachment from all places. Without even leaving the station, he catches the next train back to the city.

Although in part 1 the student seemed willing to blame the preceptor for failing his examination, he now recognizes the failure as exclusively his own. This may sound like a simple, adolescent experience—accepting one's own failures, recognizing there are consequences to one's own actions and negligence. Yet the plight of the protagonist is so integrated with the symbolism of Princeton, Broadway, and Fifth Avenue that Fitzgerald returned to all three sections of the story to borrow ideas for his first novel. In his essay "The Romantic Self and the Uses of Place," Richard Lehan correlates the story's outcome to that of the novel: "As in *This Side of Paradise*, the story ends with a sense of all that impedes the self-creating imagination. Whatever its limitations, and there are many, 'The Spire and the Gargoyle' reveals that very early in his career Fitzgerald had connected a sense of self with a sense of place, and both of these with a sense of destiny."[6]

In *This Side of Paradise*, Fitzgerald does a far superior job of developing the principal character, here named Amory Blaine; the novel also attempts to put the realm of responsibility and the significance of a social institution into a larger context than that of just the individual. Its final chapter, regardless of its weaknesses, focuses on a character who has changed personally and who wants to see society change as well. Although the book's final views are poorly presented, what is critically important is that Amory gives his lecture on socialism while returning to the towers and spires of Princeton. If "The Spire and the Gargoyle" focuses on how a place can influence an individual's fate, *This Side of Paradise* attempts to state that individuals should change the places and institutions of society. Specifically, paradise must be reclaimed when the academic community and society together redefine the mission of Princeton as an educational institution.

While Fitzgerald was expanding the core of the story into the first draft of a novel-length version, *The Education of Henry Adams* was circulating in a privately published and distributed edition (1918). Adams's text struggles to come to terms with the American educational experience in a period far removed from Puritanical religious conviction; in his case, Adams rejects the significance of Harvard classrooms as having any true positive influence on a young modernist's mind. Fitzgerald's novel similarly criticizes Princeton as an institution of higher learning, but like Adams, the young writer attempts to find grounds for modern morality in a world with "all Gods dead, all wars fought, all faiths in man shaken."

Fitzgerald's spiritual and cultural advisor, Father Sigourney Fay, the prototype for the novel's Monsignor Darcy, personally knew Adams and had perhaps discussed the autobiographical work with his young friend. Whereas Adams's treatise concludes with a comparison of the thirteenth-century Virgin and the twentieth-century Dynamo, *This Side of Paradise* ends with Amory, in a car heading back toward Princeton, lecturing to a deus ex machina on socialism. Adams tries to focus on technology as the substitute for religion; the young Fitzgerald attempted to focus on Marxist politics as a better institution for modern America than either the church or Princeton. But why does Amory take this stance en route to the university? In the final lines of his Harvard chapter, Henry Adams concludes: "As yet he [Adams, the new Harvard graduate] knew nothing. Education had not begun."[7] In effect, Amory returns to Princeton in the last pages, having realized how his formal educational experiences as well as his chance at paradise have been utter failures. But his return also represents his effort to bang on paradise's gates and seek admission on new grounds. Amory seeks the higher realm of justice, knowledge, and morality locked within Princeton's world as defined by its architecture.

What are Amory's reasons for *initially* choosing to go to Princeton? Temptations of the most superficial kind attract him: it "drew him most . . . with . . . its alluring reputation as the pleasantest country club in America."[8] Amory devotes his first two years at Princeton, before the critical examination, to the university's social traditions, specifically its clubs and organizations. From the beginning, he is a freshman advocate of the Princeton tradition. When he first develops an acquaintance with the boys in his house, he "spread the table of their future friendship with all his ideas of what college should and did mean," especially the "intricacies of the social system" (48). Yet even in these first descriptions of Amory's freshman year, Fitzgerald suggests that the true purpose of Princeton has only been partially sensed. From his first days there, Amory "loved Princeton — its lazy beauty, its half-grasped significance" (47).

The campus poet, Thomas Park d'Invilliers, first opens Amory's eyes to another side of Princeton. Based on John Peale Bishop, d'Invilliers is an avid writer and reader. Andrew Turnbull refers in his biography to the uniqueness of such literary interests: "Part of the Princeton code was not to appear to take one's studies too seriously and Bishop had an unmistakable aura of bookishness."[9] The English professors at Princeton may fail to inspire enthusiasm about poetry or modern writers, but Tom teaches Amory to enjoy reading — and writing. Several of Amory's friends, including Tom, question the Princeton social system long before Burne Holiday leads his rebellion during junior year. At one point, Tom informs Amory that he is tired of "the snobbishness of this corner of the world." He wonders if graduation from Princeton will ruin his natural intellectual curiosity: "I've learned all that Princeton has to offer. Two years more of mere pedantry and lying around a club aren't going to help me." Amory argues not why Tom must stay, but that it is useless to leave. The school has already placed its mark on the boys. As Amory explains, "For better or worse we've stamped you; you're a Princeton type!" (92).

Amory rates his own success based on his efforts outside of the classroom. The first acknowledgment of his social stature on campus is the invitation to join the staff of the newspaper: "Amory, by way of the *Princetonian*, had arrived" (78). Subsequent achievements include his admission to Cottage Club and his writing for the Triangle Club. For a while, Amory gets away with cutting class, ridiculing his professors, sleeping during lectures, and failing examinations. Of course, such a poor academic record will finally have an impact on Amory's life at Princeton. But note that it is a girlfriend, not someone on campus, who first suggests that Amory's view of Princeton is warped. The young woman is Isabelle, one of the first females to engage the young romantic's imagination. During a visit to her parents' house, Isabelle finally rejects Amory. She has grown weary of all his talk of Princeton and his self-importance: "Oh, you and Princeton! You'd think that was the world, the way you talk!" (102).

Then comes the critical examination. Fitzgerald transformed the consequences of this test from "The Spire and the Gargoyle" to *This Side of Paradise* so the focus centers on social rather than academic objectives. In the story, failing leads to banishment from Princeton. In the novel, failing results in being cut off from club memberships. The test is given during September of Amory's junior year. Completely bored with the preparation classes, Amory contemplates his relationship with Isabelle and his life as a student: "Somehow, with the defection of Isabelle the idea of undergraduate success had loosed its grasp on his imagination, and he contemplated a possible failure to pass off his condition with equanimity, even though it would arbitrarily mean his removal from the *Princetonian* board and the slaughter of his chances for the Senior Council" (105–6). Alec, one of Amory's friends, warns him unequivocally what failing the examination will mean to his social status: "Your stock will go down like an elevator at the club and on the campus" (106).

When Amory receives his examination results in the mail, it is fitting that he chooses to open the envelope in front of an audience. His manner is most sarcastic when he informs his peers that the slip is "Blue as the sky, gentlemen" (107). Universal possibilities, at least according to the social standards so important to Amory, are now shut off to him. In effect, the failed examination results shatter his world, just as they did the protagonist's in "The Spire and the Gargoyle." He has failed Princeton.

Indeed, Fitzgerald attempts to show that this is the first time in Amory's life where he recognizes how environments have affected his identity. The writer employs the device of a list in a most unusual way for this purpose. The passage reads:

> 1. The fundamental Amory.
> 2. Amory plus Beatrice.
> 3. Amory plus Beatrice plus Minneapolis.
>
> Then St. Regis' had pulled him to pieces and started him over again:
>
> 4. Amory plus St. Regis'.
> 5. Amory plus St. Regis' plus Princeton.
>
> That had been his nearest approach to success through conformity. The fundamental Amory, idle, imaginative, rebellious, had been nearly snowed under. He had conformed, he had succeeded, but as his imagination was neither satisfied nor grasped by his own success, he had listlessly, half-accidentally chucked the whole thing and become again:
>
> 6. The fundamental Amory. (108–9)

Although the list acknowledges a person's influence, his mother's, the primary influences on his life have been places, not people: Minneapolis, St. Regis',

Princeton. Essentially without those places, exiled from those places, Amory is nothing.

During Amory's subsequent time at Princeton he witnesses a body of students on campus who rise up together, questioning and refusing to join the clubs. The novel is weakened because Fitzgerald failed to intertwine sensitively the two kinds of introspections, Amory's own personal ones and Princeton's institutional ones. Amory remains only a passive observer of the revolutionary students. Then in the novel's last chapter, Amory suddenly identifies himself with a much larger rebellion—socialism. The connection between the microcosm of society at the university and society at large is loosely made at best.

Fitzgerald strove to show that art itself can be a rebellion too, but he did not let the character of Amory adequately represent this notion either. After failing the examination in his junior year, Amory grows more interested in poetry, or, in hermeneutical terms, the Word of meaning; it is, in effect, his new extracurricular activity. Amory writes, but his poems are mostly satirical commentaries on the more boring faculty members around campus. He reads more too. It is at this time that he discovers the poetry of Rupert Brooke. The novel's title and epigraph are borrowed from Brooke and highlight Amory's predicament at Princeton: "Well this side of Paradise! . . . / There's little comfort in the wise." Amory also commences a campuswide search for other poets: "Together with Tom d'Invilliers, he sought among the lights of Princeton for someone who might found the Great American Poetic Tradition" (116). Although Amory's appreciation for poetry increases during this period, he realizes his own talents are limited. He decides he does not have what it takes to be a poet, a modern artist whose words truly represent "the Word" of the twentieth century.

When war breaks out and many students enlist as soldiers, they do so because that is what is expected of Princeton men, of any college men for that matter. Only Burne Holiday, the book's true political rebel, takes a different point of view. His own choice, extremely radical for the period, is to be a pacifist. Amory has a difficult time understanding how Burne can choose this course. The Germans are such an obvious enemy, in his and most of America's eyes. But even more important, Amory has a harder time accepting Burne's fervent belief in his personal ability to make such a decision. Burne leaves Princeton on a humble bicycle. Amory feels he is "leaving everything worth while" (163) because he is choosing to leave Paradise behind. Yet as Amory watches Burne depart, he doubts his own ability to make a personal decision that goes against the grain of the establishment: "as he saw Burne's long legs propel his ridiculous bicycle out of sight beyond Alexander Hall, he knew he was going to have a bad week. Not that he doubted the war — Germany stood for everything repugnant to him; for materialism and the direction of tremendous licentious force; it was just that Burne's face stayed in his memory and he was sick of the hysteria he was beginning to hear" (163).

Just as Amory acknowledges Burne's transformation, he is also conscious that the mood of the times is changing. Princeton has done its best to shelter its students from the modern world, but Amory nonetheless detects that even Princeton will finally have to make accommodations to modernity: "The war seemed scarcely to touch them and it might have been one of the senior springs of the past, except for the drilling every other afternoon, yet Amory realized poignantly that this was the last spring under the old régime" (166). The socially conscious boy is becoming a man who recognizes that the religious beliefs and comfortable social networks of the past may no longer work in this new era. But what will replace those networks? Amory leaves Princeton in the acceptable fashion, as a soldier. But does he ever really let go of the idea of Princeton as a paradise-on-earth for the upper classes?

The correspondence between John Peale Bishop and Fitzgerald, when both were soldiers, sheds light on this question. In a letter dated December 27, 1917, Bishop justified the war. He told Fitzgerald that he personally was "fighting simply to keep the old way of things . . . fighting for Princeton, I suppose, for in spite of all its faults it somehow represents all that I want to hold on to." [10] Fighting for Princeton? Yes, because Princeton's social system may have been challenged, but the sense of Princeton as the closest-place-to-perfection on earth never fades. Although the act of publishing *This Side of Paradise* caused Princeton to exile Fitzgerald a second time, his later prose shows he never abandoned his vision of the place as paradise.

The football game sometimes represents the equivalent of a religious icon or ritual in Fitzgerald's hermeneutic of Princeton. He exploits the symbolic possibilities in both the 1927 essay "Princeton" and the 1928 *Saturday Evening Post* story "The Bowl." Whereas the story refers to specific Yale-Princeton games, the essay elevates the language of signification and equates such games with the indescribable meaning of modern life: "For at Princeton, as at Yale, football became, back in the nineties, a sort of symbol. Symbol of what? Of the eternal violence of American life? Of the eternal immaturity of the race? The failure of a culture within the walls? Who knows? It became something at first satisfactory, then essential and beautiful." [11]

Fitzgerald attempted to present the central importance of Princeton to the universe in a football song for the school. In a letter addressed to Brooks Bowman, who had written a successful Triangle production song called "East of the Sun," Fitzgerald advised the songwriter to revise the song's lyrics in the following pattern so it could be used as a Princeton cheer:

> East of the sun, west of the moon
> *Lies Princeton,*
> South of the south, north of the north
> *Lies Princeton. . . .*[12]

Ironically, Fitzgerald was scribbling notes about college football on a Princeton newsletter when he died.

Perhaps the hermeneutical significance of Princeton to Fitzgerald is best revealed in "Princeton," an essay he wrote for *College Humor*. It reflects on his undergraduate experiences, but certain passages recall the tone of invocation in the Princeton descriptions of *This Side of Paradise*. His prose is lyrical, impassioned, philosophical at times, because the author continued to be an ardent worshiper at Princeton's altar. Fitzgerald satirically noted that paradise was certainly out of place in New Jersey; he called it "a green Phoenix" rising "out of the ugliest country in the world." It is located in the East, but it is not of the East: "The busy East has already dropped away when the branch train rattles familiarly from the junction."[13]

The concluding paragraph of the essay in particular emphasizes how beautiful — and elusive — Princeton remains as time moves the student further and further away from his days there: "Looking back over a decade one sees the ideal of a university become a myth, a vision, a meadow lark among the smoke stacks. Yet perhaps it is there at Princeton, only more elusive than under the skies of the Prussian Rhineland or Oxfordshire; or perhaps some men come upon it suddenly and possess it, while others wander forever outside. Even these seek in vain through middle age for any corner of the republic that preserves so much of what is fair, gracious, charming in American life."[14]

Fitzgerald critics have for too long focused on the New York City and Long Island of *Gatsby* as the geographic key to his interpretation of American life. When we look at Princeton as the place that transformed him into a writer, we discover Fitzgerald's central hermeneutic. Princeton and the Ivy League remained a key symbol of higher order, purpose, and meaning to Fitzgerald throughout his life. He would repeatedly refocus on Princeton, not as a setting, but as a signifier of the divine, a social and institutional construction containing the highest truth, a symbol more crucial in his early work than even the individual self.

NOTES

1. Bruns, *Inventions*, 112–13; Bercovitch, " Image of America," 158.
2. Aldridge, "Fitzgerald," 33.
3. Fitzgerald, *Afternoon of an Author*, 70.
4. Donaldson, *Fool for Love*, 35.
5. Kuehl, *Apprentice Fiction*, 106. All subsequent page references to "The Spire and the Gargoyle" are to this edition and appear parenthetically in the text.
6. Lehan, " Romantic Self," 5.
7. Adams, *Education of Henry Adams*, 64.
8. Fitzgerald, *This Side of Paradise*, 40. All subsequent page references to *This Side of Paradise* are to the 1920 edition and appear parenthetically in the text.
9. Turnbull, *Scott Fitzgerald*, 52.
10. Donaldson, *Fool for Love*, 35.
11. Fitzgerald, *Afternoon of an Author*, 72.
12. Donaldson, *Fool for Love*, 34.
13. Fitzgerald, *Afternoon of an Author*, 71.
14. Ibid., 79.

WORKS CITED

Adams, Henry. *The Education of Henry Adams*. 1918. New York: Modern Library, 1931.

Aldridge, John. "Fitzgerald: The Horror and the Vision of Paradise." In *F. Scott Fitzgerald: A Collection of Critical Essays*. Ed. Arthur Mizener. Englewood Cliffs, N.J.: Prentice-Hall, 1963. 32–42.

Bercovitch, Sacvan. "The Image of America: From Hermeneutics to Symbolism." In *Early American Literature: A Collection of Critical Essays*. Ed. Michael T. Gilmore. Englewood Cliffs, N.J.: Prentice-Hall, 1980. 159–67.

Bruns, Gerald L. *Inventions: Writing, Textuality, and Understanding in Literary History*. New Haven, Conn.: Yale University Press, 1982.

Donaldson, Scott. *Fool for Love: F. Scott Fitzgerald*. New York: Congdon & Weed, 1983.

Fitzgerald, F. Scott. *Afternoon of an Author: A Selection of Uncollected Stories and Essays*. Ed. Arthur Mizener. New York: Scribners, 1958.

———. *This Side of Paradise*. New York: Scribners, 1920.

Kuehl, John, ed. *The Apprentice Fiction of F. Scott Fitzgerald: 1909–1917*. New Brunswick, N.J.: Rutgers University Press, 1965.

Lehan, Richard. "The Romantic Self and the Uses of Place in the Short Stories of F. Scott Fitzgerald." In *The Short Stories of F. Scott Fitzgerald: New Approaches in Criticism*. Ed. Jackson R. Bryer. Madison: University of Wisconsin Press, 1982. 3–21.

Turnbull, Andrew. *Scott Fitzgerald*. New York: Scribners, 1962.

Keats's Lamian Legacy

Romance and the Performance of Gender in

The Beautiful and Damned

CATHERINE B. BURROUGHS

Elizabeth Kaspar Aldrich has noted that F. Scott Fitzgerald, "more than any other American writer who comes to mind, . . . is associated in criticism as well as biography with a particular, real woman who was at once wife, muse, model and sometimes literary rival. The highly public and well-documented career of his marriage served always as addendum to or even gloss on the work."[1] This marriage "career" anchors Judith Fetterley's well-known feminist reading of *The Great Gatsby* in which Fetterley concludes that Fitzgerald's complicated relationship with his wife, Zelda Sayre, resulted in female characters in Fitzgerald's fiction who are "annihilated" and "solipsized." Arguing that the "structures of the romantic imagination . . . are affairs of the male ego from which women are excluded,"[2] Fetterley follows the trend among a number of Fitzgerald scholars by elevating the biography to the point where analyses of the fiction emerge as but reflections of a particular interpretation of Fitzgerald's life. Fetterley's reading suggests that Fitzgerald's preoccupation with romance makes his fiction suspect for women readers. Yet as many scholars have been quick to emphasize in recent years, Fitzgerald's presentation of gender is more complicated than Fetterley's comments imply.[3] Rather than portraying women as suffering only for their allegiance to an ideology that Anne K. Mellor identifies with the term "masculine romanticism"[4] — or as his fiction's only sufferers — Fitzgerald reveals that his male characters also occupy what have traditionally been considered "feminine" positions. When loving women, Fitzgerald's men often assume the posture of emotional dependents, hugging the memory of a romantic moment to their breasts like a faded nosegay, watching in horror as the beloved turns an unsentimental eye elsewhere.

In *The Beautiful and Damned* (1922), Fitzgerald describes a relationship that is equally devastating for both male and female partner. He reveals how faith in romance can seduce its believers into prescribing roles for each other guaranteed to paralyze them into caricatures of loving people. However, by evoking the inconstant narrative voice in John Keats's narrative poem *Lamia* (1819), *The Beautiful and Damned* also counters this critique of romance, alternating between judging and embracing the romantic gestures of its central characters. This narrative ambivalence is the central strategy that *The Beautiful and Damned* borrows from Keats in order to question the desirability of idealizing erotic love. While critics have commented extensively on the prevalence of the fatal woman figure in Fitzgerald's fiction and on the legacy of Keatsian romanticism in Fitzgerald's thought,[5] they have yet to explore in any detail some of the ways in which Keats's narrator in *Lamia* influences the narrative voice of Fitzgerald's second novel. Tracing this influence on *The Beautiful and Damned* as it reveals the narrative's ambivalent presentation of romantic love and the romance genre is the focus of the following argument.

A romance about the married, *The Beautiful and Damned* charts the gradual dimming of Gloria Gilbert's luster. Yet as Anthony Patch becomes more disillusioned with this "golden girl," the narrative starts to distinguish between Anthony's eventual perception of Gloria as *"la belle dame sans merci* who lived in his heart"[6] and as the very human person who comes to discover her growing powerlessness in a culture where celebrating the romance plot is a powerful means of reinforcing gender differences.

Gloria is introduced through a short playscript, "A Flash-Back in Paradise," inserted at the start of the novel from which the narrative voice is absent (except as a presenter of stage directions). She is at first portrayed as an immortal sent to earth in order to sit in waiting for Anthony Patch, whose susceptibility to the curvatures of feminine role playing will be fatal to his own sense of self. At the insistence of "The Voice," a character called "Beauty" (whom we are to associate with Gloria in her premortal state) learns that she is to be born again, this time into an American setting and this time as a "'susciety girl,'" a "sort of bogus aristocrat" (29). She "will be known during [her] fifteen years as a ragtime kid, a flapper, a jazz-baby, and a baby vamp," who will "be paid . . . as usual—in love" (29). With her mission clear and the parameters of her gender performance foreordained, Gloria's survival in this early-twentieth-century American landscape would seem to depend upon how effectively she enacts a cultural stereotype pivotal to the romance genre: the beautiful woman who seduces men from their self-possession, self-control, and self-esteem.

Initially the narrative voice focuses on Gloria primarily as she affects Anthony's progress through the world, amusedly watching him declare his faith in certain romantic ideals and then snub them in his more ironic moments. The narrative voice even competes with its hero to assert its sense of the absurdity of human existence, generally breezing along for the first part of the novel when Anthony is single and, through the chapter titles that comment ironically on the earnestness of romance ("The Connoisseur of Kisses," "The Radiant Hour"), trying to resist getting caught up in Anthony's idealization of Gloria. However, once Gloria becomes Anthony's raison d'être, the narrative seems to forget that it has introduced her to the novel in the "Flash-Back in Paradise" sequence, which itself pokes fun at idealization: the woman who would assume her place in a culture eager to idealize female beauty has been revealed as a reluctant emissary from another world. (For instance, learning that she must go to earth again, Gloria, "sighing," says "*petulantly*": "I loathe breaking into these new civilizations" [27–28]). For once Anthony acknowledges that Gloria "moved him as he had never been moved before," that the "sheath that held her soul had assumed significance," that she appealed to "that part of him that cherished all beauty and all illusion" (73), the narrative seems unable to maintain its distance from its subject and instead cherishes Gloria's responses and divulges her feelings empathetically. As in Keats's *Lamia*, the shifting perspective of the narrative voice in *The Beautiful and Damned* makes more complicated Fitzgerald's use of the fatal woman image. In fact, as she edges closer to the moment when she will become too old to be associated with romance plots and—in the terms that the playlet in which she is introduced establishes—must return to Paradise as a contemplative beauty waiting to be reborn, the narrative champions Gloria as someone deserving of compassion. This is not to suggest that the narrator turns against Anthony. On the contrary, it musters compassion for him as well, both for his allegiance to Gloria's stellar performance of the culture's feminine ideal and for his own attempt to be "masculine" in proportion to her rebellious dance. Indeed, the narrative shows that Anthony—by enshrining in his heart the performance that Gloria has given as a young debutante—is responsible for dooming himself to behavior that inevitably disappoints not only his wife and friends but also himself.

Like Jay Gatsby to follow, Anthony commits himself to performing a role that keeps him frozen in homage to a single moment of romantic ecstasy toward which he keeps trying to return. Yet, unlike Gatsby, whose priestlike dedication to the idea of a woman (whom he is destined not to have) achieves a mythic resonance through Nick Carraway's eulogy to American dreamers at that novel's end, Anthony is fated not to inspire admiration for his tenacious love. This is because his desire to hold onto romance in marriage plays havoc with the typical romance plot. Because he marries the person he idolizes and because he still wants to remain a romantic figure in marriage, Anthony poses a challenge to the narrative of the novel, which follows his story past the limits of the plot that romance narratives are designed to contain.

After Gloria and Anthony's engagement in the first book of the novel, the narrative informs readers that the lovers are "but following in the footsteps of dusty generations" (137). But the possibility that they will ever be emotionally distant from each other temporarily recedes in the face of their young-hearted surety that they can uniquely blend, merge, and meld. In the chapter of the novel titled "The Radiant Hour," the unmarried Gloria and Anthony explore the ways in which they resemble rather than differ from each other: both are "blowy clean" twins, souls "created together and—and in love before they're born" (131). When Gloria tells Anthony that she's "got a man's mind," he asserts that hers is actually like his: "not strongly gendered either way" (134); and when Anthony kisses a woman named Dorothy Raycroft during their wan affair in a later section of the novel, he muses that "Gloria and he had been equals" (333).

For much of the story, the Patches are presented as a team dedicated to freeing themselves from cultural expectations for the "correct" performance of masculinity and femininity. Though several times in the course of telling its tale the narrative tries to intimate that the desire to hold onto romance is feminine—we are told that Gloria is attracted to Galsworthy's "power of re-creating . . . that illusion of young romantic love to which *women* look forever forward and forever back" (371; emphasis added)—the narrative shows that the Patches desire equally to preserve those moments when they felt particularly free of the clichés of middle-class married life.

Fitzgerald's narrative is especially intrusive when trying to make certain that the reader recognizes as illusory Anthony's and Gloria's faith in preserving the intensity of early romance. "It seemed," the narrative says, that Gloria "had not felt the cold, warmed by the profound *banalities* burning in her heart" (146; emphasis added). But although the narrative knows more than the lovers—is indeed privy to the fact of their inevitable disappointment and dissipation—its occasional elegaic tone suggests a sporadic identification with their romantic idealism. At one moment during Gloria's and Anthony's courtship, the narrative sounds like Keats's narrator in *Lamia*, who cannot seem to help but exclaim, "Ah, happy Lycius!,"[7] a phrase tinged with longing and regret, especially since Keats's narrator knows the unhappy outcome of its story. "Halcyon days," Fitzgerald's narrative muses, "like boats drifting along slow-moving rivers; spring evenings full of a plaintive melancholy that made the past beautiful and bitter, bidding them look back and see that the loves of other summers long gone were dead with the forgotten waltzes of their years" (137). This narrator seems to possess the same degree of nostalgia that Gloria expresses for her girlhood on the evening before her wedding when she leafs through the diary that she has been keeping for seven years.

Sensing that marriage can be especially imperiling for women, Gloria uses language that conjures up the image of Keats's snake-woman; she worries about "what grubworms women are to crawl on their bellies through colorless marriages!": "Marriage was created not to be a background but to need one. Mine is going to be outstanding. It can't, shan't be the setting—it's going to be the performance, the live, lovely, glamourous performance, and the world shall be the scenery" (147).

Because they have such high expectations for how their marriage will unfold, both Gloria and Anthony are equally stunned when the other eventually "submit[s] to mediocrity" (449), when each makes choices that emphasize gendered behavior: Gloria tries to preserve her beauty on film by undergoing a screen test for the movies, which reveals her not to be "young enough for anything except a character part" (428), and Anthony tries on the role of breadwinner by becoming a salesman and pushing a little book called "Heart Talks." Since Gloria has promised to make a marriage that features her in an atypical "performance," her aim is doomed, the narrative suggests, because merely by marrying she will be perceived as embodying the cliché of the married female that so disgusts her. That Gloria knows that what she does *not* want— "to grow rotund and unseemly, to lose my self-love, to think in terms of milk, oatmeal, nurse, diapers" (147) and to live in "a hot stuffy bungalow, with a lot of babies next door and their father cutting the grass in his shirt sleeves" (171) — cannot prevent her at novel's end from being pitied by passengers aboard a cruise liner for looking "sort of dyed and *unclean*" (448). Nor can it prevent the Patches' growing estrangement from each other, their capitulation to marital clichés as each blames the other for their diminishing self-esteem. Anthony has an affair and adopts a macho posture in telling a perverse little story about having once wanted to "kick a cat" (289); he also comes to regard the immortal Gloria as "a brilliant curtain across his door-ways," who shuts "out the light of the sun" (191). With the arrival at the Patches' Marietta residence of Joe Hull—a staring silent figure whose pres-ence troubles Gloria instinctively—Gloria is suddenly made vulnerable to a "horror in the house" (233).

Keats's version of the ancient Greek myth about the lamia forecasts Fitzgerald's presentation of romance as both vital and stultifying by describing the earthly adventures of a creature who, like Gloria Gilbert in *The Beautiful and Damned,* moves between mortal and immortal worlds. A focus on the shifting attitudes of Keats's narrator toward the poem's central female character suggests the degree to which Fitzgerald's second novel expresses a conflicted response about some of the ways in which faith in romance both fulfills and depletes its followers.

At first Keats's narrator introduces Lamia empathetically: Hermes, who has come to earth to pursue a beautiful nymph, hears Lamia's voice as "lone" and "mournful"; it is the kind, readers are told, that arouses "pity" in a "gentle heart" (1.35–37). Lamia's opening words also elicit sympathy for her predica-ment as an immortal snake who wants to become a mortal female: "When from this wreathed tomb shall I awake!" she exclaims, "When move in a sweet body fit for life, / And love, and pleasure, and the ruddy strife / Of hearts and lips!" (1.38–41).

Soon, however, Keats's narrative conveys its confusion about whether to judge Lamia as compelling or threatening to the world she would inhabit: "So rainbow-sided, touched with miseries," it says, "She seemed, at once, some penanced lady elf, / Some demon's mistress, or the demon's self" (1.54–56). Because Lamia appears to be both a miserably entrapped "lady" and a "de-mon" who must be resisted, the narrator is skeptical about Lamia's motives for wanting to exchange a reptile's body for a woman's. The narrative's attitudinal shifts toward Lamia and the other major characters in the poem signal that the primary conflict of this work, as in *The Beautiful and Damned,* derives from the narrative's struggle with how to interpret this romance to an audience. Is Lamia out to beguile her lover, Lycius, or to fulfill her dreams? Is the relation-ship between the lovers one to applaud or reject? Is the move from courtship to marriage the cause of the lovers' demise?

In perhaps the poem's most memorable scene (anticipating Fitzgerald's "A Flash-Back in Paradise" segment in *The Beautiful and Damned*), when Lamia metamorphosizes into a "full-born beauty new and exquisite" (1.172), she is described in terms horrific enough to cast doubt on the desirability of her desire to shed her snake's skin:

Left to herself, the serpent now began
To change; her elfin blood in madness ran
Her mouth foamed, and the grass therewith besprent,
Withered at dew so sweet and virulent;
Her eyes in torture fixed and anguish drear,
Hot, glazed, and wide, with lid-lashes all sear,
Flashed phosphor and sharp sparks, without one cooling tear.
The colours all inflamed throughout her train,
She writhed about, convulsed with scarlet pain.
(1.146–54)

Rooted in violence, physical agony, and mental unbalance, the narrative's vocabulary portrays Lamia as erupting apocalyptically into humanhood and thus gives the reader a horrible impression of the birthing process by which Lamia becomes female. Because the snake vomits up a female body designed to captivate Lycius—the young Corinthian to whom she has become attracted during a previous transformation—in yet another variation on the fatal woman theme that finds its prototype in *Genesis's* Eve, the question of whether or not the romantic encounter with Lycius is worth such convulsions lingers over the first part of the poem.

Ultimately Keats's narrative suggests that Lamia is most dangerous to herself and to her eventual lover, Lycius, when she behaves in stereotypically feminine ways. Assuming (after her transformation) the gesture and speech of the "half retir[ing]" female, who has long been in Corinth watching Lycius with unrequited love waiting for him to notice her, Lamia's performance is compelling—the narrative tells us—precisely because she "threw the goddess off, and won his heart / More pleasantly by playing woman's part" (1.336–37). Lycius is persuaded to act the swooning lover because Lamia is practiced in whispering "woman's lore so well" (1.325). Yet though the narrative seems determined to remind readers that Lamia is playing a deceptive role, by the end of the first part of the poem the narrative confesses that were it not *compelled* to finish the tale that it has begun, it would, in what one might call a romantic impulse, like to "leave [the lovers] thus, / Shut from the busy world, of more incredulous" (1.396–97). Rather than being alarmed at what it has described as Lycius's entrapment by a magically manipulative servant, the narrative voice momentarily abandons its concern and paints an appealing picture of the lovers ensconced in their pleasure dome.

In fact, the second part of the poem reveals that the narrative has begun to get caught up in the romanticism of its own tale. Suddenly it views the impending interruption of the lovers' tryst as "a ruin," tenderly imagining their repeated eroticism on a couch "made . . . sweet" by "use" (2.23). As Lycius's senses recall him to the world beyond the palace — just as Anthony's move him to contemplate a life without Gloria in the second half of *The Beautiful and Damned* — Lamia's perspective is once again considered: we are told that she views Lycius's growing restlessness "with pain, / . . . and she began to moan and sigh / Because he mused beyond her, knowing well, / That but a moment's thought is passion's passing bell" (2.35–39).

As the poem progresses, the narrative becomes more and more attuned to the snake-woman, especially when Lamia balks at leaving the secret palace to wed Lycius in front of all of his friends and the philosopher-professor Apollonius. Leading up to the moment when Apollonius turns his "sophist's eye" (2.299) on Lamia and annihilates her with his stare (forecasting the scene in *The Beautiful and Damned* when Joe Hull disturbs Gloria at her Marietta residence), the narrative finds ways to commiserate with Lamia's sense that Apollonius threatens her existence as a mortal woman. The most striking instance of this intensifying sensitivity occurs when the narrative calls Lycius a "Madman!" asking him why he would "flout / The silent-blessing fate, warm-cloistered hours, / And show to common eyes those secret bowers" (2.147–49). In one of the poem's best-known sections, the narrative appears to have overcome its earlier ambivalence about Lamia by bursting forth with the following rhetorical question: "Do not all charms fly / At the mere touch of cold philosophy?" (2.229–30).

The nostalgia that informs the subsequent lines suggests that the narrator has lost something that it associates positively with Lamia's performance of femininity:

> There was an awful rainbow once in heaven:
> We know her woof, her texture; she is given
> In the dull catalogue of common things.
> Philosophy will clip an Angel's wings,
> Conquer all mysteries by rule and line,
> Unweave a rainbow, as it erewhile made
> The tender-personed Lamia melt into a shade.
> (2.229–38)

Now characterized as "tender-personed," an assessment prepared for by the narrative's earlier reference to Lycius's desire to "entangle, trammel up and snare" Lamia's "soul" (2.52–53), Lamia has assumed the spot reserved for Lycius in the narrative's opening moments.

Lycius, by contrast, is now described as "perverse"; he takes "delight / Luxurious in [Lamia's] sorrows"; his passion is "cruel grown"; he is guilty of "tyranny" (2.73–81). Lycius's furious possessiveness creates a scenario in which Lamia becomes the battered wife in a moment not unlike that in *The Beautiful and Damned* when Anthony Patch experiments with playing the stereotypical husband's role on the train station platform at Redgate. The difference between the two sequences is that while Lamia is said to "love" Lycius's "tyranny" (2.81), Gloria finds Anthony's manhandling spiritually crushing. In one of many Keatsian echoes, Fitzgerald's narrative shows Anthony speculating that Gloria "might hate him now, but afterward she would admire him for his dominance" (199). Yet, understandably, just the reverse occurs. "You've — you've killed any love I ever had for you, and any respect" (200), Gloria shrieks after Anthony physically prevents her from going home in order that she might visit the Barneses. This platform scene marks a turning point in *The Beautiful and Damned*, for, as in *Lamia*, once the central male character begins to flex his muscle over the heroine, the femininity that has been alternately championed and feared by the narrative is presented as a liability for women; indeed, it is also targeted as eliciting from men performances of cultural stereotypes as exaggerated as those that the women feel compelled to enact.

By the end of *Lamia*, when Lamia dies in the middle of the bridal feast, the narrative has grown compassionate to the point of reversing its perspective from the opening of the poem, describing Lamia's pride as "sweet" and summarizing her condition as "poor." Apollonius may believe that he is saving Lycius from the machinations of a deceptive supernatural creature — "shall I see thee made a serpent's prey?" (2.298), he says to Lycius — but the poem expresses ambivalence about his actions, especially since Lycius also dies in the process of "the cure." In *The Beautiful and Damned*, the narrative voice enacts a similar struggle, not only examining what happens to individuals committed to following a romantic script but also questioning the narrator's "own" involvement in (and divestment from) the romantic tale. Rather than arguing for the necessity or desirability of women's entrapment in gender stereotypes, *The Beautiful and Damned* features an indecisive narrative voice whose alternate skepticism and sentimentality about romance encourages readers to contemplate the degree to which a faith in the ideology of "masculine romanticism" works to limit the ability of both men and women to grow in love.

NOTES

1. Aldrich, "'The most poetical topic in the world,'" 131. Mary A. McCay provides an example of the tendency that Aldrich identifies by focusing on Fitzgerald's relationships with Sheilah Graham and Frances Scott Fitzgerald in order to discuss F. Scott

Fitzgerald's "highly critical attitude" toward the women in his novels ("Fitzgerald's Women," 311).

2. Fetterley, "*Great Gatsby*: Fitzgerald's 'droit de seigneur,'" 98. The crux of Fetterley's argument centers on a quotation by Fitzgerald. Fetterley observes: "The nature of the connection that *The Great Gatsby* reveals between a male sense of disadvantage and attitudes toward women is perhaps best understood if we examine a comment Fitzgerald made in recording the profound effect on him of being a poor boy trying to win his rich girl, Zelda: 'I have never been able to stop wondering where my friends' money came from, nor to stop thinking that at one time a sort of *droit de seigneur* might have been exercised to give one of them my girl'" (82–83).

3. For other articles that focus on Fitzgerald's relationship with Zelda Sayre and the actual women in his life, see Korenman, "'Only Her Hairdresser'"; Martin, "Fitzgerald's Image of Woman"; McNicholas, "Fitzgerald's Women in *Tender Is the Night*"; Person, "Fitzgerald's 'O Russet Witch!'" and "'Herstory' and Daisy Buchanan"; and Fedo, "Women in the Fiction of F. Scott Fitzgerald."

For additional readings of Fitzgerald's female characters and gender issues, see the following: Kolbenschlag, "Madness and Sexual Mythology in F. Scott Fitzgerald"; Greenwald, "Fitzgerald's Female Narrators"; Thornton, "Sexual Roles in *The Great Gatsby*"; Ryan, "F. Scott Fitzgerald and the Battle of the Sexes"; Prigozy's important essay on Rosemary Hoyt, father-daughter incest, and the films of D. W. Griffith, "From Griffith's Girls to Daddy's Girl"; Fryer's detailed discussions of Daisy Buchanan and Nicole Warren, "Beneath the Mask" and *Fitzgerald's New Women*; Settle, "Fitzgerald's Daisy"; Sipiora, "Vampires of the Heart"; and Burroughs, "Of 'Sheer Being.'" Papers presented at the first International F. Scott Fitzgerald Conference (September 1992) and the special session on "Fitzgerald and Gender" at the Midwest Modern Language Association Conference (November 1993) suggest that Fitzgerald's portrayal of male and female character is less schematic and more complicated than previously argued.

4. Mellor, *Romanticism and Gender*, 13–29. Mellor defines "masculine romanticism" as a concern "with the capacities of the creative imagination, with the limitations of language, with the possibility of transcendence or 'unity of being,' with the development of an autonomous self, with political (as opposed to social) revolution, with the role of the creative writer as political leader or religious savior" (2).

5. The long tradition in Fitzgerald scholarship of comparing Fitzgerald's work with Keats's poetry has resulted in only a few references to the similarities that exist between *Lamia* and *The Beautiful and Damned*. See especially Lehan, *F. Scott Fitzgerald and the Craft of Fiction*; Bloom, "Introduction"; and Tuttleton, "Vitality and Vampirism," who refers to *Lamia* in his discussion of *Tender Is the Night* and "female vampirism."

For comparisons of Keats's and Fitzgerald's work, see: Schoenwald, "F. Scott Fitzgerald as John Keats"; Doherty, "*Tender Is the Night* and the 'Ode to a Nightingale'"; Grube, "*Tender Is the Night*"; McCall, "'The Self-Same Song That Found a Path'";

Loftus, "John Keats in the Works of F. Scott Fitzgerald"; Monteiro, "James Gatz and John Keats"; Scherr, "Lawrence, Keats, and *Tender Is the Night*"; and Swann, "Fitzgerald Debt to Keats?"

6. Fitzgerald, *Beautiful and Damned*, 329. All subsequent page references to *The Beautiful and Damned* are to the 1922 edition and appear parenthetically in the text.

7. Keats, *Lamia, John Keats: Complete Poems*, 1.185. All subsequent references to *Lamia* are to the 1978 edition and appear parenthetically in the text.

BIBLIOGRAPHY

Aldrich, Elizabeth Kaspar. "'The most poetical topic in the world': Women in the Novels of F. Scott Fitzgerald." In *Scott Fitzgerald: The Promises of Life*. Ed. Robert A. Lee. New York: St. Martin's Press, 1989. 131–56.

Bloom, Harold. "Introduction." In *F. Scott Fitzgerald*. Ed. Harold Bloom. New York: Chelsea House, 1985. 1–5.

Burroughs, Catherine. "Of 'Sheer Being': Fitzgerald's Aesthetic Typology and the Burden of Transcription." *Modern Language Studies* 22, no. 1 (1992): 102–9.

Doherty, William E. "*Tender Is the Night* and the 'Ode to a Nightingale.'" In *Explorations of Literature*. Ed. Rima Drell Reck. Baton Rouge: Louisiana State University Press, 1966. 100–114.

Fedo, David. "Women in the Fiction of F. Scott Fitzgerald." *Ball State University Forum* 21, no. 2 (1980): 26–33.

Fetterley, Judith. "*The Great Gatsby*: Fitzgerald's 'droit de seigneur.'" *The Resisting Reader: A Feminist Approach to American Fiction*. Bloomington: Indiana University Press, 1978. 72–100.

Fitzgerald, F. Scott. *The Beautiful and Damned*. New York: Scribners, 1922.

Fryer, Sarah Beebe. "Beneath the Mask: The Plight of Daisy Buchanan." In *Critical Essays on F. Scott Fitzgerald's "The Great Gatsby."* Ed. Scott Donaldson. Boston: G. K. Hall, 1984. 153–66.

———. *Fitzgerald's New Women: Harbingers of Change*. Ann Arbor, Mich.: UMI Research Press, 1988.

Greenwald, Fay T. "Fitzgerald's Female Narrators." *Mid-Hudson Language Studies* 2 (1979): 116–33.

Grube, John. "*Tender Is the Night*: Keats and Scott Fitzgerald." In *"Tender Is the Night": Essays in Criticism*. Ed. Marvin J. LaHood. Bloomington: Indiana University Press, 1969. 179–89.

Keats, John. *Lamia. John Keats: Complete Poems*. Ed. Jack Stillinger. Cambridge, Mass.: Belknap Press of Harvard University, 1978. 342–59.

Kolbenschlag, Madonna C. "Madness and Sexual Mythology in Scott Fitzgerald." *International Journal of Women's Studies* 1 (1978): 263–71.

Korenman, Joan S. "'Only Her Hairdresser . . .': Another Look at Daisy Buchanan."

American Literature 46 (1975): 574–78.

Lehan, Richard D. *F. Scott Fitzgerald and the Craft of Fiction.* Carbondale: Southern Illinois University Press, 1966.

Loftus, Margaret Frances. "John Keats in the Works of F. Scott Fitzgerald." *KIYO-Studies in English Literature* 7 (1972): 17–26.

Martin, Marjorie. "Fitzgerald's Image of Woman: Anima Projections in *Tender Is the Night.*" *English Studies Collections* 1, no. 6 (1976): 1–17.

McCall, Dan. "'The Self-Same Song That Found a Path': Keats and *The Great Gatsby.*" *American Literature* 42 (1971): 521–30.

McCay, Mary A. "Fitzgerald's Women: Beyond Winter Dreams." In *American Novelists Revisited: Essays in Feminist Criticism.* Ed. Fritz Fleischmann. Boston: G. K. Hall, 1982. 311–24.

McNicholas, Mary V. "Fitzgerald's Women in *Tender Is the Night.*" *College Literature* 4 (1976): 40–70.

Mellor, Anne K. *Romanticism and Gender.* New York and London: Routledge, 1993.

Monteiro, George. "James Gatz and John Keats." *Fitzgerald/Hemingway Annual 1972*: 291–94.

Person, Leland S., Jr. "Fitzgerald's 'O Russet Witch!': Dangerous Women, Dangerous Art." *Studies in Short Fiction* 23 (1986): 443–48.

———. "'Herstory' and Daisy Buchanan." *American Literature* 50 (1978): 250–57.

Prigozy, Ruth. "From Griffith's Girls to Daddy's Girl: The Masks of Innocence in *Tender Is the Night.*" *Twentieth Century Literature* 26 (1980): 189–221.

Ryan, Lindel. "F. Scott Fitzgerald and the Battle of the Sexes." *Literature in North Queensland* 8, no. 3 (1980): 84–94.

Scherr, Barry J. "Lawrence, Keats, and *Tender Is the Night*: Loss of Self and 'Love Battle' Motifs." *Recovering Literature: A Journal of Contextualist Criticism* 14 (1986): 7–17.

Schoenwald, Richard L. "F. Scott Fitzgerald as John Keats." *Boston University Studies in English* 3 (1957): 12–21.

Settle, Glenn. "Fitzgerald's Daisy: The Siren Voice." *American Literature* 57 (1985): 115–24.

Sipiora, Phillip. "Vampires of the Heart: Gender Trouble in *The Great Gatsby.*" In *The Aching Heart: Family Violence in Life and Literature.* Ed. Sara Munson Deats and Lagretta Tallent Lenker. New York: Plenum, 1991. 199–220.

Swann, Charles. "A Fitzgerald Debt to Keats? From 'Isabella' into *Tender Is the Night.*" *Notes and Queries* 37 (1990): 437–38.

Thornton, Patricia. "Sexual Roles in *The Great Gatsby.*" *English Studies in Canada* 5 (1979): 457–68.

Tuttleton, James W. "Vitality and Vampirism in *Tender Is the Night.*" In *Critical Essays on F. Scott Fitzgerald's "Tender Is the Night."* Ed. Milton R. Stern. Boston: G. K. Hall, 1986. 238–46.

Fitzgerald's Catholicism Revisited

The Eucharistic Element in *The Beautiful and Damned*

STEVEN FRYE

While F. Scott Fitzgerald's Catholic background has received some limited critical attention, the bulk of this work tends to resolve itself in fairly vague terms. In exploring Fitzgerald's religious sensibility, Andrew Turnbull discusses his "sense of the infinite" and Irving Malin suggests that Fitzgerald was a writer concerned with "the unseen spiritual dimensions of life." Pointing to the significant lack of criticism dealing specifically with Fitzgerald's Catholicism, H. W. Häusermann observes an "unworldly, almost religious spirit" implicit in Fitzgerald's works, and Bernard Tanner sees Gatsby's protection of Daisy as a secularized reinterpretation of the salvation and redemption motif.[1] In an extended book-length study, Joan M. Allen reviews Fitzgerald's influences in an attempt to tally his romanticism with a mythos evolving from Augustinian thinking.[2]

All of these analyses, many of which deal both directly and indirectly with Catholicism and Fitzgerald's religious background, tend to encourage a continual concern for the author's romanticism. Although they shed a good deal of light upon his canon, they do not address, through the analysis and application of specific terms and theological precepts, the particular nature of his religiosity, which involves a curious communion of upbringing and literary technique.[3] Details of Fitzgerald's early life are too well known to rehash here;

it is sufficient to say that while his upbringing was augmented by psychological traits that perhaps transcend the influence of culture, many of his works are influenced by his Catholic upbringing. These works, particularly *The Beautiful and Damned*, manifest an imagery and structure that reflect a specific and concrete aspect of Catholic theology—the Eucharist itself. Fitzgerald's narrative treatment of concrete reality reveals a tendency to view the material world as in some sense eucharistic in nature, as a system of signs and signification processes whose referents are immaterial and mystical.

In *The Beautiful and Damned*, Fitzgerald establishes a pattern that reflects the pervasive and systematic paradox that forms the texture of much of his later work, a system of contraries that finds a direct and concrete parallel in Catholic theology. For Catholics, the Eucharist ought to be the most recondite of paradoxes: what appears to be material in objects of ritual is in fact an ahistorical spiritual reality. The concept of the Eucharist is predicated upon the idea of Real Presence. The consumption of bread and wine is not merely a ritualistic act celebrating the sacrifice of Christ. The Son of God is in fact substantially present in the sacrament, and the bread and wine are outward symbols of an interior reality. In the eucharistic sacraments, this interior reality is a manifestation not only of Grace, but of Christ, the originator of Grace. Thus there is both a literal and a symbolic dimension to the act of eucharistic expression. In a more general sense, physical objects become signs that manifest and suggest divinity. This notion of the Eucharist is useful in understanding the metaphorical systems in narrative that Fitzgerald develops in many of his works, since physical reality becomes symbolic of the transcendent. Fitzgerald's eucharistic vision involves an imaginative projection and secularization of these religious concepts and, as such, does not necessarily conform precisely to strict theological notions governing eucharistic expression. But Fitzgerald's fiction often portrays the interpenetration of physical and material realms implicit in the concept of the Eucharist, since physical objects and people become in part mystical in nature.

The Great Gatsby is the most comprehensive and successful characterization of this aspect of Fitzgerald's consciousness. Paul Giles in fact sees traces of Fitzgerald's Catholicism in Gatsby's romantic sensibility, through his "spiritualization of earthly matter."[4] But *Gatsby* is a culmination, the final outcome of an extended intellectual and artistic process that began with specific pieces of short fiction written while Fitzgerald was still at Princeton.[5] This process reaches a critical juncture in *The Beautiful and Damned*, a novel in which eucharistic elements become most obvious through an allegorical system created by Fitzgerald. Any analysis of Fitzgerald's eucharistic vision should therefore begin with this novel, and this analysis might lead to a greater understanding of the characters and thematic patterns within his other works.

The notion of *The Beautiful and Damned* as a "flawed" novel is a matter of critical consensus, especially when the text is considered in comparison to *Gatsby*.[6] Robert Sklar argues that Fitzgerald's artistic voice is "almost wholly lost" among the "echoes" of H. L. Mencken and Frank Norris. Henry Dan Piper suggests that Fitzgerald was in fact attempting to write two stories, one the tragedy of a modern marriage and the second "a brittle comedy of ideas in the manner of Shaw or Wilde." Yet in spite of its flaws, the novel has its supporters. Andrew Hook sees *The Beautiful and Damned* as "an extraordinary piece of work, an advance on *This Side of Paradise* in terms of structural unity, characterization, and control of tone." Although Richard D. Lehan reads *The Beautiful and Damned* as a "novel of unassimilated idea" since "the theme of life's meaninglessness goes against the grain of Fitzgerald's conviction in the promises of life," he suggests that the text represents a significant advancement in the author's mastery of the novel as genre, particularly in Fitzgerald's enactment of dramatic irony and "self-mockery."[7] The novel's merits, limited though they may be, result from Fitzgerald's developing skill in narrative design and control. But more than this, the novel begins to develop many of the complex ideas and concepts that come to fruition in *The Great Gatsby*.

Sergio Perosa sees *The Beautiful and Damned* as a "moral parable" which evokes a "dreamy atmosphere" dealing with a central theme — the degeneration and decay of two characters who are guilty of "excessive indulgence in illusions and dreams."[8] It is this obsession with "illusion" that strikes at the heart of the eucharistic element inherent in the novel. Through a complex interplay between dream and reality, physicality and illusion, which becomes apparent in both character and description, *The Beautiful and Damned* manifests an essentially doctrinal view of the relationship between the transcendent and the immanent. Fitzgerald displaces the philosophical and theological notions that govern eucharistic expression and ritual, bringing them into a modern social and secular realm. At the same time, the novel reveals a spiritual conflict in Fitzgerald. The intellectual influences of a secular age, figures such as H. L. Mencken and George Jean Nathan and pervasive philosophical movements such as Darwinian theory, confronted the theological notions that governed Fitzgerald's early life.[9] These movements and ideas exerted a powerful influence on Catholicism itself, and Fitzgerald personified these changes. His second novel functions as a kind of apprentice work, an early prototype, manifesting the religious themes and notions that were dealt with more fully in *The Great Gatsby*.

In *The Beautiful and Damned*, eucharistic elements begin to appear in both character and description. As in *Gatsby*, Fitzgerald's figurative passages involve what Paul Giles calls a "spiritualization of earthly matter." [10] They contain allusions to an immaterial realm of being, and, through her beauty, Gloria Patch becomes a mystical symbol, a concrete manifestation of divinity itself. The essential struggle in Fitzgerald's consciousness, with regard to his religion, comes finally to a climax through Gloria's relationship with Anthony Patch. The plot functions around Anthony's movement from hope to despair, from a promising young man to an emotional and psychological degenerate. Although he recovers his wealth at the novel's conclusion, he remains "damned," spiritually bereft, a sickening reflection of his former self. As Gloria's illusive and ineffable beauty slips away, she ceases to function metaphorically, as an intimation of divinity. Anthony then descends into hopelessness because the physical world, independent of its symbolic referent in the divine, has lost its mythic significance. This process begins in book one, chapter 2, entitled "Symposium." Here Fitzgerald links Anthony's waning attraction to Gloria to her declining youth (as she reaches the ripe old age of twenty-four). Anthony grows "faintly, imperceptibly . . . apathetic toward Gloria." [11] This change in Anthony's feelings and perceptions becomes further apparent in his violent interchange with Gloria in the train station later in the chapter. Here Gloria begins to lose that certain undefinable and immaterial quality that attracted Anthony to her. As they return home, he contemplates the potential loss of "the girl of his glory, the radiant woman who was precious and charming because she was ineffably, triumphantly, herself" (202).

Anthony's concerns become more obvious in his startling ambivalence regarding Gloria's potential pregnancy, an ambivalence that appears after she vividly reminds him of the physical effects of childbearing and its effect on her youth and physique. At first glance, these events seem to reflect a rather puerile superficiality on Anthony's part. But his fear of Gloria's loss of beauty is more complicated than it may appear. Anthony's sensibility reflects what Häusermann (in discussing Fitzgerald's Catholic sensibility) refers to as a "constant wavering between reality and illusion." [12] Early in the novel Gloria is, as the title of chapter 2 suggests, a "siren," and this term is used in more than a metaphorical sense. Her physical appearance suggests a kind of godliness. This is apparent as Anthony observes that she is "full of a heavenly glamour" (57) and it is "agony to comprehend her beauty at a glance" (57). Anthony's degeneration, his descent into dejection, dissipation, alcoholism, and infidelity, parallels directly Gloria's gradual loss of this ineffable beauty, a beauty that in Anthony's view is more than physical, but "heavenly" (57), "an illusion" (72), and immaterial, symbolic of the mystical. Anthony's physical and psychological decay continues as the novel proceeds. Fitzgerald's eucharistic vision becomes manifest through Anthony's perceptions, his linkage of the material and the immaterial.

But these eucharistic notions appear also in the narrative itself, and, to begin the exploration of eucharistic elements, a detailed analysis of a typical description is useful. In the following passage, the narrator describes the setting surrounding an encounter between Anthony and Gloria: "The night was alive with thaw; it was so nearly warm that a breeze drifting low along the sidewalk brought to Anthony a vision of an unhoped-for hyacinthine spring. . . . for a hushed moment the traffic sounds and the murmur of water flowing in the gutters seemed an illusive and rarified prolongation of that music to which they had lately danced" (101). The imagery of "night" is infused with the ineffable, and Fitzgerald's figurative language integrates concrete reality, a historically centered realm of the temporal and physical, with something less tangible, perhaps an ahistorical realm of pure being. A derivation of the word "illusion" appears, suggesting that the physical world that these characters experience exists simultaneously with something immaterial. The scene evokes an affective response in Anthony and Gloria, one not entirely sensual, but in some sense mystical, as "something breathless and desirous that the night has conceived in their two hearts" (101). Ironically, this physical description suggests the insignificance of pure materiality, and it is not a "physical" description in a literal sense. This is apparent in phrases such as "vision of an unhoped-for hyacinthine spring" and "the illusive and rarified prolongation of that music to which they had lately danced."

At other times, Fitzgerald is more direct as he portrays the tension between material and immaterial realms. His descriptions of physical reality often reflect an immaterial yet demonic realm of existence. Fitzgerald had dealt with this material before, in overtly Catholic short stories such as "The Ordeal" and "Benediction," and in *This Side of Paradise* (where Amory Blaine encounters a demonic presence in the face of Dick Humbird). In *The Beautiful and Damned* this evocation of the demonic occurs in Gloria's encounter with Joe Hull. Hull's demonic nature is primarily constructed out of Gloria's tortured imagination, suggesting that Hull functions metaphorically for her, signifying something beyond itself, something evil. Gloria is not threatened merely by a strange man in her room but by some "unimaginable force" that "would shatter her out of existence" (243). Hull recedes into an "incomprehensible light" (243) that is seemingly the source of his being. Again, Fitzgerald's description of physical reality and his character's apprehension of that reality manifest elements of the "illusory," the immaterial, reflecting Fitzgerald's religious temperament and eucharistic vision. Physical reality in this novel becomes metaphor, suggesting realms beyond itself.

The most direct and developed example of this phenomenon in the novel occurs as Fitzgerald characterizes female beauty through Gloria herself. In exploring the religious themes in "Absolution," Lawrence D. Stewart discusses Fitzgerald's characterization of women, in particular, Gatsby's view of Daisy Buchanan as "a manifestation of the divine." In doing so, he suggests that Fitzgerald saw female beauty as a kind of Platonic virtue, a mystical quality that transcends the physical.[13] Fitzgerald's women often captivate men with a material beauty that is somehow more than material. In *The Great Gatsby*, Daisy functions more successfully as a mystical symbol, since her character is intertwined with a complex metaphorical system that portrays the illusive nature of the "dream," which can itself be seen as the desire to apprehend some transcendent realm of being. In *The Beautiful and Damned*, Gloria functions for the most part allegorically. In chapter 1, Fitzgerald constructs a mythical conversation between "THE VOICE" and "BEAUTY." THE VOICE, who commands BEAUTY to enter the world, is an omnipresent deity, concretized through character and dialogue, a vaguely detheologized version of God himself. Emerging here is Fitzgerald's propensity to view the physical and the transcendent as inextricably connected, since beauty manifest physically in Gloria is the *"unity sought for by philosophers through many centuries"* (27; emphasis in original).

When Fitzgerald refers to the term "beauty" in *The Beautiful and Damned*, one should consider carefully the specific definition he develops in this dialogue. Fitzgerald's concept of beauty emanates from the stuff of his own religious temperament, and from the now fragmented theological notions he has attempted to reject, since beauty itself is tenuously linked to the Real Presence of the transcendent. At a rather superficial level, Fitzgerald rejects Catholicism through his characters themselves. This becomes apparent in the "In Darkness" section, as Maury Noble sardonically suggests that the Bible was written by men of genius who believed in nothing, their purpose being to "mock the credulity of man" (258). While this antimetaphysical stance might lead us to ignore the mystical religiosity implicit in the text, Fitzgerald's religious sense becomes apparent through the interpenetration of material and spiritual realms. This appears first in the aforementioned dialogue between THE VOICE and BEAUTY and becomes manifest in the narrative as BEAUTY in Gloria is linked to the timeless and the immaterial. In the fullness of her youth, Gloria is described as "eternally old" (51), as one whose freshness of cheek is a "gossamer projection from a land of delicate and undiscovered shades" (71), as one who "a while ago . . . had been, and presently would again be, in a higher, rarer, air" (70). In Gloria, beauty has become a rare virtue emanating directly from the divine, the essence behind a celestial unity. Beauty transcends the immanent, and, as Gloria possesses it, she manifests an essential quality that allows her to function as a religious symbol in Anthony's eyes. The mystical quality inherent in Gloria as symbol becomes apparent in her transformative power since, consistent with Fitzgerald's vaguely secularized eucharistic vision, Gloria's ineffable beauty functions somehow to provide meaning to Anthony's otherwise purposeless life.

Before their courtship and marriage, Anthony's behavior reflects the mock-eloquent cynicism of Maury Noble, who subscribes to a philosophy predicated upon "The Meaninglessness of Life" (54). While Anthony's relationship with Gloria leads to no lasting alteration in his character or behavior, he does experience a certain exuberant and energetic revival of spirit through his contact with the radiance, the timeless, evanescent, illusory, and immaterial beauty that "gilds" (341) Gloria. Considering the dialogue between THE VOICE and BEAUTY that precedes the introduction of Gloria, and considering Anthony's mystical contemplation of her, Gloria becomes for him a projection of the transcendent. Like the Eucharist itself, she is a material manifestation of divinity. One should recognize that Fitzgerald does not begin his characterization of Gloria by describing her in purely physical terms. From Anthony's point of view particularly, beauty is the essence that distinguishes Gloria from the rest of the material world. She will become "*incomprehensible, for, in her, soul and spirit were one*" (27; emphasis in original). Even in the dialogue between THE VOICE and BEAUTY, as Fitzgerald deals only in abstraction, we see his inability to separate body and spirit, the physical from the divine. As Gloria's character is introduced, we learn quickly that "*the beauty of her body was the essence of her soul*" (27; emphasis in original).

Fitzgerald then establishes Gloria's character in more concrete terms, showing how she has become the material agent of absolute Beauty. As THE VOICE sends BEAUTY into a fallen world, Fitzgerald connects the theology of redemption with this allegorical representation of an absolute virtue. Anthony is redeemed from a state of lethargy and existential angst into an almost mystical admiration for beauty manifest in Gloria, as she appears to him "a sun, radiant, growing, gathering light and storing it—then after an eternity pouring it forth at a glance" (73). But there is an implicit paradox in Fitzgerald's treatment of beauty through Gloria. Ultimately, for both Anthony Patch and Jay Gatsby, a tendency to transform women into mystical symbols becomes destructive rather than redemptive. But perhaps Fitzgerald suggests a different kind of redemption. Before these two young men descend into oblivion, each reaches a heightened sense of emotional awareness, and, although brief, the experience is nevertheless extraordinary. As he witnesses Gloria's youthful exuberance, Anthony experiences "a gorgeous sentiment" that "welled into his eyes, choked him up, set his nerves a-tingle, and filled his throat with husky and vibrant emotion" (71). In a conversation with Nick Carraway, Gatsby recalls a particular encounter with Daisy Buchanan, in which he felt that he might nearly "suck on the pap of life" and "gulp down the incomparable milk of wonder." In this passage, Gatsby recalls an experience of "mysterious excitement" in which there was for him "a stir and a bustle among the stars." [14]

One should recognize that destruction does not occur for these young men through the apprehension of beauty from afar. A certain distance from the symbolic object seems to facilitate the mystical apprehension of the transcendent, which is the essence of the eucharistic experience. For Anthony, "it was her distance, not the rare and precious distance of the soul but still distance" (18). Destruction occurs when these men achieve an immediacy, when they finally gain possession of the material object. As this occurs, Fitzgerald's women cease to possess their mysterious symbolic significance. When Gatsby comes too close to the green light it becomes tawdry, purely material, void of anything transcendent, and "his count of enchanted objects" is "diminished by one" (94).

The same process occurs for Anthony. The plot in *The Beautiful and Damned* functions around Anthony and Gloria's degeneration from a glamorous young couple to a pair of absurd and tragic figures. As Fitzgerald characterizes Anthony's emotional response, his reaction to Gloria, his adoration of her, depends entirely on distance. When he encounters her directly, the transcendent quality eludes him. In a dialogue late in the novel he reflects upon his feelings toward Gloria: "once I wanted something and got it. It was the only thing I wanted badly. . . . And when I got it it turned to dust in my hands" (341). The emotion Anthony experiences through "distances" (72) is more powerful than any sexual response, "nearer to adoration than in the deepest kiss he had ever known" (18). Thus Fitzgerald's eucharistic vision becomes apparent as Anthony responds to Gloria. In chapter 2 of book 1, "Portrait of a Siren," she exists "in a higher, rarer air" (70), maintaining the necessary separation through the "impassable distances she created about herself" (72).

The issue of distance as a transformative power in Anthony's symbol-making process reflects Fitzgerald's secularization of eucharistic notions. For Anthony, distance allows the material object to retain a physicality without becoming tawdry and purely material. Through distance, Anthony's imagination may invest Gloria with his own vision of transcendent presence. Female beauty, through Gloria, functions as the most significant metaphorical representation of the divine. This appears again as the narrator further characterizes and describes Anthony's response: "Out of the deep sophistication of Anthony an understanding formed, nothing atavistic or obscure, indeed scarcely physical at all. . . . The sheath that held her soul had assumed significance — that was all" (73). "Sophistication" as a term implicitly suggests Anthony's particular version of the mystical experience. The immaterial essence beyond the immanent evokes a reaction that is "scarcely physical at all." The apprehension of beauty through a material object is the apprehension of divinity itself. Gloria's physical self is secondary; it is "the sheath that held her soul," possessing only "assumed significance." Beauty and illusion, the physical and the spiritual, the temporal and the eternal, exist simultaneously in a single person. The Eucharist again is implicit here, since physical reality becomes a sign suggesting a mystical referent.

However, a spiritual conflict in Fitzgerald's consciousness is ever present in the narrative since Anthony's attempt to encounter God through Gloria is a tenuous one. Material objects and people may quickly lose these glimmerings of the transcendent. Gloria's loss of mystical significance is foreshadowed early in the novel as Anthony's vision "snapped like a nest of threads . . . the garish shimmer of the lights overhead became real, portentous" (72). From this passage we see not only Fitzgerald's religious temperament and eucharistic vision but the spiritual dilemma that he continually confronted, exemplified through the fragility of metaphors and mystical symbols. A variety of factors contribute to Gloria and Anthony's descent into spiritual and material oblivion. Their cultural situation is certainly a factor in their downfall, their social background, the fact that they were both indulged as children. The modern intellectual climate, the increasingly complicated secular age, might lead to crisis and confusion in sensitive young people.

But again, many of Fitzgerald's main characters expect something extraordinary from human experience, often contemplating physical experience in search of mystical apprehension. Anthony finds a mystical symbol in Gloria which becomes apparent as he (like Maury Noble) revels in Gloria's youth, while simultaneously recognizing that she is ageless, timeless, and "eternally old" (51). Anthony continually links Gloria to the ineffable, to "a land of delicate and undiscovered shades" (71), and while the text never explicitly establishes Gloria's status as a mystical symbol in Anthony's mind, his impressions and perceptions regarding Gloria are highly suggestive of eucharistic notions.

But degeneration for Anthony occurs rather quickly, as two phenomena transpire simultaneously. First, Anthony possesses Gloria; he marries her, breaching the distance necessary for the symbol to maintain its mystical significance. Second, Beauty, a transcendent Virtue, is by its very nature illusive, manifesting itself in physical objects only briefly.

In fact, Fitzgerald establishes a specific timetable. After THE VOICE has spoken to BEAUTY, Fitzgerald states, "*All this took place seven years before* ANTHONY *sat by the front windows of his apartment and listened to the chimes of St. Anne's*" (30; emphasis in original). This is a curious and timely reference to the Catholic church since Gloria functions in a symbolic sense in much the same manner as the material objects of Catholic ritual. As Gloria loses her youth and beauty, Anthony becomes increasingly confused, without direction or emotional energy, as he recognizes the illusive nature of his own mystical apprehension. This state of mind appears in his conversation with Dorothy Raycroft. He says, "desire just cheats you. It's like a sunbeam. . . . It stops and gilds some inconsequential object, and we poor fools try to grasp it—but when we do the sunbeam moves on to something else, and you've got the inconsequential part, but the glitter that made you want it is gone—" (341). Note that through his character Fitzgerald attaches "desire" to physical "objects" and people. Anthony's desire has been focused on Gloria, and the loss he experiences is central to the thematics of the novel and to the psychological sensibility of the author. In establishing his illicit relationship with Dorothy, Anthony demonstrates a growing frustration with his marriage. At one time, a "sunbeam" had "gilded" Gloria, providing her with an illusive but essential quality. Without this "sunbeam," she becomes "inconsequential" (341), since he has lost his metaphor, his "gossamer projection," his channel to the divine. Because of this, he descends into a psychological abyss, from which even the recovery of his personal fortune cannot save him.

Thus Fitzgerald suggests a fragile and tenuous relationship between the material world and its symbolic referent in the divine. This fragility suggests Fitzgerald's paradoxical attitude and his secularization of a complex Catholic theological precept. Although his eucharistic vision sees physical reality as a manifestation of the divine, Fitzgerald continually questions, through Maury Noble, the existence of any transcendent realm of being. Fitzgerald never posits a theological viewpoint in his fiction. Nor does he create, as Yeats does, a complex metaphysical system upon which his work must function. Fitzgerald was not a mystic in this sense. But in *The Beautiful and Damned* he displays an elusive religious sensibility through characterization and description. It is important to understand that Anthony alone invests Gloria with this mystical significance. In what many (somewhat too summarily) have called a post-Christian age, he becomes the author of his own mythos. The narrative passages describing Gloria are most often composed in limited omniscience from Anthony's point of view, suggesting that Anthony Patch possesses a desire to believe as well as the residue of a Catholic metaphysical view, a eucharistic vision, a tendency to transform people and objects into religious symbols. Like Jay Gatsby, Anthony Patch is an example of what Lawrence Stewart calls "the tragic, dream-haunted man." [15] The dream has a particular source in all these works, the powerful imagination of individual characters.

Fitzgerald's is an essentially tragic view, reflecting simultaneously his attraction to the physical world and his acute awareness regarding the brevity of physical life and mystical experience. His dream is illusive because in Fitzgerald's fiction the physical world possesses a transcendent quality only in a subjective sense, in the eyes of those who desire to perceive it. The desire to encounter God remains deeply rooted in the hearts of Fitzgerald's characters. In *The Great Gatsby*, Daisy is merely a woman, a rather spoiled and superficial cultural creation, framed out of the American bourgeoisie. But Gatsby's powerful imagination transforms her into a symbol of mystical significance. The same is true for Anthony, since as readers we experience a double vision of Gloria. We know that there is nothing transcendent in the beauty she possesses, and she manifests the same qualities as many of Fitzgerald's other characters, a certain tawdriness and superficiality. However, the conversation between THE VOICE and BEAUTY functions to illuminate and clarify Anthony's view of Gloria, showing that she is the focal point of a dream not unlike the one experienced by Gatsby, a dream that is in part the product of a eucharistic vision.

Fitzgerald was unable to separate his desire to apprehend a transcendent God from his desire to embrace the physical life. Experience in life was a perpetual attempt to move beyond. The "dream" explored through Anthony in *The Beautiful and Damned* is perhaps less flawlessly executed than it could be. Fitzgerald allows Anthony to capture the object of his desire too quickly, too fully, too physically. He doesn't allow distance to perform its function as in *Gatsby*, causing the "dream" to develop to more complex and mythic proportions. As a result, in *The Beautiful and Damned* the power of the "dream" is tragically overshadowed by its rapid degeneration.

However, it is this degeneration that strikes at the heart of many of Fitzgerald's works, and a recognition of eucharistic elements becomes useful in an apprehension of the specific nature of Fitzgerald's "dream." As Häusermann suggests, "That Fitzgerald was an unbeliever in his maturity is not more of an argument against the religious interpretation of his works than is the fact that the Church denied him burial in the Catholic cemetery where his father was interred."[16] Fitzgerald was influenced by the material glitter that dominated the human scene "this side of paradise." But it is his residual Catholic sensibility, his lingering belief in paradise itself, that leads him to transform these material elements. The characters in *The Beautiful and Damned* seek a kind of communion through material glitter that must be doomed to failure, particularly from a Catholic viewpoint, since it is a fatal error to invest mystical significance in just any physical object, particularly those of the secular world. The implicit agreement among believers, the community of ritualistic expression, is absent in the search in which these characters engage. Fitzgerald's characters are left alone, without the necessary mediation of the church and congregation, which for Catholics facilitates a fulfilling spiritual union. Thus, the conflict between the forces of secularization and the influence of a complex theological precept highlight and help to formulate the fundamental paradox in Fitzgerald. His romantic interpretation of reality discloses a desire that simultaneously values less and more the very nature of material things, which is to say that Fitzgerald is never an even-tempered materialist or spiritualist. The experience that Fitzgerald's characters seek is a product of modernity, of the secular age. Mystical apprehension is significantly more difficult to achieve in the secular world, and it is the attempt to separate the theological notions that govern eucharistic expression from their liturgical context that ultimately seal the doom.

NOTES

1. Turnbull, *Scott Fitzgerald*, 77; Malin, "'Absolution,'" 209; Häusermann, "Fitzgerald's Religious Sense," 82; Tanner, "Gospel of Gatsby."
2. This study, *Candles and Carnival Lights: The Catholic Sensibility of F. Scott Fitzgerald*, represents perhaps the most comprehensive treatment of Fitzgerald's Catholic influences. Allen provides a significant amount of biographical material related to Fitzgerald's schooling and his interaction with clergymen such as Cyril Webster Sigourney Fay, and Thomas Delihant, among others. Allen also includes a number of biographical readings of important texts that attest to the pervasive influence of Catholic theology in Fitzgerald's work in general.

   See Chetwood, "Father Thomas J. Delihant." See also Nevius, "Note on F. Scott Fitzgerald's Monsignor Sigourney Fay." These early but useful article-length discussions provide important specific information about Fitzgerald's Catholic influences.

3. In *The Golden Moment: The Novels of F. Scott Fitzgerald*, Milton R. Stern refers to Fitzgerald's open rejection of his Catholicism, suggesting that from this fact one may conclude that the author's religious training had only a limited influence upon his works. It is a matter of critical and biographical consensus that Fitzgerald rejected his faith. But the substance of that faith, as other critics have noted, remains an integral component of Fitzgerald's interpretation of physical reality. This becomes manifest both in Fitzgerald's particular romantic vision and in his manner of narrative description.

4. Giles, "Aquinas vs. Weber," 2.

5. Fitzgerald's early short stories "The Ordeal" and "Benediction" deal directly with Catholicism and spiritual crisis. Allen discusses them thoroughly in *Candles and Carnival Lights*, and the issues of sacramentality, mediation, and eucharistic expression are a central thematic concern in these early works.

6. This view of the novel has existed to some degree since its original reception. For a collection of reprinted contemporary reviews, see Bryer, *F. Scott Fitzgerald: The Critical Reception*, 61–137.

7. Sklar, *F. Scott Fitzgerald*, 94; Piper, *F. Scott Fitzgerald*, 87; Hook, "Cases for Reconsideration," 30; Lehan, *F. Scott Fitzgerald and the Craft of Fiction*, 81–82.

8. Perosa, *"The Beautiful and Damned,"* 49, 50, 48.

9. For an insight into the secular intellectual influences on Fitzgerald, see Mencken, "National Letters." For a discussion of these influences in biographical form, see Mizener, *Far Side of Paradise*; and Stern, *Golden Moment*.

10. Giles, "Aquinas vs. Weber," 2. Giles attempts to contextualize Fitzgerald's religious perceptions in a historically specific ideological frame. Giles points specifically to the conflicts and debates that altered American Catholicism in the early twentieth century. He states that "Scott Fitzgerald interacted with the materialist orientation of the American Dream in a climate in which the Church itself was debating whether the well-being of the Institution within the United States was best served through resistance to that dream or cooperation with it" (2). The debate itself centered around the Church's traditional antimaterialist ideological stance and the rise of high capitalism in America.

11. Fitzgerald, *Beautiful and Damned*, 192. All subsequent page references to *The Beautiful and Damned* are to the 1922 edition and appear parenthetically in the text.

12. Häusermann, "Fitzgerald's Religious Sense," 82.

13. Stewart, "'Absolution' and *The Great Gatsby*," 185.

14. Fitzgerald, *Great Gatsby*, 112. All subsequent page references to *The Great Gatsby* are to the 1925 edition and appear parenthetically in the text.

15. Stewart, "'Absolution' and *The Great Gatsby*," 183. Through a detailed analysis of characterization and description, Stewart's article attempts to explore the thematic relationship between *The Great Gatsby* and "Absolution." Stewart reminds us that "Absolution" was originally intended to be an early chapter in *Gatsby*, and that the young boy Rudolph originally represented Gatsby as a child. In discussing Father

Schwartz's crisis, Stewart states that he "desperately needs an object to symbolize his yearning for God" (185). Thus, while Stewart deemphasizes the Catholic sensibility in *Gatsby* in place of more secular and modernist concerns, he observes a distinct similarity between the Catholic priest in "Absolution" and Gatsby. Both can be seen as "tragic, dream-haunted" men (185). From his interaction and interpretation of Gloria coupled with his personal degeneration, one can certainly characterize Anthony Patch in the same manner.

16. Häusermann, "Fitzgerald's Religious Sense," 82.

WORKS CITED

Allen, Joan M. *Candles and Carnival Lights: The Catholic Sensibility of F. Scott Fitzgerald.* New York: New York University Press, 1978.

Bryer, Jackson R., ed. *F. Scott Fitzgerald: The Critical Reception.* New York: Burt Franklin, 1978.

Chetwood, T. B., S.J. "Father Thomas Delihant, S.J. 1878–1949." *Woodstock Letters* 78 (1949): 351–54.

Fitzgerald, F. Scott. "Absolution." In *The Short Stories of F. Scott Fitzgerald: A New Collection.* Ed. Matthew J. Bruccoli. New York: Scribners, 1989. 259–72.

——. *The Beautiful and Damned.* New York: Scribners, 1922.

——. "Benediction." *Flappers and Philosophers.* New York: Scribners, 1920. 141–56.

——. *The Great Gatsby.* New York: Scribners, 1925.

——. "The Ordeal." In *The Apprentice Fiction of F. Scott Fitzgerald: 1909–1917.* Ed. John Kuehl. New Brunswick, N.J.: Rutgers University Press, 1965. 78–87.

——. *This Side of Paradise.* New York: Scribners, 1920.

Giles, Paul. "Aquinas vs. Weber: Ideological Esthetics in *The Great Gatsby.*" *Mosaic: A Journal for the Interdisciplinary Study of Literature* 22, no. 4 (1989): 2–12.

Häusermann, H. W. "Fitzgerald's Religious Sense: Note and Query." *Modern Fiction Studies* 2 (1956): 81–82.

Hook, Andrew. "Cases for Reconsideration: Fitzgerald's *This Side of Paradise* and *The Beautiful and Damned.*" In *Scott Fitzgerald: The Promises of Life.* Ed. A. Robert Lee. New York: St. Martin's Press, 1989. 17–37.

Lehan, Richard D. *F. Scott Fitzgerald and the Craft of Fiction.* Carbondale: Southern Illinois University Press, 1966.

Malin, Irving. "'Absolution': Absolving Lies." In *The Short Stories of F. Scott Fitzgerald: New Approaches in Criticism.* Ed. Jackson R. Bryer. Madison: University of Wisconsin Press, 1982. 209–16.

Mencken, H. L. "The National Letters." *Prejudices: Second Series.* New York: Knopf, 1920. 9–101.

Mizener, Arthur. *The Far Side of Paradise.* 1951. Boston: Houghton Mifflin, 1965.

Nevius, Rev. R. C. "A Note on F. Scott Fitzgerald's Monsignor Sigourney Fay and His Early Career as an Episcopalian." *Fitzgerald/Hemingway Annual* 1971: 105–13.

Perosa, Sergio. "*The Beautiful and Damned.*" In *F. Scott Fitzgerald: A Collection of Criticism.* Ed. Kenneth E. Eble. New York: McGraw-Hill, 1973. 48–59.

Piper, Henry Dan. *F. Scott Fitzgerald: A Critical Portrait.* New York: Holt, Rinehart and Winston, 1965.

Sklar, Robert. *F. Scott Fitzgerald: The Last Laocoön.* New York: Oxford University Press, 1967.

Stern, Milton R. *The Golden Moment: The Novels of F. Scott Fitzgerald.* Urbana: University of Illinois Press, 1970.

Stewart, Lawrence D. "'Absolution' and *The Great Gatsby.*" *Fitzgerald/Hemingway Annual 1973*: 181–87.

Tanner, Bernard. "The Gospel of Gatsby." *English Journal* 54 (1965): 467–74.

Turnbull, Andrew. *Scott Fitzgerald.* New York: Ballantine, 1962.

The Great Gatsby—The Text as Construct

Narrative Knots and Narrative Unfolding

RICHARD LEHAN

I have always been slightly puzzled about why a novel as carefully constructed as Fitzgerald's *The Great Gatsby* has so many inconsistencies within it. The novel takes on the verbal complexity of a poem, and Fitzgerald skillfully tells a compelling story at the same time as he brilliantly compresses elements involving American history and Western culture into the fifty thousand words that make up the novel. It is a novel, the meaning of which refuses to be limited: every reading offers a new insight, and seventy-five years after publication the criticism often offers us something new; and yet this is a novel in which Fitzgerald inconsistently describes a character, confuses key dates, compresses action to the point that it perhaps strains credulity, and offers statements that are often simply confusing in relation to each other. Moreover, it is a novel in which the motives of perhaps the most important scene in the novel are left vague, if not totally ambivalent, and in which the ending puzzles us by the behavior of the narrator as well as the difficulty of assessing that behavior in moral terms.

I will come back to these matters. But before I do, I should like to say a few words about *The Great Gatsby* as a constructed text. The idea of textual construct is fairly recent. Previously, most of the critics had brought a concept of organic form, the old New Criticism idea of the inseparable relationship between part and whole, to a reading of the novel. This assumption had proven to be a useful one, since so much of the meaning in *Gatsby* comes out of its imagery, its texture, and the complexity of its motifs, all of which establish constellations of meaning that make up the universe of the novel. And yet in looking at the novel rather obsessively in these terms, we have, until recently, been somewhat casual about the cultural meaning of the text.

In order to read *The Great Gatsby* as a textual construct we must realize that, like every text, it was first pretextualized—that is, it was first the product of literary conventions that were in place before it was written. Such conventions became codified and expressed as literary modes, creating their own system of literary reality. These modes were brought into being in a historical context and served cultural agendas (and are thus ideological). Since the narrative mode is always larger than the text to which it applies, we have variation between texts in the same mode, at the same time that no text will ever be identical with the way it exists conceptually.

To see *Gatsby* in this context is to see first the way it draws its being from modernism—that is, in what way it organizes itself within terms of the narrative discourses that Fitzgerald, as a modernist, had at his disposal. We know that there were really two narrative modes that Fitzgerald could have drawn from. One was an aesthetic tradition that owed much of its being to the romantic movement. As Edmund Wilson has told us, modernism was simply the second stage of romanticism, modifying the mythic with the symbolic, working in the main within cyclical theories of history, and foregrounding a sense of subjectivity and consciousness often connected with philosophies of consciousness such as Bergson's. The other tradition, of course, was literary naturalism, a realistic tradition that emphasized the deterministic effects of environment, heredity, and a pregiven temperament. Fitzgerald had never worked within the mainstream of either tradition. In *This Side of Paradise* he brought an aesthetic discourse to his novel, retelling Compton Mackenzie's bildungsroman *Sinister Street*, which allowed Fitzgerald to saturate Amory Blaine's consciousness in the high romantic poetry from Keats and Shelley to Pater and Dowson. In *The Beautiful and Damned* he moved in the other direction and told a story of physical decline in the manner of Norris and Dreiser that Mencken, whom he admired at the time, had advocated. In *Gatsby* he attempted to bring the two traditions together, creating a realm of personal romantic intensity and cultural destiny told against a world of physical force embodied by Tom Buchanan and the mechanics of the new city, the new megalopolis.

That *Gatsby* is a product of visionary romanticism is a point important enough to emphasize. We know of Fitzgerald's interest in the subject from the famous course in romanticism he took with Christian Gauss at Princeton, a course the subject matter of which Edmund Wilson comes back to time and time again in *Axel's Castle* to suggest the bedrock upon which modernism rests. In Gauss's course, works like Pater's *Greek Studies* were read, especially Pater's famous essay on Dionysus. The Dionysus myth informs Western culture from Aeschylus and Euripides's Bacchae to Keats's later poetry and Nietzsche's *The Birth of Tragedy*. Historically, Dionysus was a re-presentation of the man-god figure that came out of Asia Minor embodied in Tammuz. The tradition was carried on in the Adonis figure, primarily Greek but with Hebrew origins, and was also inscribed in the Osiris figure in Egypt and Africa. In Greek legend, Dionysus is conceived by the God Zeus in the human Semele, the daughter of King Cadmus. When Semele dies she gives premature birth to her baby, who is brought to term by Zeus who sews the baby into the folds of his own flesh. Most of the readings of Dionysus connect him with vegetative and fertility rituals, with seasonal change, the earth renewing itself as do the vines of wine. But Dionysus was also connected with a cult organized around women who became frenzied to the point that they were capable of murder, as in Euripides when Agave murders Pentheus, her own son. Dionysus is usually seen as the opposite of Christ, since Christ calls for self-control rather than self-abandonment. But the connection between Christ and Dionysus is that both are born of woman/God—that is, they bridge the space between the earthly and the transcendent.

In the eighteenth century, the mythic nature of Dionysus was transformed, and his function was "re-presented" (that is, historically reembodied) by the carnival and later by the mysterious stranger and the man in the crowd. Joyce's Macintosh man carries much of the original meaning. Both Poe and Twain make use of such a figure in their fiction. While the vampire legend stems from a different mythology, its function is very much the same: Dracula, supported by at least three women, stalks the night, disrupting the ordered Victorian London that he has mysteriously entered. Fitzgerald's Gatsby embodies many of these elements: he emerges from the carnivalesque crowd of his own parties as a mysterious stranger, especially when seen at night. Fitzgerald cut eighteen thousand words describing Gatsby's childhood and background in order to give him this intensified sense of mystery. These elements play an important part in modernism in general, as we can see with poets like H.D., who translated from the Greek and used the Dionysus myth in her poetry, and dramatists like Eugene O'Neill, who employs a version of the Dionysus myth in *The Great God Brown*.

A slightly different use of the man-god figure informs *The Great Gatsby*:

Gatsby is the embodiment of his own godlike vision, or as the text tells us, "He was a son of God."[1] Such a creation implies vision, and the novel keeps coming back to the matter of sight through the eyes of T. J. Eckleburg, the eyes of the owl-eyed man, and the eyes of Nick that get more myopic as the novel proceeds, until we end with the eyes of Gatsby whose sight is transformed from the resplendent to the ordinary the day he loses Daisy, and a rose simply becomes a rose.[2] Like Dionysus and Christ, Gatsby becomes the dual product of his own creation. Like both the Greeks and the early Christians, Fitzgerald realized that the real story of God is not in the heavens or on earth, but in the reconciliation of the two—in the romantic intensity that transforms the physical.

If such intensity makes up one-half of Gatsby's character in the novel, the other half is given over to the physical powers that undo it, and here the novel is played out in the physical realm of Tom Buchanan and the city. Henry Adams had discussed the connection between these two realms in his "Virgin and the Dynamo" chapter in *The Education of Henry Adams*. The Virgin is a mythic vision—the vision of self that Gatsby uses to create himself and that organizes the medieval culture according to Adams. The dynamo is the random physical power that feeds off the natural universe and goes beyond romantic containment, giving rise to the diversity and multiplicity that fragments self as well as culture. Fitzgerald's novel clearly takes place within these narrative parameters. Before it is anything else it is a romantic/naturalistic battle between the visionary and the physical realms. The visions that give direction to life are indeed perishable, Fitzgerald tells us, perhaps destined in materialistic America to fail because they soon become outworn, soon are taken over by the past, which means that we are often looking backward when we think we are looking forward: "So we beat on, boats against the current, borne back ceaselessly into the past" (182).

Such is the story of Gatsby who projects an image of Daisy five years too late to be realized. And such is the story of Gatsby's America. Just before Fitzgerald began writing *Gatsby*, Frederick Jackson Turner's book involving the frontier thesis was published, based on the famous paper he had read in 1893 at the meeting of the American Historical Society at the World's Exposition in Chicago. Turner argued, based on census figures, that the frontier was now closed, the frontier that made America unique by allowing the nation to accommodate the vision of what it could be. So long as the frontier was open, everything was in the realm of the potential, waiting to be realized. James J. Hill had gone to the frontier and remade himself; so had Dan Cody, whose name suggests the beginning and end of the frontier (Daniel Boone who entered the true wilderness and Buffalo Bill Cody who transformed the frontier experience into a Disney-like Wild West show). Gatsby models himself on both Hill and especially Cody, and takes his frontier vision not to the frontier but to the city, where he plays it out in a world of new physical force, the end product of which is the Valley of Ashes. Fitzgerald not only saw the vision as allowing new ways of seeing and creating new forms of energy but he saw the loss of the vision as leading to forms of cultural blindness and to the entropy that leaves us with physical waste. It is for these reasons that the blind eyes of T. J. Eckleburg look out over the Valley of Ashes, and for these reasons that its custodian is the burnt-out, sickly George Wilson, whose name suggests another burnt-out visionary (Woodrow Wilson) and who blindly becomes the agent of Gatsby's death when he looks into the eyes of T. J. Eckleburg, tells us that God knows everything, and then goes out and kills the wrong man.

As a constructed text, *Gatsby* takes its meaning from the play between romantic and naturalistic narrative modes, between a belief in the visionary and the limits set on such transcendent desire by a realm of physical force. And clearly Fitzgerald felt that these motives took us to the very heart of what was meant by America—the world to which the Dutch sailors brought a new-world vision and the corruption of that vision from the end of the Civil War when the idealistic views of Jefferson, who carried so much of the visionary meaning for Fitzgerald, gave way to the more materialistic views of Hamilton.[3] Fitzgerald, of course, saw that other writers had anticipated him in this theme, especially Mark Twain in works like *A Connecticut Yankee in King Arthur's Court* and *The Gilded Age*, but also critics like Van Wyck Brooks who saw idealized and materialized elements at war within America like viruses might war within the physical body.

The critics who have made the connection between Fitzgerald and Twain anticipate what I mean by the constructed text—a text that takes its being from what is dominant at a historical moment in narrative modes. My only objection is that those critics seldom make the connections in these terms. Robert Sklar, in *F. Scott Fitzgerald: The Last Laocoön*, takes us to Twain with what seems to me the misguided belief that Fitzgerald was playing out the genteel ideals that pervaded late-nineteenth-century America. What someone like Sklar misses is how close, if not identical, Fitzgerald's view of culture came to that of the old historicism—the belief that every culture has an inbred meaning, a spirit or *geist* that gives it identity, a kind of essential being organized in terms of a period of time (as in Burkhardt's history of the Renaissance) or in terms of a national culture (as in von Ranke's history of Bismarck's Germany).

Fitzgerald, I believe, did see America in historicist terms, but they were the terms of Spengler, who saw American destiny as part of the larger destiny of the West. Within this destiny the process of decay and degeneration had already set in, a theme that Max Nordau and Cesare Lombroso made abundantly clear, suggesting that historical evolution had become inverted as Adams did in his theory of entropy, and which twilight poets like Dawson and Pater reinforced. From Adams's dynamo to Eliot's wasteland, to Fitzgerald's valley of ashes, to Pynchon's Trystero is a straight line in the development of this idea. The flip side of visionary history is the entropic, and both are built into the workings of the old historicism, to which Fitzgerald gave consent when he gave consent to Spengler, an idea I have documented elsewhere and which Fitzgerald documented himself in a long interview that he gave in April of 1927 to Harry Salpeter of the *New York World*.[4] Vision and decline, energy and waste—here are the key elements that Fitzgerald brought to his fiction, not only in the novels that precede *Gatsby* (*This Side of Paradise* and *The Beautiful and Damned*) but also in the novels that follow (*Tender Is the Night* and *The Last Tycoon*, as well as in the series of long short stories that make up the novella "Philippe, Count of Darkness").[5]

Along with a sense of the mythic/symbolic, and a historicist's sense of time, the modernist had a theory of consciousness (that is, subjectivity) that also becomes embedded in a novel like *Gatsby*. Clearly it is a tradition of thought that moves through Henry James and Joseph Conrad before it informs the mind of Nick Carraway. In his preface to *The Nigger of the Narcissus*, Conrad discussed his own aesthetics of fiction. Fitzgerald was moved by Conrad's critique, and it led to his idea of the "dying fall," the term he used to convey the sense of sadness and melancholy that came about when the intensity of the romantic visionary was deflected by opposing materialistic forces. Such romantic intensity stemmed in turn from special moments of experience that lived sharply in memory, informed our very sense of self, and which gave time a quality of being—or so Bergson said in his modernistic theory of time. And while Fitzgerald did not know Bergson directly, he certainly did indirectly, at least to the extent that he knew that the same experience could never be repeated. Once informed by consciousness, such an experience could never again be innocent of such consciousness. When Nick tells Gatsby, you can't repeat the past, he is unlocking another modernist truth.

Once we posit Fitzgerald among the moderns, we can begin to see how the narrative elements of *Gatsby* (what I have been calling the constructed text) supply a source of power beyond themselves, allowing Fitzgerald to draw from the strong spring and diverse currents of modernism itself. But most looks at *Gatsby* do not begin from this end of the telescope; instead, they examine particular scenes and passages within the text on the assumption that such matters have meaning in their own right. In the hope of suggesting how matters of critical indeterminacy might be mediated by the idea of the constructed text, I would like now to return to some of the questions that I raised initially, and to look specifically at *Gatsby* in terms of some of the more obvious narrative problems we encounter.

One of the more obvious problems in the novel involves the discrepancies of Daisy's hair.[6] At one point, Daisy refers to her daughter's "yellow hair" and says, "She's got my hair and shape of face" (117); but, at another point, when Daisy and Gatsby first fall in love, we are told "he kissed her dark shining hair" (150). Obviously, this inconsistency was not intentional; my guess is that Fitzgerald had two women in mind as he wrote about Daisy, and that she began as Ginevra King (who had brown hair) and was transformed on occasion into Zelda (who had blonde hair). But the problem here has much larger ramifications, and points to the fact that Daisy's physical characteristics are left vague throughout the novel. Daisy lacks physical presence because it is more important that she embody romantic expectation and lost time.

Daisy's vagueness and impalpability lead to mistakes in accounting for her chronology. We are told that Daisy and Gatsby fall in love in the summer and autumn of 1917 when Daisy is eighteen years old. The next autumn, 1918, she makes her debut "after the armistice" (November 11, 1918), is engaged to a man from New Orleans in February 1919, and in June 1919 she marries Tom Buchanan (76–77). Tom and Daisy honeymoon in the South Seas through June and July of 1919 and in August they are in Santa Barbara, where Tom gets into an accident on the Ventura highway with a chambermaid from the hotel (78). The next April, 1920, Daisy gives birth to her child. The novel, we know, takes place in the summer of 1922, and we are told that the child is three years old. But if the child was born in April of 1920, it would be two years and two months old.[7] Such a significant mistake has no meaning in and of itself, but it does suggest to me that Fitzgerald was far more concerned with symbolic rather than physical chronology in this novel. Movement from spring to autumn, from youth to adulthood, from romantic expectation to disillusionment, from life to death, from pastoral to tragic, from the ideal to the grotesque, from the spiritual to the material — these are symbolic elements that get narrative priority in *Gatsby* and literary modernism.

Once within the discourse of modernism, Fitzgerald could write at a physical distance from the world he was describing, even if it led to certain inconsistencies, even incredulity in plot. This happens when Fitzgerald revises the order of his narrative. In an earlier draft, Fitzgerald put the scene at Gatsby's party before the scene involving Tom and Myrtle Wilson in the apartment on 158th Street. This order gives Tom a slightly longer time to renew his acquaintance with Nick. By reversing these scenes, we have Tom taking Nick almost immediately into his confidence and inviting him to a moment of his lovemaking in New York. We know that Tom has not seen Nick for at least seven years, and we also know that Nick is Daisy's cousin. Such behavior on Tom's part does not seem very credible, but Fitzgerald braved it anyway, because he wanted to delay the appearance of Gatsby until the present chapter 3 in order to make Gatsby more mysterious and to make his eventual presence more strange in keeping with the mythic nature of the novel.

It is this desire for mystery, as well as the desire to give Gatsby a dual nature, that gets Fitzgerald into more narrative trouble. He has really created two Gatsbys: One is the man who has turned himself into God, the other is the Dakota farm boy who is still a roughneck. The latter tells Nick he is from San Francisco in the Midwest, while the former has been around the continent three times in Dan Cody's yacht and surely knows where to find San Francisco. Here the realistic and romantic elements of the novel pull the character away from any kind of consolidated meaning. Fitzgerald did not want us to bring these narrative elements together because they were not always in narrative synchronization with each other, as we can see if we allow Gatsby's account of the accident that killed Myrtle Wilson to get too detailed. To be sure, Daisy was driving, but Gatsby does manage to stop the car with the emergency brake. He clearly has the option of returning to the scene of the accident, but as Gatsby tells Nick, Daisy "fell over into my lap and I drove on" (145). Gatsby's participation in Myrtle's death gets almost no attention from the critics because, I would argue, they have been caught up in the sweep of Fitzgerald's romantic modernism and read this scene very differently than they do a comparable scene in Dreiser's *An American Tragedy*, when the car wreck near the beginning of the novel realistically establishes the meaning of Clyde Griffiths as a character.

But these are minor discrepancies in contrast to those that involve Nick. We never come to understand, for example, how Nick knows in such detail what went on in Wilson's garage the night and morning after Myrtle's death, since Nick was not there. And, more important, we never really come to know whether Tom Buchanan knew that Daisy was driving the car when he allows George Wilson to believe that Gatsby had run over Myrtle. And despite the fact that much of the meaning of the whole novel turns on how you answer this question, no critic, to my knowledge, looks upon it as a major narrative problem, but all instead assume either that Tom knows or that Tom does not know. Perhaps the latter interpretation is in the ascendancy, although to read the novel this way gives a certain justification to Tom's actions that reverses (at least for me) the narrative force and meaning of the novel. I believe Fitzgerald gives us an answer of sorts when he sends Nick around to the back of the Buchanans' house where he observes Tom and Daisy talking at the kitchen table over an uneaten plate of chicken and untouched bottles of ale. He tells us they looked as if they were "conspiring," a word that suggests Tom is aware of Daisy's involvement in the accident. On this one word, then, so much of the meaning of the novel turns, because if Tom sends Wilson to Gatsby's house knowing that Daisy was driving the car, then Tom is as responsible for Gatsby's death as is Wilson. The fact that Fitzgerald can let so much of the meaning of his story ride on the ambiguity of one word tells us as much about the narrative mode in which he was writing as it does about the story itself.

What is equally puzzling is the passage Nick gives us before he witnesses Tom and Daisy at the kitchen table: "A new point of view," he tells us, "occurred to me. Suppose Tom found out that Daisy had been driving. He might think he saw a connection in it—he might think anything" (145). What can this mean? What is the connection? Possibly that Daisy had intentionally run over Myrtle? Possibly at an inquest that his own name will become linked to Myrtle as her lover? The ending of the novel is not much more helpful in answering some of these questions. Here Nick confronts Tom and asks him directly what he told Wilson. His question stems from a guess—a correct guess—that Tom had sent Wilson in pursuit of Gatsby. But Tom insists that he told Wilson "the truth": "I told him the truth. . . . He was crazy enough to kill me if I hadn't told him who owned the car" (180). Tom lets Nick believe that he did not know that Daisy was driving: "He [Gatsby] ran over Myrtle like you'd run over a dog and never even stopped the car" (180). That Tom says this means nothing, since he does not know that Gatsby has told Nick that Daisy was driving. But what is more puzzling is Nick's response: "there was nothing I could say, except the one unutterable fact that it wasn't true" (180). Why is this fact unutterable? What has Nick to gain by letting Tom think that he has acted correctly, finally shaking hands with him as they part? This scene makes the actual ending of the novel all the more ambiguous. Nick leaves the East and retreats back to the West, the scene of his youth, with all the nostalgia that Fitzgerald brings to that world. Nick, in other words, seems intent on repeating the past, just what he told Gatsby he could not do, and the novel supposedly ends on a note of both contradiction and defeat.

Such inconsistencies are a part of the ending of The Great Gatsby, and yet they have seldom been discussed as serious lapses in the novel. While they must remain lapses, I think they are softened in their effect and can be explained by the modernist intentions that Fitzgerald brought to his novel, especially his desire to end the novel on a note of the "dying fall": he wanted to increase the sense of sadness and pathos that come with Gatsby's death, a pathos that in part also stems from Nick's feeling of helplessness in the face of Tom and in the East—that is, in New York—the realm and source of Tom's power. His desire to create a dying fall, a sense of life sadly running out for both Gatsby and Nick, is also the reason that Fitzgerald tells his story against the seasons of the year, moving from late spring (the novel begins on June 7, 1922) to late autumn (Nick last meets Tom "one afternoon late in October" [179]). That the fate of Gatsby is inseparable from the seasons of the year only intensifies his mythic character and suggests another parallel to the Dionysus story—and another connection to modern narrative discourse. While reading *Gatsby* as a modernist text does not wash away the narrative blemishes it may have, it helps explain those blemishes and allows us to see better the narrative problems Fitzgerald had to encounter in writing this brilliant novel.

In suggesting that Fitzgerald had access to a narrative realm that preceded his writing of the novel, I am, of course, coming very close to an aspect of Michel Foucault's theory of discourse. While I am willing to acknowledge this debt, I also want to say, by way of conclusion, that there are many differences between Foucault and me: the most important would be my insistence on the need to historicize discourse, lock it into a historical moment, into a specific culture, and into the diachronic. *The Great Gatsby*, like so much of modern American fiction, is a postwar novel that comes with the closing of the frontier and the rise of urban America, written at a time when romanticism still had mythic import and when a historicist sense of the past could still inform creative consciousness. Also, unlike Foucault, I make no claim for the death of the author; I argue just the opposite: that *The Great Gatsby* becomes *The Great Gatsby* only when the elements of modernism are filtered through the special consciousness of Fitzgerald himself. I have no desire to eliminate agency from history or from the act of creating fiction but insist on seeing how an author and a historical moment come together. Whatever blemishes we may find in *The Great Gatsby*, whatever may be its narrative knots and its puzzling unfolding, Fitzgerald gave life to a historical moment of which he himself was also the product, and produced a modernist text that we have long recognized (and I hope—in this time of canon reformation—we will continue to recognize) as one of the supreme achievements of American literature.

NOTES

1. Fitzgerald, *Great Gatsby*, 99. All subsequent page references to *The Great Gatsby* are to the 1957 edition and appear parenthetically in the text.
2. The wording here suggests Gertrude Stein. Stein's intent was to deflate the romantic vision, and her theory is the basis for another tradition of language in modernism — namely, imagism and later the idea of the vortex, although in trying to find an equivalent to the cubism of art, she broke company with Pound and especially Wyndham Lewis, whose *Time and Western Man* is a direct attack on modernist theories of time and consciousness — simultaneity and durée.
3. The dispute between Jefferson and Hamilton runs deeply throughout American literature, especially in the modernist period. Pound, Faulkner, and Dos Passos all shared Fitzgerald's sympathy for the Jeffersonian over the Hamiltonian vision.
4. Lehan, *"The Great Gatsby": The Limits of Wonder*, 80–90; Salpeter, "Fitzgerald, Spenglerian."
5. "Philippe, Count of Darkness" is a sequence of short stories, originally published in *Redbook Magazine*, October 1934 ("In the Darkest Hour"), June 1935 ("The Count of Darkness"), August 1935 ("The Kingdom in the Dark"), and posthumously in November 1941 ("Gods of Darkness").
6. Joan S. Korenman has pointed out the inconsistency in the color of Daisy's hair in "'Only Her Hairdresser.'"
7. In the new Cambridge edition of *Gatsby*, Matthew J. Bruccoli silently changes the dates in the text to bring them into synchronization with each other. Such an editorial policy, I believe, is dangerous, because it hides from the reader the various time lines Fitzgerald confused. The text Fitzgerald gave us seventy-five years ago has an integrity that should not be violated by modern editors, especially when there are no notes to reveal that an editor's hand — and not Fitzgerald's — is at work.

WORKS CITED

Adams, Henry. *The Education.* 1918. Ed. Ernest Samuels. Boston: Houghton Mifflin, 1973.

Detienne, Marcel. *Dionysus at Large.* Cambridge, Mass.: Harvard University Press, 1989.

———. *Dionysus Slain.* Baltimore: Johns Hopkins University Press, 1979.

Deutsch, Helene. *A Psychoanalytic Study of the Myth of Dionysus and Apollo.* New York: International University Press, 1969.

Ebel, Henry. *After Dionysus.* Rutherford, N.J.: Fairleigh Dickinson University Press, 1972.

Evans, Arthur. *The God of Ecstasy: Sex Roles and the Madness of Dionysus.* New York: St. Martin's Press, 1988.

Fitzgerald, F. Scott. *The Great Gatsby.* 1925. New York: Scribners, 1957.

———. *The Great Gatsby*. 1925. Ed. Matthew J. Bruccoli. New York: Cambridge University Press, 1991.

———. *The Last Tycoon*. New York: Scribners, 1941.

———. "My Lost City." In *The Crack-up*. Ed. Edmund Wilson. New York: New Directions, 1945. 23–33.

———. ["Philippe, Count of Darkness"]. "In the Darkest Hour," *Redbook Magazine* (October 1934): 15–19, 94–98; "The Count of Darkness," *Redbook Magazine* (June 1935): 20–23, 68, 70, 72; "The Kingdom in the Dark," *Redbook Magazine* (August 1935): 58–62, 64, 66–68; "Gods of Darkness," *Redbook Magazine* (November 1941): 30–33, 88–91.

———. *Tender Is the Night*. New York: Scribners, 1934.

Foster, John Burt. *Heirs to Dionysus: A Nietzschean Current in Literary Modernism*. Princeton, N.J.: Princeton University Press, 1981.

Korenman, Joan S. "'Only her Hairdresser . . .' : Another Look at Daisy Buchanan." *American Literature* 46 (1975): 574–78.

Lehan, Richard D. *F. Scott Fitzgerald and the Craft of Fiction*. Carbondale: Southern Illinois University Press, 1966.

———. "F. Scott Fitzgerald and Romantic Destiny," *Twentieth Century Literature* 26 (1980): 137–56.

———. *"The Great Gatsby": The Limits of Wonder*. Boston: G. K. Hall, 1990.

Salpeter, Harry. "Fitzgerald, Spenglerian." *New York World*, April 3, 1927: 12M.

Spengler, Oswald. *The Decline of the West*. 2 vols. Tr. Charles F. Atkinson. 1918; 1922. New York: Knopf, 1926; 1928.

Taylor, George Rogers. *The Turner Thesis*. Boston: D. C. Heath, 1956.

Turner, Frederick Jackson. *The Frontier in American History*. New York: Henry Holt, 1920.

Wilson, Edmund. *Axel's Castle: A Study in the Imaginative Literature of 1870–1930*. 1931. New York: Scribners, 1959.

Fitzgerald and Proust

Connoisseurs of Kisses

ANDRÉ LE VOT

Nothing seems farther from Fitzgerald's sparseness and allusiveness in *The Great Gatsby* than the profuse explicitness and the leisurely unfolding of Proust's hyperboles. Fitzgerald and Proust apparently share little in common save, in vastly different contexts, their exposure of the rich and their interest in the delusions of love. Still, the exploration of a few analogous correlatives by both writers points to further resemblances. The analysis of common technical approaches deepens our understanding of *The Great Gatsby*. It is as if the very differences were revealing, as if Proust, in his fuller, more explicit treatment of the same theme, offers an enlightening commentary on what is merely suggested in Fitzgerald.

My attention was first drawn to several similarities regarding women and love, too close in their symbolic functions to be considered coincidences.[1] Fitzgerald and Proust use the same objects, a voucher for a kiss and a little yellow pencil given as a compensation, to illustrate the same notions. They also describe a very unusual way of kissing, a point that is the main focus here.

The idea of a card valid for a kiss is suggested by Proust's Marcel: "If you really don't mind my kissing you, I'd rather put it off for a while and choose a good moment. Only you mustn't forget that you've said I may. I want a *voucher*:

'valid for one kiss.'"[2] And by Fitzgerald's Daisy: "If you want to kiss me any time during the evening, Nick, let me know and I'll be glad to arrange it for you. Just mention my name. Or present a green card. I'm giving out green."[3]

In Proust, Albertine gives a little gold pencil as a compensatory gesture to Marcel when she meets him after she has refused to be kissed: "She was genuinely distressed by her failure to gratify me, and gave me a little gold pencil, with the virtuous perverseness of people who, touched by your kindness but not prepared to grant what it clamours for, nevertheless want to do something on your behalf."[4]

In the revised galleys of *The Great Gatsby*, during his party, Gatsby asks Daisy to give the Star the address of her hairdresser: "here's a chance to become famous. . . . you'll be the originator of a new vogue all over the country." She refuses, but at the end of the party she notices Gatsby's sadness:

> "Have I said something that you—Here——!"
> With her little gold pencil she wrote an address on the table-cloth. "There's where I get my hair cut. Is that what she wanted to know?"
> But there was no such intimacy between them as would allow them to criticize each other's friends. Gatsby took out his pencil and slowly obliterated her marking with his own.[5]

In the printed version, there is no indication that she feels superior to the Star. On the contrary, the Star is the only person Daisy likes at the party. In the same compensatory spirit, Daisy gives her gold pencil to Tom, "to take down any addresses" (107), as if to make up for the moments she is going to spend with Gatsby.

The third common point is Proust's and Fitzgerald's status as "connoisseurs in kisses." Witness the enigmatic but apparently knowledgeable way the director postpones his kiss of the Star, a procedure that echoes the kiss of Albertine in *The Guermantes Way*, certainly one of the most famous in French literature.

Daisy and Gatsby's only significant kiss in the novel, the pivotal decisive moment in their story, is a remembered kiss, a five-year-old kiss. When they meet again, only a formalized, ritualistic projection of the act can do justice to Gatsby's mystical conception of their love. The traditional contact between lovers is displaced by an elaborate, highly symbolic ceremony, apparently enacted by the servants of a cult, the Star and her director.

To kiss or not to kiss Albertine seems to be the main question for Marcel, Proust's narrator. It is not a trivial question, notwithstanding appearances, as it implies either the past will be redeemed, fulfilled, or left barren of its significance. The kiss between Gatsby and Daisy in the November night is also a crucial experience that determines their future.

Why to kiss, how to kiss, when to kiss: these are three other relevant questions when considering the significance of kissing for both Gatsby and Marcel.

Why: The Proustian or the Fitzgeraldian kiss (in *Gatsby*) is not, to misquote a French wit, the contact of two skins and the exchange of two whims. It has very little to do, as a matter of fact, with skin and with desire; nor, to put it more succinctly, does it have much to do with eroticism. It is not a matter of sensuality, but a *cosa mentale*, a thing of the mind. It is not the expression of a physical urge but the token of a spiritual debate.

How: There is nothing of the unbridled, prolonged contact associated with romantic kisses. On the contrary, it is a very dilatory, deliberate movement, as of one celestial body attracted by another, a slow conjunction accompanied by an intense mental activity. It involves no fierce contact of two lips but the chaste, almost reluctant, slightly absurd pecking at a cheek.

When: The importance of this symbolic act calls for an intense concentration that cannot be found in a casual encounter. It requires the right mood, the exact pitch of awareness, to the point of being postponed in Proust if the right conditions cannot be summoned — hence, the "voucher for a kiss." The kiss for Proust is a focusing (or refocusing) in space and time of all the scattered, ephemeral, conflicting personalities within the beloved; it is an attempt to recapture the wholeness, the singleness, of the first impression. The kiss is the vehicle for a deliberate seeking of things past.

Fitzgerald and Proust are not concerned with something happening for the first time but with its reenactment. Their emphasis is not on a "fresh encounter" but on a ritualistic celebration. Time has stopped at a certain point and the Beloved is replaced by an idealized image, an icon. Further, the making of such an icon merges with the very method used by both writers for characterization — through condensation, replacements, and echoes. Their common approach, which poses the problematic quality of identity, can be summed up by the definition Madame Merle, in James's *The Portrait of a Lady*, gives of her own personality: "I know that a large part of myself is in the dresses I choose to wear. . . . One's self — for other people — is one's expression of one's self; and one's house, one's clothes, the book one reads, the company one keeps — these things are all expressive."[6]

Here, novelistic technique reflects the novelist's conception of character; it is an allusive way of defining people through their objects, houses, friends, and so forth, an oblique characterization that achieves economy through a series of analogues. It also reflects reality as perceived by the main character:

for Gatsby, Daisy *is* Louisville; for Marcel, Albertine *is* Balbec. Each character is thus defined by a series of factors that determine the nature of his (or her) relationship with others.

Gatsby is not in love with Daisy alone but with what she stands for—her house, the prestige of her social position, her wealth, the quality of those in love with her, her city and the South. His "irresistible" (152) pilgrimage to Louisville when he is back from Europe is the nearest he can get to her: "He left, feeling that if he had searched harder, he might have found her" (153). Last, but not least, when he settles in West Egg opposite the green light at Daisy's landing, one of a number of *"enchanted objects"* (94; emphasis added), it becomes the heart of the icon that subsumes all those elements. This icon is what Gatsby, while trying desperately to recapture its components and ignoring the changes, is really in love with. The living Daisy is only the shadow of this archetype, something merely "personal" (152), accidental, not affecting the essential. Like Albertine, she becomes a "captive" of and a "fugitive" from a too-exacting love.

Marcel, in a similar way, does not fall in love with Albertine at first but with the whole group of girls he meets in Balbec—with the holiday spirit and with the Grand Hotel and the seaside. Into his love goes his nostalgia for those moments when the young girls formed an anonymous and inextricably entangled "bunch of roses": "rose-sprigs whose principal charm was that they were silhouetted against the sea" (WBG 1007). "I cannot say whether it was the desire for Balbec or for her that took possession of me then; perhaps my desire for her was itself a lazy, cowardly, and incomplete form of possessing Balbec" (GW 364).

The silhouettes against the sea, Marcel's leitmotif, is, like the green light, the ultimate icon that contains all others. Each girl adds to this knowledge of Albertine. Andrée, Rosemonde, Gisele, and Berthe are all facets of her personality: "it was a genuine wish to love that wavered between them all, to such an extent was *each the natural substitute for the others*" (WBG 1007; emphasis added). What is true of Marcel's illusion is also true of Gatsby's: "He had thrown himself into it with a creative passion, adding to it all the time, decking it out with every bright feather that drifted his way" (97).

The story of Marcel's relationship with Albertine follows a twofold movement: (1) A *diversification*, not only from the other girls, but from the various contradictory aspects she presents to him. She simultaneously remains part of a sensuous collective body and, as time goes by, she undergoes a process of extreme diversification, enhanced by her talents for acting and lying. She becomes many characters in one, "a many-headed goddess" (GW 379). (2) A *concentration* of those various contradictory aspects she presents to him, an attempt at singleness and synthesis. The offered kiss will be the occasion for a momentous attempt to recapture unity.

In Fitzgerald, we can observe an analogous treatment of Daisy through a series of variations. What is said of other women in the novel, somehow, though to a different degree, often applies to her. Three different readings of her personality are thus suggested: a matter-of-fact copy, Jordan, her younger double, an understudy, who always admired her; a degraded stage, Myrtle Wilson, also a liar and a cheater like Jordan; an opposite, the Star, a legendary, archetypal projection, who expresses her external prestige.

Fitzgerald and Proust also share a similar treatment of *couples* who exemplify variations of a fundamental situation. In Proust, the couples Marcel-Albertine, Swann-Odette, Marcel-Gilberte, and Saint-Loup–Rachel are all based, to different degrees, on female treachery and male jealousy. In *Gatsby*, the gamut runs from the couple Daisy-Gatsby (romantic love) to Jordan-Nick (trivial affair), to Myrtle Wilson-George Wilson (degraded married life), to the contrapuntal Court of Love ironical image offered by the couple Star-director. Accordingly, *the kissing procedure*, as will be seen, follows the same hierarchy from the trivial (Nick-Jordan) to the sublime and the symbolic (Star-director).

Before coming to this essential point, it is necessary to go a little deeper into the similarities between the iconic features in Daisy and Albertine, otherwise vastly different from each other.

First there is the floral imagery: Daisy is seen as a greenhouse flower, an orchid "opening up again in a flower-like way" (20); "she blossomed for him like a flower" (112); "her artificial world was redolent of orchids" (151). Albertine is consistently referred to as a rose, more carnal and sensual.

Another similarity is voice: Daisy's voice is "full of aching, grieving beauty" (90); it has a "fluctuating, feverish warmth" (97). It might betray her sensuality: "Perhaps Daisy never went for amour at all—and yet there's something in that voice of hers" (78–79). As for Albertine, her "way of pronouncing her words was so carnal, so seductive that merely in speaking to you she seemed to be caressing you. A word from her was a favour, and her conversation covered you with kisses" (GW 374).

Both are actresses: Daisy uses her voice to subdue those around her. At Gatsby's party, the Star is the only person she can identify with: both are orchids, both are actresses. In the revised galleys, she is described as "a gorgeous, scarcely human orchid of a woman who sat in state under a white-plum tree."[7] Daisy has played all the roles: "I've been everywhere and seen everything and done everything. . . . Sophisticated—God I'm sophisticated!" (18). She has also become an idol, "gleaming like silver, safe and proud above the hot struggles of the poor" (105). The last part she has played, that of Gatsby's mistress, is discarded when reality breaks in, "as though she had never, all along, intended doing anything at all" (132–33). Meanwhile, Gatsby plays the role of her director. He stages the setting (his house directly across the bay from Daisy's), fixes the meeting at Nick's, and wants to go on with the script: when Daisy leaves Tom, they will return to Louisville for their wedding.

Albertine is implicitly compared to actresses, understudies, and projections also, their archetypal models being the Star and Proust's Lea, the lesbian actress: "I remembered Albertine first of all on the beach, almost painted upon a background of sea, having for me no more real an existence than those theatrical tableaux in which one does not know whether one is looking at the *actress* herself who is supposed to appear, at an *understudy* who for the moment is taking her part, or simply at a *projection*" (emphasis added). Among the other girls, Albertine appears as a leading actress, the Star who has created the part: "in the infinite series of imaginary Albertines who followed one after the other in my fancy hour by hour, the real Albertine, glimpsed on the beach, figured only at the head, just as the actress who 'creates' a role, *the star*, appears, out of a long series of performances, in the *few* first alone" (WBG 917; emphasis added).

A fourth similarity is the feeling of unreality: the woman's iconic image rarely coincides with reality. This blurring of two planes, the real and the ideal, is best experienced when meeting the Star, producing "that peculiarly unreal feeling that accompanies the recognition of a hitherto ghostly celebrity of the movies" (106). This "unreal feeling" also affects Gatsby: "the expression of bewilderment had come back into Gatsby's face, as though a faint *doubt* had occurred to him as to the *quality* of his present happiness" (97; emphasis added). In Proust, it takes the form of a state of puzzlement as to who the *real* Albertine is. The kiss seems to be the only way to break the spell.

Fifth is disappointment: a sense of disappointment is found in Albertine ("when she was no longer swaying in my imagination before a horizon of sea, but motionless in a room beside me, she seemed to me often a very poor specimen of a rose" [GW 364]) and in Daisy ("There must have been moments . . . when Daisy tumbled short of his dreams" [97]). Gatsby realizes that "his mind would never romp again like the mind of God" (112). The sense of the inadequacy between his *"unutterable visions"* and Daisy's *"perishable breath"* (112; emphasis added) finds its counterpart in Marcel's realization of something lacking that justifies the kiss: "I should have liked, before kissing her, to be able to breathe into her anew the mystery which she had had for me on the beach before I knew her" (GW 378–79).

To conclude the list of similarities, both heroines are submitted to a peculiar kissing procedure, an elaborate way of being kissed by their lover (emphasized in the symbolic projection of the Star and her director). Three characteristics are to be found in Proust and Fitzgerald: the kiss is preceded by a hesitation between the impulse and the act, as a token of its tremendous importance; it is slow, as if to emphasize its uniqueness; and while being protracted, an intense mental activity is going on in the mind of the male character.

Gatsby and Marcel are in love with an icon, a product of their nostalgia and imagination. The function of the kiss is to trigger a moment of incarnation and knowledge. With nothing frivolous in it, it partakes of the seriousness of a prayer or a sacrament. It is a high moment of expectancy, abstraction, and concentration, pushing aside the accidental, conjuring up the essence, waiting for a revelation, an epiphany.

The iconic nature of the epiphany is explicitly stated in Proust. Marcel is not after the woman in front of him, but tries to "reproduce experimentally the phenomenon which diversifies the individuality of a fellow-creature," to get hold of a composite image, "to draw out one from another, like a nest of boxes, all the possibilities that it contains — so now, during the brief journey of my lips towards her cheeks, it was ten Albertines that I saw, this one girl being like a many-headed goddess" (GW 378–79). The tension is broken by the ludicrous when Marcel is transfixed by the bell or blunders into physical obstacles. Fitzgerald's early conception (in the manuscript) of the Star is also farcical, with the facetious suggestion that her escort, the director, might "spoil her hair."[8] We still feel a subdued irony left over in the published version.

Starting from there, we can distinguish five different types of kisses — with similarities in the motivations and differences in the reasons for delaying the act. What is similar is that the kiss, far from being a prelude, or a euphemistic form of sexuality, is dissociated from sensuality. In *The Great Gatsby*, the actual sexual act takes place *before* Gatsby falls in love, before the mythical November kiss: "He took what he could get, ravenously, unscrupulously . . . one still October night" (149). For Gatsby, it means a realization and acceptance of having to give up a loftier future of imagined glory after a half-reluctant abandonment of his former illusions. As for Proust's Marcel, after first attempting to force himself on Albertine (like Gatsby, "ravenously" [149], close to a rape), he transmogrifies the kiss into an aesthetic quest, an end in itself, to recapture the lost world of Balbec, to reduce multiplicity into unity.

The three kisses in *The Great Gatsby* point to three degrees of love. Except in the first case, they don't reflect the usual erotic impulse, the sense of urgency ("You can't live forever" [36]) expressed by Myrtle when she first meets Tom. This norm is stated when Nick, healthily sensual, kisses Jordan, for him no "disembodied face," but the proximity of a demanding body— "I drew up the girl beside me, tightening my arms" (81).

No kiss between Gatsby and Daisy occurs in the present, except for a brief defiant one in her house when Tom leaves the room to answer the telephone (116). All that remains is the memory of the slow autumn kiss in the moonlight five years before: "He knew that when he kissed this girl and forever wed his unutterable visions to her perishable breath, his mind would never romp again like the mind of God. So he *waited*, listening for a *moment longer* to the tuning fork that had been struck upon a star. *Then* he kissed her. At his lips' touch she blossomed for him like a flower and the incarnation was complete" (112; emphasis added). Their kiss, after an intense moment of deliberation, is a crucial gesture, the sealing of a fundamental choice, involving "the following of a grail" (149).

The third avatar of the kiss is that of the Star and her director, a kind of vision, the celebration of an archetypal ceremony linking Star to director, lover to beloved. The contrast between the outer uproar of the party and their inner calm and mastery is striking. Both are professionals slowly and solemnly performing an emblematic representation of incorporeal, spiritualized love: "their faces were touching except for a pale, thin ray of moonlight between. It occurred to me that he had been *very slowly* bending toward her *all evening* to attain this proximity, and even while I watched I saw him stoop *one ultimate degree and kiss at her cheek*" (108; emphasis added).[9] This sublimated kiss reflects the essence of Gatsby's commitment. Its meaning is emphasized by the procession of Platonic shadows on a window blind: "Sometimes a shadow moved against a dressing-room blind above, gave way to another shadow, an indefinite procession of shadows, that rouged and powdered in an invisible glass" (19). Those pathetic solitary shadows represent the last stage, after the kiss of the Star, in the poetical handling of Gatsby's predicament. There are no such symbolical projections in Proust, whose characters are handled in purely psychological terms.

A parallel presents itself between these three types of kisses and the two kisses between Marcel and Albertine, the first in *Within a Budding Grove* and the second in *The Guermantes Way*. The attempt at a first unsolicited kiss, with sexual undertones, reminds us of Anthony's kiss in the section entitled "The Connoisseur of Kisses" in *The Beautiful and Damned*, when Gloria icily refuses him.[10] It parallels Albertine's reluctance, suspended contact, and denied revelation:[11]

> in the *state of exaltation* in which I was, Albertine's round face, lit by an inner flame as by a night-light, stood out in such relief that, imitating the rotation of a glowing sphere, it seemed to me to be turning, like those Michelangelo figures which are being swept away in a stationary and vertiginous whirlwind. I was about to discover the fragrance, the flavour which *this strange pink fruit*[12] contained. I heard a sound, abrupt, prolonged and shrill. Albertine had pulled the bell with all her might. (WBG 996; emphasis added)

The second kiss, in Paris, meets with her acquiescence. It is encouraged and obligingly postponed (a "voucher," to be used at the right moment, has been presented). Between the cup and the lips, there is a slow deliberate introspection, as in the Fitzgeraldian November night: "Albertine had often appeared different to me, so now—as if, prodigiously accelerating the speed of the change of perspective . . . which a person presents to us in the course of our various encounters, I had sought to contain them all in the space of a few seconds" (GW 378).

At this point, Proust goes a stage further and makes explicitly clear the meaning that Fitzgerald leaves implicitly suspended, the failure to achieve fusion through physical contact, however chaste (a kiss on the cheek in both cases). The "ultimate degree" achieved by the director in *Gatsby*, only suggested by the disappearance of the "thin ray of moonlight" between the faces, is realistically documented in Proust, beyond the mere suggestion of a contact obscuring the vision.

In *The Guermantes Way* the long-expected kiss ends in anticlimax, abased by the coarseness of proximity and the ludicrous reality of noses and cheeks interfering with the act:

> At first, as my mouth began gradually to approach the cheeks which my eyes had recommended it to kiss, my eyes, in changing position, saw a different pair of cheeks; the neck, observed at closer range and as though through a magnifying glass, showed in its coarser grain a robustness which modified the character of the face. . . . suddenly my eyes ceased to see, then my nose, crushed by the collision, no longer perceived any odour, and, without thereby gaining any clearer idea of the taste of the rose of my desire, I learned, from these *obnoxious signs*, that at last I was in the act of kissing Albertine's cheek. (GW 378–79; emphasis added)

The two botched attempts to kiss Albertine — one denied, the other offered, postponed, and resolved into a comical failure (as was suggested with the Star in the manuscript version of *Gatsby*) — dispel the illusion of a possible communion.

So the ultimate proximity means the end of illusions, as Fitzgerald deftly suggests when obliquely referring to the central icon, Daisy's green light: "Compared to the great distance that had separated him from Daisy, it had seemed very near to her, almost touching her. It had seemed as close as a star to the moon. Now it was again a green light on a dock" (94).

Gatsby's sense of frustration ("he wanted to recover something, some idea of himself perhaps that had gone into loving Daisy. His life had been confused and disordered since" [112]) corresponds to Marcel's realization of something lacking in Albertine: "I should have liked, before kissing her, to be able to breathe into her anew the mystery which she had had for me on the beach before I knew her" (GW 377).

In both cases, nothing satisfactory comes out of the consummation. Is it better to abstain? Such is the message of Keats's *Ode on a Grecian Urn*, which Fitzgerald knew by heart, illustrating the merciful compensations of unfulfilled love:

> Bold lover, never, never canst thou kiss,
> Though winning near the goal—yet, do not grieve;
> She cannot fade, though thou hast not thy bliss,
> For ever wilt thou love, and she be fair![13]

NOTES

1. *Swann's Way* was first published in 1913; the English translation appeared in 1924. Extracts from *The Guermantes Way* (Balbec) were first published in June 1914 (*Nouvelle Revue Français*); the full novel first appeared in French in 1918. The complete English translation appeared in 1925. *Within a Budding Grove* was originally published in 1918 and published in English in 1924, the year that Fitzgerald was working on *The Great Gatsby* on the Riviera. It is possible that Christian Gauss, Fitzgerald's French literature teacher at Princeton in the fall of 1915 and 1916, introduced his classes to passages of these novels. On his influence, see Le Vot, F. *Scott Fitzgerald: A Biography*, 37–38.

2. Proust, *Guermantes Way*, 376; emphasis added. All subsequent page references to *The Guermantes Way* are to the 1982 edition, are cited as GW, and appear parenthetically in the text. The English text of *Remembrance of Things Past* has the same distribution in three volumes as the French text: *Within a Budding Grove* is located in the first, *The Guermantes Way* in the second. The third volume (*The Captive*

[1923], *The Fugitive* [1925]), although dealing again partly with the Albertine cycle (*The Prisoner* [1923], *The Fugitive* [1925]), presents little relevance to the theme of this paper, which is centered on *The Great Gatsby.*

3. Fitzgerald, *Great Gatsby,* 105. All subsequent references to *The Great Gatsby* are to the 1953 edition and appear parenthetically in the text.

4. Proust, *Within a Budding Grove,* 1003–4. All subsequent page references to *Within a Budding Grove* are to the 1981 edition, are cited as WBG, and appear parenthetically in the text.

5. Fitzgerald, *F. Scott Fitzgerald Manuscripts III,* 102–3.

6. James, *Portrait of a Lady,* 397–98.

7. Fitzgerald, *F. Scott Fitzgerald Manuscripts III,* 89.

8. Ibid., 43.

9. The November kiss takes place on a sidewalk "white with moonlight" (112). Romance is associated with moonlight and darkness with consummation. In *The Last Tycoon,* "four feet of moonlight" separate the lovers when they first meet (Fitzgerald, *Last Tycoon,* 26). On their second meeting, there is only "one foot" between them (66); when they finally kiss, "the inch between them melted into darkness" (86).

10. Fitzgerald, *Beautiful and Damned,* 113–15.

11. Cf. *Beautiful and Damned:*

> Anthony pulled her quickly to her feet and held her helpless, without breath, *in a kiss that was neither a game nor a tribute.*
>
> Her arms fell to her side. In an instant she was free.
>
> "Don't" she said quietly. "I don't want that."
>
> She sat down on the far side of the lounge and gazed straight before her. A frown had gathered between her eyes. (113–14; emphasis added)

12. Cf. what Jordan says about New York: "There's something very sensuous about it— overripe, as if *all sorts of funny fruits* were going to fall into your hands" (124; emphasis added).

13. Keats, *Poems and Verses of John Keats,* 365.

WORKS CITED

Fitzgerald, F. Scott. *The Beautiful and Damned.* 1922. New York: Scribners, 1950.

——. *F. Scott Fitzgerald Manuscripts III: "The Great Gatsby": The Revised and Rewritten Galleys.* Introduced and arranged by Matthew J. Bruccoli. New York: Garland, 1990.

——. *The Great Gatsby.* 1925. New York: Scribners, 1953.

——. *"The Great Gatsby": A Facsimile of the Manuscript.* Ed. Matthew J. Bruccoli. Washington, D.C.: Microcard Editions, 1973.

——. *The Last Tycoon.* Ed. Edmund Wilson. 1941. In *Three Novels of F. Scott Fitzgerald.* New York: Scribners, 1953.

James, Henry. *The Portrait of a Lady.* 1881. In *Novels, 1881–1886.* Ed. William T. Stafford. New York: Library of America, 1986. 193–800.

Keats, John. *The Poems and Verses of John Keats.* Ed. John Middleton Murry. Rev. ed. London: Eyre & Spottiswoode, 1949.

Le Vot, André. *F. Scott Fitzgerald.* Tr. William Byron. Garden City, N.Y.: Doubleday, 1983.

Proust, Marcel. *Within a Budding Grove.* 1918. *Remembrance of Things Past,* vol. 1. Tr. C. K. Scott Moncrieff and Terence Kilmartin. London: Penguin Books, 1981. [465]–1018.

———. *The Guermantes Way.* 1920. *Remembrance of Things Past,* vol. 2. Tr. C. K. Scott Moncrieff and Terence Kilmartin. London: Penguin Books, 1981. 3–620.

Redirecting Fitzgerald's "Gaze"

Masculine Perception and Cinematic License in

The Great Gatsby

SCOTT F. STODDART

With his move to Hollywood in 1937, F. Scott Fitzgerald's fascination with moving pictures transcended interest in a paycheck; he keenly believed that an understanding of this medium would enable him to compose screenplays of substance.[1] Perhaps it is this simple desire to understand the medium that eludes Hollywood moguls who desperately purchase the rights to film American classics. Sadly, Hollywood maintains a long history of transforming novels into films, altering novels to create revisionist "classics," all in the name of "art" or "big bucks." Such proves the fate of Fitzgerald's *The Great Gatsby*; filmed on three separate occasions, no version approximates the novel's complexity, causing director Peter Bogdanovich to agree "that this Fitzgerald novel is all but unfilmable."[2] This essay focuses on the technicolor tragedy of Jack Clayton's 1974 version, as the reasons for its failure, in my estimation, reflect Hollywood's inability to filmically replicate the written word. In *The Great Gatsby*, Fitzgerald uses Nick Carraway to weave a tale of shallow materialism and misplaced obsession; Hollywood, in turn, reweaves this subtle tapestry cinematically to revise it as another tale, one of unrequited passion, a melodramatic love story of epic proportions.

Fitzgerald's genius of characterization lies in the subtle quality of Nick Carraway's narration, what I term "masculine perception," a form, oddly enough, similar in scope to the "gaze" identified by feminist film critics.[3] In the novel, Nick's voice gradually changes in his discussions of Daisy Buchanan and Jay Gatsby. As Daisy illicitly involves herself with Gatsby, Nick's "gaze" becomes bitter, almost jealous toward Daisy, yet grows even more gracious and understanding with respect to Gatsby. However, by altering Nick's "gaze," director Clayton uses "cinematic license" to strip Nick of his narrative power to film a marketable Jazz Age melodrama.

The Critical Reception: Twenty Years of Change

While contemporary reviews of Clayton's *The Great Gatsby* seem anything but glowing, a moderate change within the scholarly climate in the past twenty years since its release should cause us to reexamine the film from the novelistic perspective. *Variety* notes that by 1974, America was in the midst of "a nostalgia craze"; the producers at Paramount realized the potential of a period piece like *The Great Gatsby*.[4] Contextualizing this marketing strategy, we can see the brilliance in such an assumption. Americans steadily realized the "no-win" situation of the ever-present Vietnam conflict; questions surrounding Nixon's involvement in "Watergate" continued to infiltrate the evening news; tensions mounted on the academic front between men and women because of the newly strengthened feminist movement. It is little wonder that middle America eagerly bought into Paramount's nostalgia campaign designed to "Gatsbyize" America. In fact, *Time* magazine dedicated a cover story, "Ready or Not, Here Comes Gatsby" (March 18, 1974), to revealing the marketing tactics Paramount employed to insure the film's "blockbuster status." Paramount signed four companies to market a selection of "Gatsby products" linked through their advertising to the film: Glenby International hair salons ("After you've seen *The Great Gatsby*, get the cut"); Robert Bruce Sportswear for men (which landed Robert Redford on the cover of *Gentleman's Quarterly* for March 1974); Ballantine's "21" Brands Scotch (which ran ads touting "Gatsby's parties . . . we were there . . . illegally, of course!"); and E. I. du Pont (which marketed "Classic White" Teflon cookware "in the tradition of *The Great Gatsby*").[5] This campaign, now recognized as the prototype for Hollywood's marketing of its blockbusters, proved quite successful. *The Great Gatsby* broke all records in prerelease ticket sales, an unprecedented $18.6 million in advance bookings alone. The anticipation, playing off the need for the romance of the carefree 1920s, was reflected in the trade posters: "Gone is the romance that was so divine." With such promise, it is little wonder that Americans bought so eagerly into this "American Dream."[6]

However, most contemporary reviews generally found fault with the film. The *Washington Post* criticized it for its "many verbal as well as visual clichés, its poor acting (especially the two principal stars), its sluggish pacing, and its fundamental vulgarity," while the *Saturday Review* believed "the production failed as soon as Mia Farrow indicated her interest in playing Daisy." In his *New York Times* review, Vincent Canby found "the substance of the novel has largely vanished" and its "gut-clutching moments" became "just more starry-eyed photography." *Time's* Jay Cocks simply called it "a dull and dreadful movie."[7] But many scholarly critics disagree with these assessments from the popular press. Revisionists point to the contemporary reviewers' collective resistance to Paramount's publicity campaign; they feel their distanced perspectives read the film more fairly. In an early analysis, Edward T. Jones justifies Clayton's version, placing blame on the complexity of the novel: "Clayton has presented what he can of the original, testing his material whenever possible against the literature he has filmed." Another early reading, by Penelope Houston, argues that the film's "fastidious, literally faithful, meticulous concern" with the novel passed over most critics' heads. Along similar lines, Marjorie Rosen's attitude that, "given time, much of the rather hysterical criticism will prove to be entirely wrong" has generally proven true.[8]

As early as 1975, revisionist articles including J. Teegarden's "The Joke's On Us: *Gatsby* is Great" and Louis Giannetti's "The *Gatsby* Flap" attest that contemporary responses were to the merchandising instead of the filmic text. Giannetti writes, "On the whole, this film is certainly one of the most faithful attempts in film history to adhere to the spirit, and whenever possible, to the letter, of a great novel." Even more important, two film theory texts praise Clayton's filmic text. Giannetti's *Understanding Movies* uses *The Great Gatsby* to illustrate proper use of color filters, tracking shots, subtext, and costumes. Frank Magill's *Cinema: The Novel into Film* declares *Gatsby* subject to a misguided critical elite: Farrow's Daisy becomes "bold and sharp"; Redford's Gatsby "is more in keeping with Fitzgerald's intent . . . [while] the film's beautiful visual techniques may have been partly responsible for its lack of critical success."[9] Distancing the film from the historical moment of its release allows revisionist critics to revel in the romance of Clayton's *Gatsby*; it is for this reason alone it becomes important to reassess the filmic text with respect to Fitzgerald's original.

Nick's "Gaze": Reading Daisy Buchanan

Granted, from its opening paragraphs, the novel exhibits many filmic qualities, teasing any director to capture its essence: sumptuous sets, detailed costumes, even a musical soundtrack in chapter 3.[10] But Fitzgerald's use of Nick to tell his story of "that summer" in 1922 (61) in West Egg, to narrate the consciously written screenplay of Gatsby's fall from his self-made facade, and Daisy's subsequent involvement in that fall, is, in essence, a filmic "gaze." Laura Mulvey explains this as a method whereby "Woman stands in patriarchal culture as signifier for the male other, bound by a symbolic order in which man can live out his fantasies and obsessions through linguistic command by imposing them on the silent image of woman still tied to her place."[11] The novel's plot follows these lines closely as Daisy finds herself physically positioned between Gatsby's fanciful "woman-worship" and her husband Tom's selfish machinations, orchestrated once again by the phallocentric order of Nick's storytelling. Take, for example, Nick's opening commentary on Daisy. Initially, he introduces her through Tom: "I drove over there to have dinner with the Tom Buchanans" (5). We hear of *his* family, *his* money, even the "enormous leverage" of *his* body (7). The stifling presence of Tom cleverly leads to the unforgettably languid first impression we receive of Daisy, sprawled upon "an enormous couch . . . as though upon an anchored balloon" (8). Not only does the repetition of the word "enormous" remind us of Nick's controlled fascination with Tom, but "anchored" becomes a key word of judgment in respect to Tom's physical force over Daisy in their marriage.[12]

However, Nick soon regains semantic control as he details Daisy's voice for us after we have heard her utter only a single four-word sentence. In his metaphor, her voice "is an arrangement of notes that will never be played again" (9). Naturally, this can be read as a compliment to its musical quality; but it is in seemingly simple phrases like this that Nick flexes his own narrative muscle, revealing to us that Daisy consciously performs as she speaks, much the opposite of Tom's continual off-the-cuff racist ramblings. Soon thereafter, Daisy arranges her own analogy: "I love to see you at my table, Nick. You remind me of a — of a rose, an absolute rose" (15). But here again, we pass from Daisy's insecure observation to Nick's present-day response: "This was untrue. I am not even faintly like a rose" (15). Nick negates Daisy's phrase and, in effect, takes away any creative control of her own rhetoric. In her most dramatic outburst of this first chapter, Daisy tells Nick of her newly "cynical" attitude toward her role as wife and mother. Recounting the birth of her daughter,

Pammy, Daisy articulates with disgust a woman's position: "'She told me it was a girl, and so I turned my head away and wept. "All right," I said, "I'm glad it's a girl. And I hope she'll be a fool—that's the best thing a girl can be in this world, a beautiful little fool"'" (17). Just as it appears that Nick will allow Daisy some control, some power, he qualifies this moment with his own caustic commentary, noting "the basic insincerity of what she had said," the "absolute smirk on her lovely face" tipping the reader off, in essence, to the inherently superficial qualities Daisy later comes blatantly to represent. Realizing that "the whole evening had been a trick of some sort to exact a contributory emotion from me" (18), Nick leaves Daisy after he sets the stage, warning us to beware.

Clayton's cinematic version renders Nick an impotent onlooker from the start as the director elevates our impression of Daisy for his own melodramatic purpose through a traditional filmic male "gaze." Beginning immediately, Daisy's image as the romantic ideal provides the viewer with Clayton's interpretation—that Gatsby (Robert Redford) and Daisy (Mia Farrow) were meant for each other in a positive way. After some heavy foreshadowing during the opening credits—images of Gatsby's palatial home, the infamous yellow car, the ominous pool—the image cuts to a scrapbook of three sepia photos of Daisy Buchanan. It is here that the haunting music begins to swell, and the lens slowly zooms in to fill the frame with Daisy's fawnlike eyes, dreamily looking directly at the spectator. The camera then cuts to an old framed photograph of a southern mansion. When it pulls away we see that it rests on a nightstand by Gatsby's bed, emblazoned with a pretentious "JG" embroidered on its center. We casually drift onto the other nightstand, which holds yet another large, gauzy photo of Daisy, a close-up in a white picture hat. We cut next to a dressing table on the other side of the room. Here we see valet ornaments neatly displayed with a tiny ring and a curiously large medal. Once again, another large photograph of Daisy, in a rather ornate frame, watches over the items. While the casual observer might see these as an expeditious manner of capturing mise-en-scène, we must recognize that Clayton's constant, loving focus on the image of Daisy introduces us to *his* image of Daisy in a manner much the opposite of Nick's "gaze." Using the traditional cinematic gaze, Clayton obviously desires his audience to draw a connection with his romantic representation of the novel. The music that echoes throughout the credits calls attention not only to the tragic plot that involves Gatsby but also to the tragedy of these two "star-crossed" lovers.

The film's use of the events from chapter 1 similarly alters the viewer's perception of Daisy; however, this empowering of Daisy forces Nick into the position of a passive participant, an ineffective voice-over. The film's opening narrative parallels the novel's opening events with glaring exceptions. We first see Nick (Sam Waterston) manipulating a motored punt across a bay to enjoy dinner with Daisy and Tom Buchanan (Bruce Dern). While Nick recounts (via voice-over) the wisdom imparted by his caring father, he carelessly weaves his boat in and out of the paths of more experienced yachtsmen, losing his dapper white fedora along the way. This clumsy image of Nick underscores Clayton's intention of stripping Nick of his narrative control. While we obviously lose character delineation from the narrator's perspective in the film, Clayton's blatant disengaging of Nick's judgmental eye forces Daisy into a more romantically charged and sympathetic light. From her flirtatious manner as she reclines on her own white sofa (with Jordan Baker safely placed on the opposite side of the room, thus avoiding innuendo) to the extreme close-up of her gasping face the moment Jordan mentions her casual knowledge of Nick's next-door neighbor, Clayton's Daisy becomes a caricature of the Jazz Age doll. His Daisy takes control by pouting and gleefully gabbing like some child-woman. Without Nick's perception, there is no glimpse of the calculatingly selfish woman.

The dinner party shows a fine example of this transference of power as Daisy tells Nick he is "like a rose." Instead of Nick's verbal reaction to both speaker and remark, he lovingly smiles and clutches her hand; he becomes another flaccid victim to the southern-bred charms of his idealistic cousin. Soon thereafter, she floats out of the scene, returning to remark upon a "romantic" nightingale that walks upon the lawn. An added scene in the film, the golf tournament where Jordan (Lois Chiles) cheats, departs from the original as well. It is here that Clayton chooses to film Daisy's revelation of her postpartum depression as she cries about the fate of her newly born daughter. Once again, Nick passively listens without critical comment. However, this scene ends on a comic note: We watch Jordan move her golf ball out of a sand trap as Daisy exclaims, "She is the most immoral young lady I have ever seen!" This reveals a moral streak within Daisy, rather than the questionable ethical status highlighted by Nick early in the novel. In this light, Clayton obviously wants his viewers morally to align themselves with the romantic, moral notions of Daisy and the soon-to-be-revealed aspirations of Gatsby; he disengages Nick's "gaze" for the sake of his love story.[13]

Flashback: The Essence of Cinematic Romance

The telling of the Gatsby/Daisy history provides another glaring discrepancy between novel and film. The novel's recounting of their past takes place twice: once when Jordan speaks to Nick in chapter 4, in an effort to persuade him to invite Daisy to tea; the second, in chapter 8, the night of Myrtle Wilson's death, when Gatsby tells his version of their past to Nick. In both instances, Nick employs his "gaze" to force a distinct reading of Daisy rather than of Gatsby. In a curious, uncharacteristic move, Nick uses Jordan's voice solely to provide romantic details. While we might believe that Nick relinquishes his narrative to provide an honest account in an effort to capture the growth of his own awareness, I believe it is a much more subtle means of narrative control over Daisy. We instantly recall Jordan as the woman who holds herself "as if she were balancing something on it [her chin] which was quite likely to fall" (8); she is, after all, the subject of "a critical, unpleasant story" (19). Constantly reminding us of her reputation, Nick forces us to question whatever she says; in this light, we question whatever positive intentions Jordan entertains. After Jordan recounts these romanticized details about Daisy, Nick questions Daisy's motives. On the other hand, he avoids criticizing Gatsby's sophomoric attraction (as exemplified in his buying a house opposite Daisy's) as nothing more than "a strange coincidence" (79). Nick continues to emulate Gatsby's romantic determination: "He came alive to me, delivered suddenly from the womb of his purposeless splendor" (79), an understatement of sorts, emphasizing Nick's own growing fascination with his hero. Jordan's version of Daisy's past momentarily places Daisy at the center of the drama, soliciting sympathy for its femme fatale of abject circumstance. Instead, Nick interprets this as a tragedy for Gatsby: "He had waited five years and bought a mansion where he dispensed starlight to casual moths—so that he could 'come over' some afternoon to a stranger's garden" (80). Consequently, Nick's own fantasies begin to take hold. He turns to Jordan, "this clean, hard, limited person, who dealt in universal skepticism" (81), reducing her, in short, to a sexual object to suit his own repressed passions.[14]

Later, after the calamity at the Plaza Hotel, Gatsby admits to Nick his past association with Daisy. Again, instead of finding fault with Gatsby's unreasonable behavior, Nick condemns Daisy through his own critical filter. The description of Daisy as "the first 'nice' girl he [Gatsby] had ever known" (148) highlights Nick's sarcastic intention. Gatsby even admits deceit while telling of his seduction of Daisy, which Nick casually brushes off: "He might have despised himself, for he had certainly taken her under false pretenses . . . he had deliberately given Daisy a sense of security. . . . When they met again, two days later, it was Gatsby who was breathless, who was, somehow, betrayed" (149). Nick's constant support of Gatsby, his "gaze" of misogynistic intent, further influences our own judgment of Daisy, who now appears heartless at the center of "her artificial world," impatiently wanting "her life shaped, now, immediately" (151). It is only at the end of Nick's narrative that we recall with bitterness his voyeuristic scene of the night before. Looking in through "the pantry window," Nick describes Daisy for the last time we actually see her in the novel: "Daisy and Tom were sitting opposite each other at the kitchen table, with a plate of cold fried chicken between them, and two bottles of ale. . . . his hand had fallen upon and covered her own. . . . There was an unmistakable air of natural intimacy about the picture, and anybody would have said that they were conspiring together" (146). Throughout his narrative, Nick's qualifiers form a negative perception of Daisy; his narrative "gaze" assures that we see Daisy for what *he* understands her to be. This last scene, suggesting the clandestine conspiracy that destroys Gatsby, increases our negative impression of Daisy.

In mounting his more marketable melodrama, Clayton removes Nick even further from the storytelling when we learn of the couple's "past." Although Nick accompanies Gatsby and Daisy during their teatime tryst, he witnesses Daisy's infamous reaction to Gatsby's shirts in silence. However, more important, Clayton's decision to film the relationship's past and present paints a markedly different portrait of Daisy. In these two montages, we are present, while Nick is not. Instead of viewing this as Gatsby's materialized obsession, we view an erotically suggestive, emotionally mutual relationship between Gatsby and Daisy — one we obviously want to succeed. After finding the scrapbooks featured in the film's opening credits, Daisy becomes our typical filmic heroine. She mentions their relationship of 1917, which begins a romanticized montage mixing their past and present: She recalls that the other soldiers "meant nothing"; she wishes her "sweet young lieutenant" still had his uniform; she tells Gatsby he has her heart completely. However, this idealized vision is Daisy's, which runs counter to the harsher version of Nick's narrative. This sequence only strays once from Daisy and Gatsby when Clayton cuts to a close-up of Myrtle Wilson (Karen Black) applying lipstick in her New York flat — with Tom Buchanan lying on her bed watching. This obviously draws a real line of distinction between the two affairs: Tom's and Myrtle's, placed in the realities of the New York apartment, is a one-sided passion, as Tom continues to deceive both women; Gatsby's and Daisy's, bathed in the romance of his palace, is the "something" that Jordan claims Daisy deserves — their mutual romance *is* moral to the audience. As the montage continues, it is Daisy who recounts the facts of her ill-fated wedding to Tom. Although Gatsby begins to apply pressure here, sympathy builds for Daisy as she looks into the camera to wail "Rich girls don't marry poor boys, Jay Gatsby!" In this light, the cinema's Daisy captures our heart. We, too, want her to have something in her life, and Gatsby arrives as the perfect vehicle for her happiness.

A second montage captures the fruition of Gatsby's obsession; however, the depiction allows us to witness Daisy's romantic desires coming true as well. The sequence, in the present, begins with Daisy's jeweled hand caressing a display of copper molds in Gatsby's rather large, yet simple kitchen. It is logical to begin here, the traditional woman's domain, because Daisy now begins to control the sequence as she says to Gatsby, in a coy way, "Let's be foolish; put on your uniform." Clayton's next cut, a close-up of a single, erect candlestick glowing, cues us to the sexual extent of Daisy and Gatsby's relations. The camera gradually pulls back to show them waltzing in his darkened ballroom, a Victrola echoing throughout the room as a close-up of the couple dissolves into a memory of their courting days. We now see from Gatsby's perspective a stately southern mansion beside which a younger Gatsby and Daisy (still Farrow and Redford) walk to its door. It is during this portion of the sequence that we root for Gatsby as he tells her again, "I felt married to you ever since." This honorable statement once again places his obsession in a positive light. When Gatsby later reveals his desire to be her "husband," complete with the token of a ring whose stone is "the color of the light on your dock," we naturally want our noble hero and deserving heroine united in morally correct matrimony. In a subsequent scene, the two lovers lounge beside a pool of goldfish, promising each other eternal love in an ultimate moment of cinematic melodrama. At this point, we can see that the absence of Nick's narratorial "gaze" causes us to envision Daisy positively; the careless Daisy of the novel becomes, in the film, the willing victim of the erotic dream which is Jay Gatsby.

Of course, this helps to make the film's ending all the more tragic. After the chaos of the Plaza Hotel (one scene shows Tom yelling an accusation about Gatsby's bootlegging operation across a crowded lobby; another offers a significantly boraxed version of Myrtle Wilson's demise), we follow Gatsby, rather than Nick, as he watches outside the Buchanan home for Daisy's light. He then goes to Nick's house to report that Daisy drove the car from the Plaza, which should prepare us finally to judge Daisy in the light cast by Nick's narration in the novel. However, this scene cuts to the Buchanans at breakfast,

Tom hovering over the table as Daisy sits in a stupor. As Tom reaches for her hand, we see nothing of Nick's "conspiracy"; instead, we have a couple consoling each other, one reaching to help the other put past indiscretions behind. Then Daisy gasps as the shadow of George Wilson darkens the table. She rushes from the room screaming while her maid identifies Wilson. As Daisy enters the next room, the angelic Pammy runs into her arms weeping about a smock she wants to wear that day. In response, Daisy sobs, "You can wear any color you want! Beautiful little fools can wear any color they wish!" Naturally, this scene reinforces the image of Daisy as a victim of the traditional, cinematic gaze; she is positioned between the two rival men as a trophy of their conquest.

Conclusion

From Fitzgerald's original text to Clayton's cinematic text, Daisy Buchanan becomes a different woman. Using a traditionally phallocentric gaze, the film creates a moral tragedy with Gatsby and Daisy rather than Nick Carraway at its moral center. The final scene shows both Tom and Daisy taking leave of Nick in the lobby of the Plaza some few months after Gatsby's funeral. Daisy's last line, barely whispered to Nick, "You know how I love to see you at my table," highlights her fragile nature; she now becomes the film's tragically broken shell, another contrast to the novel's pervasive image of Nick's "gaze" of disgust at the "careless" people of East Egg.

NOTES

1. Bruccoli, *Some Sort of Epic Grandeur*, 426.
2. Gaston, *Jack Clayton*, 76. *The Great Gatsby* was first filmed in 1926 in a silent film version starring Warner Baxter as Gatsby and Lois Wilson as Daisy. A second version appeared in 1949 with Alan Ladd as Gatsby and Betty Field as Daisy. For an in-depth analysis of these versions, see Margolies, "Novel to Play to Film."
3. Laura Mulvey's "Visual Pleasure and Narrative Cinema" is the seminal article concerning the male cinematic gaze. Mulvey's discussion highlights the psychoanalytic tendency of Hollywood to produce an image of women in one of two ways — either as the fetishistic object of man's desire or as sociopathic victim of man's inherent fear of "the castrating female." Both of these images restrict women's power within the gaze, regulating her to the position of enjoyment for the male spectator (198–209). Since its initial publication in 1975, many feminist film critics argue

that these "positions" can regulate a limited form of power to woman. These include Kuhn, *Power of the Image*, Kaplan, *Women and Film*, and Doane, *Femme Fatale*.

4. *"Great Gatsby,"* 14.

5. "Ready or Not, Here Comes Gatsby," 86, 87; Spada, *Films of Robert Redford*, 205.

6. Although Mia Farrow and Robert Redford were Clayton's initial choices for the role of Daisy and Gatsby, they were not Paramount's favorites. According to Spada, Bob Evans, Paramount's production chief, solicited Broadway producer David Merrick to secure the film rights to *The Great Gatsby* as a token to his then-wife, Ali McGraw, who keenly wished to play Daisy after having just received an Oscar nomination for *Love Story*.

After paying $350,000 to Scottie Smith, Fitzgerald's daughter, for the rights, Evans and Merrick approached Marlon Brando, Jack Nicholson, and Warren Beatty for the role of Gatsby. McGraw's lack of "star power," however, caused more established male actors to pass on the project, leaving Redford the studio's only choice for a role he desperately wanted: "I wanted Gatsby badly. . . . He is not fleshed out in the book, and the implied parts of his character are fascinating" (204). After McGraw left the project and left her husband, Evans, for actor Steve McQueen, the search for a new Daisy began. Even though Candice Bergen, Katherine Ross, and Faye Dunaway were approached for the role, Clayton selected Farrow because, in the words of Bob Evans, "She brought a mystical quality, a kind of spoiled arrogance, that made her especially interesting" (205).

7. Arnold, *"Gatsby? Poor Scott!"* 1; Alpert, "Lost Tycoon," 57; Canby, "They've Turned *Gatsby* to Goo," 1; Cocks, "Crackup." For a more detailed contemporary response to Clayton's *Great Gatsby*, see Margolies, "Novel to Play to Film" and Gaston, *Jack Clayton*.

8. Jones, "Green Thoughts in a Technicolor Shade," 229; Houston, "Great Gatsby," 177; Gaston, *Jack Clayton*, 85.

9. Giannetti, " *Gatsby* Flap," 13; idem, *Understanding Movies*, 36; Magill, *Cinema*, 226–27. In more recent years, scholarly articles appearing in *Focus on Film* (Atkins, "Melody Lingers On"), and *La Revue du Cinema* (Lajeunesse, "*Gatsby le Magnifique*") include positive revisionist readings of the film. Also, the National Council of Teachers of English (NCTE), in their "Literature and Film" series for high school teachers, recommends the film as a good method of introducing Fitzgerald's *The Great Gatsby* to their students.

Of course, I do not mean to imply that all critics who have written about Clayton's *The Great Gatsby* sing its praises. Gaston's *Jack Clayton* catalogs many negative responses; however, he lists only one scholarly entry after 1975, Maslin's "Ballantine's Scotch."

10. The novel actually cites two "soundtrack" possibilities: Vladimir Tostoff's "Jazz History of the World" (Fitzgerald, *Great Gatsby*, 50; all subsequent page references to

The Great Gatsby are to the 1990 edition and appear parenthetically in the text), and "Three O'Clock in the Morning," "a neat, sad little waltz of that year" (110).

11. Mulvey, "Visual Pleasure and Narrative Cinema," 199.

12. Fraser's "Another Reading of *The Great Gatsby*" hypothesizes that Nick Carraway may constantly question his sexuality throughout the summer of 1922; to prove Nick's insecurity with his own homosexuality, Fraser's essay looks at Fitzgerald's original draft and the words Nick uses to describe Tom and Gatsby.

13. The *Time* cover story on the making of Clayton's *The Great Gatsby* suggests a possible reason for some of these changes ("Ready or Not, Here Comes *Gatsby*"). Paramount, the studio producing and marketing *Gatsby*, had just experienced its first real blockbuster the year before with Arthur Hiller's *Love Story*; it appears that the studio suggested that *Gatsby* should pursue the same romantic lines as *Love Story* in order to prove attractive to the same audience.

This notion also supports the reasons Paramount offered the project to Jack Clayton instead of its "A-list" of "up-and-coming" directors including Peter Bogdanovich, Arthur Penn, and Mike Nichols (Spada, *Films of Robert Redford*, 204). In a predecision interview, Clayton told executives he read the book when he was fifteen and had always wanted to bring it to the screen; at one time, he even tried to secure the film rights: "What was it about the novel that attracted him so much, that made him say at times that he 'adored' it and that it 'made a great impression' on him? He saw Fitzgerald's story as one 'of a man with an incredible obsession. I love the idea of obsessional people, possibly because I am one'" (Gaston, *Jack Clayton*, 5). He understood that Gatsby's "greatest mistake was that he was a romantic," but he also believed that "being a romantic is actually the totally correct thing to be in life" (Ibid., 14). Perhaps this is why Clayton took *The Great Gatsby*'s critical failure so much to heart.

14. It is interesting to note here that Truman Capote, initially hired to compose the screenplay for Clayton, focused his version around Nick's repression; insiders claimed that Capote's screenplay made more overt overtures to Nick's homosexuality (and re-created Jordan as a lesbian). When Paramount refused to film Capote's version, he sued the studio; they agreed to an out-of-court settlement, and Francis Ford Coppola came on board to compose a new version from scratch (Spada, *Films of Robert Redford*, 204).

WORKS CITED

Alpert, Hollis. "The Lost Tycoon." *Saturday Review/World*, May 4, 1974, 57–60.

Arnold, Gary. "*Gatsby*? Poor Scott!" *Washington Post*, April 3, 1974, B1, B9.

Atkins, Irene Kahn. "The Melody Lingers On: Source Music in Films of the American Past." *Focus on Film* 26 (1977): 29–37.

Bauche, Freddy. *Le Cinema Anglais*. Lausanne: Editions L'Age D'Homme, 1978.

Bruccoli, Matthew J. *Some Sort of Epic Grandeur: The Life of F. Scott Fitzgerald.* San Diego: Harcourt Brace Jovanovich, 1981.

Canby, Vincent. "They've Turned *Gatsby* to Goo." *New York Times,* March 31, 1974, sect. 2, pp. 1, 3.

Clayton, Jack. *The Great Gatsby.* Hollywood: Paramount Pictures, 1974. Film.

Cocks, Jay. "The Crackup." *Time,* April 1, 1974, 88.

Doane, Mary Ann. *Femme Fatale: Feminism, Psychoanalysis, and Cinema.* New York: Routledge, 1991.

Fitzgerald, F. Scott. *The Great Gatsby.* 1925. New York: Macmillian, 1990.

Fraser, Keath. "Another Reading of *The Great Gatsby.*" In *Modern Critical Interpretations of "The Great Gatsby."* Ed. Harold Bloom. New York: Chelsea House, 1986. 57–70.

Gaston, Georg M. A. *Jack Clayton: A Guide to References and Resources.* Boston: G. K. Hall, 1981.

Giannetti, Louis. "The *Gatsby* Flap." *Literature/Film Quarterly* 3 (1975): 13–22.

———. *Understanding Movies.* Englewood Cliffs, N.J.: Prentice-Hall, 1976.

"*The Great Gatsby.*" *Variety,* March 27, 1974, 14.

Houston, Penelope. "The Great Gatsby." *Sight and Sound* 43 (1974): 177–78.

Jones, Edward T. "Green Thoughts in a Technicolor Shade: A Revaluation of *The Great Gatsby.*" *Literature/Film Quarterly* 3 (1974): 229–36.

Kaplan, E. Ann. *Women and Film: Both Sides of the Camera.* New York: Routledge, 1988.

Kuhn, Annette. *The Power of the Image: Essays on Representation and Sexuality.* Boston: Routledge, 1985.

Lajeunesse, J. "*Gatsby le Magnifique.*" *La Revue du Cinema* 299 (1974): 158–59.

Magill, Frank N. *Cinema: The Novel Into Film.* Pasadena, Calif.: Salem, 1980.

Margolies, Alan. "Novel to Play to Film: Four Versions of *The Great Gatsby.*" In *Critical Essays on "The Great Gatsby."* Ed. Scott Donaldson. Boston: G. K. Hall, 1984. 187–200.

Maslin, Janet. "Ballantine's Scotch, Glemby Haircuts, White Suits, and White Teflon: *Gatsby* 1974." In *The Classic American Novel and the Movies.* Ed. Gerald Peary. New York: Frederick Ungar, 1977. 261–67.

Mulvey, Laura. "Visual Pleasure and Narrative Cinema." *Screen* 16, no. 3 (1974): 198–209.

"Ready or Not, Here Comes *Gatsby.*" *Time,* March 18, 1974, 82–91.

Rosen, Marjorie. "Francis Ford Coppola." *Film Comment* 10, no. 4 (1974): 43–49.

———. "'I'm Proud of That Film': Jack Clayton Interviewed by Marjorie Rosen." *Film Comment* 10, no. 4 (1974): 49–51.

Spada, James. *The Films of Robert Redford.* Secaucus, N.J.: Citadel, 1977.

Teegarden, J. "The Joke's on Us: *Gatsby* Is Great." *Audience* 7 (1974): 9.

The Rendering of Proper Names, Titles, and Allusions in the French Translations of *The Great Gatsby*

MICHEL VIEL

Fitzgerald was a lover of names. The list of Gatsby's guests at the beginning of chapter 4 of *The Great Gatsby* is a well-known illustration of this interest. Less conspicuous are the other names in the book, including place names, some fictional, most real. The characters move a lot as the story unfolds, and it is always very clear where they are, or where they are going. Indeed, one could draw a reasonably detailed map of New York and Long Island only by using the names of the places mentioned.

The author's involvement with names might seem of doubtful relevance to a translator. "How do you say 'bootlegger' in French?" might be a problem, but "How do you say 'Gatsby?'" is a question that does not make sense. "Gatsby" does not mean something. As Jordan Baker puts it, "[Gatsby] is just a man named Gatsby,"[1] or in Jakobsonian terms, "['Gatsby'] means a person named [Gatsby]."[2] Place names, names of events or institutions, titles of books and periodicals are in no way different. All have single, unambiguous references. Logically, translating names should be a simple matter. Either these names have conventional lexicalized foreign equivalents (La Nouvelle-Orléans for New Orleans) or they do not and the English terms are to be used (Long Island). Thus questions like "How do you say West Egg in French?" or even "How do you say New York in French?" should not arise.

And yet there are several reasons that the question of the rendering of proper names and the like in translation does arise: First, as in the examples above, proper names are frequently based on compounds that include a common name. It is often difficult to decide whether this common name should be preserved or translated. Fitzgerald himself illustrates this dilemma by referring practically in the same breath to the "Bois de Boulogne" (GG 52) and to "the Argonne Forest" (GG 53). Which pattern should *we* follow? Second, proper names are the essence of the cultural background of the novel. What can a translator do about references to the American experience or allusions to the cultures of the English-speaking peoples? Should we use "Yale" when Fitzgerald writes New Haven, assuming that the university is better known to foreign readers than its seat? Finally, a translator's job is not limited to rendering meaning. We also have to render form. This duty has a bearing on names.

As it seems impossible to separate linguistic, cultural, and stylistic problems, I have chosen to write about the title of the novel, place names, personal names, and allusions — in that order. Also, a short essay like this cannot aim at a detailed treatment of the subject. I have just picked out a few examples that I found puzzling or interesting.

There are two French translations of *The Great Gatsby*, the first by Victor Llona and the second by myself.[3]

The Title

The Great Gatsby came out in April 1925, and before the year was over, Victor Llona had completed his work. Fitzgerald, who was delighted to have one of his works in translation, said it sounded "wonderful."[4] Ever since 1926, for better or for worse, *The Great Gatsby* has been known to French readers as *Gatsby le Magnifique*. Technically, this type of equivalence is called an overtranslation: "Gatsby the Magnificent." How good was that choice?

The history of the title is well-known. *The Great Gatsby* was one among many suggestions. For want of an idea that could satisfy his editors and boost the sales, Fitzgerald reluctantly resigned himself to the choice of "The Great Gatsby" while commenting: *"The Great Gatsby* is weak because there's no emphasis even ironically on his greatness or lack of it" (January 24, 1925). Three weeks before the book was due for publication, he wired to Maxwell Perkins: "CRAZY ABOUT TITLE UNDER RED WHITE AND BLUE" (March 19, 1925), but Perkins did not follow suit (GG 206–8).

What can a translator do with a title that both did not enthuse the author and contains a linguistic difficulty? Like most languages, English formally differentiates between physical size (large) and moral or intellectual greatness (great). In French, there is only one word ("grand") for size and greatness. "Le Grand Gatsby" would have been ambiguous, with a strong suggestion that the man was particularly tall. Furthermore it would have sounded like *Le Grand Meaulnes*, the novel by Alain-Fournier, then recently published (1913), in which "grand" means big, referring to age: Meaulnes is originally referred to as "le grand Meaulnes" because he is older than the boys who call him so.[5] "Gatsby le Grand," in which the inversion has the effect of restricting the meaning to greatness, is a regal translation, reminiscent of Louis, Peter, and Napoleon. Victor Llona preferred to view his Gatsby as a prince, like Lorenzo dei Medici, usually known in French as "Laurent le Magnifique." Lorenzo is mainly remembered as a patron of the arts while Gatsby, unlike many of the Gold Coast millionaires, has no such interest. Thus the connotation is misleading.

Oddly enough, considering the suggested inappropriateness of the original title, and ignoring Florentine history, *Gatsby le Magnifique* may be the only part in the translation that might sound better than the original, especially in Llona's version, because Llona chose to render "gorgeous" in the prologue as "magnifique": "If personality is an unbroken series of successful gestures, then there was something gorgeous about him" (GG 6); "S'il est vrai que la personnalité est une suite ininterrompue de gestes réussis, il y avait en cet homme quelque chose de magnifique" (Llona 24). Gorgeous would be better translated as "splendide" in French, but "magnifique" as an equivalent fares well too, to such an extent that Llona manages to give the impression that Fitzgerald took the trouble to justify the title as early as the second page of the novel. This simply is not true, and in fact "magnifique," in Llona's translation, corresponds to two different, unconnected words. This choice thus runs counter both to text and title history, if we take into consideration Fitzgerald's own doubts and final belated unsuccessful rejection.

For practical reasons I retained "Gatsby le Magnifique" because this is how the novel (not to mention the film) has come to be known in French. I knowingly used "splendide" for gorgeous on the assumption that the echo of "magnifique," although a very shrewd idea, came close to betraying the author and cheating the readers.

If I had felt free to go my own way, I would have rendered the title as "L'illustre Gatsby" (the renowned, or celebrated, Gatsby). This, I am ready to admit, is also an overtranslation but one semantically and stylistically closer to the original than the "authorized" version.

If Fitzgerald had been willing or able to impose "Under the Red, White, and Blue" on his editors, I think I might have translated the title as "Sous la bannière étoilée" (literally "Under the star-spangled banner"), because the red, white, and blue (admittedly in reverse order) are the colors of France, and thus a literal translation would have been misleading. In the body of the book "the red, white and blue banners in front of all the houses" (GG 59) does read "les drapeaux rouges, blancs, et bleus qui pavoisaient toutes les maisons" (Viel 71)—this without too much harm, although I am not absolutely certain that all readers will take the hint.

As I was progressing in my translation, I became aware that the initial syllable of Gatsby was a slang word for pistol. This connotation is lost to foreign readers, and the repeated accusation that "il a tué un homme" ("he killed a man") will be the poorer for the suppression of the gunshot echo in Gatsby's name.

West Egg and East Egg, and the Problem of Determinatives

If we believe linguists and logicians, West Egg and East Egg, as place names (that is, as names) mean nothing more than the places named respectively West Egg and East Egg. And yet one should remember the case of Humpty Dumpty, the egg-shaped creature of *Through the Looking-Glass*: "My name means the shape I am."[6] The names of these places denote their contour and respective position. The "eggness" of West Egg and East Egg is discussed at length in a passage (GG 7–8) in which the word "egg" as a common noun is used three times.

Assuming that the words East and West are known to the reader, the translator is left with the hope that Fitzgerald gave sufficient clues for him or her to deduce the meaning of egg from the context. Yet Victor Llona squeezed in a surreptitious translation: "Je demeurais à West Egg—l'œuf occidental—qui est, avouons-le, le moins chic des deux" (Llona, 28): "I lived in West Egg—the western egg—which admittedly is the less fashionable of the two." Translating the book for a readership of the 1990s, more familiar with Western culture and the Wild West than that of the 1920s, I decided that one could simply borrow West and East, and furthermore resorted to a more oblique translation of egg: "J'habitais à West Egg, qui est, disons, le moins chic des deux œufs" (Viel 14): "I lived in West Egg, which—shall we say—is the less fashionable of the two eggs."

The Eggs are just an instance of a more general problem. Should one translate determinatives in place names, for instance, common nouns and adjectives which are parts of compound names? I found it impossible to follow the same course everywhere.

When the noun under consideration does not retain its original meaning, it is preferable to leave it untouched. Let us hope that the reader will not think that Lake Forest is a lake or a forest and that the Punch Bowl is a bar. On the whole, I am afraid, there is no general fixed rule. Conventionally, Fifth Avenue and Fifty-ninth Street are translated as "la Cinquième Avenue" and "la Cinquante-neuvième Rue." Contrariwise, both Victor Llona and I opted for Madison Avenue, not "l'Avenue Madison." When I think back why I intuitively opted for a borrowing in the latter case and a literal translation in the former, it seems to me that inasmuch as there are no numbers for streets and avenues in my country, the preservation of English forms is not necessary to suggest a foreign place. On the other hand, l'avenue Wilson (if not l'avenue Madison) was quite a common name in the aftermath of the Great War for a street in French cities, later to be joined by the numerous avenues Roosevelt and avenues Kennedy. So one way or another, we have to retain a foreign element in Madison Avenue, better to keep it at arm's length from our home experience.

Admittedly there are many borderline cases. Llona translated both Pennsylvania Station and Union Station (la gare de Pennsylvanie and la gare de l'Union), unquestionably a sensible choice. I chose to translate Union Station while leaving Pennsylvania Station in its English form. I still wish I could find a good reason to account for the difference. Times Square must be made explicit: "la station de métro Times Square." Queensboro Bridge, the Plaza Hotel, and so forth fare better in translation: "le pont de Queensboro," "l'hôtel Plaza," or even "le Plaza" — or so it seems to me. Knowing that translation, as opposed to borrowing, means a loss in local color counterbalanced by a gain in rhythm and intelligibility, the question is to decide which is the lesser of two evils.

Gatsby's Guests, with a Special Reference to Tom's Acquaintance, "Blocks" Biloxi

Whatever has been said so far, some names are intended to be meaningful. This is unquestionably the case with nicknames, of which there are at least three in the novel: Owl Eyes, the visitor in Gatsby's library; James B.

("Rot-Gut") Ferret, one of the seventy-seven in the list of guests at the beginning of chapter 4; and "Blocks" Biloxi, an acquaintance of Tom's who "made boxes" and "came from Biloxi" (GG 99).

Both Victor Llona and I chose to translate Owl Eyes as Oeil-de-Hibou, and "Rot-Gut" as Tord-boyaux: "James B. Ferret dit Tord-boyaux." The original translator went as far as rendering "Blocks" Biloxi by "Biloxi, dit 'La Boîte' [literally 'Box' Biloxi], parce qu'il en fabriquait" (Llona 163). I stuck to a more conservative "Biloxi dit 'Blocks' Biloxi, parce que c'était un fabriquant de boîtes" (Viel 114). If I ever have the opportunity of revising my translation, I propose to resort to a more imaginative rendering of this name: "Biloxi dit Bille-en-bois [literally 'Blockhead Biloxi'], qui fabriquait des boîtes—je n'invente rien, et qui était originaire de Biloxi," or playing on another alliteration, "Biloxi dit le Caisson [slang for head], qui était fabriquant de caisses [big strong box]."

Nicknames are rather convenient. One way or another, a satisfactory solution can be found. On the other hand, there is little that we can do about the list of Gatsby's guests. To a very great extent, a name like Mrs. Ulysses Swett, who exists practically only as a name in the novel, means a lot more than the person named "Mrs. Ulysses Swett." It is obviously a mistake to correct the spelling back to Sweet (Llona 90). On the contrary, a name like this suggests that the person who bears it is physically squalid or morally repulsive. But Swett does not mean anything to a French reader. Should we supply a translation as we often do on the stage with "tag-names" like Snake or even Lady Sneerwell? Translators enjoy such exercises: "Madame Ulysse Lesueur," "la famille Sangsue" (the Leeches), "Simon Durot" (S. W. Belcher), and "Mademoiselle Cauchon" (Miss Haag) could be put forward as candidates for a few of these names. If we do this, however, we make Gatsby's guests foreigners—not Americans—a choice that simply is not true to the story. There is nothing we can do either about the Hornbeams, the Smirkes, Edgar Beaver, the Fishguards, S. B. Whitebait, Cecil Roebuck, George Duckweed, Francis Bull—all complex, suggestive, not to say meaningful, names.

The French readers will be lucky if they notice the presence of Clarence Endive, Doctor Civet, the Willie Voltaires and Ed Legros among the guests. To my linguistic consciousness the first two are freaks—Frenchified freaks if you like, but nonetheless freaks. Willie Voltaire sounds like a joke because Voltaire is the anagram of Arouet l[e] i[eune], and no one bears this name in France. Besides the Great Will will not be recognized—if he should—under the pet name Willie. Legros is a common French name but in itself it is of little interest. Indeed it not individual names that are meaningful but the accumulation of these. As in nuclear physics, a critical mass has to be reached to make each individual name trigger a chain reaction that catches the reader's attention.

Assuming a reader's viewpoint on Gatsby's guests, one will find that there is a scale of understanding of their names. At the top of the scale, you have a hypersophisticated (but improbable) super reader-critic, personified by Ruth Prigozy, for whom each name has a value that is at least connotative.[7] At the bottom, you have my helpless monolingual French readers, for whom the Hammerheads and the Catlips are just as ordinary people as the Buchanans and the Wilsons. If you do not know the words or associations underlying the names, Gatsby's guest list, suggestive and brilliant as it may be, simply amounts to name-dropping.

This inability of ours to understand the gist of the list of Gatsby's guests' names has far-reaching consequences: when Tom complains that "women run around too much these days. They meet all kinds of crazy fish" (GG 81),[8] when he refers to Gatsby's house as a "menagerie" (GG 84), when he says that Gatsby's car is "a circus wagon" (GG 94), when he claims that "you've got to make your house into a pigsty in order to have any friends" (GG 101), he is entirely justified given the names of Gatsby's guests. All the while, the foreign reader will remain unaware that these accusations are literally founded, and will think that Tom is just misbehaving, or showing his animosity toward Gatsby.

Besides linguistic problems, there are cultural problems. French readers might pick out Jewish family names with waspish first names (Clyde Cohen, Lester Myer), and think that there is something awkward about such combinations; that was undoubtedly part of Fitzgerald's intention. They might even overreact to Irish family names with classical first names like Horace O'Donavan, while I am not so sure that there is much here to attract the attention of an American reader.

Yet the same French readers will miss the point about the Stonewall Jackson Abrams of Georgia. Victor Llona hazarded an audacious rendering, "les George Washington Cohen, de Georgie" (Llona 90). In this name, George Washington is his own invention, and Cohen is borrowed from Clyde Cohen, further down on the list (Clyde Cohen himself becomes Clyde Abrams in French). The translator assumed — rightly — that no one in France had ever heard of General Stonewall Jackson. Barring all moral judgment on this controversial choice, I think that both George Washington and Cohen are a mistake here. The name "Stonewall Jackson" can only be a deliberate choice on Fitzgerald's part. It clearly indicates that those who bear such first and middle names are militant southerners. This point is confirmed by the examination of the galley proofs, in which the author had crossed out (the Stonewall Jackson Abrams of Georgia) "still violently impassioned about the Civil War."[9] George Washington's politics and patriotism, despite the fact that he himself was a Virginian like Stonewall Jackson, seem to me totally adverse to those of the Confederate general. Not only this but Stonewall Jackson is mentioned in *This Side of Paradise*, where Fitzgerald precisely emphasizes his significance[10] — another reason to stick to it in *The Great Gatsby*.

The second mistake about substituting George Washington Cohen for Stonewall Jackson Abrams is that the possibility that the Stonewall Jackson Abrams should be Jews is not proven. In their authoritative dictionary, Reaney and Wilson state that "[this name is] not confined to Jews."[11] If there is any doubt about the couple's gentility, the ambiguity of the name Abrams is sufficient in the translation.

As we draw farther from personal names to common nouns, we come across ranks, titles, and the like. Nobility titles are to be translated: the Dukes of Buccleuch will become les ducs de Buccleuch, and the Earl of Doncaster le comte de Doncaster. On the whole there is a certain amount of flexibility with such words. Victor Llona chose to retain Gatsby's rank on the medal from Montenegro "au major Jay Gatsby" (Llona 95). I made Gatsby a "commandant" (Viel 65).

Syntax puts pressure on the translator to give a French version: the article is necessary in *le* docteur Eckleburg, *le* docteur Civet, an obligation which makes le Dr. Civet or Dr. Civet a little awkward. Victor Llona rendered Mr. as M. (reads "monsieur") while I chose to stick to the English form: Mr. Gatsby, Mr. Sloane. This choice is possible because Mr. has become part of the French language. It seems preferable to M. because it has the advantage of preserving the characters' Americanness. Still I was compelled to get back to "monsieur" to translate "sir" in an apostrophe: "After a pause he added 'sir' in a dilatory, grudging way" (GG 88).

References to the Contemporary Scene and Literary Allusions

The titles of books and periodicals raise problems that are similar to those of determinatives in place names. Whether *Yale News* — in reality the *Yale Daily News* — will appear as *Yale News* or as les *Nouvelles de Yale* is very much a matter of taste: again, what should have precedence, local color (preserved by borrowing) or readability (obtained by a literal translation)? Better-known newspapers can retain their original titles, the more so as chance has it that the words tribune and journal have the same graphic forms in English and in French. Respecting italicizing or inverted commas, one should not be too anxious about the use of the French article in la *Tribune* and *Le Journal*. On the other hand, what sort of magazine *Town Tattle* must be is an important detail, and the word "tattle," if used as such, will give no clue about this. Llona used the literal but derogatory *Les Potins de New York* (Llona 51, 54), while I switched point of view to *Les coulisses de la ville* ("City backstage," Viel 32, 34), assuming that a derogatory word like "potins" was unlikely to be used in the title of a magazine.[12]

As for books, Llona made the hypallage explicit in his translation of *The Rise of the Colored Empires* as *L'Ascension des Empires des gens de couleur* (Llona 37), while I stuck to the original figure *La Montée des empires de couleur* (Viel 20), in which "montée" was intended to be an echo of "la montée des périls," itself reminiscent of "le péril jaune" (yellow peril), all common phrases in the first half of this century. *Simon Called Peter*, a bestseller of the 1920s, by a popular author named Robert Keable (1887–1927), a novel that Fitzgerald specifically denounced as immoral,[13] is said to be "un roman douceâtre" in the original French translation (Llona 54). Knowing as we do Fitzgerald's opinion of it, we cannot be satisfied with a qualification like "a sweetish novel," whatever is meant here. On the other hand, it is also true that a literal translation (Viel 34) is of no avail to the reader. It remains for a new translator to find a better idea.

Hopalong Cassidy and *Simon Called Peter* are real books. *The Rise of the Colored Empires* is not.[14] How can French readers know this? Many allusions and cultural references are bound to be lost to foreign readers, all the more so as it is difficult for them to separate fact and fiction. In some cases, though, we may be comforted with the certainty that the American readers of today will be just as much at a loss as their foreign counterparts. It is doubtful that Peter's fame has reached to the Myrtles of the 1990s.

The same identification problem arises with people. Frisco, Gilda Gray, Belasco, and Stoddard are real people; Goddard and Vladimir Tostoff are fictional. You need an insider's — or a scholar's — view of the American scene of the 1920s to be able to say which of these is real, and which is fiction.

It would be a mistake to assume that this situation has no bearing on the translation. Sometimes the translator will be tempted to smuggle in information about real people: "moving her hands like Frisco" (GG 34) is rendered by Llona as "agitant les mains comme *le danseur* Frisco" (Llona 67; emphasis added), "Gilda Gray's understudy from the Follies" (GG 34) becomes "la doublure de Gilda Gray, *l'étoile* des *Ziegfeld* Follies" (Viel 45; emphasis added).

The case of Belasco is still more interesting. The name is used by Owl Eyes during his visit to the "Merton College Library" as a common noun: "This fella's a regular Belasco" (GG 38). I explained in a footnote (Viel 48) who Belasco was, while the sentence had originally been translated as "Ce type est un metteur en scène de premier ordre" (Llona 73). Undoubtedly Llona got the gist of what Owl Eyes meant, but his version, if translated back into English, would yield "The fella's a first-rate director." I think that names as such are part of what makes Fitzgerald's style so personal, and they should not be left out on the spurious pretext that it is sufficient to preserve meaning. By switching information from Gatsby to Gatsby's library, it is possible to maintain Belasco and render the idea. If I am offered a second chance with the translation, I will change it to: "C'est une mise en scène digne de Belasco" (It's a setting/production worthy of Belasco).

Among dozens, I have selected two allusions that seem to me to be of particular interest: "the world and its mistress" (GG 49) and *Castle Rackrent* (GG 67), especially as Matthew J. Bruccoli ignores the former altogether, and does not, in my opinion, give a fully satisfactory explanation of the latter.

Chapter 4 begins like this: "On Sunday morning while church bells rang in the villages alongshore, the world and its mistress returned to Gatsby's house and twinkled hilariously on his lawn" (GG 49). There is no record of "the world and its mistress" in the *Oxford English Dictionary*, 2nd ed., nor in *Webster's New International Dictionary*, 3d ed.; but under the word "wife" the former does record "all the world and his wife" as "(humorous colloq.), all men and women, everybody: usually hyperbolically for a large and miscellaneous body or company of people of both sexes." This definition is followed by quotations from Swift (1731), Byron (1822), Dickens (1865), and *The World* (1912). Most interesting is the reference to Dickens (*Our Mutual Friend*) because the passage the quotation is taken from comes as close as possible to a guest list, thus making Dickens a possible source of inspiration for Fitzgerald:

> Foremost among those leaving cards at the eminently aristocratic door before it is quite painted, are the Veneerings. . . . One copper-plate Mrs Veneering, two copper-plate Mr Veneerings, and a connubial copper-plate Mr and Mrs Veneering, requesting the honour of Mr and Mrs Boffin's company at dinner. . . . The enchanting Lady Tippins leaves a card. Twemlow leaves cards. A tall custard-coloured phaeton tooling up in a solemn manner leaves four cards, to wit, a couple of Mr Podsnaps, a Mrs Podsnap, and a Miss Podsnap. *All the world and his wife and daughter leave cards. Sometimes the world's wife has so many daughters, that her card reads rather like a Miscellaneous Lot at an Auction;* comprising Mrs Tapkins, Miss Tapkins, Miss Frederica Tapkins, Miss Antonina Tapkins, Miss Malvina Tap-

kins, and Miss Euphemia Tapkins; at the same time the same lady leaves the card of Mrs Henry George Alfred Swoshle, *née* Tapkins; also a card, Mrs Tapkins at home, Wednesdays, Music, Portland Place.[15]

Another possible source for Fitzgerald's distortion of the world and his wife is a satirical work little-known today, *The New Bath Guide*, in which the author features a Lord Ruggamuffenn, a dubious nobleman, who opens his Bath residence to a miscellaneous company:

> This Place is enchantingly pretty;
> We never can see such a Thing in the City;
> You may spend all your Life-Time in *Cateaton*-Street
> And never so civil a Gentleman meet;
> You may talk what you please, you may search *London* thro',
> You may go to *Carlisle's* and to *Almanac* too;
> And I'll give you my Head if you find such a Host,
> For Coffee, Tea, Chocolate, Butter, and Toast;
> How He welcomes at once *all the World and his Wife*
> And how civil to folk he ne'er saw in his *life*.[16]

The host described in this passage and Gatsby have a similar attitude to visitors: "People were not invited—they went there. . . . Sometimes they came and went without having met Gatsby at all" (GG 34). The difference is in the number of illegitimate couples that tread Gatsby's lawns. Some are mentioned in the list: the Chrysties (or rather Hubert Auerbach and Mr. Chrystie's wife), Beluga and his girls, Benny McClenahan and his, Mr. Albrucksburger and Miss Haag, Ardita FitzPeters and Mr. P. Jewett (GG 49–50). Others are pointed out toward the end of chapter 3:

> "She had a fight with a man who says he's her husband," explained a girl at my elbow.
>
> I looked around. Most of the remaining women were now having fights with men said to be their husbands. (GG 42)

Victor Llona gives a word-for-word translation: "Le dimanche matin, tandis que sonnaient les cloches dans les villages de la côte, tout le monde et sa maîtresse revenait [*sic*] chez Gatsby et scintillait [*sic*] gaiement sur la pelouse" (Llona 89).[17] In the absence of "tout le monde et sa femme," the expression "tout le monde et sa maîtresse" does not make sense in French. I chose to make "the world and its mistress" more explicit: "Le dimanche matin, tandis que sonnaient les cloches des églises dans les villages côtiers, le tout-New-York, bonne société et libertins réunis, retournait chez Gatsby et les rires scintillaient gaiement sur sa pelouse" (Viel 61) ("New York's people of fashion, both well-thinking society and debauchees.").

The other reference is to Castle Rackrent in chapter 5:

> "Are you in love with me," she said in my ear. "Or why did I have to come alone?"
>
> "That's the secret of Castle Rackrent." (GG 67)

Bruccoli says this is "an allusion to the English novel by Maria Edgeworth (1767–1849), published in 1801."[18] I am not so sure. It is true that the noun "rack rent" means a high, excessive rent, and Maria Edgeworth did write a novel entitled *Castle Rackrent*, which features an extortionist landlord, but I cannot find any specific allusion to this novel in Nick's reply to Daisy. Containing the word "rack" as it does, Rackrent has various overtones such as the rack, an instrument of torture likely to be found in a Gothic castle, and the phrase to go to rack and ruin (to go to destruction), a common fate for such a place. Nick's Castle Rackrent evokes some undefined Gothic castle in which some dark secret is hidden. Llona translated Castle Rackrent by "le manoir à l'envers" (Llona 116) — a translation also adopted in a subtitle in the film directed by Jack Clayton. This phrase is based on "le monde à l'envers," literally the world upside down, used in a sentence like "C'est le monde à l'envers" to refer to a situation where the usual order of things is not respected (as, for instance, when children give orders to their parents, or the secretary makes decisions for her boss). But Nick's house is not a "manoir" (a castle), and Nick himself does not infringe on social order or precedence in inviting Daisy to tea. If we stick to Castle Rackrent in French, though, the reader will be at a loss as to what it is all about, and miss the jocular threat in Nick's reply to Daisy. I chose "le Château de Barbe-bleue" (Viel 80) (Blue-Beard's Castle), because of the terrifying secret that is hidden in it. Blue-Beard is well-known to French readers, and I hoped that the allusion would more appropriately speak to their imagination.

Conclusion

In the course of translating, the translator manages one way or another to solve so many problems that at first seemed insoluble that he always hopes against hope that eventually all will come right. Yet his task is a hopeless one. If he did not cling to the illusion that this time he will finally crack the nut, he would never begin in the first place.

Faced with the difficulties of proper names and allusions, many translators are tempted to don editors' gowns and write footnotes. The use of footnotes is a great help, but it is also an easy way out; and it cannot reflect the integrity of the original. Literature is not commentary, and footnotes are just that. Fitzgerald did not use notes; why should we? More often than not we have to be satisfied with approximations. Thus the World Series becomes "le championnat de baseball," which if translated back will yield "the baseball championship," an obvious misrendering.

Like a John Fowles novel, this essay will be graced with two endings. The first ending, the sad ending, concludes that misrenderings like "the baseball championship" are bound to be numerous in translations. The second ending, the happy ending, claims that our intuitions and failures as translators are of some relevance to scholars. Try to read *Gatsby* in French. Very likely you will find that the translation is a poorer version of the work, yet it may also tell you a lot about the original.

NOTES

1. Fitzgerald, *Great Gatsby*, 40. All subsequent page references to *The Great Gatsby* are to the 1991 edition, are cited as GG, and appear parenthetically in the text.
2. Jakobson, *Selected Writings*, 2:131.
3. Fitzgerald, *Gatsby le Magnifique*. Tr. Victor Llona; all subsequent page references to this translation are to the Le Livre de Poche edition, are cited as Llona, and appear parenthetically in the text. Fitzgerald, *Gatsby le Magnifique*. Tr. Michel Viel; all subsequent page references to this translation are cited as Viel and appear parenthetically in the text. Since this essay was written, a third French translation, by Jacques Tournier, appeared in 1996, published in Paris by Grasset.
4. Kuehl and Bryer, *Dear Scott/Dear Max*, 129.
5. Alain-Fournier, *Le Grand Meaulnes*, 20, 24.
6. Carroll, *Through the Looking-Glass*, 263.
7. Prigozy, "Gatsby's Guest List." It would be more correct to say that there is no actual "top" to this scale. Prigozy sees Miss Claudia Hip as "a daring and wealthy socialite," and she goes on to comment: "the absence of superfluity in the surname suggests directness and willingness—to 'try' anything—even a man 'reputed to be her chauffeur'" (105). Until I read this explanation I had assumed that Miss Claudia Hip had a defective hip (Latin *claudicare*, to limp). It is the privilege of connotative meaning to accept contradiction.

There is more on this subject in Long, "Vogue of Gatsby's Guest List," and in Stone, "More About Gatsby's Guest List." For an interpretation of the list as a reflection of the narrator's point of view, see also Suhamy, *Stylistique anglaise*, 281–84.

8. Prigozy points out the "fishiness" of many of the names ("Gatsby's Guest List," 103).

9. Fitzgerald, *F. Scott Fitzgerald Manuscripts III*, 47. The suppression is an obvious case of self-censorship. There is another example like this. In his marked copy of the novel, Fitzgerald crossed out the italicized part in this sentence: "Americans, while willing, *even eager*, to be serfs, have always been obstinate about being peasantry" (emphasis added), and added "occasionally" before "willing" (69).

10. "Even Foch hasn't half the significance of Stonewall Jackson" (Fitzgerald, *This Side of Paradise*, 103). The continuity between *This Side of Paradise* and *The Great Gatsby* is exemplified by the verse inscribed at the beginning of the latter novel, allegedly by Thomas Parke d'Invilliers, a character in the former. The lines have been left out in Llona's translation.

11. Reaney and Wilson, *Dictionary of English Surnames*, s.v. Abrams.

12. Fitzgerald took his inspiration from *Town Topics* (Fitzgerald, *Great Gatsby*, 185).

13. See his statement on censorship in the *Literary Digest* (June 23, 1923), quoted in Turnbull, *Letters*, 476, and in Bruccoli and Bryer, *F. Scott Fitzgerald in His Own Time*, 170. *Simon Called Peter* is the story of a young curate named Peter Graham who joins the army as a chaplain and forsakes his London upper middle-class fiancée for the love of an alluring South African nurse. The latter eventually declines to marry him, convinced as she is that she would stand between him and God. The novel alternates drinking bouts, naughty episodes, and considerations about religion. Romantic, moralizing, and sexy, it has the kind of true vulgarity that would appeal to Myrtle Wilson. The title (which remains unexplained in the work) can be construed as a reference to Peter's apostolic mission.

14. Like *Town Tattle*, it is inspired by a real publication, *The Rising Tide of Color* by Lothrop Stoddard (see Fitzgerald, *Great Gatsby*, 183).

15. Charles Dickens, *Our Mutual Friend*, 157; emphasis added.

16. [Anstey], *New Bath Guide*, letter 12, 1:111–20; emphasis added. This possible source is more fully documented in Viel, "Notes on the Origin of Gatsby's Guest List."

17. It is interesting that the double spelling mistake has escaped so many reprints and new editions. The verbs should agree in the plural, but the addition of "et sa maîtresse" sounds so strange that the translator and editors have left the verbs to agree with "tout le monde" only.

18. Fitzgerald, *Great Gatsby*, 132.

WORKS CITED

Alain-Fournier, [Henri]. *Le Grand Meaulnes*. Paris: Emile-Paul, 1913.

[Anstey, Christopher.] *The New Bath Guide: or, Memoirs of the B-r-d family. In a series of poetical epistles*. London: J. Dodsley, 1766.

Bruccoli, Matthew J., and Jackson R. Bryer, eds. *F. Scott Fitzgerald in His Own Time: A Miscellany.* Kent, Ohio: Kent State University Press, 1971.

Carroll, Lewis. *Through the Looking-Glass, and What Alice Found There.* 1871. Rev. ed. Ed. Martin Gardner. Harmondsworth, England: Penguin, 1970. 166–345.

Dickens, Charles. *Our Mutual Friend.* London: Chapman and Hall, 1865.

Fitzgerald, F. Scott. *F. Scott Fitzgerald Manuscripts III: "The Great Gatsby": Revised and Rewritten Galleys.* Introduced and arranged by Matthew J. Bruccoli. New York: Garland, 1990.

——. *The Great Gatsby.* 1925. Ed. Matthew J. Bruccoli. New York: Cambridge University Press, 1991.

——. *Gatsby le Magnifique.* Tr. Victor Llona. 1926. Paris: Le Livre de Poche, n.d.

——. *Gatsby le Magnifique.* Tr. Michel Viel. Lausanne: L'Age d'Homme, 1991.

——. *This Side of Paradise.* 1920. Harmondsworth, England: Penguin, 1963.

Jakobson, Roman. *Selected Writings. II: Word and Language.* The Hague: Mouton, 1971.

Keable, Robert. *Simon Called Peter.* London: Constable, 1921.

Kuehl, John, and Jackson R. Bryer, eds. *Dear Scott/Dear Max: The Fitzgerald-Perkins Correspondence.* New York: Scribners, 1971.

Long, Robert Emmet. "The Vogue of Gatsby's Guest List." *Fitzgerald/Hemingway Annual* 1969: 23–25.

Prigozy, Ruth. "Gatsby's Guest List and Fitzgerald's Technique of Naming." *Fitzgerald/ Hemingway Annual* 1972: 99–112.

Reaney, P. H., and R. M. Wilson. *A Dictionary of English Surnames.* London: Routledge, 1991.

Stone, Edward. "More About Gatsby's Guest List." *Fitzgerald/ Hemingway Annual* 1972: 315–16.

Suhamy, Henri. *Stylistique anglaise.* Paris: Presses Universitaires de France, 1994.

Turnbull, Andrew, ed. *The Letters of F. Scott Fitzgerald.* New York: Scribners, 1963.

Viel, Michel, "Notes on the Origin of Gatsby's Guest List." *F. Scott Fitzgerald Society Newsletter* 3 (1993): 6–8.

Tourism and Modernity in *Tender Is The Night*

DANA BRAND

In addition to all of the other things it is, *Tender Is the Night* is a novel about tourism. Much of it is devoted to a representation of the ways in which Americans traveled through and experienced Europe in the 1920s, during an American tourist invasion that swamped all previous invasions and that to Fitzgerald and many of his contemporaries seemed to have a particular historical significance.[1] In *Tender Is the Night*, Fitzgerald uses American tourism in Europe as a metaphor for "modernity." When I refer to modernity here, I am using the term as it has been used within a tradition of discourse about modernity that extends back into the nineteenth century and that has been particularly prominent in contemporary criticism. As such recent cultural critics as Jurgen Habermas and Marshall Berman have noted, there are some common features to the way in which modernity has been described in writers as diverse as Wordsworth, Baudelaire, Marx, Nietzsche, Benjamin, Lefebvre, and others. All have observed that, in the modern world, the phenomenological character of experience is less unified, coherent, or continuous than it was in earlier historical periods. Although the resources of capitalism and modern industrial technology have made possible the production of an immensely rich and perpetually renewing spectacle of experience, the weakening of traditional social and philosophical structures has made it more difficult to connect or assign meaning or value to individual experiences. As we engage in any of the various spectatorial experiences that define modern life, we therefore develop, as Walter Benjamin has suggested, a relationship to experience that can best be characterized as a form of collecting. Modern experience is a collection of lived moments, connected only by the fact that they are part of the same hoard, piled up inside the all-inclusive dome of a cosmopolitan subjectivity.

The various writers who have written about modernity in this way have offered different models for the characteristic consciousness of modernity. Baudelaire and Benjamin found the consciousness of modernity exemplified in the *flaneur*, the strolling spectator who reads and collects the sights and sounds of the metropolis.[2] Writers like Marx, Spengler, and Henry Adams find modernity represented most effectively by a somewhat different figure, the tourist, who shares the *flaneur*'s omnivorous yet superficial openness, but who adds the dimension of economically powerful consumption.[3] The tourist, in their conception, is not content to be a detached spectator, a collector of impressions. He or she must also be a detached purchaser, a collector of exotic goods, experiences, and souvenirs. In writing *Tender Is the Night*, attempting to provide, as he wrote to Maxwell Perkins, a "model for the age,"[4] Fitzgerald appears to have been influenced by the conception of modernity, and the understanding of the modern significance of tourism, that he found in Spengler, Marx, and Adams. Though the influence of these sources is evident in Fitzgerald's most intellectually ambitious novel, what makes *Tender Is the Night* so impressive is the vividness and concreteness with which he animates, expands upon, and combines these ideas. Representing the splendid motion and glamour of "stupid, unaging"[5] American tourism, Fitzgerald offers some extraordinary images of tourism as the characteristic process of the modern mind.

The centrality of American tourism as a metaphor in *Tender Is the Night* is established in the opening chapters, where we learn that the Divers have set in motion a process that will be complete by the end of the book, a process that was in fact a significant development in the history of American tourism. Having persuaded Gausse to keep his hotel open in summer, they help to bring about the transformation of the French Riviera from a winter resort frequented primarily by British and Russians to a summer resort with a particularly prominent American presence. Americans, as Dick explains to Rosemary, are used to a different climate from the older civilizations. Figuratively, this is what will enable the replacement. Americans, as the entire book demonstrates, are more suited than the older cultures to the climate of the modern world.

In the opening chapters of *Tender Is the Night*, the tourism of Americans is presented against a backdrop of the ruins and traces of the tourism of the imperial civilizations that have preceded them. The book opens with images of the three British nannies "knitting the slow pattern of Victorian England . . . into sweaters and socks" (11), with the "closed book shops and grocery stores" (22) of the Russians, the ruined aqueducts of the Romans. These ruins contextualize the imperviousness and restless motion of the Americans, who seem unable to conceive of time or history, to recognize that their own dominion is likely to be as transient as that of Rome, Britain, or Russia. In the first general description of Americans as a group, on the platforms of the Gare St. Lazare, Fitzgerald describes how their faces appear "intelligent" and "considerate," yet also "new," "thoughtless," and "thought-for" (96). As Franz Gregorovius says of Dick, they have "stupid, unaging American" (117) faces, yet like Dick, they are not stupid. It is simply that, in spite of their intelligence, they do not think. Their faces do not register the effects of experience. "Thoughtless" and "thought-for," responding to the strongest external influence at the moment, their ideas and personalities are fluid. They have been in Europe, but now they are going home. Already they are "leaning a little over the ocean . . . undergoing a sea change" (96).

Here and elsewhere in the book, Americans seem peculiarly detached from their own consumption of Europe. This detachment is figured throughout the book by the prominence of the sort of conveyances in which tourists customarily travel. In this instance, the Americans are boarding trains. Trains are ubiquitous in *Tender Is the Night*, and they are often associated with a departure from the boundaries of a stable identity. Nicole holds hands with her father on a train, Rosemary may have had her first sexual experience on a train, Maria Wallis fires her gun as a train is pulling out of the station, Dick falls permanently in love with Nicole on a train trip, and so on. Some of the meanings that constellate around trains in this book are established in the third chapter, when Rosemary travels by train to Cannes. Fitzgerald writes: "Unlike American trains that were absorbed in an intense destiny of their own, and scornful of people on another world less swift and breathless, this train was part of the country through which it passed. . . . Rosemary was sure she could lean from the window and pull flowers with her hand" (21). Americans, absorbed in their "intense" historical destiny, impatient in a "world less swift and breathless," have no connection to or comprehension of the world over which they establish economic dominion. Like Rosemary and her mother, they are uncomfortable with quiet, foreign places or with the obstacle a landscape presents to their movement. They are always figuratively on American trains, where all things are possible and behavior need not be rooted in anything significant or substantial.

In addition to trains, Fitzgerald uses airplanes and ocean liners to represent the abstraction of Americans from time, space, and culture. When Dick flies from Zurich to Munich, he delights in "looking at the earth from far off . . . descend[ing] in his imagination into the villages" to "shake hands with the rural characters" (219). He feels in this moment as if he can experience the detachment of "statesmen and commanders and all retired people" (219), and he feels his own detachment from his past as well, from the world of his father, as he imagines the churches of the Alpine villagers to resemble his father's church in Buffalo. A few pages later, when Dick is boarding a steamship to return to Europe, after the funeral of his father, he experiences a similar detachment. When one boards a ship, Fitzgerald writes, "the past, the continent, is behind; the future is the glowing mouth in the side of the ship; the dim turbulent alley is too confusedly the present" (229). Aboard ship, "One is a citizen of a commonwealth smaller than Andorra, no longer sure of anything" (230).

Enclosed within their various conveyances, Americans view Europe as if from "the margin," and it is presumably significant that one of the conveyances in the book, Golding's yacht, is actually given this name. The repeated image of enclosure within a moving, self-contained space represents the nature of their marginality. Unable to break out of their moving enclosures, the Americans in this book exemplify the cosmopolitan condition that Spengler described as typical of a "civilization" as it consumes the "culture" that gave birth to it. In *The Decline of the West*, Spengler writes that in the earlier phase of the life-cycle of a society that he designated with the word "culture," life is the selective integration of experiences for the purpose of constructing a consistent and socially connected identity. The individuals of a culture are content to stay in one place and express the genius of their culture. When the culture develops and declines into a civilization, life acquires a cosmopolitan character, as the restless, wealthy, and uprooted inhabitants of the civilization leave behind their national boundaries in order to appropriate what other cultures have created. "Thoughtless" and "thought-for" tourism, rather than the production of culture, becomes the defining activity of the civilization. Spengler observes that this pattern, of superficial consumption of the culture by the civilization, has been repeated throughout history and is being repeated in the twentieth century. "The mob of parvenu tourists from Rome," Spengler writes, "gaped at the works of the Periclean age with as little understanding as the American globetrotter in the Sistine Chapel at those of Michelangelo."[6]

Throughout *Tender Is the Night*, Fitzgerald illustrates the paradoxical quality of economically powerful tourism as he would have known about it from his own experience, and as he would have read about it in Spengler. The power of their money gives American tourists an apparently unlimited access to Europe. At the same time, it insulates them. The American newspaper dealer, who appears at two crucial points in *Tender Is the Night*, shows a clipping of "a stream of Americans pouring from the gangplank of a liner freighted with gold" (107). In the course of the book, we see them pouring from their gangplanks to fill hotels, trains, beaches, and sanitariums. In a book almost entirely set in Europe, Europeans are visible only as providers of services to be paid, and just as often, to be paid off. As Augustine, the fired cook, observes "with the voice of the commune" (296), Dick and Nicole, to her, are nothing but "disgusting Americans who come here and drink up our finest wines" (296). Like Augustine, who puts down her kitchen knife for one hundred francs, the Europeans in this book will get money out of Americans any way they can, with contempt and resentment toward the cosmopolitan foreigners who consume their heritage. This is true of the French doctor who demands his payment after the duel, the constable bribed in the Peterson affair, and the police and families, who pretend to be upset when Mary North and Lady Caroline Sibley-Biers, dressed as sailors, pick up two French girls. The Swiss psychiatrists, who live off the mental illness of wealthy Americans, are only somewhat more sophisticated examples of this. Franz Gregorovius is careful to protect what he has gotten out of the Americans, after he perceives that Dick is no longer a "serious" man. The European participants at the conference Dick attends in Berlin are contemptuous of the crude empiricism and naiveté of the Americans, but they are suitably respectful when "the Americans . . . play their trump card," announcing "collosal gifts and endowments . . . great new plants and training schools" (218–19). At every stage in the book, Americans are only given respect because of their money. They enter into no relationships more substantial or more firmly grounded than that between an employer and a wage earner.

Just as the money of the Americans in Europe reduces all human relationships to economic ones, so does it reduce all objects and many forms of human interaction to commodities. Much of the representation of tourism in *Tender Is the Night* seems to illustrate some passages that drew Fitzgerald's notice in Marx and Engel's *The Communist Manifesto*. In the advanced stages of capitalism, Marx and Engels write: "In place of the old wants, satisfied by the production of the country, we find new wants, requiring for their satisfaction the products of distant lands and climes." To satisfy their new desires, the bourgeoisie must move "over the whole surface of the globe. It must nestle everywhere, settle everywhere, establish connections everywhere. The bourgeoisie has through its exploitation of the world-market given a cosmopolitan character to production and consumption in every country."[7] This idea is illustrated not only by the famous epic catalog of Nicole's purchases in Paris but by the fact that throughout the book the Divers are represented as, first and foremost, pioneer consumers, the kind of individuals who create a taste for new commodities. Their beach appurtenances, including "a portable bath house for dressing" and a "pneumatic rubber horse," are examples of the "first burst of luxury manufacturing after the War" (26). Shortly after this, Dick calls Nicole with a megaphone and we are told that Dick "had many light mechanical devices" (35), most of them, presumably, as novel and unnecessary as the megaphone. There is also an apparently gratuitous reference to "the sailor trunks and sweaters [the Divers] had bought in a Nice back street—garments that afterward ran through a vogue in silk among the Paris couturiers" (312). The entire book is set against the backdrop of a process the Divers have set in motion, the commoditization of the summer Riviera; and it also deals extensively with a similar process in which both of them are involved, the commoditization of mental health with the establishment of psychiatric clinics.

The reduction of all objects to commodities, and the reduction of all human relationships to economic ones, produces the detachment from European cultural forms that is visible in the faces of the Americans on the railway platform and is exemplified in the behavior of Americans throughout the book. Since everything can be bought and either hoarded or left behind, everything becomes interchangeable. Nothing is permanent and nothing has an intrinsic value. For Rosemary, Collis Clay, and most of the American tourist hordes, the sense of the world's availability and interchangeability produces a blank imperviousness. For the Divers and their entourage, it produces a more sophisticated sense of the arbitrariness of all values. This is evident early in the book, in the opening pages of the Divers' dinner party at the Villa Diana. Dick Diver is throwing a party, a socially constructive act, but he doesn't care for whom he throws it, and he hopes that it will be a really bad party. Tommy Barban is going to war. He is participating in an activity that builds and destroys civilizations. Yet he doesn't care for whom or for what he is fighting. Abe North boasts that he is a moral person and then facetiously identifies his moral code as opposition to the burning of witches. Fitzgerald offers a remarkable image of this general detachment when Nicole gives Rosemary's mother a yellow pocketbook. Delighting in the arbitrariness of it, Nicole fills the pocketbook only with yellow things. With a great deal of cleverness, Nicole finds new principles of association, as a kind of party game, in a world in which older principles of association have fallen into disuse.

As objects and values are represented as arbitrary, so too are the emotions and social gestures of the characters in *Tender Is the Night*. Things are done and felt for their own sake, for the tourist's pleasure they provide, not for what they mean. Rosemary falls in love with Dick for the experience of it. She can move on to other lovers, other experiences in her life, as easily as she can board a train for another city. The Americans who frequented the salon in the former palace of the Cardinal de Retz were "very quiet and lethargic at certain hours and then they exploded into sudden quarrels and breakdowns and seductions" (84). Dick too presides over a world of arbitrary emotion experienced for its own sake, and he contemplates the "waste and extravagance" of "the carnivals of affection" he has given, "as a general might gaze upon a massacre he had ordered to satisfy an impersonal blood lust" (36). The cultural tone of all of this arbitrary experience is connected, Fitzgerald implies, to the most characteristic American art form of the period. As Kaethe Gregorovius says, while she observes what she believes to be Nicole's self-indulgent theatricality, Nicole "ought to be in the cinema, like your Norma Talmadge — that's where all American women would be happy" (268).

One of the most interesting contributions Fitzgerald makes to the analysis of modernity he found in his various sources is his suggestion that the quintessential American art form, the cinema, epitomizes the modern tourist's consciousness evident in all American interactions with Europe. In many ways, the best model the book offers for Fitzgerald's conception of the American consciousness is the movie studio at Monte Carlo, where Rosemary goes to meet Brady. In the studio, Rosemary is described as feeling as if she is in Los Angeles, a place outside of history and culture. Objects like an Indian street, a cardboard whale, and a gigantic cherry tree lie about, ripped from contexts, available, like everything else in the world and in history, for use as images. The studio is an emblem of the American mind in that, like Nicole's shopping trip, it is an accumulation of things that can be "owned" but are otherwise unconnected by any coherent principle of association. It is a heap, a hoard, a catalog. Like other American stage sets mentioned in the novel — the Villa Diana, the former palace of the Cardinal de Retz, or the gigantic set on which *The Grandeur That Was Rome* is being filmed — it is a renovation and appropriation of the past. It is absolutely detached from the land on which it is built and the culture that surrounds it.

The studio represents, in Europe, an institution that is referred to throughout the book as creating the minds and characters of Americans. Violet McKisco's "soul" is described as having been "born dismally in the movie houses of a small town in Idaho" (231). Rosemary has literally stepped down from a movie screen. Tommy Barban thinks he is Ronald Colman. It is because they learn of the world and the possibilities of life through film that Americans can assume such a wide range of roles. They can marry Oriental potentates, fight in exotic wars, make love with anyone they please, as easily as Rosemary slips from one film role to another. In the image of the film studio, and in the cinematic references throughout the book, Fitzgerald connects American tourism with what is its most significant cultural product: Hollywood's touristic re-creation of the whole world and all of history.

The modern world represented in *Tender Is the Night* is one in which only a certain type of subjectivity can thrive — one that is modeled on the movie studio at Monte Carlo, that cannot remember, that can only contain, that is not structured, like Dick Diver's, around a fixed self or permanent loyalties. The perfect subjectivity for cosmopolitan capitalism is one that is perennially open to new objects and experiences, that, because of its fluidity, is capable of changing form, acting differently in different situations. In *Tender Is the Night*, Fitzgerald associates this subjectivity with Americans, but he goes further than this. He also implies throughout the book that the people who are most suited to the world he is representing are women.

Throughout *Tender Is the Night*, women are associated with the cosmopolitan fluidity exemplified by American tourism, film, and shopping. Nicole's purchase of everything there is to be had on the Rue de Rivoli is represented as a characteristically female process, one that Rosemary is learning. In the scene at Voisins, in which the intrinsic insecurity of American men is discussed, Rosemary, Mary, and Nicole exemplify the intrinsic security of American women. They are at ease with "the enormous flux of American life" (63), and unlike Dick, they will be at ease throughout the remainder of the book as they assume a great variety of roles.[8] It is this natural fluidity that makes them naturally suited to the cinema, which Dick refers to as "a fine profession for a woman" but one that would not be suited to him because, unlike a woman, and certainly unlike the women in this book, he is incapable of being "all out of character" (320).

In a wide range of references, Fitzgerald suggests that American women are naturally and comfortably alienated from language, memory, form — from anything that is associated with the creation of order or stability. "Talk is men" (183), Nicole observes, as is memory, since she and the other women in the book are all described as having very poor memories. Nicole is healthiest when she flows and forgets. Walking through her garden near the end of the book, contemplating the possibilities presented by Tommy Barban, "the inhibitions of the male world disappeared and she reasoned as gaily as a flower, while the wind blew her hair until her head moved with it. Other women have had lovers—the same forces that last night had made her yield to Dick up to the point of death, now kept her head nodding to the wind, content and happy with the logic of, Why shouldn't I?" (307). Uncomfortable with form, memory, or permanence, the women in this book seem completely and unproblematically comfortable with shopping, being in movies, or with the general process of traveling through life like a tourist, accumulating experiences of all kinds as "loot" (307) or as "stops" that may be counted "on a string of beads" (119).

Representing women's subjectivity in this way, Fitzgerald is likely to have been influenced by misogynistic theories of female consciousness he would have encountered in Spengler and in D. H. Lawrence's *Fantasia of the Unconscious*.[9] Emphasizing the connection between American women and American tourism, he is also likely to have been influenced by such passages as the following from Henry Adams's *Education:* "in America . . . The woman had been set free—volatilized like Clerk Maxwell's perfect gas; almost brought to the point of explosion, like steam. One had but to pass a week in Florida, or on any of a hundred huge ocean steamers, or walk through the Place Vendome, or join a party of Cook's tourists to Jerusalem, to see that the woman had been set free; but these swarms were ephemeral like clouds of butterflies in season, blown away and lost, while the reproductive sources lay hidden."[10] In this passage, Adams suggests, as such authors as Henry James and William Dean Howells had suggested before him, that American tourism in Europe is a characteristically female—and for men, feminizing—process.[11]

Though a full treatment of this issue is beyond the scope of this essay, I believe it is legitimate to observe that Fitzgerald ties together many of his ideas about the consciousness of modernity by suggesting something very similar. Women, *Tender Is the Night* implies, are the sex most suited to enjoy the experience of modernity, the sex most suited to dominate American culture in the era of advanced capitalism. Since men like Abe North and Dick Diver have failed to create a fixed world continuous with the past, it is only natural, Fitzgerald implies, that women like Nicole Diver, Rosemary Hoyt, and Mary North abandon them to flow in the direction of the future. As the Spenglerian world-civilization of the twentieth century, America was, as Fitzgerald said in an interview as he was working on *Tender Is the Night*, "a woman's country."[12] Though I think it is unfortunate that Fitzgerald's fascinating and even trenchant representation of modernity involves such assumptions about women, it is clear that this question of the gendering of the process of American tourism deserves study, as part of a general process by which, in the 1920s, important cultural questions were "eroticized." It should also be noted that Fitzgerald, unlike Lawrence or Adams, represents the easy female embrace of modernity in *Tender Is the Night* in at least dispassionate and possibly admiring terms. Even if his quasi-scientific analysis of the problems posed by modernity involve stereotypical conceptions of the mental attributes of both genders, he refrains from unambiguously condemning the transition he describes. He seems rather to be recording the inevitable decline of a man like Dick and the inevitable ascent of a woman like Nicole in history as it is evolving according to laws as immutable as the laws of Nature. In the end, it is because of both its achievements and its limitations that *Tender Is the Night* is what Fitzgerald hoped it would be, "a model of the age," a cultural analysis shaped by the assumptions of its time.

NOTES

1. For an account of American tourism in Europe in the 1920s, its significance, as perceived by contemporary sources, and its relation to previous waves of American tourism in Europe, see Sutton, *Travellers*, chap. 5; and Turner and Ash, *Golden Hordes*, chap. 5.
2. See Baudelaire's essay "Painter of Modern Life" and Benjamin's essays "The Flaneur" and "On Some Motifs in Baudelaire"; the latter two are collected in Benjamin, *Charles Baudelaire*.
3. Fitzgerald read the first volume of Spengler in early 1927 on the recommendation of Maxwell Perkins, and he read the second volume late in 1928 (Sklar, *F. Scott Fitzgerald*, 222). In a 1940 letter to Perkins, he claimed to have been reading Spengler during the summer of 1924, when he was completing *Gatsby* (Turnbull, *Letters*, 289). This is impossible since *The Decline of the West* was not published in English translation until 1926 and Fitzgerald did not know German. His assertion, however, indicates how important Fitzgerald believed Spengler had been in his intellectual life, and as an influence on his work. Fitzgerald wrote to Perkins that after reading Spengler, he never "quite recovered from him" (Turnbull, *Letters*, 289). When asked at the age of thirty, in 1927, to identify the books that had the greatest effect on him at various points in his life, he identified *The Decline of the West* as the most important book to him at age thirty (Bruccoli and Bryer, *F. Scott Fitzgerald in His Own Time*, 275). When Fitzgerald later made up a reading list to educate Sheilah Graham, he even constructed the list as a preparation for reading Spengler. Kathleen, in *The Last Tycoon*, who is largely based on Sheilah Graham, refers to a lover who had been educating her to read Spengler. For useful discussions of the Spenglerian elements in *Tender Is the Night*, see Lehan, *F. Scott Fitzgerald and the Craft of Fiction*, 33–36, and Sklar, *F. Scott Fitzgerald*, 222–26.

The degree to which Fitzgerald read Marx is inevitably controversial. At the very least, he had read *The Communist Manifesto* (his marked copy is in the Fitzgerald Papers at Princeton). He also probably read some of *Capital*, though it is impossible to know exactly how much. It is clear from the outline of *Tender Is the Night* that he prepared in 1932 that Fitzgerald was strongly influenced by Marx when writing the novel, even if he apparently dropped several of the most important Marxist ideas in the 1932 outline when he completed the final version of the book (see Sklar, *F. Scott Fitzgerald*, 264, and Bruccoli, *Composition of "Tender Is the Night*," 76–77).

Fitzgerald had been influenced by Henry Adams from the time that he was at Princeton. His early mentor, Father Sigourney Webster Fay, had known and collaborated on an article with Adams. In a letter to Maxwell Perkins, Fitzgerald claimed to have based Thornton Hancock, a character in *This Side of Paradise*, on Henry Adams (Turnbull, *Letters*, 138).

4. Turnbull, *Letters*, 182.

5. Fitzgerald, *Tender Is the Night*, 117. All subsequent page references to *Tender Is the Night* are to the 1962 edition and appear parenthetically in the text.

6. Spengler, *Decline of the West*, 1:34.

7. Marx and Engels, *Communist Manifesto*, 8, 7.

8. Nicole, of course, is not comfortable throughout the book, but she does become comfortable at the end, when she becomes cured by adopting, in her relationship with people, the fluid attitude of Rosemary and Mary North, a modern posture toward experience that she herself had exemplified in her shopping.

9. Fitzgerald read Lawrence's *Fantasia* early in 1930 and it became very important to him (Sklar, *F. Scott Fitzgerald*, 216). As he wrote to Mrs. Bayard Turnbull while writing the final version of *Tender Is the Night*: "I believe that if one is interested in the world in which willy-nilly one's children will grow up the most accurate data can be found in the European leaders, such as Lawrence, Jung, and Spengler" (Turnbull, *Letters*, 433).

10. Adams, *Education of Henry Adams*, 444.

11. In a project I am currently working on having to do with the American representation of Venice, I find assertions of this idea to be astonishingly common, in the works of "serious" writers like James and Howells, and in popular sources and travel guides as well.

12. Fitzgerald said this in an article entitled "Fitzgerald, Spenglerian," originally published in the *New York World* on April 3, 1927, and republished in Bruccoli and Bryer, *F. Scott Fitzgerald in His Own Time*, 276.

WORKS CITED

Adams, Henry. *The Education of Henry Adams: An Autobiography*. 1918. Boston: Houghton Mifflin, 1961.

Baudelaire, Charles. "The Painter of Modern Life." In *Selected Writings on Art and Literature*. Ed. and tr. P. E. Charvet. London: Penguin, 1972. 390–435.

Benjamin, Walter. *Charles Baudelaire: Lyric Poet in the Era of High Capitalism*. Tr. Harry Zohn. London: New Left Books, 1973.

Berman, Marshall. *All That Is Solid Melts into Air*. New York: Simon and Schuster, 1981.

Bruccoli, Matthew, J. *The Composition of "Tender Is the Night."* Pittsburgh: University of Pittsburgh Press, 1963.

Bruccoli, Matthew J., and Jackson R. Bryer, eds. *F. Scott Fitzgerald in His Own Time: A Miscellany*. Kent, Ohio: Kent State University Press, 1971.

Fitzgerald, F. Scott. *Tender Is the Night*. 1934. New York: Scribners, 1962.

Habermas, Jurgen. *The Philosophical Discourse of Modernity: Twelve Lectures*. Tr. Frederick Lawrence. Cambridge, Mass.: MIT Press, 1987.

Lawrence, D. H. *Fantasia of the Unconscious*. 1922. New York: Viking Press, 1967.

Lehan, Richard D. *F. Scott Fitzgerald and the Craft of Fiction*. Carbondale: Southern Illinois University Press, 1969.

Marx, Karl, and Friedrich Engels. *The Communist Manifesto*. Ed. and tr. Leo Huberman and Paul M. Sweezy. New York: Monthly Review Press, 1968.

Sklar, Robert. *F. Scott Fitzgerald: The Last Laocoön*. New York: Oxford University Press, 1967.

Spengler, Oswald. *The Decline of the West*. Tr. Charles Frances Atkinson. London: George Allen and Unwin Ltd., 1926.

Sutton, Horace. *Travellers: The American Tourist from Stagecoach to Space Shuttle*. New York: William Morrow, 1980.

Turnbull, Andrew, ed. *The Letters of F. Scott Fitzgerald*. New York: Scribners, 1963.

Turner, Louis, and John Ash. *The Golden Hordes: International Tourism and the Pleasure Periphery*. New York: St. Martin's Press, 1976.

Fitzgerald's Use of History in *The Last Tycoon*

ROBERT A. MARTIN

My room is covered with charts like it used to be for *Tender Is the Night*, telling the different movements of the characters and their histories.

—F. Scott Fitzgerald to Zelda Fitzgerald, October 19, 1940 [1]

Fitzgerald scholars have long been aware that a large part of Fitzgerald's "magic suggestiveness" comes from the unique blending of time, place, and character set against the larger framework of history and specific references to recognizable events. Most of the historical studies done so far are centered on *The Great Gatsby* and *Tender Is the Night*. My own reading, however, suggests that Fitzgerald's use of history generally divides itself into two very distinct categories. The first—for want of a better term—could be called mythical history; the second I would call factual history, particularly as it is used in *Tender* and *The Last Tycoon*. *Gatsby* has a suggestive, almost metaphorical, sense of history in which one is led to understand that the Dutch sailors are really veiled references to Henry Hudson's voyage of discovery in 1609 when he sailed up the Hudson River as far as Albany looking for the Northwest Passage, presumably passing through the channel of Long Island Sound, where we first see Gatsby stretching "out his arms toward the dark water in a curious way." [2] By the same token we learn (or have been taught) that Dan Cody is intended to suggest the spirit of two American frontiersmen — Daniel Boone and Buffalo Bill Cody — bringing Gatsby into focus as a Westerner descended from the frontier myth and legend that even Nick realizes is a dream "already behind him" (GG 141).

But the most remarked on and remarkable passage in *Gatsby* is Nick's awed summary of the transcendent connection between the Dutch sailors' first view of the New World and Gatsby's parallel sense of wonder over Daisy — the discovery of an "aesthetic contemplation he neither understood nor desired, face to face for the last time in history with something commensurate to his capacity for wonder" (GG 140). If it was, indeed, "the last time in history," this passage alone would be enough to support the hypothesis that Fitzgerald was using history as a thematic subtext to connect the American past and present — the dream turned cynical and corrupt, the ambiguous morality of life in East Egg and West Egg as paradigm. But, as everyone knows, the *Gatsby* map is much larger and the distances in time and space much greater.

Fitzgerald, however, was a careful craftsman who used popular myth and history to give his tale the exact amount of general historicism that his vision required. Indeed, the title that most aptly sums up *Gatsby* is that of an essay by Kermit W. Moyer, "*The Great Gatsby*: Fitzgerald's Meditation on American History," or a similar suggestion in Alan Trachtenberg's "The Journey Back: Myth and History in *Tender Is the Night*," in which Trachtenberg sees Fitzgerald's fiction as an "extended meditation on America, its history and its notorious dreams."[3]

This is by no means to disagree with the obvious — that Fitzgerald always had a sense of history, especially from *Gatsby* forward; but history in *Gatsby* is largely myth as history, not the history of the past. Events in *Gatsby* are primarily what was in the newspapers and popular press of the time: the Fuller-McGee case, Prohibition and its gangsters, the popular myths of Daniel Boone and Buffalo Bill. Fitzgerald did not comment on these references in his notes and rarely did so in his letters except to associate a character with the real person, for example, Arnold Rothstein as the model for Meyer Wolfshiem or Edith Cummings for Jordan Baker.[4] Further, this is not to say that Fitzgerald had not previously used historical names and events as background and reference. In many of his short stories, such as "May Day," "The Ice Palace," and "The Last of the Belles," there are historical settings and characters. Their function, however, is to locate and define the characters and settings in place and time rather than to integrate the past with the present through a historical parallel.

It is, however, as arguable as one wishes to make it, not until *Tender Is the Night* that Fitzgerald began more directly and frequently to merge history and fiction, to meditate more consciously on history itself, and to write about specific parallels between American history and characters and situation in his work. In *Tender*, he refers to Ulysses S. Grant in a comparison with Dick Diver's stalled career, which "was biding its time, again like Grant in Galena";[5] to the Battle of the Somme in World War I; and to Dick Diver's family background: "My great-grandfather was Governor of North Carolina and I'm a direct descendant of Mad Anthony Wayne" (158). The most historical reference in *Tender* is, in fact, Mad Anthony Wayne, who is today almost totally obscure.[6]

Fitzgerald from his youngest days was well aware that he was related to Francis Scott Key through his paternal grandmother, whose grandfather, Philip Barton Key, was Francis Scott Key's uncle.[7] A tenuous relationship to be sure, but firmly established enough to make a young boy from St. Paul conscious of his heritage. In addition, Fitzgerald recorded in one of his notebooks that "My great grandmother visted [sic] Dolly [sic] Madison,"[8] as if to remind himself of his connection to American history and personalities, and indirectly to President James Madison. Perhaps Fitzgerald was thinking about history in his work every day, but I believe he only became fully serious about his use of history in his fiction when he began to write *The Last Tycoon*. Fitzgerald's true meditation on American history, however, was never published during his lifetime; it was written to himself in one of his notes for this last novel: "I look out at it—and I think it is the most beautiful history in the world. It is the history of me and of my people. And if I came here yesterday like Sheilah I should still think so. It is the history of all aspiration—not just the American dream but the human dream and if I came at the end of it that too is a place in the line of the pioneers."[9]

There are at least three primary and related levels of American history that Fitzgerald uses in *Tycoon*. The first is exemplified by the immediate focus on the Hermitage, the home of Andrew Jackson outside Nashville, Tennessee. On this level, Fitzgerald uses factual history, the physical solidity of place, which needs no further enlargement or detail since it exists; the name itself is enough to provide an association. The second is the symbolic association of presidential names scattered throughout the book, some of which are given either directly (Monroe Stahr) or indirectly (President Roosevelt), or with a historical association by evocation (Jackson, Lincoln, McKinley). And third, he uses history in a parodic and comedic sense to contrast the genuine tycoons of the past with the shallow Hollywood illusionists of the present. In this last usage, history becomes distorted and is turned into myth, illusion, and metaphor—the transformation of the American Dream and history into the dream factories of Hollywood, the triumph of mass entertainment over reality. As Henry Dan Piper has noted, "In Hollywood Fitzgerald, at any rate, had found his greatest theme." [10] Fitzgerald might well have realized that he was not only at the end of the pioneer line in time but also geographically at the end of the pioneering place, the California of Hollywood make-believe rather than the reality of a physical land of tycoons and settlers of an earlier day. The only place in America in 1937 where he could earn a substantial wage, repay his debts, and provide for his family was on the far western edge of the continent.

It is, of course, not a whimsical choice that the first major scene in *The Last Tycoon* takes place at Andrew Jackson's Hermitage just outside Nashville, Tennessee. When their plane is grounded by bad weather, Cecelia, Wylie White, and Manny Schwartze undertake a visit to the Hermitage and a one-hour taxi ride for no real reason other than Wylie White's desire "to take you out to The Hermitage, Home of Andrew Jackson" [11] at 2:30 in the morning. This is clearly a device on Fitzgerald's part to get the characters out to the Hermitage since Wylie has said, just one page earlier, that "I was born in Nashville" and "I've kept away for fifteen years. I hope I'll never see it again" (7), and Manny Schwartze does not know or care about the history of the Hermitage or Andrew Jackson judging from his remarks on the way out.

But Wylie reveals that his interest in the area is more than merely tourist curiosity: "I was born near here—the son of impoverished southern paupers. The family mansion is now used as an outhouse. We had four servants—my father, my mother and my two sisters" (10). Wylie is clearly bitter and reflects not on Jackson, the man of the people, but on the political success story of a man whose house represents what Wylie wishes to forget. When Schwartze suddenly appears, he tells him: "'Just in time, Mr. Schwartze,' he said. 'The tour is just starting. Home of Old Hickory—America's tenth president. The victor of New Orleans, opponent of the National Bank, and inventor of the Spoils System'" (12). Fitzgerald never makes clear how Wylie regards Jackson or his political life except in this scene, which is hardly complimentary. It is nevertheless also the location of Schwartze's suicide, with the Hermitage as representative of some better part of American history and the American Dream. Cecelia ponders Schwartze's belief in the symbolic nature of the house rather than the man: "It was doubtful if he knew who Andrew Jackson was as he wandered around, but perhaps he figured that if people had preserved his house Andrew Jackson must have been someone who was large and merciful, able to understand" (13).

The irony is, of course, that Schwartze kills himself because of an imagined or real slight from "Mr. Smith," who is actually Monroe Stahr. Although Fitzgerald based Stahr somewhat loosely on the character of Irving Thalberg and not on his actual life, Thalberg's position as head of production at a major movie studio allowed Fitzgerald to invent freely and to develop complications. In an inscription intended for Norma Shearer, Thalberg's widow, probably drafted during a late stage of the writing, Fitzgerald explained the Thalberg-Stahr mixture:

DEAR NORMA:

You told me you read little because of your eyes but I think this book will interest you—and though the story is purely imaginary perhaps you could see it as an attempt to preserve something of Irving[.] My own impression of him shortly recorded but very dazzling in its effect on me, inspired the best part of the character of Stahr—though I have put in somethings [sic] drawn from . . . other men and, inevitably, much of myself.

Fitzgerald's rendering of Stahr and his story, then, was based on imagination and a "very dazzling . . . effect." In a final paragraph of the letter to Shearer, Fitzgerald adds, "I invented a tragic story and Irvings [sic] life was, of course, not tragic except his struggle against ill health, because no one has ever written a tragedy about Hollywood." [12] Fitzgerald's desire to keep the subject of his novel, as well as Thalberg's identity, secret is revealed in a September 29, 1939, letter to Kenneth Littauer, the fiction editor of Collier's magazine, a letter probably written when Fitzgerald had composed not much more than the first chapter. In proposing the sale of serial rights to Collier's, Fitzgerald, in outlining the story, noted that Cecelia was to be the narrator who "focuses our attention upon two principal characters—Milton Stahr (who is Irving Thalberg—and this is my great secret) and Thalia, the girl he loves. Thalberg has always fascinated me. . . . The events I have built around him are fiction, but all of them are things which might very well have happened, and I am pretty sure that I saw deep enough into the character of the man so that his reactions are authentically what they would have been in life" (LLT xxxi; emphasis in original).

In his letters to Norma Shearer and to Littauer, Fitzgerald makes it a point to emphasize that he is drawing on Thalberg's character primarily, and to Shearer he says that Stahr consists of "somethings [sic] drawn from . . . other men." These are revealing comments since it has too often been assumed by subsequent critics that Stahr was mostly Thalberg. Given the very prominent place of the Hermitage in the story's early and symbolic development, it is not beyond possibility that Andrew Jackson would also in some way be involved as a historical presence linking the past to the present of the story. Fitzgerald's increasing interest in the American past and the parallels he probably saw between Jackson as president and Stahr as head of a studio—the end of aristocratic ascendancy and the rise of a new mass industry—with all of the power and money represented by the democratic promise of the American Dream, were surely to be a part of the plan. Why else would he devote a major episode to the events that take place at the Hermitage?

With this connection in mind, it appears more than likely that Fitzgerald also modeled Stahr to an extent on Jackson, not just physically, but politically and historically. Although superficially resembling Thalberg, the parallels with Jackson are a bit too numerous to be coincidental. Fitzgerald owned *Andrew Jackson: The Gentle Savage* (1929) by David Karsner. In addition, in 1938 *Andrew Jackson: Portrait of a President* by Marquis James won a Pulitzer Prize only a year before Fitzgerald began to work intensely on *The Last Tycoon*. Given his interest in the best-sellers and prizes of his contemporaries, it seems likely he would have read the book.

Both Jackson and Stahr (like Thalberg) had limited educations and no inherited social positions; but Jackson is considered the first presidential model to represent the democratic ideal of birth from humble circumstances, the experience of the American frontier, military experience, belief in the common man, and devotion to democracy. Stahr's military experience is not on the frontier of history but on the new frontier of Hollywood. Part of his success is that he, like Jackson, knows what people want. Fitzgerald makes this comparison explicit through Lincoln in still another way when he has Boxley recognize: "Stahr like Lincoln was a leader carrying on a long war on many fronts; almost single-handed he had moved pictures forward through a decade, to a point where the content of the 'A productions' was wider and richer than that of the stage. Stahr was an artist only, as Mr. Lincoln was a general, perforce and as a layman" (107).

Stahr, like Thalberg, also is seen generally as being frail and thin, and describes himself as having "very thin" legs (79); Jackson is described by all biographers as frail and thin near the end of his life. Claude G. Bowers, for one, like Karsner, says, "His long straight legs were thin, and . . . his shoulders were a little bowed by the burdens he had borne." [13] Like Jackson, Stahr has suffered through the death of his wife and still mourns her, but unlike Jackson he finds Kathleen when "smiling faintly at him from not four feet away was the face of his dead wife, identical even to the expression. Across the four feet of moonlight, the eyes he knew looked back at him, a curl blew a little on a familiar forehead; the smile lingered, changed a little according to a pattern; the lips parted—the same" (26).

In his notes, Fitzgerald indicated his intention was to have Brady blackmail Stahr over his affair with Kathleen. Jackson and his wife had to be remarried in 1794 due to a questionable divorce from her first husband, which was later used as a political weapon against Jackson. The incidents seem parallel enough to suggest a general rather than a specific correlation, and put together with other Hollywood social and political common events such as blackmail, the labor unions' rise, studio intrigue, and the fear of Communism, can be seen as modern-day equivalents of the Spoils System, the National Bank controversy, and the political and social scandals of the time.

Without going into specific details, Henry Dan Piper also believes that Fitzgerald planned to use Jackson as a model for Stahr:

> Fitzgerald also planned to emphasize certain parallels between his hero and two potent American political executives: Abraham Lincoln and Andrew Jackson. Jackson was intended to illustrate the ruthless, autocratic elements in Stahr's personality. Old Hickory was the first strong American president, and Stahr was a general waging war on a dozen fronts at once — against lazy subordinates, jealous associates, penny-pinching financiers, power-hungry labor unions. . . . At one stage in Fitzgerald's planning, he intended to have Stahr meet his death in front of the capitol in Washington. When Fitzgerald himself died, he was still not certain how he was going to work out the full implications of the Lincoln-Jackson association that he had so far indicated only in crude terms.[14]

An obvious connection to the American past is made through Fitzgerald's use of historical names of presidents and having Stahr's actions associated with historical figures. Presidential names, particularly Jackson, Monroe, Lincoln, and McKinley, represent the larger historical images in American history, and by association reflect Stahr's unique qualities. In *College of One*, Sheilah Graham reports that Fitzgerald explained to her why Stahr's first name was Monroe: "Jewish parents often give their sons the names of American Presidents." Robert Roulston, however, believes that the name "Monroe" had a more direct connection with Fitzgerald and that the decision to use his last name as Stahr's first name was deliberate and a part of a larger plan: "By assigning his hero the name of the fifth president, Fitzgerald links Monroe Stahr with the upper reaches of the Chesapeake Bay area aristocracy from which Fitzgerald himself was descended. Then, too, he explicitly identifies Stahr with the era that aristocracy was at its zenith — the late eighteenth century."[15]

In invoking the name and figure of James Monroe, Fitzgerald also manages to link Stahr with other distinguished Virginians, such as George Washington and Thomas Jefferson, who became president. One wonders here why the party of tourists went to the Hermitage and not to Monticello if a link to history was the sole purpose. The answer is obviously that Jefferson himself was an aristocrat and hardly a man of the people. Stahr—the last tycoon—"had just managed to climb out of a thousand years of Jewry into the late eighteenth century" (119), and Stahr clearly aligns himself philosophically with those earlier patrician values: "he had learned tolerance, kindness, forbearance, and even affection like lessons" (97). Fitzgerald could never quite resist writing himself into his characters, and according to Robert Sklar, while he was writing *Tycoon* he "cast his mind back over his family heritage, pondering the sources of the values he had inherited and put to such important uses in his art. 'What a sense of honor and duty,' he wrote of his father's generation, '—almost eighteenth century rather than Victorian.'"[16]

James Monroe and Stahr also have similar qualities and similar challenges. Monroe, according to Noble E. Cunningham Jr., faced very different challenges from any of his predecessors. Like Monroe, Stahr is portrayed as a "rationalist" (*LLT* 119), and when he agrees to meet with Brimmer, who represents the Communist Party and philosophy, Fitzgerald, in several ways, shows him as being acutely aware of the political divisions of the 1930s. In the face of impending unionization of the studios, Stahr attempts to develop an understanding between himself as a paternalistic studio head and the writers and directors who work under his authority and direction. According to Cunningham, James Monroe presided over an "era of good feelings during his presidency."[17] Stahr, like Monroe, tries to establish "good feelings" by working out new and better relationships. The major challenge for Monroe was to work well with Congress and the members of his cabinet.

The broad parallels between the political struggles would no doubt have been expanded and refined as Fitzgerald worked over the final draft of *Tycoon*. The point is that even in its unfinished state, there is enough of a mix between Monroe, Jackson, Lincoln, and Stahr through a process of historical transformation to suggest—if not entirely document—the firm historical basis that Fitzgerald intended to develop for the novel. Both Jackson and Stahr are bound by a class code, and both are egalitarian in temperament and philosophy; both are also believers in democracy, the common man, and the American Dream. Like Jackson, who opposed and defeated a coalition of southern nationalists who defied federal authority in the name of states' rights, Stahr was to react in a similar way in a scene Fitzgerald planned to write in which Stahr would become angry with the writers and directors who attempt to organize a union against the studio. Stahr initially was to seem to side with

Bradogue (Brady) and the studio, raising the question of individual rights versus a paternalistic establishment and a benevolent dictator, another similarity to the beliefs of Jackson.[18]

By establishing the central image of the Hermitage as both emblematic and symptomatic of dream and denial simultaneously, it is the place, according to Roulston, where "Mount Vernon, in effect, merges with the Alger myth. The result is a relic which, while principally southern in its evocations, connotes glories of pre-Civil War America which are northern as well as southern. It also conjures up the failings of antebellum America, because Jackson was a slaveholder and, as Wylie White reminds Cecilia [sic], the inventor of the spoils system."[19] Neither Cecelia, Wylie White, nor Manny Schwartze can gain entry to the Hermitage. The significance seems apparent: the tycoons and self-made leaders of the past are now subsumed within the confines of a materialistic, cynical, and corrupt society. Even to "the coastal rich . . . who casually alighted from our cloud in mid-America" (8), the airports seem depressing and sterile. In brief, the American Dream is closed off both from the twentieth century and from the past—the preindustrial world of trees, cows, roosters at dawn, and "blue-green shadows stirring every time we passed a farmhouse" (10), as Cecelia remarks with some amazement. Wylie White's error in identifying Andrew Jackson as "America's tenth president" (he was actually the seventh, 1829–37) suggests—since I do not believe that Fitzgerald made an error in the number or the dates—that Americans have lost a sense of self and direction concerning their own past. Wylie White is a writer and educated, yet he misses Jackson's actual presidential sequence widely.

Since Fitzgerald is writing about Hollywood, his view of history and historical figures, once they become part of a movie script, is part and parcel of his sense of contrast between what is real and what is illusory. Although the Hermitage, and its association with Andrew Jackson, is bedrock reality, all of the other presidential references in Hollywood are calculated to create a sense of not only illusion but also a tawdry misuse of history. As Fitzgerald gradually moves away from Jackson and toward Lincoln after chapter 1, some sense of his larger indictment of Hollywood becomes apparent. When Stahr picks up his phone at his beach house, he is momentarily impressed when he receives what he thinks is a call from the president, who at the time would have been Franklin D. Roosevelt. He acts a bit for Kathleen's benefit:

> "It's the President," he said to her, almost stiffly.
> "Of your company?"

"No, of the United States."

He was trying to be casual for her benefit but his voice was eager.

"All right, I'll wait," he said into the phone, and then to Kathleen, "I've talked to him before." (83)

Fitzgerald is here using history in the traditional sense to show the effect of the call on both Stahr and Kathleen. Stahr speaks "almost stiffly," and his "voice was eager." But when he learns a second later that it is an orangutan who, its owner claims, looks like President McKinley and who can supposedly talk, Stahr's mood and tone change as he becomes not amused but annoyed: "because he had thought it was the President and had changed his manner, acting as if it were. He felt a little ridiculous" (84).

Robert Sklar has observed that "In the completed portion of *The Last Tycoon* Lincoln is viewed as a symbol of the past through three separate perspectives, gradually broadening out to a perception of the essential links between the present and the past." Sklar fails to mention, however, that in each of those three perspectives the references to Lincoln are calculated to reveal the shallowness of the Hollywood mentality. Sklar does note that "Hollywood admires Lincoln as a clever entertainer" and has appropriated "the past for its entertainment purposes."[20] But this seems to me to be the point Fitzgerald was making — that Hollywood has no conception of history, either of itself or of the national past. In the first scene, Stahr asks gag man Mike Van Dyke to show Boxley, an Englishman (supposedly based on Aldous Huxley), "a double wing, clutch, kick, and scram." After explaining to Boxley that "It was a routine . . . back in the Keystone days," Mike asks Stahr if Boxley knows what a routine is. "'It means an act,' Stahr explained. 'Georgie Jessel talks about "Lincoln's Gettysburg routine"'" (33). To Stahr, who never refers to himself as a modern-day Lincoln, the point of Lincoln and Gettysburg is reduced to "an act," one that can only be explained by reference to a stand-up comedian, the historical past either not existing at all or simply irretrievable in any way that Boxley can understand.

The second reference occurs as Stahr and Prince Agge pass through a corner of the studio commissary filled with the casts and costumes of various period films. When Agge sees an actor dressed as Abraham Lincoln, "his whole feeling suddenly changed":

Nicolay's biography was much read. He had been told Lincoln was a great man whom he should admire and he had hated him instead because he was forced upon him. But now seeing him sitting here, his legs crossed, his kindly face fixed on a forty cent dinner, including dessert, his shawl wrapped around him as if to protect himself from the erratic air-cooling — now Prince Agge, who was in America at last, stared as a tourist. . . . This then was Lincoln. . . .

Lincoln suddenly raised a triangle of pie and jammed it in his mouth and, a little frightened, Prince Agge hurried to join Stahr. (*LLT* 48–49) [21]

By using a foreigner and a prince as observers whose inner reactions we are allowed to experience, Fitzgerald places this scene in opposition to both the image of "Lincoln's Gettysburg routine" and the passage already discussed in which the English writer Boxley recognizes that "Stahr like Lincoln was a leader carrying on a long war" (107). It is important to recognize that both Prince Agge and Boxley are visitors from other countries who nevertheless manage to place Lincoln and Stahr in their respective historical contexts effortlessly. Both men, presumably, are well-educated and capable of making historical analogies. They both see Stahr in a way that no other character does in relation to Lincoln, who represents something much more important to a foreigner than to Hollywood moviemakers. Lincoln comes momentarily alive for Agge, which is a silent comment on both the power of films to make an event visual and the shock of realizing that once the illusion is broken, the figure becomes as insignificant as the actor eating pie.

Michael Millgate has perceptively noted several additional points of similarity between Lincoln and Stahr that reinforce the idea of Fitzgerald's intention to parallel the two leaders:

Both are men of humble origins and little education but of great ability and vision; both practice in their relations with subordinates complete accessibility and an unforced personal democracy; both accept without hesitation the full responsibility of their position while disliking many of the duties involved. As Fitzgerald saw, there is an obvious analogy to be drawn between Stahr's position and Lincoln's: Stahr can be seen as the commander-in-chief, receiving reports from the battleline, issuing orders to his generals (the directors), overseeing work which has to be done in detail by others. [22]

Ironically, perhaps, the only other person to see Stahr historically is Pete Zavras, a Greek cameraman, who tells him, "You are the Aeschylus and the Diogenes of the moving picture. . . . Also the Asclepius and the Menander" (61). By placing another foreigner in the position of commentator and historical comparativist — even though Zavras does not equate Stahr with figures from American history — Fitzgerald once again used and relied on an extended framework of historical references. By suggesting parallels between the political struggles of Jackson, Monroe, and Lincoln, and Stahr's political struggles with the studios, Fitzgerald was defining the end not only of a pioneering era but also of an attitude and aspiration — "not just the American dream but the human dream." All that remained for Fitzgerald to complete his story of Stahr was to write the scene in which "Stahr wants to see Washington. Goes there and is sick the whole time and sees it only as he leaves."[23] This scene was never written, but one can see where it was headed: Stahr wanders around Washington sick, looking at presidential monuments and, in effect, realizing for himself the American dream of poor boy becomes rich and powerful. American history has come full circle from the eighteenth to the twentieth centuries; the Dream has turned finally into nightmare and disillusionment.

The Last Tycoon uses history to a much greater degree and with much more complexity than any of Fitzgerald's previous works.[24] In spite of recent biographies by Jeffrey Meyers and James R. Mellow, plus numerous articles and specialized studies, the close textual and manuscript examination of *Tycoon* has only just begun to occur with the publication of *The Love of The Last Tycoon: A Western*, Matthew J. Bruccoli's critical edition of the work-in-progress as Fitzgerald left it at his death. With this text now in print, perhaps serious attention can at last be paid to Fitzgerald's final novel, which, even in its unfinished state, is certainly one of his very best.

NOTES

1. Turnbull, *Letters*, 127.
2. Fitzgerald, *Great Gatsby*, 20. All subsequent page references to *The Great Gatsby* are to the 1991 edition, are cited as GG, and appear parenthetically in the text.
3. Trachtenberg, "Journey Back," 170.
4. Turnbull, *Letters*, 551, 173.
5. Fitzgerald, *Tender Is the Night*, 315. All subsequent page references are to the 1934 edition and appear parenthetically in the text.
6. "Mad" Anthony Wayne (1745–96) was not crazy as Baby Warren seems to think but was a prominent American general who was known for taking risks where others hesitated, hence the epithet "Mad." During the Revolution he was engaged in many prominent battles; afterward, in 1792, he was commissioned as commander in chief of the army to act against Ohio Indians under the Militia Act. On August 20, 1794, he engaged a large force of Indians led by Chief Turkey Foot, who was killed at the Battle of Fallen Timbers near the present-day location of Maumee, Ohio, near Toledo. Wayne's victory in the battle ended Indian resistance in the area and opened up the Northwest Territory to settlement. Where Fitzgerald

picked up Mad Anthony Wayne as a danger signal for Baby Warren's conversation with Dick Diver is subject to speculation, but it is another example of his historical knowledge. For accounts of Wayne's military career, see Schlesinger, *Almanac of American History*, 126, 131, 134, 161, 165; and Morris, *Encyclopedia of American History*, 95, 100, 101, 106, 124, 442.

7. See Scottie Fitzgerald Smith's "The Colonial Ancestors of Francis Scott Key Fitzgerald" in Bruccoli, *Some Sort of Epic Grandeur*, 496–510. Smith includes a genealogical chart of the Key and Fitzgerald families. A note on the chart says that "Francis Scott Key Fitzgerald and Francis Scott Key were second cousins, three times removed."

8. Fitzgerald, *Notebooks*, 267.

9. Ibid., 332.

10. Piper, *F. Scott Fitzgerald*, 280.

11. Fitzgerald, *Love of the Last Tycoon*, 9. All subsequent page references are to the 1993 edition, are cited as *LLT*, and appear parenthetically in the text.

12. Bruccoli, *"Last of the Novelists,"* 14.

13. Bowers, *Making Democracy a Reality*, 33.

14. Piper, *F. Scott Fitzgerald*, 268–69. Fitzgerald may have been aware of other correspondences between himself and Andrew Jackson. Both were descended from immigrant Irish families; both had lost spouses (by 1938 Zelda was spending much of her time in institutions); both were born in places far beyond the center of politics, culture, or influence; both were suspicious of and hostile toward (or jealous of) wealth and the privileged class; both were outside the aristocratic circles of their day; and both were constantly short of money. For details on Jackson, I have drawn on several standard biographies as well as Sean Wilentz's entry on Jackson in *Reader's Companion*, 579–80, 582–86. Also helpful is Shaw and Bremer, *Andrew Jackson, 1767–1845, Chronology—Documents—Bibliographical Aids.*

David Karsner, in *Andrew Jackson*, also provides some details on Jackson that might have caught Fitzgerald's attention. A few examples: Jackson was "a scrapper as a boy" (26); "an atrocious speller" (28); had "contracted small pox at 15 while a prisoner of war of the British and was seriously ill and an invalid for one year" (45). Jackson was honored at a banquet by Thomas Jefferson in Lynchburg, Virginia, and returned his toast by offering the same to James Monroe after becoming a military hero (251); in Washington, D.C., Jackson was the guest of President Madison at the White House and was honored by "a gorgeous feast" prepared by Dolley Madison (251). In his final years, Jackson had tuberculosis and died of it (393).

15. Graham, *College of One*, 73; Roulston, "Whistling 'Dixie' in Encino," 360.

16. Sklar, *F. Scott Fitzgerald*, 332.

17. Cunningham, "Monroe, James," 741–42.

18. Wilentz, "Jackson, Andrew," 579–80; Bruccoli, *"Last of the Novelists,"* 138–40.

19. Roulston, "Whistling 'Dixie' in Encino," 362.

20. Sklar, *F. Scott Fitzgerald*, 335–36.

21. "Nicolay's biography" is a passing reference to John G. Nicolay and John Hay's *Abraham Lincoln: A History* (1890), a book not among those sent to the Princeton University Library after Fitzgerald's death. Fitzgerald did own Carl Sandburg's five-volume set, *Abraham Lincoln*; Lord Charnwood's *Abraham Lincoln*; and Edgar Lee Masters's *Lincoln the Man*.

22. Millgate, "Scott Fitzgerald as Social Novelist," 85–86.

23. Fitzgerald, *Notebooks*, 332; Bruccoli, "*Last of the Novelists*," 138.

24. In addition to a careful search of *This Side of Paradise, The Beautiful and Damned,* and *The Great Gatsby* versus *Tender Is the Night* and *The Last Tycoon,* my argument for Fitzgerald's later and more serious use of history beginning with *Tender* is based on a reading of *The Letters of F. Scott Fitzgerald, Correspondence of F. Scott Fitzgerald, The Notebooks of F. Scott Fitzgerald* (which cover 1932–40 only, but do suggest his thinking during those years, if only fragmentarily), and the several lists of his books sent to the Princeton University Library after his death. Of the one thousand or so books sent to Princeton, Fitzgerald's library contained about 10 percent of a historical nature, with an emphasis on Napoleon and his era, the American Civil War, and World War I.

WORKS CITED

Bowers, Claude G. *Making Democracy a Reality.* Jackson, Tenn.: Memphis State College Press, 1954.

Bruccoli, Matthew J. *The Composition of "Tender Is the Night."* Pittsburgh: University of Pittsburgh Press, 1963.

———. "*The Last of the Novelists*": *F. Scott Fitzgerald and "The Last Tycoon."* Carbondale: Southern Illinois University Press, 1977.

———. *Some Sort of Epic Grandeur: The Life of F. Scott Fitzgerald.* New York: Harcourt Brace Jovanovich, 1981.

Bruccoli, Matthew J., and Margaret M. Duggan, eds., with the assistance of Susan Walker. *Correspondence of F. Scott Fitzgerald.* New York: Random House, 1980.

Cunningham, Noble E., Jr. "Monroe, James." In *The Reader's Companion to American History.* Ed. Eric Foner and John A. Garraty. Boston: Houghton Mifflin, 1991. 741–42.

Fitzgerald, F. Scott. *The Great Gatsby.* 1925. Ed. Matthew J. Bruccoli. New York: Cambridge University Press, 1991.

———. *The Love of The Last Tycoon: A Western.* 1941. Ed. Matthew J. Bruccoli. New York: Cambridge University Press, 1993.

———. *The Notebooks of F. Scott Fitzgerald.* Ed. Matthew J. Bruccoli. New York: Harcourt Brace Jovanovich/Bruccoli Clark, 1978.

———. *Tender Is the Night.* New York: Scribners, 1934.

Graham, Sheilah. *College of One.* New York: Viking Press, 1967.

James, Marquis. *Andrew Jackson: Portrait of a President*. New York: Grosset, 1937.

Karsner, David. *Andrew Jackson: The Gentle Savage*. New York: Brentano, 1929.

Mellow, James R. *Invented Lives: F. Scott and Zelda Fitzgerald*. Boston: Houghton Mifflin, 1984.

Meyers, Jeffrey. *Scott Fitzgerald: A Biography*. New York: HarperCollins, 1994.

Millgate, Michael. "Scott Fitzgerald as Social Novelist: Statement and Technique in *The Last Tycoon*." In *F. Scott Fitzgerald*. Ed. Harold Bloom. New York: Chelsea House, 1985. 81–87.

Morris, Richard B., ed. *The Encyclopedia of American History*. New York: Harper & Row, 1965.

Moyer, Kermit W. "*The Great Gatsby*: Fitzgerald's Meditation on American History." *Fitzgerald/Hemingway Annual 1972*: 43–57.

Nicolay, John G., and John Hay. *Abraham Lincoln: A History*. New York: Century, 1890.

Piper, Henry Dan. *F. Scott Fitzgerald: A Critical Portrait*. New York: Holt, Rinehart and Winston, 1965.

Roulston, Robert. "Whistling 'Dixie' in Encino: *The Last Tycoon* and Fitzgerald's Two Souths." *South Atlantic Quarterly* 79 (1980): 355–63.

Schlesinger, Arthur M., Jr. *The Almanac of American History*. New York: G. P. Putnam, 1983.

Shaw, Ronald E., and Howard F. Bremer, eds. *Andrew Jackson 1767–1845, Chronology—Documents—Bibliographical Aids*. Dobbs Ferry, N.Y.: Oceana, 1969.

Sklar, Robert. *F. Scott Fitzgerald: The Last Laocoön*. New York: Oxford University Press, 1967.

Trachtenberg, Alan. "The Journey Back: Myth and History in *Tender Is the Night*." In *Critical Essays on Fitzgerald's "Tender Is the Night*." Ed. Milton R. Stern. Boston: G. K. Hall, 1986. 170–85.

Turnbull, Andrew, ed. *The Letters of F. Scott Fitzgerald*. New York: Scribners, 1963.

Wilentz, Sean. "Jackson, Andrew." In *The Reader's Companion to American History*. Ed. Eric Foner and John A. Garraty. Boston: Houghton Mifflin, 1991. 579–80.

PART THREE

The Stories and Essays

Tamed or Idealized

Judy Jones's Dilemma in "Winter Dreams"

QUENTIN E. MARTIN

Critics, especially feminist ones, have recently been taking a closer look at the female characters in F. Scott Fitzgerald's fiction, and several have found an author who, as one critic says, is "extremely unsympathetic" toward those characters. David Fedo writes that "the notion that women are predators, that they are capable of destroying even the men they want most, becomes a central idea in nearly all of Fitzgerald's fiction." Judith Fetterley argues that *The Great Gatsby* is a "dishonest book" because it is "based on the lie of a double standard that makes female characters in our 'classic' literature not persons but symbols and makes women's experience no part of that literature's concern"; this dishonesty, she adds, "goes unrecognized by Fitzgerald." *The Norton Anthology of American Literature* has institutionalized this view, saying that Fitzgerald, along with other leading twentieth-century male writers, interprets "the 'New Woman' as an ominous sign of social breakdown." [1]

Other critics, though, have a more measured perspective on the matter, believing that Fitzgerald's view of women is too complex to be written off so summarily. Mary McCay, directly responding to Fetterley's criticism, maintains that Fitzgerald's "fiction, at its best, runs deeper than she [Fetterley] describes. His women are seldom as passive as Fetterley implies, nor are they static seduction figures simply luring men to destruction." Sarah Beebe Fryer, among others, agrees, writing that Fitzgerald's treatment of women "deserves reconsideration." [2]

Although these and other critics have ably defended Fitzgerald, their arguments are generally supported by the cases they make for the female characters of his novels, specifically Daisy Buchanan and Nicole Warren, and they have tended to ignore or overlook the women of his short stories. Part of the explanation for this may lie in the still prevailing belief that Fitzgerald's short stories are shoddy stuff that he churned out for cash so that he could concentrate on his serious work, the novels. Critics in general, subsequently, either neglect the stories or dismiss them as poor relatives of the novels. Jackson R. Bryer notes the "deplorable absence of worthwhile commentary" on the stories and says that "the single greatest need in Fitzgerald studies has long been for close attention to the style and artistry of the texts themselves." Alice Hall Petry, in a recent study of Fitzgerald's short stories, echoes Bryer's point. After listing some of Fitzgerald's best stories, she notes that they have "inexplicably . . . been ignored or dismissed lightly by Fitzgerald scholars." [3]

The rich and complex "Winter Dreams" is a striking example of this inexplicable lack of critical attention. Only a handful of full-length studies have been written about it, and it is barely mentioned in most of the major books about Fitzgerald. Not only would a closer look at "Winter Dreams" reveal the vitality of much of Fitzgerald's short fiction, it would also help overturn the fashionable Fitzgerald-as-misogynist reading and add to the healthy trend of revisionist studies of Fitzgerald's female characters.

But for now, Judy Jones of "Winter Dreams" is still seen as a static seduction figure who lures Dexter Green into unhappiness and despair. Matthew J. Bruccoli compares Judy's "inconstancy" with Dexter's "faithfulness," while John Kuehl claims that Judy, reckless, violent, and dishonest, is one of those "golden femmes fatales who ensnare, then abandon, suitors"; and Sergio Perosa calls Judy "irresponsible" and, like many critics, dismisses the story as one of the "preliminary studies" for The Great Gatsby. Similarly, John A. Higgins, who sees genuine merit in "Winter Dreams," nonetheless considers Judy "insatiable," the "arch–femme fatale," and a "girl . . . not worth the having"; K. G. W. Cross says that Judy is "selfish and wilful . . . [and] toys with her victim long enough to destroy his chance of happiness"; Herbie Butterfield argues that Judy is "a spoiled child, playful and fanciful"; and William Fahey writes that "Fitzgerald presents Dexter's idol as a puppet." Clinton S. Burhans, who has written the most thorough evaluation of the story, remarks on Judy's "roller-coaster inconstancy" and her treatment of men as "playthings." [4]

This is the unfortunately unanimous view of Judy, with only Petry questioning the femme fatale label.[5] But is it the correct view? Or is it another symptom of the failure to see how deep, as Mary McCay argues, Fitzgerald's best fiction runs? I believe that Judy, like Daisy Buchanan, can in fact be more accurately seen as a victim of a world that makes, or tries to make, puppets out of women, and that Fitzgerald is aware of and sympathetic toward Judy's plight. I will argue that "Winter Dreams" has been consistently misread and woefully shortchanged; that Fitzgerald is lamenting the lost dreams of Judy as much as he laments those of Dexter; that, indeed, the loss of Judy's dreams is the more profound and painful one in the story; and, finally, that the story contains a precise and impassioned critique of the habits and attitudes that served to circumscribe women. Fitzgerald, in short, did not fear the New Woman, as the Norton editors flashily argue. Instead, he, with his sure and careful touch, created female characters, like Judy Jones, so subtle and probing that today's hasty commentators miss the point entirely.

That women and views of women were going through revolutionary change was obvious to Fitzgerald and his contemporaries. The previous fifty to one hundred years had witnessed, especially in America, the epochal move of millions of women out of the house and into the world, whether it had been to schools and colleges (as students and teachers) or to a variety of jobs and professions. In 1900, for example, 40 percent of American college students were women, and the census of that year listed 303 occupations, with women represented in 296 of them. In all, 5.3 million women were working in 1900, a number that grew to 8.1 million in 1910, 8.5 million in 1920, and 10.8 million in 1930. The number of women in white-collar employment nearly doubled during each of those ten-year periods up to 1920, with 3.35 million female white-collar workers in 1920 and 4.76 million in 1930.[6] Of course the majority of these women worked in jobs that were extensions of domestic work—textiles, nursing, elementary school teaching, office support—and most were paid less than men doing comparable work; nonetheless, the amount and dispersal of female employment were revolutionary.

Women were also making political and legal gains, having by the turn of the century abolished nearly all the restrictions of the common-law doctrine of *femme couverte*. Among these gains was a liberalization in divorce laws; Arthur M. Schlesinger notes that "twice as many divorces in the period 1878–1898 were granted upon the wife's complaint as the husband's, [reflecting] a greater self respect among women and unwillingness to put up with conditions which their mothers would have accepted in silence." In 1916, there was one divorce for every nine marriages as compared to one in twenty-one in 1880.[7] Sexual liberation was occurring as well. Despite the myths, late-nineteenth-century women were not uniformly counseled to ignore or be embarrassed about their bodies,[8] and this liberalization increased in the new century. William Chafe notes that "women born after the century were twice as likely to have experienced premarital sex as those born before 1900."[9]

These and other changes resulted in the New Woman, and this creature soon entered serious and popular culture. William Dean Howells and Henry James, among others, brought into their works female characters who worked, talked freely and frankly, and questioned the rules of society. Indeed, for not presenting women as passive, prettified, homebound angels, both writers were attacked on the grounds that young and impressionable readers would be tainted.[10] The fact that Tom Corey in Howells's *The Rise of Silas Lapham* prefers the plain-looking and plain-speaking Penelope over the blonde, beautiful, blushing Irene is an indication of the changing nature of what constituted attractiveness in women. Fetterley's claim that women are mere symbols in the supposedly patriarchal world of American literature becomes absurd when one actually reads the books themselves. (Gerald Graff notes that Fetterley's "'resisting reader' does not always stop to read before resisting."[11]) From Daisy Miller to Celia Madden to Rose Dutcher to Carrie Meeber to Lady Brett Ashley, scores of female characters speak and behave "immodestly" — and these new, undomesticated creatures, though of course morally complex, were clearly not proffered as mere symbols of a decaying social order.

The New Woman appeared in popular culture as well. James R. McGovern notes the changes in how women were presented in advertisements in popular magazines: in the July 1915 *Ladies Home Journal*, an ad "depicts a young woman driving a speedboat while her boyfriend sits next to her," whereas just ten years previously, "when young lovers trysted in advertisements, they met at Horlick's Malted Milk Bar; he with his guitar and she with her parasol." McGovern also cites, among other examples, a popular song of 1916 called "A Dangerous Girl," whose lyrics read in part, "You dare me, you scare me, and still I like you more each day."[12] Again, what constituted attractiveness in women was changing: to be daring, to drive instead of being driven, was what portions of society were beginning to welcome and desire.

Fitzgerald himself was, as said, acutely aware of this transformation from an "angel in the house," to use Coventry Patmore's notorious phrase, to a working woman. And in many ways, Fitzgerald welcomed this change. He wrote to his daughter, Scottie, that "I never wanted to see again in this world women who were brought up to be idlers." In a later letter, he hopefully predicted that "every girl your age in America will have the experience of working for a living."[13] Fitzgerald, in his personal life, was of course ambivalent about these changes in women: he both supported and was exasperated by his wife Zelda's dancing, drawing, and writing. But the point is that he was deeply interested and involved in this transformation in women's social, economic, and political status, and this awareness suffuses his fiction, especially "Winter Dreams," though critics have been slow to recognize it.

But it is a complex awareness, for this transformation of women was by no means complete — it was, in fact, producing profound complications and problems. It was still considered unusual if not improper for middle- and upper-class women (such as Judy Jones) and for most married women to work. Twenty percent of adult women may have been working in 1900, but only 5 percent of married women were employed outside the house.[14] In Sinclair Lewis's *Main Street*, Carol Kennicott "could not have outside employment. To the village doctor's wife it was taboo. She was a woman with a working brain and no work." Chafe remarks that "a woman who consciously endeavored to share more of her husband's world succeeded only at the price of isolation from the rest of the female community." In the classic 1929 study *Middletown*, the authors make clear that a large part of society still thought of and classified women in preliberation terms: "Middletown husbands . . . are likely to speak of women as creatures purer and morally better than men but as relatively impractical, emotional, unstable, given to prejudice, easily hurt, and largely incapable of facing facts or doing hard thinking."[15]

Hence, this new behavior of the New Woman, though welcomed by some, such as Dexter (the daring Judy is more attractive than the stolid Irene Scheerer), still puzzled or displeased men like the Middletown husbands and many of the characters in the fiction of Fitzgerald and others. To many men and women, the New Woman was an additional threat to the social fabric, one already thinned by immigration, labor unrest, religious indifference, and other factors. "Countless citizens," as Robert Wiebe points out, "sensed that something fundamental was happening to their lives, something they had not willed and did not want, and they responded by striking out at whatever enemies their view of the world allowed them to see."[16] And among those that were struck — often literally, as I will show — was the New Woman.

Judy, then, is caught in the dilemma of having the newfound freedom to act frankly and to treat men as equals — she presumably thumbs through magazines that show women driving motorboats, listens to popular songs about the attractiveness of daring women, reads about strong, frank, independent women in novels — but at the same time being stigmatized as a threat to the established order. This is especially so because she is from the upper class, which, as noted, had not yet given its women the freedom to seek lives outside the home.

Judy, as the critics argue, *is* an unpredictable, flirtatious, and at times rude woman who apparently uses men as playthings in order to escape boredom; she does indeed seem to be the static seduction figure that many critics and the other characters in the story see her as. What is missed by both groups is that there are some powerful *causes* for her behavior, and in her reaction to those causes she shows uncommon awareness, intelligence, and complexity. In her fight against the forces of her society, she is anything but a puppet or femme fatale; she is more sinned against than sinning.

In her first appearance, Judy is a "beautifully ugly" eleven-year-old whose behavior is unpredictable and outrageous (ordering people around, raising a golf club against her nurse).[17] Also in this first scene she is described as "passionate" and "radiant," and as having "vitality" (128). When she's next seen, at age twenty, she is again described as having "passionate vitality" (the word "passionate" is used three times in these first two descriptions, and later her "passionate energy" is noted); she gives an impression of "intense life" (132).

And how do the men in the story react to her passionate vitality? "All she needs," says Mr. T. A. Hedrick, "is to be turned up and spanked for six months and then to be married off to an old-fashioned cavalry captain" (132). Hedrick echoes the attitude of many other fictional characters, and those in society, who want to tame this New Woman. Dr. Ledsmar in *The Damnation of Theron Ware* believes that the outspoken and independent Celia Madden should be "whipped." In *The Awakening*, Edna Pontellier's father, "the Colonel," counsels Edna's husband that "authority, coercion are what is needed" to tame the wayward Edna; "Put your foot down good and hard," the Colonel says; that's "the only way to manage a wife." And, to cite one more example, a character in *Main Street* tells Carol's husband, Dr. Kennicott, that "the way to handle wives, like the fellow says, is to catch 'em early, treat 'em rough, and tell 'em nothing." [18]

Vitality and passion, though attractive, threaten the ability of men to contain women, so men like Hedrick want to beat those qualities out of them and render them childish ("spanked") in their subservience and docility. In short, they want to tame these new creatures. Women, according to Hedrick, should be passive and silent (and, incidentally, not allowed on golf courses), active only in their service to men and children. Hedrick is perhaps most offended because Judy is a fiery young woman and not a wife-and-mother-in-waiting. "Contemptuously," he points out her propensity for "turning those big cow-eyes on every calf in town!" And the narrator says that "it was doubtful if Mr. Hedrick intended a reference to the maternal instinct" (132). Dexter has similar thoughts: while trying to convince himself that Judy is unworthy, "he enumerated her glaring deficiencies as a wife" (139). The irony is that Judy does turn out to be a loyal wife and mother; she loves her husband even though "he drinks and runs around," and she "stays at home with her kids" (144). Her married life is admittedly not developed in the story, but it can be tentatively cited as making another point: that vitality and individuality in a woman do not necessarily negate her ability to be a good wife and mother, as Mr. Hedrick and Dexter believe.

But men not only try to tame and control women like Judy; they also, paradoxically, idealize them. On the night that Judy and Dexter go motorboating, Judy introduces herself and explains why she's riding alone on the lake: "I live in a house over there on the Island, and in that house there is a man waiting for me. When he drove up at the door I drove out of the dock because he says I'm his ideal" (133–34). This is the most explicit reference to the tendency of men to idealize Judy, but other attempts occur throughout the story and they, along with the attempts to tame Judy, create an intractable dilemma for her. She desperately wants to be treated fairly, not trampled over by "an old-fashioned cavalry captain" (132) and not absurdly idealized, as by the man waiting in her house. But these are the only ways men know how to react to her—either to tame or to idealize.

Olive Chancellor in James's *The Bostonians* feels a similar frustration, believing that most men can be divided into two groups, "palterers and bullies." This Scylla-and-Charybdis dilemma also exists for Daisy Buchanan, whose "choices," as Fetterley writes, "amount in reality to no more than the choice of which form she wishes her oppression to take."[19] Just as Daisy is trapped between the tamer (Buchanan) and the idealizer (Gatsby), so Judy is caught between the cavalry captain (Hedrick) and the idealizers (the man at her house and others). Therefore, she fights back with the only weapon she has— her beauty. Since "she was not a girl who could be 'won'" like some trophy, she fights off these men by "immediately resolv[ing] the affair to a physical basis" (137). She forces them to play *"her game and not their own"* (137; emphasis added), and as a result they become frustrated, confused, bitter, and angry. To call her behavior selfish, spoiled, dishonest, irresponsible, or flirtatious is to confuse a counterpunch for a punch. She reacts to the "youthful lovers" and "youthful" love affairs. As the narrator surmises: "Perhaps from so much youthful love, so many youthful lovers, she had come, in *self-defense*, to nourish herself wholly from within" (137; emphasis added).

All Judy wants is to find one man who is not "youthful" or immature—she calls men "children" (142) later—and who does not have the urge to tame or idealize her. This explains why "when a new man came to town every one dropped out" (137) and why she has in her young life stepped into so many cars, sat in so many leather seats, rested her elbow on so many doors — "waiting" for a man who will not view her and treat her as all previous men have (140). In addition, it's made clear that she is not just waiting for a rich man. A story she tells Dexter seems to indicate that she is a gold digger (it's the type of label that might be turned against her). She says that her relations with "a man I cared about" ended when "he told me out of a clear sky that he was poor as a church-mouse. He'd never even hinted it before" (135). But she did not end the relationship because of his poverty — "I've been mad about loads of poor men," she says — but because he tried to conceal it, tried to be something he was not. In short, he was not able to provide what Judy is looking for: a fair, honest, forthright, and mature man who will not try to tame or idealize her, someone with whom she can develop "individual camraderie [sic]" (141). By lying, this man without money "didn't start right" (135).

It's Dexter's apparent lack of artificiality, especially about his money, that first attracts Judy to him. When Dexter finishes telling her how rich he is, "There was a pause. Then she smiled" (136). She smiles not for the money but for the frankness. And soon after that the "unpredictable compound" (136) of her lips — not the presumably predictable compound of a tamed or idealized woman's lips — initiates the affair.

The manner in which Judy then seems to "toy with Dexter," as Cross says, convinces Dexter and most readers that Judy is a heartless flirt (another label that might be used to categorize her). The narrator's comments about Judy seem to support that reading: she has "the most direct and unprincipled personality with which [Dexter] had ever come in contact" (136); "there was a very little mental side to any of her affairs" (136); "she was entertained only by the gratification of her desires" (137); "she had beckoned . . . and yawned at [Dexter]" (138). Within a week she is running off with another man, and Dexter soon discovers that a dozen men "circulated about her" (137). Dexter's "first exhilaration" turns into "restlessness and dissatisfaction" (137). It seems that the sole cause of this dissatisfaction is Judy's inconstant behavior, but again Judy's behavior is being misread; again a counterpunch is seen as a punch, self-defense as attack. For Dexter has, subtly, played the same game that other men have played with Judy. His apparent lack of artificiality is just that — apparent. His frank start had given Judy hope that he would be different, and when he turned out not to be different, her treatment of him is "revenge for having ever cared for him at all" (138).

How is Dexter like all the other men? First, he has the same urge to tame Judy. On that first night of those kisses, the night after the motorboat ride, he feels "that for the moment he controlled and owned" that "exquisite excitability" of Judy (136). With this feeling, this attempt to own and control a woman who could not be "won," he too does not start right. He also commits the other sin, namely that of idealizing her. On this first date, he sees that Judy is wearing a casual dress, which makes him "disappointed at first that she had not put on something more elaborate. This feeling was accentuated when, after a brief greeting, she went to the door of a butler's pantry and pushing it open called: 'You can serve dinner, Martha.' He had rather expected that a butler would announce dinner, that there would be a cocktail" (135). Already, in what she wears and how she acts, Dexter senses a gap between what she is and what—as a pretty rich girl from an important family—she should be. And this gap, this failure to be the girl he wants her to be, makes him "disappointed." While they eat, he grows more disappointed because she does not act like a predictable and tamed beauty. She slips into "a moody depression," smiles at unconnected things— "at him, at a chicken liver, at nothing" (135)—and speaks petulantly. And Dexter's reaction is not an increased interest or attraction; rather, he feels an "uneasiness" and becomes "worried" and "disturbed" (135). She is untamed and does not match Dexter's idealized picture of her; hence he is "disturbed."

Dexter cannot deal with Judy's individuality, unpredictability, and unconventional behavior. Such behavior makes him disappointed, uneasy, worried— all on their first date. And though it is not explicitly stated that Judy senses and reacts to Dexter's ideas and feelings, it is certainly not implausible that she feels Dexter's unease, his idealization and attempt to tame (if not own) her, since she has seen such behavior in every other man she's met. In this light, her subsequent treatment of him is at least partially understandable.

Dexter's unnaturalness, his attempt to be what he is not, is brought up throughout the story and is a trait that Judy might also have perceived. Dexter, like Gatsby, is embarrassed about his past: his mother's name and her origins as "a Bohemian of the peasant class" bother him; he insists on calling his hometown Keble and not Black Bear Village because Keble is not a "footstool" for a fashionable lake (135). As a successful businessman, he becomes interested in music and books because "he had a rather priggish notion that he— the young and already fabulously successful Dexter Green—should know more about such things" (139). Since he idealizes himself, tries to fit the complications of his past into a neat contemporary portrait, and even refers to himself in the third person, it is no surprise that he similarly idealizes and compartmentalizes—and hence misunderstands—Judy.

That Judy reacts against Dexter's behavior is revealed at a later meeting when, "for almost the first time since they had met," he acts naturally with her, does not parrot the things all the men usually say to her: "he did not ask her to sit out with him or tell her that she was lovely." And she, significantly, "did not miss these things" (139). She is tired of conventional behavior and words. At a later meeting, furthermore, he will "find no casual word with which to profane the hour" (141), and this, in part, leads to a resumption of their affair.

The male characters, to repeat, are bewildered and made miserable by Judy because she cannot be tamed and because she resists idealization; yet, almost unconsciously, they are enormously attracted to her. Her passion and vitality, her "unpredictable compound" (136), set her off from other women. Her smile is so radiant that "at least a dozen men were to carry [the memory of it] into middle age" (129); her inexpressible loveliness brings "no end of misery to a great number of men" (128). Men are enraptured by her because the women of their creation — tamed, protected, idealized — are pallid in comparison. Indeed, "light-haired" (138) Irene, the woman Dexter becomes engaged to, is literally pallid.

But though men help to create women like Irene, they don't like them because they're boring, as Dexter's feelings about Irene show. Just four months into his engagement to Irene, he marvels "that so soon, with so little done, so much of ecstasy had gone from him" (139). Imagining his future with her, he "knew that Irene would be no more than a curtain spread behind him, a hand moving among gleaming teacups, a voice calling to children" (139). Here is the angel in the house, yet what is the result: "fire and loveliness were gone, the magic of nights and the wonder of the varying hours and seasons" (139). The engagement is to be announced soon, one that "no one would be surprised at" (140). Dexter is doing the expected thing, following the standard pattern, marrying the "right" girl; there will be no more surprises in his life, no more distracting "fire" and "magic." In a late scene in the story, while looking at some people dance (he is no longer dancing himself) and thinking of this future, "he leaned against the door-post, nodded at a man or two — yawned." Then he hears, "Hello, darling" (140).

At the moment that Dexter is yawning into a solid, predictable life of no surprises, Judy appears, slender and golden, and "he could have wept at the wonder of her return" (140) when all weeping and wonder seemed lost from his life. For when Judy left, "all mysterious happenings, all fresh and quickening hopes, had gone away with her" (140). It is Judy and women like her who provide the compound that make life a mysterious happening, and make Dexter "magnificently attune to life" (133). Yet the men in the story do all they can to deny and eliminate that mystery, that unpredictable compound, by taming it or making it unreal by idealizing it.

The second act between Dexter and Judy lasts only a month, and once more Fitzgerald implies that Dexter's urge to control and own Judy—and not Judy's mere toying and mindless flirtation—is what dooms the affair. Dexter again starts off wrong by thinking "this was his girl who was speaking, his own, his beautiful, his pride" (142); significantly, the word "his" is used four times in this one sentence. Moreover, during this affair or after (the story does not make this clear), Dexter realizes that "he did not possess in himself the power to move fundamentally or to hold Judy Jones" (143), implying again that Dexter has tried to control and own a person who refuses to be owned. Other taming and idealizing behavior may also have resurfaced during this monthlong second affair, behavior that Judy reacted to. And when this affair ends and he does not "bear any malice toward her" (143), it's left unsaid whether Judy might have borne any malice toward him for trying again to control and own her, for falling into a predictable pattern of male behavior, for hinting at but not fulfilling the possibility of creating "a deep and spontaneous mutual attraction" (137), for disappointing *her*.

Eventually, however, Judy gives up her search. Though it's not told, since this is ostensibly the story of Dexter's lost dreams and not Judy's, it can be deduced that Judy kept looking, kept trying any new man in town (and in her trips to Florida and Hot Springs), and finally discarded *her* dreams. "I'm awfully tired of everything," she says late in the story (141). She's tired of those youthful love affairs and youthful lovers and of those "idiotic dance[s]" filled "with those children" (142). She's worn out from fighting men who try to tame and idealize her. Dexter at this late point sees her cry for the first time; something, too, has perhaps broken in her. She asks, "why can't I be happy?" (142). So she marries Lud Simms—his name alone indicates a lack of grace, if not a cavalry captain—who "drinks and runs around," who can be "particularly outrageous," and who "treats [Judy] like the devil" (144). Yet, apparently resigned to not realizing her own dreams, she forgives and perhaps even loves him, and stays home with her children. She never finds a life that is not dominated by children.

Thus, at the end of the story, one can say, as the narrator says about Dexter, that Judy Jones—like many other women in Fitzgerald's fiction and in American society at the time (her name has an Everywoman aspect to it)—also had something in her long ago, a desire for mature camaraderie, for a man who would not try to tame or idealize her, for a life where her passion and vitality would not be resented and curbed, but that thing is gone, and it will come back no more.

Fitzgerald, as McCay has argued, was a "chronicler and critic of the world in which he lived," a world "not entirely of Fitzgerald's fictional making." He was committed, almost to the point of obsession, to transcribing the reality of his times. "More than any other writer," Malcolm Cowley argues, "Fitzgerald had the sense of living in history. He tried hard to catch the color of every passing year: its distinctive slang, its dance steps, its songs (he kept making lists of them in his notebooks), its favorite quarterbacks, and the sort of clothes and emotions its people wore. He felt in the beginning that his own life was not merely typical but representative of a new generation."[20]

The characterization of Judy Jones, then, is a part of Fitzgerald's attempt to bring a representative figure of his generation into literature, a woman, like many women, caught between contradictory forces. To accuse him of being sexist or misogynist because he portrays male characters as bewildered by and at times antagonistic toward unconventional women and because he portrays female characters as oftentimes confused and crippled by this society is the logical equivalent of shooting the messenger. Yet this is the thought process of many critics of Fitzgerald (and of other writers of the time) and one that blinds them to the complexity of Fitzgerald's views of women and his sympathy for their plight.

The failure to understand Fitzgerald's view of Judy Jones is linked to the mistaken impression that Fitzgerald is somehow a part of the reactionary forces that were intent on putting down the New Woman, as the *Norton* editors argue. Fitzgerald has become as misunderstood as Judy Jones herself, and this intellectual sloppiness has resulted in a grievous cheapening and trivialization of one of this country's greatest writers.

NOTES

1. Fryer, "Nicole Warren Diver and Alabama Beggs Knight," 325; Fedo, "Women in the Fiction of F. Scott Fitzgerald," 27; Fetterley, *Resisting Reader*, 94, 96–97, 94; Baym et al., *Norton Anthology of American Literature*, 2:941.
2. McCay, "Fitzgerald's Women," 312; Fryer, "Nicole Warren Diver and Alabama Beggs Knight," 325.
3. Bryer, *Short Stories of F. Scott Fitzgerald*, xiii, xvi; Petry, *Fitzgerald's Craft of Short Fiction*, 1–2.
4. Bruccoli, *Some Sort of Epic Grandeur*, 173; Kuehl, *F. Scott Fitzgerald*, 64; Perosa, *Art of F. Scott Fitzgerald*, 57; Higgins, *F. Scott Fitzgerald*, 60–61; Cross, *F. Scott Fitzgerald*, 73; Butterfield, "'All Very Rich and Sad,'" 102; Fahey, *F. Scott Fitzgerald and the American Dream*, 148; Burhans, "'Magnificently Attune to Life,'" 409, 403.
5. Petry, *Fitzgerald's Craft of Short Fiction*, 123.
6. Divine et al., *America Past and Present*, 574, 543; United States Department of Commerce, *Historical Statistics*, 129, 140.
7. Schlesinger, *Rise of the City*, 156; Divine et al., *America Past and Present*, 654.

8. See Carl Degler's essay, "What Ought to Be and What Was."
9. Chafe, *American Woman*, 95.
10. See Kolb, *Illusion of Life*, 46.
11. Graff, "American Criticism Left and Right," 111.
12. McGovern, " American Woman's Pre–World War I Freedom in Manners and Morals," 255, 242.
13. Fitzgerald, *Letters to His Daughter*, 52, 57.
14. Divine et al., *America Past and Present*, 544.
15. Lewis, *Main Street*, 89; Chafe, *American Dream*, 98; Lynd and Lynd, *Middletown*, 117.
16. Wiebe, *Search for Order*, 44.
17. Fitzgerald, *Stories of F. Scott Fitzgerald*, 128–29. All subsequent page references to "Winter Dreams" are to the 1951 edition and appear parenthetically in the text.
18. Frederic, *Damnation of Theron Ware*, 224; Chopin, *Awakening*, 125; Lewis, *Main Street*, 335.
19. James, *Bostonians*, 931; Fetterley, *Resisting Reader*, 100.
20. McCay, "Fitzgerald's Women," 311; Cowley, "Third Act and Epilogue," 148.

WORKS CITED

Baym, Nina, et. al., eds. *The Norton Anthology of American Literature*. 4th ed. 2 vols. New York: W. W. Norton, 1994.

Bruccoli, Matthew J. *Some Sort of Epic Grandeur: The Life of F. Scott Fitzgerald*. New York: Harcourt Brace Jovanovich, 1981.

Bryer, Jackson R., ed. *The Short Stories of F. Scott Fitzgerald: New Approaches in Criticism*. Madison: University of Wisconsin Press, 1982.

Burhans, Clinton S., Jr. "'Magnificently Attune to Life': The Value of 'Winter Dreams.'" *Studies in Short Fiction* 6 (1969): 401–12

Butterfield, Herbie. "'All Very Rich and Sad': A Decade of Fitzgerald Short Stories." In *Scott Fitzgerald: The Promises of Life*. Ed. A. Robert Lee. New York: St. Martin's Press, 1989. 94–112.

Chafe, William H. *The American Woman: Her Changing Social, Economic, and Political Roles, 1920–1970*. New York: Oxford University Press, 1972.

Chopin, Kate. *The Awakening*. 1899. London: Penguin, 1984.

Cowley, Malcolm. "Third Act and Epilogue." In *F. Scott Fitzgerald: The Man and His Work*. Ed. Alfred Kazin. 1951. New York: Collier, 1962. 147–54.

Cross, K. G. W. *F. Scott Fitzgerald*. New York: Grove Press, 1964.

Degler, Carl. "What Ought to Be and What Was: Woman's Sexuality in the Nineteenth Century." *American Historical Review* 79 (1974): 1467–90.

Divine, Robert A., et al. *America Past and Present*. 3rd ed. New York: HarperCollins, 1991.

Fahey, William A. *F. Scott Fitzgerald and the American Dream*. New York: Thomas Y. Crowell, 1973.

Fedo, David. "Women in the Fiction of F. Scott Fitzgerald." *Ball State University Forum* 21, no. 2 (1980): 26–33.

Fetterley, Judith. *The Resisting Reader: A Feminist Approach to American Fiction.* Bloomington: Indiana University Press, 1978.

Fitzgerald, F. Scott. *Letters to His Daughter.* Ed. Andrew Turnbull. New York: Scribners, 1965.

———. *The Stories of F. Scott Fitzgerald.* New York: Scribners, 1951.

Frederic, Harold. *The Damnation of Theron Ware.* 1896. London: Penguin, 1986.

Fryer, Sarah Beebe. "Nicole Warren Diver and Alabama Beggs Knight: Women on the Threshold of Freedom." *Modern Fiction Studies* 31 (1985): 318–25.

Graff, Gerald. "American Criticism: Left and Right." In *Ideology and Classic American Literature.* Ed. Sacvan Bercovitch and Myra Jehlen. New York: Cambridge University Press, 1986. 99–121.

Higgins, John A. *F. Scott Fitzgerald: A Study of the Stories.* Jamaica, N.Y.: St. John's University Press, 1971.

James, Henry. *The Bostonians.* 1886. In *Henry James: Novels, 1881–1886.* Ed. William T. Stafford. New York: Library of America, 1986. 801–1219.

Kolb, Harold H., Jr. *The Illusion of Life: American Realism as a Literary Form.* Charlottesville: University Press of Virginia, 1969.

Kuehl, John. *F. Scott Fitzgerald: A Study of the Short Fiction.* Boston: Twayne, 1991.

Lewis, Sinclair. *Main Street.* 1920. San Diego: Harcourt, Brace, n.d.

Lynd, Robert S., and Helen Merrell Lynd. *Middletown: A Study of Modern American Culture.* 1929. San Diego: Harcourt, Brace, n.d.

McCay, Mary A. "Fitzgerald's Women: Beyond Winter Dreams." In *American Novelists Revisited: Essays in Feminist Criticism.* Ed. Fritz Fleischmann. Boston: G. K. Hall, 1982. 311–24.

McGovern, James R. "The American Woman's Pre–World War I Freedom in Manners and Morals." In *Our American Sisters: Women in American Life and Thought.* Ed. Jean E. Friedman and William G. Slade. Boston: Allyn and Bacon, 1973. 237–59.

Perosa, Sergio. *The Art of F. Scott Fitzgerald.* Tr. Charles Matz and Sergio Perosa. Ann Arbor: University of Michigan Press, 1965.

Petry, Alice Hall. *Fitzgerald's Craft of Short Fiction: The Collected Stories — 1920 – 1935.* Ann Arbor, Mich.: UMI Research Press, 1989.

Schlesinger, Arthur M. *The Rise of the City, 1878–1898.* Chicago: Quadrangle Books, 1933.

United States Department of Commerce. *Historical Statistics of the United States: Colonial Times to 1970.* Washington, D.C.: Government Printing Office, 1975.

Wiebe, Robert. *The Search for Order, 1877–1920.* New York: Hill and Wang, 1967.

Inside "Outside the Cabinet-Maker's"

JOHN KUEHL

Scott Fitzgerald's short-short story "Outside the Cabinet-Maker's" has
been neglected in part because its availability has been limited. Written in
1927 and published in *Century Magazine* in December 1928 for merely $150
after it had been rejected by seven other magazines, the piece was finally included in *Afternoon of an Author* (1957, 1958), then in two 1963 collections,
The Bodley Head Scott Fitzgerald and *The Fitzgerald Reader*. Both American
volumes were assembled by Arthur Mizener; *Afternoon of an Author* was reis-
sued by Macmillan in 1987 as an inexpensive Scribner Classic. Mizener was
the first critic to assess the story adequately. Writing in *The Sense of Life in the
Modern Novel*, he said:

> "Outside the Cabinet-Maker's" is, both in substance and technique, a wholly
> mature story. Only a writer who had seen that the significant values of experience
> exist in all experience could have said so much with material so magnificently
> homely and familiar; only a writer who had known and could remember what
> it felt like to see and had completely accepted the blindness of middle age could
> have presented that little girl's murderous innocence without romantic irony; only
> a writer with the most delicate sense of how meaning inheres in events could have
> kept his story so unpretentious; only a writer whose dramatic sense was a function
> of his understanding could have managed the ending of this story without leaving
> an impression of technical trickiness.[1]

Another critic, John A. Higgins, has claimed that "Outside the Cabinet-Maker's" is "generally acknowledged as one of [Fitzgerald's] finest short pieces," yet his assertion was based upon brief allusions like Sergio Perosa's one-paragraph analysis of this "beautiful little sketch" in *The Art of F. Scott Fitzgerald*.[2] Even now, thirty-five years after Mizener's evaluation and twenty-eight years after Higgins's claim, there is only one critical essay devoted exclusively to "Outside the Cabinet-Maker's."[3]

A second reason for such neglect is the length of the story. Although written in 1927, it contains only about 1,300 words, thus challenging the usual view concerning Fitzgerald's so-called "late style" — that this emerged during the mid-1930s when *Esquire*, which paid $250 per submission but would accept 2,000 words or less, displaced the *Post*, which paid $2,000–$4,000 per submission but expected 5,000 words or more. Clearly, his economical prose was not necessarily a late development, nor did it supplant the rhetorical prose altogether. The two styles were antithetical: one marked by brevity, objectivity, indirection, simplicity, and dialogue; the other by the reverse of these. Yet they sometimes overlapped, with "Outside the Cabinet-Maker's" appearing in the *Post* era (1928) and the seven-part "Trouble" in the *Esquire* era (1937), for example.

According to Mizener, "Outside the Cabinet-Maker's" "belongs to the period when the Fitzgeralds were living at Ellerslie, in Wilmington, and their daughter was six."[4] There is no reason to doubt him, though, except for an allusion to "les Du Ponts" (141), who resided nearby, the story's cityscape, like its chief characters, remains nameless. Three persons — "the man," "the lady," and "the little girl" — park "at the corner of Sixteenth and some dingy-looking street" (137) one "fine November day" (138). Aside from sporadic references providing Jamesian "solidity of specification," such as Market Street, Mr. Miller, and The Del Upholstery Co., the people are generic (boy, woman, men, "darkies") and the two focal edifices vague. Therefore, the establishment that the three outsiders visit is marked "Cabinet-Maker" and the dwelling that inspires "Daddy's" fairy tale is "a flat in the back of a shop" (138) neither he nor the little girl recognizes. This pervasive anonymity causes the representative nature of the story to transcend its private experiences, though Fitzgerald loads it with references from the actual world such as President Coolidge, Iceland, Miss Television, and the Land of Oz.

Whereas the fairy tale or story-within-a-story is all action, "Outside the Cabinet-Maker's" itself is more structured than plotted, a framework narrative employing Fitzgerald's favorite arrival-departure pattern. The opening frame, during which "The automobile stopped" (137), and the closing frame, during which "They drove off" (141), bracket the fairy tale. Had the first of the story's two spatial breaks occurred after the lady "disappeared up a small stairs" (138) rather than later, the reader would see more plainly how coming and going enclose this embedded yarn. However, the author does remind us of their inextricability when the lady, who otherwise functions mostly within the framework, interrupts the framed material by calling down from the cabinet-maker's upper story, "He's busy. . . . Gosh, what a nice day!" (138) and when the little girl extends the fairy tale into the closing frame. Since the framed material focuses on the latter's relationship with Daddy, this relationship becomes central, as in "Babylon Revisited," where framework narrative and arrival-departure pattern are also used. Though father and daughter both call the ambiguous lady only "you," minimizing her importance, she must be the man's wife and the little girl's mother, for the group evidently constitutes a nuclear family.

The allusion to the "Murphys" (137) in the opening frame probably confirms that the framed fairy tale was inspired by an incident Honoria Murphy Donnelly recorded fifty-six years later in her biography of her parents: "It was always fun when the Fitzgeralds came for dinner. One particular evening, Scott said he had an exciting plan for the three of us, and he took two lead soldiers from his pocket. He told us there was to be a party for Scottie, the Fitzgeralds' four-year-old daughter, at which one of the soldiers, who was secretly a prince, would attempt to rescue a princess he intended to marry. The princess, he explained, was being held prisoner by a wicked witch in a castle, which was guarded by a dragon. The other soldier was a member of the witch's army."[5]

During the published story, Daddy tells the little girl that an Ogre has entrapped the Fairy Princess in the flat behind the shop and has imprisoned the King and Queen "ten thousand miles below the earth" (138); that her release depends upon three stones: "The Prince has already found one stone in President Coolidge's collar-box. He's looking for the second in Iceland. Every time he finds a stone the room where the Princess is kept turns blue" (139); that the King and Queen are now free and the King, along with Witch, soldiers, and fairies, is presently involved; and that one soldier will "put the ice on the Ogre's head and freeze his brains so he can't do any more harm" (140).

Daddy's fictional and Fitzgerald's actual account of this fairy tale are quite similar with regard to setting, characters, and plot. But whereas the lady vanishes in the story, Zelda, her life model, became an important presence in the incident, which was both narrated and enacted. She contributed "a castle . . . made of *papier-maché*" and imitated "the voices of the witch, the princess, and her lady-in-waiting," whose dresses she had spent weeks fashioning, so that Donnelly rightly called this performance "Scott and Zelda's make-believe world."[6]

When Fitzgerald embellished the tale told at the Juan-les-Pins party in "Outside the Cabinet-Maker's," he excluded Zelda (and Honoria — the name he gave to the character modeled on Scottie in "Babylon Revisited") to focus on the central father-daughter relationship. Thus, the fairy tale, originally a mere entertainment, acquired greater significance. To begin with, the man, whose ennui is projected through recurrent yawning, makes the mundane world fabulous because of his love for the little girl. We learn immediately that "The neighborhood was red brick, vague, quiet. There were a few darkies doing something or other up the street and an occasional automobile went by" (138). But soon all this changes as the unfamiliar flat becomes the Princess's prison and various passersby become Ogre, King, Witch, and soldiers in a transformed environment where good and bad fairies appear with magical signs and stones.

His fantasy, which inspires the little girl to employ her own imagination, depresses the man, who "was old enough to know that he would look back to that time — the tranquil street and the pleasant weather and the mystery playing before the child's eyes, mystery which he had created, but whose luster and texture he could never see or touch any more himself. Again he touched his daughter's cheek instead and in payment fitted another small boy and limping man into the story" (140). This painful irony finally ends: "For a moment he closed his eyes and tried to see with her but he couldn't see — those ragged blinds were drawn against him forever" (141).

Unable to derive even vicarious pleasure from this act of creation, the father also fails at keeping it an unconscious vehicle for wish fulfillment. His narration projects the traditional happy ending, with Prince freeing King and Queen as well as Fairy Princess, or, respectively, himself, the lady, and the little girl. However, in the little girl's version, which occurs later, "The King and Queen and Prince were killed and now the Princess is queen" (141).

Daddy, who "had liked his King and Queen and felt that they had been too summarily disposed of," reacts "rather impatiently": "You had to have a heroine." Whereupon the little girl matter-of-factly declares her independence by responding, "She'll marry somebody and make him Prince" (141). This exchange is prefigured on at least three occasions in the framed material, with the father playing thwarted suitor and the daughter incipient femme fatale:

"Listen," said the man to the little girl, "I love you."
"I love you too," said the little girl, smiling politely. (138)

. . . He looked at the little girl. "You're my good fairy."

"Yes. Look, Daddy! What is that man?" (140)

"Oh, I love you," he said.

"I know, Daddy," she answered abstractedly. (141)

Even when a child is more receptive to her father, she must, through the inexorable process of time, reject him as most important male. The following conversation between Charles and Honoria Wales in "Babylon Revisited," published three years after "Outside the Cabinet-Maker's," illustrates this:

"Daddy, I want to come and live with you," she said suddenly.

His heart leaped; he had wanted it to come like this.

"Aren't you perfectly happy?"

"Yes, but I love you better than anybody. And you love me better than anybody, don't you, now that mummy's dead?"

"Of course I do. But you won't always like me best, honey. You'll grow up and meet somebody your own age and go marry him and forget you ever had a daddy."

"Yes, that's true," she agreed tranquilly.[7]

A lesser writer might have focused on the father-daughter relationship as an end in itself, but Fitzgerald, the consummate artist, invokes this relationship in both stories to convey larger concerns. In "Babylon Revisited," where there are numerous stock-market allusions, "selling short" tacitly equates public financial and private moral transactions; protagonist and market collapse together as inseparable entities, for emotional bankruptcy (*crack-up*) mirrors economic bankruptcy (*crash*). While the world at large recovered from its public depression, "Good Time Charlie" Wales — representative of boom and bust — occupied a sanitarium. Eventually, though affluent again, he cannot recuperate from his private depression until he regains the child he lost — along with his wife and his money — through dissipation.

Whereas "Babylon Revisited" uses the father-daughter relationship to dramatize a historical crisis, its predecessor uses it to dramatize the universal predicament of human loneliness. Accordingly, the first brief paragraph of "Outside the Cabinet-Maker's" introduces familial separation: "The automobile stopped at the corner of Sixteenth and some dingy-looking street. The lady got out. The man and the little girl stayed in the car" (137).

Before entering the shop "lettered 'Cabinet-Maker'" (138), where she will remain until the end of the framed material, this "lady" carries on a conversation in French with the man, thus excluding the little girl, who protests. But they ignore her, presumably because the purpose of their visit here is to purchase a surprise gift doll's house for the little girl, although the phrase "*les maisons de poupée"* (141) is not uttered and the price not mentioned until the lady returns. Meanwhile, disenchanted Daddy courts the little girl as his Prince courts the Fairy Princess. She finally disposes of both parents, slaying the King/Prince (father/suitor) and Queen (mother). Then their innocent child boldly declares: "now the Princess is queen" (141).

Fitzgerald's *mise en scène* subtly reinforces his ironic pattern of familial alienation. After the lady goes upstairs, father and daughter view their desolate environment. The unfamiliar flat that inspires his tale is hidden behind "curtains" and "a loose shutter," where "part of a yellow dress" (138) becomes the Princess. The only human contact transpiring in this neighborhood involves a small boy (Ogre) outside the flat and a woman (Witch) inside, whose attempts to communicate are abortive. When nobody answers his knock, "he didn't seem . . . to be greatly disappointed." And when he calls "an unintelligible word" at the window, "the crisp wind" blows her answer away. The chalk pictures the small boy draws are interpreted by Daddy and his daughter as "magic signs." Other people appear, including a jeweler's clerk and a man carrying ice, but none of them connects. For instance, two men who become "King's soldiers" (140) silently "crossed the street ahead and passed out of sight" (139).

"Outside the Cabinet-Maker's" resembles the stories in *Dubliners* (1922), a book Fitzgerald ranked among "the great English classics," writing on the back cover, "I am interested in the individual only in his rel [relation] to society. We have wondered [*sic*] in imaginary lonliness [*sic*] for a hundred years." He had already published "Absolution" (1924), which was obviously influenced by "The Sisters" and "Araby," so this similarity should surprise no one.[8] His 1928 piece could be considered a Joycean epiphany too. It is static as well as brief. Three anonymous persons park before an anonymous shop in an anonymous town on an unspecified fall day. Except for their errand, nothing actually happens to this nuclear family prior to its departure. Daddy and daughter are frozen in time like the archetypal fairy tale they jointly create, or the doll's house — another replication of domestic life — produced by another artificer.

During the closing frame, one can perceive the true significance of Fitzgerald's seemingly trivial situation, since there, if nowhere else, "its soul, its whatness leaps to us from the vestment of its appearance."[9] "Outside the Cabinet-Maker's" ends with a paragraph directly projecting the solitariness of human existence implied throughout the text. Here, each character is preoccupied with his or her own world: "They rode on abstractedly. The lady thought about the doll's house, for she had been poor and had never had one as a child, the man thought about how he almost had a million dollars and the little girl thought about the odd doings on the dingy street that they had left behind" (141).

These three lonely people, whose point of origin remains unknown, thus depart for an equally obscure destination, leaving us to ponder one of Scott Fitzgerald's most neglected and most brilliant short stories.

NOTES

1. Mizener, *Sense of Life in the Modern Novel*, 189–90.
2. Higgins, *F. Scott Fitzgerald*, 102; Perosa, *Art of F. Scott Fitzgerald*, 95.
3. Grenberg, "'Outside the Cabinet-Maker's': Fitzgerald's 'Ode to a Nightingale.'" My approach to the story is quite different from Grenberg's.
4. Fitzgerald, *Afternoon of an Author*, 137. All subsequent references to "Outside the Cabinet-Maker's" are to the 1987 edition and appear parenthetically in the text.
5. Donnelly, *Sara and Gerald*, 26.
6. Ibid., 26–27. This "make-believe world" is frequently alluded to in Eleanor Lanahan's *Scottie, The Daughter of . . . : The Life of Frances Scott Fitzgerald Lanahan Smith*, especially in chapter 1, "A Golden Childhood."
7. Fitzgerald, *Babylon Revisited and Other Stories*, 218.
8. Kuehl, *F. Scott Fitzgerald*, 57–64.
9. Joyce, *Stephen Hero*, 213.

WORKS CITED

Donnelly, Honoria Murphy, with Richard N. Billings. *Sara and Gerald: Villa America and After*. New York: Times Books, 1982.

Fitzgerald, F. Scott. *Afternoon of an Author: A Selection of Uncollected Stories and Essays*. Ed. Arthur Mizener. 1957. New York: Macmillan, 1987.

———. *Babylon Revisited and Other Stories*. New York: Macmillan, 1987.

Grenberg, Bruce L. "'Outside the Cabinet-Maker's': Fitzgerald's 'Ode to a Nightingale.'" In *New Essays on F. Scott Fitzgerald's Neglected Stories*. Ed. Jackson R. Bryer. Columbia: University of Missouri Press, 1996. 118–29.

Higgins, John A. *F. Scott Fitzgerald: A Study of the Stories*. Jamaica, N.Y.: St. John's University Press, 1971.

Joyce, James. *Stephen Hero*. New York: New Directions, 1944.

Kuehl, John. *F. Scott Fitzgerald: A Study of the Short Fiction*. Boston: Twayne, 1991.

Lanahan, Eleanor. *Scottie, the Daughter of . . . : The Life of Frances Scott Fitzgerald Lanahan Smith*. New York: HarperCollins, 1993.

Mizener, Arthur. *The Sense of Life in the Modern Novel*. Boston: Houghton Mifflin, 1964.

Perosa, Sergio. *The Art of F. Scott Fitzgerald*. Tr. by Charles Matz and Sergio Perosa. Ann Arbor: University of Michigan Press, 1965.

Whose "Babylon Revisited" Are We Teaching?

Cowley's Fortunate Corruption—

and Others Not So Fortunate

BARBARA SYLVESTER

Although F. Scott Fitzgerald's novels have long benefited from the crusading efforts of textual critic Matthew J. Bruccoli, Fitzgerald's short stories, most of them published initially in popular magazines of the 1920s and 1930s, have received relatively little textual attention. "Babylon Revisited," the story generally acknowledged to be the best of several short masterpieces,[1] is customarily reprinted in two different versions, one partially corrupt, the other marred by what I will suggest was a transmission error at Scribners. Yet each version cites the supposedly authoritative text of the story as printed in *Taps at Reveille.* The textual variants not only belie Fitzgerald's reputation for careful craftsmanship, but, more startling, also offer contradictory details that confuse a crucial thematic issue: the change in Charlie Wales occasioned by his ability to identify a unifying purpose in his life.

The most important substantive variant occurs in the last line of Charlie Wales's early rumination on his commitment to guide his daughter and his belief in the sustaining value of character: "Everything else wore out."[2] The line is printed thus in the Macmillan anthology and in *The American Tradition in Literature,* as well as in many other books used in our classrooms. Ironically, these collections and the many scholarly studies using this version of the line imply that they cite the 1935 edition of *Taps at Reveille*, edited by Fitzgerald personally. But the word "else" is in fact an accretion, silently added in Malcolm Cowley's 1951 collection, *The Stories of F. Scott Fitzgerald*. In *Taps at Reveille* the line reads simply, "Everything wore out."[3]

The Cowley insertion is thematically essential, of course, and supports Fitzgerald's apparent intention. If Charlie Wales believed that *everything* "wore out," he could not be thinking, in the story's concluding paragraph, that "he wanted his child, and nothing was much good now, *beside that fact*" (*Taps* 341; emphasis added). The very point of the story is that Charlie Wales is a changed man precisely because he can now identify an ordering purpose in his life. Adversity has taught him that in the twentieth century all accomplishments are transitory or illusory except for the commitment to human relationships, specifically to the protective and shaping parental relationship taken for granted in an earlier age. That is a commitment — a value — that does not wear out. The story's conclusion implies that Charlie may not actually get custody of his child, may never stop being "so alone" (*Taps* 341). But even so, he has discovered a commitment to something worth trying for. Everything "else" passes, but that commitment gives him structure in his defeat. And it is this stripped-down perspective that allows Wales to demonstrate grace under the pressure of modern reality, making "Babylon Revisited" the equal of Ernest Hemingway's finest portrayals of bleak redemption.

One wonders, therefore, how Fitzgerald could have allowed this contradiction in the essential thrust of his greatest short story. That it is an inadvertency, as I believe, can be partially accounted for by a review of Fitzgerald's circumstances and work habits during the times when he produced his original texts: the revised typescript he sent to the *Saturday Evening Post*, the published *Post* version of 1931, and the revised version published in the *Taps* collection in 1935. Since much of the literary criticism of "Babylon Revisited" deals with its autobiographical nature, such a review may be especially appropriate. Fitzgerald has left behind enough material to allow us to fix almost exactly the date of his composition of "Babylon Revisited." Following his usual practice of writing a short story in "one jump [day] or three," Fitzgerald evidently started and completed "Babylon Revisited" in Paris in December of 1930. He wrote in longhand, sent the story to a stenographer to be typed, penciled in final revisions on the completed typescript, and mailed it to his agent, Harold Ober, in New York. The Fitzgerald-Ober correspondence confirms that the revised typescript and letter arrived in Ober's office on January 2, 1931.[4]

It is remarkable that Fitzgerald could write at all during what must have been an unusually painful year. In April, Zelda Fitzgerald had suffered the first of the mental breakdowns that would continue until her death. She was in and out of hospitals and clinics throughout 1930 and most of 1931. Pressing hard to secure cash for her treatment, Fitzgerald wrote seven stories in 1930, one of the last being "Babylon Revisited." This important story led off the February 21, 1931, *Post* issue with a front-page, full-page illustration, traditionally a mark of the value of a story.[5]

Soon after the publication of *Tender Is the Night* on April 12, 1934, Scribners requested from Fitzgerald a collection of short stories to publish in the fall. Although Fitzgerald agreed to a fall 1934 publication date, he repeatedly delayed the necessary work. Initially, he had conceived big plans for the collection,[6] but his work on the volume was impeded by his deepening depression both over Zelda's continuing illness and over the poor reception of *Tender Is the Night*. Amid mounting debts and increasing drinking bouts, he eventually decided on the stories, arranged and revised them, and sent them off. In March 1935, *Taps at Reveille* was finally published.

No documentary record survives of Fitzgerald's revisions to "Babylon Revisited" for the *Taps* collection. But the evidence suggests that the puzzling substantive variant evolved through either an initial oversight by Fitzgerald or an error of transmission at Scribners. In making the revisions, Fitzgerald deleted more than half of the original passage dealing with Charlie Wales's meditation on Honoria and his value to her as a parent. The full passage, in both the 1930 typescript and the published 1931 *Post* version, catalogs the traditional social values children could no longer receive from their parents:

> He thought he knew what to do for her. He believed in character, he wanted to jump back a whole generation and trust in character again as the eternally valuable element. Everything wore out now. Parents expected genius, or at least brilliance, and both the forcing of children and the fear of forcing them, the fear of warping natural abilities, were poor substitutes for that long careful watchfulness, that checking and balancing and reckoning of accounts, the end of which was that there should be no slipping below a certain level of duty and integrity. That was what the elders had been unable to teach plausibly since the great break between the generations ten or twelve years ago . . .[7]

For *Taps at Reveille*, Fitzgerald deleted the two long sentences following "Everything wore out now." The deletion is aesthetically useful because the didactic passage slows the quick flow of the scene. But Fitzgerald made the cut for a more important reason. He had published one of those sentences, altered only slightly, in book 3 of *Tender Is the Night*: "He managed to reach them over the heads of employees on the principle that *both the forcing of children and the fear of forcing them were inadequate substitutes for that long, careful watchfulness, the checking and balancing and reckoning of accounts, to the end that there should be no slip beyond a certain level of duty."* [8] We know that Fitzgerald regularly culled his magazine stories for passages to use in his novels. Given his horror of recycling "used" passages in further publications of the stories, he customarily deleted any "used" passage and wrote a new one. There is no reason to doubt that he intended to revise and replace this passage in "Babylon Revisited" and so remedy the inconsistency left by the deletion.

In the context of the complete *Post* passage, the sentence "Everything wore out now" does not contradict the thrust of the story, as it does when it stands alone. In the original context, it is clear that "now" refers to present-day values, while Charlie Wales adheres to the values of an earlier generation. Including the word "now" somewhat modifies the contradiction occurring otherwise. Furthermore, the omission in the *Taps* version even of the final word "now" reinforces the suspicion that Fitzgerald meant to tinker with the sentence. Of course, it is also possible that the "now" was inadvertently deleted during the transmission process at Scribners, an accident not unlikely given the deliberate deletion of the lines immediately succeeding the word. At that time, Fitzgerald would not likely have caught an inadvertent deletion because he was unwilling to examine the second galley proofs of *Taps at Reveille*. We know that he blew up at a "dumb" copy editor in December 1934 and complained to Maxwell Perkins at Scribners: "I did not *want* a second galley and did not ask for it—these stories have been corrected *once* for myself, *once* for the *Post* and the third time on your first galleys and *that is all I can do.*" [9] Since no documentary record survives of Fitzgerald's revisions for the *Taps* collection, the chances are we will never know the exact details.

However, we do know that even during this turbulent period of Zelda's accelerating mental degeneration and his own despondency over the poor reception of *Tender Is the Night,* Fitzgerald retained his earlier belief in human character and a parent's responsibility for shaping it in a child. Dick Diver echoes that belief in *Tender Is the Night:* "The factor that gave purposefulness to the period was the children." And Fitzgerald himself stated the belief clearly in a 1935 newspaper interview: "This generation should be held close to whatever elements of character we have been able to find and develop in ourselves." [10]

Even though Fitzgerald's views on purpose and character are expressed by Charlie Wales in "Babylon Revisited," critics have often emphasized the protagonist's disillusionment rather than his hope. Critics have made much of

Fitzgerald's 1939 remark, "You see, I not only announced the birth of my young illusions in *This Side of Paradise* but pretty much the death of them in some of my last *Post* stories like 'Babylon Revisited.'" Walter Allen's statement exemplifies the typical view of both Fitzgerald and the story: "He is the poet of regret for opportunities lost and of remorse for action wrongly or unheedingly taken. In this respect, his masterpiece is probably the tragic 'Babylon Revisited.' . . . It is an intolerably moving story."[11] Yet it is a moving story precisely because it is a story in which hope and renewed purpose register more powerfully than regret. Evidence for such authorial intention resounds in the story itself and in the biographical details of Fitzgerald's life. The emphasis on the perseverance of the protagonist, Charlie Wales, bespeaks the belief that became increasingly important to Fitzgerald as he composed "Babylon Revisited" and tried to hold the remnants of his own family together during the disastrous early part of the decade of the 1930s. He summed up his feelings for the year September 1930 to September 1931 (he began and ended his annual year always in September, the month of his birth) and duly recorded it in his annual ledger: "Waiting. From Darkness to Hope."[12]

Thus, Cowley's insertion years later of the clarifying word "else" is the kind of repair Fitzgerald himself would have made at the time, we must assume, had he not been revising during one of the most distracting periods in his hectic life. The insertion is a fortunate corruption, therefore. But it is a corruption; and because it was done silently, it has concealed a contradiction in the *Taps* version of "Babylon Revisited" that might otherwise have led us to appreciate, more than we have, the theme of hope in the story.

The fact that Cowley's emendation in this instance almost certainly honors authorial intention—and certainly honors the intention of the work—does not mean that the reader should be sanguine about this editor's interference in general. We know from his own remarks in a 1951 *Saturday Review of Literature* article that Cowley considered Fitzgerald to be "not a thinker" but rather a "poet who never learned some of the elementary rules for writing prose." Such an attitude would naturally convince Cowley that he had a right to "clean up" Fitzgerald's manuscripts without informing his readers. Matthew J. Bruccoli reports that Cowley's 1951 edition of *Tender Is the Night* includes "more than 900 variants from the first edition—but less than thirty of these he [Cowley] identifies in his notes." Moreover, Bruccoli warns that Cowley's "liberal position on silent emendation" leaves the unwary reader of the novel with "something less than straight Fitzgerald."[13]

This warning is equally relevant for readers of the Cowley version of "Babylon Revisited." For despite the "fortunate" emendation we have just observed, other Cowley emendations serve to undercut, albeit in a minor way, thematic issues in the story. William White has noted Cowley's omission of an entire line.[14] In both Fitzgerald's typescript and *Taps*, Charlie Wales replies firmly to his sister-in-law's bitter suggestion that he may start "throwing away money" again: "'Oh, no,' he said. 'I've learned. I worked hard for ten years, you know — until I got lucky in the market, like so many people. Terribly lucky. It didn't seem any use working any more, so I quit. It won't happen again'" (*Taps* 333). Cowley omits the penultimate line: "It didn't seem any use working any more, so I quit."[15] Without this line, the passage merely suggests that Charlie will not get lucky again or will not throw his money around. With the line, the passage highlights the fact that Charlie will not *quit* again, will not quit either working or persevering in his purpose. With the line included, the passage enriches our understanding of Charlie's shift from passive to active participation in shaping his life, and underscores the emphasis on his newfound discipline and sense of purpose. The overall cumulative effect, then, of such silent emendation by Cowley is to corrupt the text in ways that obscure not only Fitzgerald's precise thematic concerns but also his genuine strengths as a craftsman.

Fitzgerald also suffered at the hands of printers and copy editors at the Curtis Publishing Company and at Scribners. Many of Fitzgerald's perfectly grammatical and artistically rhythmical sentences were arbitrarily modified by copy editors at the *Saturday Evening Post* to conform to the Curtis in-house style, a style that Fitzgerald never followed, despite his ten-year association with the *Post*. Instead, Fitzgerald frequently used rhetorical punctuation to accentuate meaning in a line, for he believed intensely, as John Kuehl has observed, that "form and economy are essential to good writing."[16] The evidence also suggests that many changes in the *Taps* version of "Babylon Revisited" were errors of transmission occurring at Scribners when Fitzgerald's heavily revised proofs were set into print. Two or three examples of the progression of "Babylon Revisited" from Fitzgerald's original typescript through publication first in the *Post* and then in the Scribners *Taps at Reveille* will suffice to illustrate typical corruptions, both with single words and with punctuation. Although many might be considered minor, they often distort or destroy subtle reinforcement of the story's themes, thereby obscuring the craftsmanship of an artist who had a "healthy respect for the single word and the single line."[17]

The subtle shifts in meaning brought about by changing a single word are exemplified in an early line of dialogue that takes place when Charlie Wales returns to the Ritz Bar after a long absence. In Fitzgerald's revised typescript, Charlie Wales asks the barman, "And the snow-bird?"[18] According to the *OED*, the word "snowbird" was first noted in 1914 as a slang term for a cocaine addict. Although Fitzgerald should have omitted the hyphen, his spelling is more accurate than is the *Post*'s "correction" in making it two words: "snow bird." [19] The additional *Taps* "correction" adds capitals— "Snow Bird" — designating a proper nickname and detracting attention from the character's drug use (*Taps* 321). But there can be no doubt that Fitzgerald used the word "snow-bird" with its slang meaning in mind. In "The Hotel Child," a story published just one month earlier than "Babylon Revisited," he refers to cocaine users. By using the slang term "snow-bird" in "Babylon Revisited," Fitzgerald quickly associates the opening setting, the Ritz Bar, with a "Babylon," where the usual connotations evoked by natural snow—whiteness, freshness, purity—are perverted into those of darkness and debauchery connected with drug addiction. Further, the term reverberates in the story as the details of Helen's final wanderings through a snow-filled night are recounted; there, too, the natural snow is both beautiful and terrible and hastens Helen's death. It is inconceivable, then, that Fitzgerald, given his belief that *"a single word . . . can throw a new emphasis or give a new value to the exact same scene or setting,"* [20] would have changed the sense of "snow-bird" by adding those capital letters as he revised "Babylon Revisited" for the *Taps at Reveille* collection. But artistic reasons aside, we know that Fitzgerald never bothered with accidentals when he revised. Numerous biographers have observed that Fitzgerald's care for accidentals — matters of spelling and punctuation — went into his first preparation of a story. His later revisions of printed texts consisted solely of substantive changes.

Editors who "fixed" Fitzgerald's spelling also took liberties with his punctuation. A typical example of Fitzgerald's rhetorical punctuation occurs in a passage describing Charlie Wales's interior monologue as he rides in a taxi along the Left Bank: [21] "'I spoiled this city for myself,' he thought. 'I didn't realize it but the days came along one after another and then two years were gone and everything was gone and I was gone.'" [22] By omitting commas, Fitzgerald allows no resting places for the reader, forces the reader to move steadily in lockstep through the series, and thus simulates the character's feeling. For here, after all, Charlie Wales is reflecting on the steady march of time and the relentlessness of its destructive power. But despite the optional nature of comma use in such a sentence, the *Post* copy editors added commas, conventionally breaking the long series of coordinate clauses: "'I didn't realize it, but the days came along one after another, and then two years were gone, and everything was gone, and I was gone.'" [23] The resulting tidy breaks in the sentence completely obliterate the accentuated meaning and heightened intensity created by Fitzgerald.

The most poignant rhetorical punctuation marks in "Babylon Revisited" are the exclamation points used to punctuate the child Honoria's greeting of her father: "Daddy! . . . Oh, daddy, daddy, daddy, daddy, dads, dads, dads!" (*Taps* 323). Although all printed versions understandably use the normal exclamation mark, the ones in Fitzgerald's typescript are meticulously hand-drawn, double the height of the line.[24] These exclamation marks highlight the daughter's passionate anticipation of her father and her magnified expectations of him. But the outsized marks also emphasize, by contrast, the father's sense of diminished possibilities as dramatized by Charlie's reflection on time in the preceding passage.

These are only some of the many variants in accidentals in the printed texts. Some are matters of grammar and syntax that intimate that Fitzgerald was not especially meticulous about the elementary rules of grammar. But at least some of the grammatical errors occurred when words were accidentally dropped in transmission. And the evidence suggests that Fitzgerald was an infinitely better grammarian than Cowley would have us believe.

The final effect of such corruptions, whether occurring intentionally through the actions of editors or unintentionally through accidents of transmission, has been to compromise Fitzgerald's reputation as a craftsman and to obscure his precise thematic concerns. Moreover, Cowley's silence long masked the actual chain of events editorial specialists needed to know in order properly to establish any text. Although Lindfors, McCollom, and White have identified other inconsistencies between the *Post* and *Taps* versions of the story, neither they nor other readers of the *Taps* version have publicly emphasized discussion of the crucial thematic contradiction in its text.[25] In his 1989 edition of the stories, Matthew J. Bruccoli returns to the *Taps* version, thus deleting Cowley's accretion. The line in the Bruccoli edition reads "Everything wore out,"[26] but Bruccoli offers no explanation for the specific thematic contradiction thus reinstated.

In "Babylon Revisited," we must not only identify but also understand the thematic inconsistency so long masked by Cowley's fortunate corruption. To do so is to gain a lesson in the tricks of oversight our ordering minds can play on us as we read a text. Early readers must simply have glossed over the contradiction Cowley noticed and silently eliminated. Whatever our editorial philosophy, Cowley's emendation leads us to contemplate a more representative text of "Babylon Revisited" than we might otherwise have envisioned. But we should also recognize the many unfortunate corruptions that plague Fitzgerald's classic short story, the story most often anthologized and taught in our colleges and universities. The presence of corruptions, both fortunate and unfortunate, underscores the need for a critical edition of Fitzgerald's stories, an edition that will fully represent Fitzgerald's artistry to the countless readers who encounter him *first* in his short fiction.[27]

APPENDIX

The "Babylon Revisited" paragraph is printed below, as it appears in *Taps at Reveille*. Following the paragraph are the various versions of its ending as found in Fitzgerald's revised typescript, the *Post*, *Taps*, and Cowley's edition.

At dinner he couldn't decide whether Honoria was most like him or her mother. Fortunate if she didn't combine the traits of both that had brought them to disaster. A great wave of protectiveness went over him. He thought he knew what to do for her. He believed in character; he wanted to jump back a whole generation and trust in character again as the eternally valuable element. Everything wore out.

FSF typescript Dec. 1930	*Post* Feb. 1931	*Taps* Mar. 1935	Cowley ed. 1951
Everything wore out now. Parents expected genius or at least brilliance, and both the forcing of children and the fear of forcing them, the fear of warping natural abilities, were poor substitutes for that long careful watchfulness, that checking and balancing and reckoning of accounts, the end of which was that there should be no slipping below a certain level of duty and integrity. That was what the elders had been unable to teach plausibly	Everything wore out now. Parents expected genius, or at least brilliance, and both the forcing of children and the fear of forcing them, the fear of warping natural abilities, were poor substitutes for that long careful watchfulness, that checking and balancing and reckoning of accounts, the end of which was that there should be no slipping below a certain level of duty and integrity. That was	Everything wore out.	Everything else wore out.

FSF typescript	*Post*	*Taps*	Cowley ed.
Dec. 1930	Feb. 1931	Mar. 1935	1951
since the great	what the elders		
break between	had been un-		
the generations	able to teach		
ten or twelve	plausibly since		
years ago . . .	the great break		
	between the		
	generations ten		
	or twelve years		
	ago.		

NOTES

1. See Bruccoli, *Some Sort of Epic Grandeur*, 309.
2. Fitzgerald, *Stories of F. Scott Fitzgerald*, 388. This 1951 edition, assembled by Malcolm Cowley, has long been considered the standard edition of the stories.
3. Fitzgerald, *Taps at Reveille*, 325. Except where otherwise noted, all subsequent page references to the *Taps at Reveille* text of "Babylon Revisited" are to the 1960 edition, are cited as *Taps*, and appear parenthetically in the text.
4. Turnbull, *Letters*, 93; Bruccoli, *As Ever*, 175.
5. Gundell, *Writing—From Idea to Printed Page*, 340.
6. Kuehl and Bryer, *Dear Scott/Dear Max*, 195–202.
7. Fitzgerald, *F. Scott Fitzgerald Manuscripts* VI, 427. Note that the ellipsis is part of Fitzgerald's typescript. The *Post* changed the ellipsis to a period. See the appendix to this essay for a copy of the paragraph under discussion and for comparison of all versions of its ending: those from Fitzgerald's revised typescript, from the *Saturday Evening Post*, from *Taps at Reveille*, and from Cowley's 1951 collection of the stories.
8. Fitzgerald, *Tender Is the Night*, 257; emphasis added. Given the different page numbers in the many editions of *Tender Is the Night*, note that the sentence is found in the second paragraph of book 3, chapter 4.
9. Kuehl and Bryer, *Dear Scott/Dear Max*, 215–16.
10. Fitzgerald, *Tender Is the Night*, 257; Buttitta, "'The Less the Parents of Today Try to Tell Their Children,'" 294.
11. Turnbull, *Letters*, 588; Allen, *Short Story in English*, 141–42.
12. Fitzgerald, *F. Scott Fitzgerald's Ledger*, 185.
13. Cowley, "Fitzgerald," 10; Bruccoli, "Material for a Centenary Edition," 178, 179.
14. White, "Two Versions."
15. Fitzgerald, *Stories*, 395. In the manuscript, the passage reads: "'Oh, no,' he said, 'I've learned. I worked hard for ten years, you know—until I got lucky in the market like so many people. Terribly lucky—it didn't seem any use working any more,

so I quit. It won't happen again" (Fitzgerald, *F. Scott Fitzgerald Manuscripts VI,* 449).

16. Kuehl, "Scott Fitzgerald's Critical Opinions," 22.
17. Ibid., 25.
18. Fitzgerald, *F. Scott Fitzgerald Manuscripts VI,* 417.
19. Fitzgerald, "Babylon Revisited," 3.
20. Turnbull, *Letters,* 540–41; emphasis added.
21. For distinctions between rhetorical and syntactical punctuation, see Shillingsburg, *Scholarly Editing in the Computer Age,* 59–67.
22. Fitzgerald, *F. Scott Fitzgerald Manuscripts VI,* 421.
23. Fitzgerald, "Babylon Revisited," 4.
24. Fitzgerald, *F. Scott Fitzgerald Manuscripts VI,* 422.
25. In addition to White, see also Lindfors, "Paris Revisited," and McCollum, "'Babylon Revisited' Revisited."
26. Fitzgerald, *Short Stories,* 619.
27. Although discussion of the disciplinary debates concerning scholarly editing does not fall within the purview of this essay, I believe that certain editorial principles should guide preparation of a critical edition of "Babylon Revisited." G. Thomas Tanselle explains these principles in "Problems and Accomplishments in the Editing of the Novel." Tanselle applauds the editorial theory used by the Center for Editions of American Authors (CEAA) to produce their outstanding critical editions:

> The editorial theory behind them is Greg's rationale of copy-text: as a rule, therefore, the text chosen as the basis for the newly edited text is the fair-copy manuscript or, if it does not survive, the earliest printed edition based on that manuscript. If there is convincing evidence that an author gave careful attention to all details of a later edition, that edition would be the copy-text; but normally authors, even when they make changes in words (substantives) in later editions, do not reexamine all the punctuation, capitalization, and spelling (accidentals) with the result that later editions generally exhibit a progressive deterioration of accidentals. An editor who accepts the accidentals of the manuscript or earliest edition and emends that text with authoritative revisions from later editions is recognizing this divided authority. (333)

Given the publication history of "Babylon Revisited" and our knowledge of Fitzgerald's revising habits, I would use Fitzgerald's revised typescript as copy-text, emend that text with authoritative substantive revisions from the *Taps at Reveille* edition, and account as fully as possible for each such emendation.

WORKS CITED

Allen, Walter. *The Short Story in English.* New York: Oxford University Press, 1981.
Bruccoli, Matthew J. "Material for a Centenary Edition of *Tender Is the Night.*" *Studies in Bibliography* 17 (1964): 177–93.

————. *Some Sort of Epic Grandeur: The Life of F. Scott Fitzgerald*. New York: Harcourt Brace Jovanovich, 1981.

Bruccoli, Matthew J., ed., with the assistance of Jennifer McCabe Atkinson. *As Ever, Scott Fitz—: Letters Between F. Scott Fitzgerald and His Literary Agent, Harold Ober—1919–1940*. Philadelphia: J. B. Lippincott, 1972.

Buttitta, Anthony. "'The Less the Parents of Today Try to Tell Their Children, the More Effective They Can Be in Making Them Believe in a Few Old Truths.'" In *F. Scott Fitzgerald: in His Own Time: A Miscellany*. Ed. Matthew J. Bruccoli and Jackson R. Bryer. Kent, Ohio: Kent State University Press, 1971. 292–94.

Cowley, Malcolm. "Fitzgerald: The Double Man." *Saturday Review of Literature*, February 24, 1951, 9–10, 42–44.

Fitzgerald, F. Scott. "Babylon Revisited." *Saturday Evening Post*, February 21, 1931, 3–5, 82–84.

————. *F. Scott Fitzgerald Manuscripts VI, part 2: "The Vegetable," Stories, and Articles*. Introduced and arranged by Matthew J. Bruccoli. New York: Garland, 1991.

————. *F. Scott Fitzgerald's Ledger, A Facsimile*. Washington, D.C.: NCR/Microcard Editions, 1972.

————. *The Short Stories of F. Scott Fitzgerald*. Ed. Matthew J. Bruccoli. New York: Scribners, 1989.

————. *The Stories of F. Scott Fitzgerald*. New York: Scribners, 1951.

————. *Taps at Reveille*. 1935. New York: Scribners, 1960.

————. *Tender Is the Night*. 1934. New York: Scribners, 1960.

Gundell, Glenn. *Writing—From Idea to Printed Page*. New York: Greenwood, 1969.

Kuehl, John. "Scott Fitzgerald's Critical Opinions." In *Profile of F. Scott Fitzgerald*. Ed. Matthew J. Bruccoli. Columbus, Ohio: Charles E. Merrill, 1971. 21–39.

Kuehl, John, and Jackson R. Bryer, eds. *Dear Scott/Dear Max: The Fitzgerald-Perkins Correspondence*. New York: Scribners, 1971.

Lindfors, Bernth. "Paris Revisited." *Fitzgerald Newsletter* 16 (1962): 4.

McCollum, Kenneth. "'Babylon Revisited' Revisited." *Fitzgerald/Hemingway Annual 1971*: 314–16.

Shillingsburg, Peter L. *Scholarly Editing in the Computer Age*. Athens: University of Georgia Press, 1986.

Tanselle, G. Thomas. "Problems and Accomplishments in the Editing of the Novel." *Studies in the Novel* 7 (1975): 323–60.

Turnbull, Andrew, ed. *The Letters of F. Scott Fitzgerald*. New York: Scribners, 1963.

White, William. "Two Versions of F. Scott Fitzgerald's 'Babylon Revisited': A Textual and Bibliographical Study." *Papers of the Bibliographical Society of America* 60 (1966): 439–52.

————. "'The Text of 'Babylon Revisited.'" *Fitzgerald Newsletter* 28 (Winter 1965): 4–7.

Art and Autobiography in Fitzgerald's "Babylon Revisited"

RICHARD ALLAN DAVISON

"Babylon Revisited" is F. Scott Fitzgerald's most acclaimed short story. That it is also one of his best is due to his brilliant stylistic and structural control[1] and the haunting complexity of the main character, Charlie Wales, alias Charles J. Wales of Prague. In his creation of a character whose ambivalences encompass hope, courage, nostalgia, anger, restraint, self-pity, pathos, regeneration, resignation, and self-destructive tragedy — virtually everything but humor — Fitzgerald has drawn more heavily from his own life experiences than critics have acknowledged. Fitzgerald's letters and essays about an analogous period in his life reflect his own agonized mind and demonstrate his deep sympathy for Wales, who is, more than most of Fitzgerald's characters, his alter ego. A 1979 interview with Fitzgerald's daughter, Scottie Fitzgerald Smith, and new information from one of Scottie's childhood friends and playmates reinforce these strong autobiographical overtones and undercurrents in "Babylon Revisited."

In her 1982 memoir, the daughter of Fitzgerald's friends Gerald and Sara Murphy, Honoria Murphy Donnelly, recalled:

Mother expressed her discomfort at being subjected to Scott's "analysis, subanalysis, and criticism," which she found "on the whole unfriendly." The purpose of Scott's scrutiny, she soon realized, was to gather material for characterizations in his writing, which in my parents' case appeared in *Tender Is the Night*. Mother resented being used in such a way. No matter how fond she was of Scott—and her affection for both Scott and Zelda was very genuine—she believed that her privacy had been violated.

I too was a subject of Scott's analytical approach. I was only eight in the summer of 1926, but I well remember him as a man, very handsome in a delicate way, who would stare at me and ask penetrating questions. Why, he insisted on knowing, did I like the color red. Because my dress is red, or because I like the pink and red flowers in the garden, I would reply in my struggling way. I later became aware, as Mother had, that Scott had studied me for the purpose of fictional character depictions. The little girl in *Babylon Revisited* [*sic*] is probably more Scottie Fitzgerald than I, but it is not insignificant that he named her Honoria.[2]

A year later in an October 16, 1983, letter to me that accompanied her annotated copy of "Babylon Revisited," Honoria Murphy Donnelly cited more specific parallels: "the role playing game they [Charlie and his daughter Honoria] have is rather like Scottie as a child." The annotations argue for a pastiche of autobiographical echoes in "Babylon Revisited": "I didn't act demonstrative[ly] . . . as a child . . . Scottie [unlike Honoria Murphy, but like Honoria Wales] call[ed] her father 'Daddy.'" "Both Scott and my father [like Charlie to the fictional Honoria] were warm to us." "[R]ole playing [like Honoria Wales's] was typical of Scottie when she was young . . . I recall with great pleasure what fun it was to play with her." "Scott had a collection of lead soldiers [like those Charlie gives to the Peterses]." In the side margin next to Charlie's and Honoria's discussion of lunch opening section 2, Donnelly wrote: "This is a conversation that could conceivably have come up with *either* Fitz's or Murphys." And in the side margin next to Lincoln Peters's "You children go in and start your soup,"[3] she added: "Murphys maybe[;] both families kept a strict food schedule for our own good." Her letter and annotations (which Eleanor Lanahan's new biography of Scottie corroborates)[4] make clear her belief that much of Fitzgerald's story is a blend of biographical data from both the Fitzgeralds and the Murphys.

With a rare creative blending Fitzgerald has crafted in "Babylon Revisited" the life models of himself, Zelda, Scottie, Honoria Murphy, Aunt Rosalind, and Uncle Newman (Zelda's sister and brother-in-law) into redoubtable actors in a trial for which the reader must share the agonies as both judge and jury. The emotional lives of both Wales and Fitzgerald stand as defendants. It is a shattering ordeal for all. Almost masochistically, Fitzgerald has placed Wales in an atmosphere of an impending doom, a doom as inevitable as that of Stephen Crane's Swede in "The Blue Hotel." He has adroitly manipulated most readers into both liking and sympathizing with Charlie while suggesting at the very outset that Charlie will, at least temporarily, fail in his battle for his daughter Honoria, fail in his attempt to recapture his daughter, if not his honor.

Charlie would like custody of this child he is in Paris to regain, and in many ways he deserves to have Honoria back, to spirit her away to be the daughter of his current self, the financially secure and respected Charles J. Wales of Prague. What is even clearer is Honoria's strong desire to be with her father. Honoria throws herself joyfully and lovingly into his arms. She asks him, without prompting, when she will be coming to live with him. She reveals her qualified regard for Marion Peters, her maternal aunt and (with Lincoln Peters) dutiful guardian. It becomes apparent in her initial refusal of Charlie's offer of expensive gifts that love for her father transcends that of material goods. Charlie, not surprisingly for a father who has not seen his daughter in ten months, brings Honoria a doll at their first meeting at the Peterses. The next day, over lunch, however, he raises the ante, announcing to her: "First we're going to the toy store in the Rue Saint-Honoré and buy you anything you like. And then we're going to the vaudeville at the Empire" (307). Honoria answers: "I like it about the vaudeville, but not the toy store" (307). She appreciates that she already "had lots of things" and, worried that they are not "rich anymore" and wanting him more than his possessions, only reluctantly and "resignedly" (307) agrees to accept his offer of more material gifts.

Charlie's love for Honoria is equally clear. Charlie continually refuses that second drink. It is evident that he is deeply disturbed by Duncan Schaeffer's and Lorraine Quarrles's "unwelcome" intrusion into the loving intimacy of his luncheon with Honoria and horrified by their drunken disruption of his quiet triumph at the Peterses' apartment, where, for a time, victory in the quest for Honoria seems his. Charlie, then, would like very much to have Honoria, and Fitzgerald prompts most readers to sympathize with his desire.

Yet as several critics have argued so forcefully, Charlie's ambivalent urges and his persistent need for self-justification tend to undermine his good intentions.[5] His reluctance to accept his share of the blame for the destructive period in his past that placed Honoria in the custody of the Peterses, himself in a sanitarium and his wife, Helen, in an early grave, undercuts his apparent reformation. Charlie nowhere acknowledges that he was partly to blame for Helen's death. This reluctance to accept proper responsibility for his faults and make full atonement for them is apparent in most of what he says and does. Why else does he long so for echoes of his turbulent past—the tempting cafés, the nostalgic music, the colored lights, the names of discredited friends who shared them? Why does he make his nostalgic journey through the streets of Paris?[6] Why does he insist upon that one drink a day? (Isn't it an unnecessary temptation much like that of the quart bottle of whiskey Doc keeps in the kitchen cabinet in William Inge's play *Come Back, Little Sheba*?[7]) And why does Charlie at the very beginning of the story plant the seed of his own destruction by leaving the Peterses' address with the Ritz barman after inquiring about former acquaintances, willing accomplices from his period of dissipation? Why, in a word, is he at the Ritz bar at all? If he is attempting to demonstrate his triumph over past weaknesses, trying to prove to himself that they cannot engulf him, it is a questionable attempt at best. For the story begins and ends with Charlie at the scene of his most reprehensible moments, in an atmosphere as precarious as that of Hemingway's "The Sea Change." In Hemingway's story (also published in 1931), the main character, stunned by the departure of his girlfriend, who has abandoned him for a lesbian affair, is left drinking in the company of an accommodating bartender and what a 1930s audience would view as effete homosexuals. Charlie's bartender is equally accommodating in a bar that is almost empty but for "a group of strident queens" Charlie watches "installing themselves in a corner" (303). Although Charlie waves away the bartender's offer of a second drink (and everyone else's for that matter), his psychological state at the story's end is, like Phil's at the end of Hemingway's story, one of stunned desperation.

A more positive reading of Wales's scribbling of Lincoln Peters's address for the barman at the beginning of "Babylon Revisited" might include self-punishment, the threshold to his admission of guilt.[8] The act is much like Silas Lapham's "accidental" burning of his new house, which, as partial atonement for his own guilt, does lead to Lapham's moral rise and redemptive sacrificial act. Charles does not progress this far. There is a deeper desperation in his need for Honoria. He deems it necessary to buy her expensive presents. There is desperation and pathos in his dreamlike return to his dead wife, who is first envisioned in a white dress, as if in willful contrast to Marion's funereal black. Fitzgerald points up this contrast in his revisions of the magazine version of "Babylon Revisited" by making Marion a more formidable and somewhat more domestic opponent to Charlie, which makes clearer her ability to take adequate care of Honoria. Instead of *"fiddling"* with "the *glass grapes* on her necklace,"[9] Marion *"plays"* "with the *black stars* on her necklace" (*Reader* 311; emphasis added), suggesting a more potent control over Charlie's destiny. Instead of sitting "behind empty coffee cups" (*Post* 82) she sits "behind the coffee service" (*Reader* 311), suggesting a firmer control over her household. Instead of coming "back into the little salon" (*Post* 4) she comes "back from the kitchen" (*Reader* 305), suggesting a more intimate involvement with the day-to-day rituals affecting Honoria's life with the Peterses. In "half sleep" Charlie also sees the deceased Helen in a swing that moves faster and faster, blurring the past, present, and future as well as merging them.[10] At the end of the story he assures himself defensively that she wouldn't want him to be so alone, that if she were with him now she would approve of his desire for Honoria. But as far as Wales's life is concerned the present is no bastion against his past. For Charlie all time is one time. Events of the past ultimately sour the present and complicate the future.

Not surprisingly, much has been made of Fitzgerald's handling of time in "Babylon Revisited."[11] It is clear that acts of the past haunt the present and threaten defilement of the future. Charlie's memories of Helen evoked in the image of the pendulum movement of her swing do influence his present actions, which will in turn help determine his future with Honoria. The ritual of the daily drink contains both the past and the present and threatens in itself to poison the future. The final irony, however, is not so much that Charlie "sees himself in the eternal present, alone,"[12] but that the past that defeats him is only a *small segment* of his past, that past as defined by Marion and so dreaded by his conscience. That Charlie's proclaimed definition of the past is so different from Marion's indicates both his strength and his weakness. For although Charlie stresses the distant past, a far more extensive time period, in an attempt to refute Marion's emphasis on the much briefer, more immediate past, the considerable merits of the longer time period are relentlessly obscured by the tragic mistakes of the shorter one.

To Marion the past is his year and a half or so of dissipation. She seizes on that one night when Charlie locked Helen out in the snow as a metaphor of his irresponsibility. Fitzgerald seems to be using snow as a part of the central motif of moral laxity, of dissipation, of spiritual bankruptcy. Snow is also a slang term for cocaine and "the Snow Bird" (*Reader* 302) Charlie asks about in the beginning of the opening scene may be a cocaine user or connection.[13] The "snow of twenty-nine" that "wasn't real snow," recalled by Charlie in the final scene, may also refer to the drugs dispensed along with alcohol during those boom days: "If you didn't want it to be snow, you just paid some money" (321). It is especially appropriate that Charlie locks his wife out in "a snowstorm in which she wandered about in slippers" (315). It may be that both snow and cocaine render Helen vulnerable to her fatal "heart trouble" (314), which Marion blames wholly on Charlie. Fitzgerald continually suggests a drug-blurred society in which money was vainly purported to buy not only escape from moral responsibility but immutability from the very laws of nature and from time itself. Placing

Charlie's and Helen's marital difficulties in a social scene immersed in both alcohol *and* drugs lends more credence to Marion's condemnations. Although she behaves neurotically during his visits, her importunate brother-in-law's immersion in a destructive lifestyle has given her ample reason to distrust him. On several occasions, Charlie tries to counter Marion's litany of that one terrible night with his own definition of the past. He sees that one night and the year and a half of profligate living as atypical, arguing that he has worked hard for most of his thirty-five years, maintaining that for most of his life he *has been* a responsible person, sober and hardworking.

Charlie Wales (along with hosts of fictional characters under extraordinary pressures, including the protagonists in Dante's *Divine Comedy* and Hemingway's "The Short Happy Life of Francis Macomber") is, at age thirty-five, at the very center of his life, poised between his past and his future, success and failure, heaven and hell. His present claim of reform is more believable because of his long record of past responsibility. The durability of his most recent success in business in Prague is as believable as the likelihood of his overall reform, if one sees as the true norm these many years of sobriety before his relatively brief period of dissipation during the boom years of Paris. The inconsistencies in the numbering of the years before Charlie's stock market success (mistakes which could be either Charlie's or Fitzgerald's) make it difficult to determine some chronological details with certainty. At times the boundary between Charlie's more recent past is as blurred as those scenes that suggest the ambivalence or confusion of values. In any case, Charlie's apparent reform is no more able to prevent Honoria from remaining with the Peterses, away from her father, than Fitzgerald's own self-control was able to overcome Zelda's illness and his own periods of dissipation and prevent him from sending Scottie away from the circle of her true family to the surrogate families of distant boarding schools.

Writing this story around the same time as his brilliant essays "Echoes of the Jazz Age" and "My Lost City," and while Zelda was intermittently institutionalized, Fitzgerald clearly transmutes some of his own guilt feelings, his need for self-justification, his near despair. Concerning this debilitating period he later recorded a haunting summary of his frustrations: how he had "left [his] capacity for hoping on the little roads that led to Zelda's sanitarium."[14] Around the summer (?) of 1930 he imparted to Oscar Forel, Zelda's Swiss psychiatrist, a self-defense whose essence was to be echoed in Charlie Wales's own rationalizations. Fitzgerald wrote: "*During my young manhood* for *seven years I worked extremely hard,* in six years bringing myself by tireless literary self-discipline to a position of unquestioned preeminence among younger

American writers; also by additional 'hack-work' for the cinema, ect. [*sic*]. I gave my wife a comfortable and luxurious life such as few European writers ever achieve." [15]

In a 1979 interview, Scottie Fitzgerald Smith describes how the complexity of the shared guilt between her parents did indeed carry over into the story:

> Question: "Your father said of himself and your mother, Zelda: 'We ruined ourselves. I've never honestly thought we ruined each other.' Does that seem like a basically accurate assessment of their relationship to you?"
>
> Scottie: "Yes. My Aunt Rosalind, my mother's oldest sister, who is portrayed [as Helen's sister] in *Babylon Revisited* [*sic*], was forever trying to prove my father ruined my mother's life. I don't believe that and I don't believe she ruined his life. I think they were singularly mismatched. . . . There's no question but that each needed stability and clearly neither one was able to give the other stability. They encouraged each other's most self-destructive tendencies." [16]

Fitzgerald himself confessed to Scottie (in a letter of June 7, 1940): "I told you once it was an old *Saturday Evening Post* story called 'Babylon Revisited' that I wrote in 1931. You were one of the principal characters." The painful closeness of life and art is even more apparent in Fitzgerald's November 18, 1930, letter to his literary agent Harold Ober, in which he implored: "*Very important* Please *immediately* send me back carbon copy of this story ['Babylon Revisited']. It's terribly important because this is founded on a real quarrel with my sister-in-law + I have to square her." [17] Although he felt his share of the mutual responsibility for the disaster in his own marriage, Fitzgerald may be trying to bury much of the guilt in his fictive counterpart. He works hard to make his alter ego sympathetic. He may also be trying to expiate his own guilt through Charlie's explanations and his rationalizations. Helen's kissing of young Webb is but one indication (perhaps the tip of the iceberg) of her share in the mutual destruction of their marriage and her life.

It is significant that most of Fitzgerald's revisions for the *Taps at Reveille* version of "Babylon Revisited" make Charlie's language more decisive and his character less uncertain. Fitzgerald indicates more precisely in *Taps at Reveille* Charlie's desire to concentrate on the present and change his perspectives. The change from two years since his drinking to three years increases Charlie's separation from his recent past and reinforces his connection with his more distant past as a sober, hardworking husband and father.

But just as Fitzgerald's letter to Dr. Forel contains some of the truth but not the whole truth about the hard work that may not have been sufficient to redeem Fitzgerald's own life, so Charlie Wales's most recent efforts and the stability of his larger past seem not enough to assuage his guilt and repair the damage of the year and a half of shared irresponsibility. And Charlie is up against a fictive force in Helen that is even more formidable than Zelda's Aunt Rosalind, who, according to Scottie, was "forever trying to prove" Fitzgerald had ruined Zelda's life. In the end, Charlie is forced to wait at least six months longer for another chance as Honoria continues to grow out of his fatherly grasp. He must forestall his "desire of putting a little of himself into her before she crystallized utterly" (310). Charlie's fear of Honoria's imminent crystallization may be spawned in part by his memory of that supposedly unreal "snow of twenty-nine" that was, in fact, real enough to threaten the life of another loved one, Helen, his own wife and Honoria's mother. Fitzgerald's letters to Scottie, filled with a poignant urgency, were his attempts from long distance to reach *her* before she "crystallized utterly" without benefit of his stern but loving counsel. For no one believed in strength of character more than Fitzgerald did.

Another important change in the *Taps at Reveille* version of "Babylon Revisited" reinforces the picture of a Charlie struggling toward character reform. Fitzgerald revised the sentence "character, like everything wears out" (*Post* 5) to the more optimistic view of character as an "eternally valuable element" worthy of his trust (*Reader* 306). Some seven years later (July 1938), in a letter to a sixteen-year-old Scottie, Fitzgerald praised "the old virtues of work and courage and the old graces of courtesy and politeness" that came from "my generation of radicals and breakers-down" even though it was a past "that produced Barbara Hutton."[18] We note that Charlie "wanted to jump back a whole generation and trust in character again as the eternally valuable element" (*Reader* 306). Fitzgerald, like Charlie, wanted to be in a position to give Scottie the kind of unassailable love and security that seemed (in 1931) to be epitomized in the home life of Honoria Murphy.

Charlie's desire to repeat his earlier past is charged with the same desperate optimism as Jay Gatsby's attempt to roll back time. Most readers side with Charlie for a variety of reasons. They like him for his optimism, his tenacity of purpose, his hopefulness. They like him for some of the same reasons they like Gatsby. But they also sense his doom. For just as surely as no redemptive phone rings for Gatsby as he lies in the pool of his imminent death, so no testament from the past will save Charlie, who will be forced to forswear, perhaps forever, his hope of regaining Honoria. Nor is Charlie's mask of Charles J. Wales of Prague any more successful in his quest to regain Honoria than was Jimmy Gatz's Gatsby mask in his misguided attempt to regain Daisy. At best he can continue to arrange her life from afar, for, unlike Gatsby, whose own gnawing sense of loss is mercifully foreshortened, Charlie remains alive in the harbor of his hopes. Fitzgerald also tried to remain alive and arrange his daughter's life. Except for brief periodic visits, he too was an absentee bread-winner. Along with Zelda's expensive medical care he gave Scottie's education top priority. At his premature death Scottie's college bills were paid, his legacy of a life insurance policy intact. A kind of model of concern, Charlie also will continue to send Honoria presents, letters, hope. Still, he too seems doomed to "beat on . . . against the current, borne back ceaselessly into the past." And what is as painful to the reader as it is to Charlie is the growing sense that the past gripping him most powerfully is that past so narrowly circumscribed by the prejudiced judgment of Marion. The hope that he can regain legal custody of Honoria is as fleeting as are the highs and lows of his moods that fluctuate throughout the story as a barometer of his complexity.

Yet it is clear as the story ends that the widowed Charlie will continue to provide for his daughter and battle to sustain his own beleaguered sense of honor. For his creator has furnished him an apt model. As a diligent provider for his absentee daughter and institutionalized wife until his poignant death in the prime of his life, Fitzgerald proved himself a superb example of the values he extolled — those old virtues, those old graces, of work and of courage.

NOTES

1. If there is a flaw in "Babylon Revisited" it may be, as my colleague Charles H. Bohner has suggested, in Fitzgerald's fleeting glimpse into Marion's mind (toward the end of section 3) that is inconsistent with the third-person point of view that otherwise remains with Charlie's center of consciousness.
2. Donnelly, *Sara and Gerald*, 148.
3. Fitzgerald, *Reader*, 320. Unless otherwise noted, all subsequent page references to "Babylon Revisited" are to the 1963 edition, are cited as *Reader*, and appear parenthetically in the text.
4. Lanahan, *Scottie*, 45.
5. For a strong case for Charlie's unsuccessful efforts to come to terms with his life, see Toor, "Guilt and Retribution."
6. To the *Taps at Reveille* version of "Babylon Revisited" Fitzgerald added a whole paragraph (his most extensive revision in the story) detailing Charlie's nostalgic tour of Paris (Fitzgerald, *Reader*, 303). It is important to acknowledge that Charlie would, of course, be less than human if his nostalgic memories of those parties of his past were not somewhat sweet as well as bitter, but at this point a rejection of that period of dissipation, even if it be a puritan rejection, is necessary to retain Honoria, the declared purpose of this return visit to Paris.

7. Doc does ultimately give into temptation and drains the bottle. Although Alcoholics Anonymous was not founded until 1935, its firm belief in such total abstinence for alcoholics was established by the 1920s through such organizations as the Oxford Group.

8. For a defense of Wales, in part an answer to Toor, see Twitchell, "'Babylon Revisited': Chronology and Characters."

9. Fitzgerald, "Babylon Revisited," 82; emphasis added. All subsequent page references to the *Saturday Evening Post* version of the story are cited as *Post* and appear parenthetically in the text.

10. Often when Fitzgerald describes physical blurring in many other stories, as well as his novels, he is also implying moral and spiritual uncertainty, weakness, or corruption. It is also clear in, for instance, *The Great Gatsby* and *The Last Tycoon* that attempts to repeat or return to the past are either futile or disastrous.

11. See, for instance, Gross, "Fitzgerald's 'Babylon Revisited'"; and Staley, "Time and Structure." Gross's seminal article remains one of the soundest readings of "Babylon Revisited."

12. Staley, "Time and Structure," 388.

13. For a treatment of Charlie's sense of loss and regret regarding his recent past that also touches upon Fitzgerald's reference to cocaine, see Gervais, "Snow of Twenty-Nine."

14. Fitzgerald, *Notebooks*, 204.

15. Bruccoli and Duggan, *Correspondence of F. Scott Fitzgerald*, 242; emphasis in original.

16. Smith, "Interview," 2–3.

17. Turnbull, *Letters*, 78; Bruccoli, *As Ever*, 175; emphasis in original.

18. Turnbull, *Letters*, 36.

WORKS CITED

Bruccoli, Matthew J., ed., with the assistance of Jennifer McCabe Atkinson. *As Ever, Scott Fitz—: Letters Between F. Scott Fitzgerald and His Literary Agent, Harold Ober—1919–1940*. New York: J. B. Lippincott, 1972.

Bruccoli, Matthew J., and Margaret M. Duggan, eds., with the assistance of Susan Walker. *Correspondence of F. Scott Fitzgerald*. New York: Random House, 1980.

Donnelly, Honoria Murphy. Letter to author, October 16, 1983.

——, with Richard N. Billings. *Sara and Gerald: Villa America and After*. New York: Times Books, 1982.

Fitzgerald, F. Scott. "Babylon Revisited." *Saturday Evening Post*, February 21, 1931, 3–5, 82–84.

——. *The Fitzgerald Reader*. Ed. Arthur Mizener. New York: Scribners, 1963.

———. *The Notebooks of F. Scott Fitzgerald.* Ed. Matthew J. Bruccoli. New York: Harcourt Brace Jovanovich, 1978.

Gervais, Ronald J. "The Snow of Twenty-Nine: 'Babylon Revisited' as *Ubi Sunt* Lament." *College Literature* 7 (1980): 47–52.

Gross, Seymour L. "Fitzgerald's 'Babylon Revisited.'" *College English* 25 (1963): 128–35.

Lanahan, Eleanor. *Scottie the Daughter of . . . : The Life of Frances Scott Fitzgerald Lanahan Smith.* New York: HarperCollins, 1995.

Smith, Scottie Fitzgerald. "An Interview with Scottie Fitzgerald Smith." Philadelphia's *WUHY Press Release*, September 1979: 1–4.

Staley, Thomas F. "Time and Structure in Fitzgerald's 'Babylon Revisited.'" *Modern Fiction Studies* 10 (1964–65): 386–88.

Toor, David. "Guilt and Retribution." *Fitzgerald/Hemingway Annual* 1973: 155–64.

Turnbull, Andrew, ed. *The Letters of F. Scott Fitzgerald.* New York: Scribners, 1963.

Twitchell, James B. "'Babylon Revisited': Chronology and Characters." *Fitzgerald/Hemingway Annual* 1979: 155–360.

Fitzgerald's "Crack-up" Essays Revisited

Fictions of the Self, Mirrors for a Nation

BRUCE L. GRENBERG

Almost everyone interested in understanding Fitzgerald's career in the 1930s has recognized some certain significance in the "Crack-up" essays (published in *Esquire* in February, March, and April 1936). Literary criticism being what it is, however, there is little agreement about what that significance might be.

Andrew Turnbull saw in the essays "casual nakedness and candor" and viewed them as both a "post-mortem on [Fitzgerald's] nervous and psychological breakdown" and as "the work of a lapsed Catholic, for whom confession was a rhythm of the soul." Henry Dan Piper, in his early but still persuasive *F. Scott Fitzgerald: A Critical Portrait*, devoted a major chapter to the essays, which he viewed basically as Fitzgerald's attempt "to come to terms with his private experience," enabling him "after two years . . . to examine his recent past and his present situation with detachment and clarity." Piper goes on to argue that "with these 'Crack-Up' essays, Fitzgerald commenced the last and most mature period of his career." Dissenting from these views, Milton Hindus sees the "real emotions and ideas of his confession" obscured by "a mist of verbal artifice" and observes that "the greatest confessional writing contains more concrete evidence than does *The Crack-Up* that its author was burned in the fire of reality." Brian Way goes even further in his criticism, lamenting Fitzgerald's "distinct superficiality in carrying on the business of self-analysis" and concluding that "these essays, far from being rigorous exercises in self-scrutiny, are, rather, exercises in self-dramatization and self-pity." Much closer to my view is Robert Sklar, who argues that the essays were a "means of drawing the line between future and past, a ritual gesture to separate a new life from the old."[1]

However divergent the above sampling of critical opinion might appear, there is a common ground that underlies the postures of these critics and other like-minded commentators. For whether the "Crack-up" essays are viewed as a resurgence of Fitzgerald's artistic powers, as Piper would have it, or as evidence of Fitzgerald's "lesion of confidence" as Bruccoli so trenchantly puts it, the initial assumption, erroneous and fatally flawed, is that the essays are Fitzgerald's naive, "unmediated" personal confession of a mental and psychological breakdown in the 1930s — a kind of psychiatric, literary mea culpa.[2]

The origins of this misdirecting and critically debilitating assumption are not far to seek. When Edmund Wilson published The Crack-up in 1945, the full weight of his critical reputation as well as his celebrated longtime friendship with Fitzgerald gave an authority to his judgments that has proved a mixed blessing. The slim volume did much to rekindle interest in Fitzgerald certainly, but at the expense of seeing him clearly. For Wilson's "poetic" dedication to the book, whose title focuses our attention on the "Crack-up" essays, depicts a Fitzgerald who "fed on drink for weeks," who "lent a lyric voice / To all the tongueless knavish tavern boys, / The liquor-ridden, the illiterate,"[3] a Fitzgerald who produced but "Two emeralds" (one of them "half-cut" [9]) and but a handful of jewels characterized as "Flawed," "milky," "chill," "shifty" (8), "tinsel," and, finally, "common" (9). More directly to the point of the "Crack-up" essays, Wilson's dedication mourns a Fitzgerald who was "Betrayed, but self-betrayed by stealthy sins — / And faded to the sound of violins" (7). No doubt the relationship between Fitzgerald and Wilson begs closer scrutiny, but here it suffices to point out that Wilson's own stealthy sin as a critic, and as a friend, is that of naively mistaking the writing for the writer, the autobiography for the autobiographer.[4]

Recent studies in the genre of autobiographical, confessional writing suggest that the form is anything but simple, and my purpose in this essay is to suggest some of the depths of Fitzgerald's imagination that heretofore have remained unexamined. However large a role personal experience played in Fitzgerald's creative imagination, he was scarcely ever merely "personal" in his quasi-autobiographical essays. Ruth Prigozy argues persuasively that in the 1930s Fitzgerald turned to the past "to interpret not merely an individual's life but the national experience as well," while James L. W. West III emphasizes the critical axiom that "Fitzgerald had long felt that the cycles of his own life paralleled the rises and falls of American society in the 1920s and 1930s." Indeed, Fitzgerald persistently identifies himself with America and his life's course with America's history, and much of the chromatic depth of his essays, as well as his fiction, derives from this definition of his expanded "self." Given these, and many other, views of Fitzgerald's historicizing imagination, it is all the more remarkable that criticism of the "Crack-up" essays has remained so recalcitrantly rooted in the "biographical." Even Brian Way, who in general opposes the excessively biographical approach to Fitzgerald's works, dismisses the "Crack-up" essays as Fitzgerald's "autobiographical account of his own collapse," which "fails to move," and argues that "the importance of these pieces has been consistently overrated."[5]

In sharp contrast, I would like to suggest that the "Crack-up" essays are not overrated but under-read. They are best seen not (as Way would have it) as "the last resource of a man who feels he cannot obtain a hearing by any less desperate means," but as sophisticated *fiction* written in the genre of "confession-anatomy" as defined by Northrop Frye in *The Anatomy of Criticism*, combining the *"introverted*-intellectual" voice of the confession with the *"extroverted*-intellectual" voice of the anatomy.[6] Indeed, Frye's definition and discussion of the interaction between autobiography, confession, satire, and anatomy provide some much-needed illumination of Fitzgerald's manifold purposes in the "Crack-up" essays, for in them Fitzgerald successfully fuses the commentary on his own crisis in the 1930s, with his rich, various, and suggestive commentary on the crisis of the nation during the same fraught period.

Susanna Egan, in *Patterns of Experience in Autobiography*, makes some further judgments about the genre that are very telling and relevant to this discussion. First, she argues convincingly that the autobiographical form is in its essence a fiction, one in which the author-autobiographer, through reflection, selection, and the implication of form, attempts to convey a sense of "virtual" reality out of the chaotic, disordered, "actual" reality of the life as it was lived. Thus, the autobiographer is not the person (Fitzgerald in this case) but the persona adopted for a literary, fictive purpose.[7] The "Crack-up" essays aptly illustrate Egan's point in the most palpable way, for there, in the putative account of his personal breakdown, Fitzgerald, remarkably, does not even mention Zelda's illness and the draining effect it had on him, and mentions only peripherally his own serious and persistent drinking problem. Egan's second, corollary observation is equally valuable: autobiography, particularly in its avatar as confession, is by its very nature a dialogue—the confessor speaking to someone in order to elicit a response.[8] Thus, in reading the "Crack-up" essays we must bear in mind that Fitzgerald was challenging the specific readership of *Esquire* to recognize the disintegration not only of F. Scott Fitzgerald but of themselves and the American identity. To get to some of the depths of the "Crack-up" essays, then, we must determine the nature of the persona that Fitzgerald adopts, and recognize the role of that persona within the context of the confessional drama that the essays act out.

At the very outset of the first essay, "The Crack-up," Fitzgerald makes clear that his theme is to be more than a mere personal lament. He calls the essay a short *history*" (69; emphasis added), and in the same, second paragraph of the essay he defines "a first-rate intelligence" as one possessing "the ability to hold two opposed ideas in the mind at the same time, and still retain the ability to function" (69). Although this dictum is oft-quoted, it is usually cited in the abstract with little or no attention given to its contextual value and its prominence in the "Crack-up" essays themselves. But this definition is, in fact, at once an assertion of Fitzgerald's complex intelligence in the essays that follow and a complementary directive to the reader to look beyond the simple surface of the essays. It indirectly, but surely, instructs the reader to view Fitzgerald's "short history" (the *three* "Crack-up" essays, as it turns out) as a *compound* record of disintegration—not merely of Fitzgerald, but of the audience to which he writes—and, by extension, of America itself. It is this complexity of purpose that produces the shifting tonalities of the essays—which move from self-pity to accusation, to threat, from quasi-clinical analysis, to myth making, to irony and satire.

Fitzgerald points the reader toward this complex purpose directly, in what purports to be a "clinical history" of his own "crack-up." After summarizing his two years of wanting to be alone, not wanting "to see any people at all" (71), Fitzgerald tells us that "suddenly, surprisingly, I got better" (72). And it is *then* that he "cracked like an old plate as soon as I heard the news" (72). Surely Fitzgerald has something other than clinical accuracy in mind by thus linking his crack-up to his "getting better," for the anomaly of this summary analysis, in fact, dissociates his personal well-being from the subject of his essay—cracking up. As Fitzgerald relates it, his *recovery*-induced cracking seems remarkably akin to a Jamesian consciousness of the ineluctability of life's events—a consciousness that is at once painful and morally elevating. And Fitzgerald immediately tells us, only three pages into the first of the essays, "That is the real end of this story. What was to be done about it will have to rest in what used to be called the 'womb of time'" (72). The image of time's womb is, of course, primarily historical rather than psychiatric, or even psychological, and, thus, Fitzgerald once again suggests to his readers that his essay and the ones that follow, are to illuminate not merely a personal crack-up and "failure" but the larger, more important crack-up and failure of the American self, viewed within a historical context.

Throughout the essays Fitzgerald makes a number of specific identifications between his own crack-up and the crisis experienced by the nation in the crash of 1929 and the economic-social depression that followed. In the opening paragraph of "The Crack-up" he distinguishes between blows that come "from outside" (the depression, I suggest) and the "sort of blow that comes from within" (his depression) (69). That abstraction is given substance two paragraphs later when Fitzgerald explicitly identifies the historical and personal contexts in the essay: "As the twenties passed, with my own twenties marching a little ahead of them" (70), he begins his third paragraph. And, even more definitively, Fitzgerald delineates that historical context in the penultimate paragraph of the third essay, "Handle With Care." There, he explicitly identifies his personal history with the history of the nation; he calls his "own happiness in the past" not "the natural thing but the unnatural—unnatural as the Boom; and *my recent experience parallels the wave of despair that swept the nation when the Boom was over*" (84; emphasis added).

A focal point of the encompassing historical dimension of the essays is provided at the end of the first essay, in the dialogue/drama recounting Fitzgerald's confession to his friend Nora Flynn, who is cast in the role of "Job's comforter" (73). Nora remarks suggestively (or cryptically, apparently—since few, with the exception of André Le Vot, have commented on this passage),[9] "Suppose this wasn't a crack in you—suppose it was a crack in the Grand Canyon" (74). The metaphor is indirect to be sure, but it is all the more revealing because of its indirection. What is the Grand Canyon but a very large crack in *America?*—a simple but telling gloss, consistent with the speaker's further comment: "The world only exists through your apprehension of it, and so it's much better to say that it's not you that's cracked—it's the Grand Canyon" (74). Fitzgerald rejects this notion "heroically" by asserting, "The crack's in me" (74). Nora's further accusation that Fitzgerald is "trying to be a little puny individual" elicits his ironic question: "Baby et up all her Spinoza?" (74), and like all good irony, this question preserves as it rejects. Rejecting the "easy," face-saving explanation of his depression (as caused by something outside himself), the persona nevertheless embeds in his rejection the opposed idea that Nora is also right. For Spinozism is summarily defined as the "doctrine . . . that there is one sole and infinite substance of which extension and thought are attributes and individual beings are changing forms" (*OED*). And this allusion to Spinozism is intended to illuminate the identity, rather than the distinction, that exists in Fitzgerald's mind between individual lives (his own in particular) and what we normally refer to in the abstract as "history."

These identifications between "self" and "history" are not merely ornamental, then, and not at all peripheral to the central "confessional" theme of the essays. Rather, they signify overtly the conceptual framework of the essays, a framework in which Fitzgerald asserts the reciprocating values of self, culture, and nation, and thereby establishes his autobiographical persona as an American moralist-Everyman who has directly experienced what Fitzgerald terms (at the end of "Handle With Care") the "end that comes to our [N.B., not my] youth and hope" (84).

The first essay ends with the quotation from Matthew 5:13: "*Ye are the salt of the earth. But if the salt hath lost its savour, wherewith shall it be salted?*" (74). This may well be "one of the saddest verses in the Bible," as Piper would have it,[10] but defeatism is not the crux of the passage. Syntactically conditional and rhetorically admonitory, Matthew 5:13, in context and in spirit, is essentially exhortative. For it points backward to Matthew 5:11–12:

> Blessed are ye when men shall revile you, and persecute you, and shall say all manner of evil against you falsely, for my sake.
>
> Rejoice and be exceeding glad; for great is your reward in heaven: for so persecuted they the prophets which were before you.

And it points ahead to the rhapsodic verse that follows (5:14): "*Ye are the light of the world. A city that is set on a hill cannot be hid*" (emphasis added). The true implication of the passage from Matthew is that at the close of the first essay Fitzgerald establishes his persona as an authentic prophet, ignored in his own land, expressing to his countrymen an unwelcome and unheeded truth.

Perhaps one should say that the "Crack-up" essays stand as prophecy in the past tense, for the pervasive theme of the essays is the crack-up of America, which had already taken place in the Boom of the 1920s, the economic and social collapse of 1929, and the depression that followed. A pained observer and reluctant recorder of the demise of "old America," Fitzgerald found himself having to adopt new perspectives on the nation whose fortunes seemed to be radically changing.

Although Fitzgerald's fiction up to 1930 was frequently touched by disaster, as he reminds us in "Early Success" (1937), essentially it was predicated upon expectation and hope, or, at least, "the contradiction between the dead hand of the past and the high intentions of the future" ("Crack-up" 70). But Fitzgerald's major work in the 1930s (for example, "Echoes of the Jazz Age" [1931], "Babylon Revisited" [1931], the "Crack-up" essays themselves, and *Tender Is the Night* [1934]) are all reflective, "elegiac" works, founded upon Fitzgerald's conviction that not just he but America had reached a climacteric in 1929. And I must reaffirm here that, in this context, *Tender Is the Night* is Fitzgerald's greatest achievement, precisely because it is his comprehensive fictional statement on the demise of "old America." [11]

Fitzgerald's disappointment with the reception of *Tender Is the Night* is well documented, and again it is strange that critics have not taken an extra step and recognized in the sequence of events the connection between the apparent "failure" of *Tender Is the Night* and Fitzgerald's essential purposes in the "Crack-up" essays. Charting once again, and more directly this time, the decline and fall of "Old America," the essays, indeed, serve as an explicatory gloss on the novel's main concerns, which critics like Edwin Fussell, Milton Stern, Alan Trachtenberg, John F. Callahan, and I have argued are essentially historical.

The parallels between the "Crack-up" persona and Dick Diver, between the essays and the novel, are numerous and emphatic. Fitzgerald retraces in his persona's decline the essential terms of Dick Diver's fall in the course of the novel. Like Diver, the Fitzgerald-persona of the essays *had* believed that "life was something you dominated if you were any good" ("Crack-up" 69); like the Diver of Switzerland who wanted to be the best psychiatrist that ever lived, the persona had believed that "ego would continue as an arrow shot from nothingness to nothingness with such force that only gravity would bring it to earth at last" ("Crack-up" 70). Like Diver, the persona had been "more than average in a tendency to identify myself, my ideas, my destiny, with those . . . that I came in contact with" ("Crack-up" 71); like Diver at the Villa Diana or on the Somme battlefield—attempting to order a fractured world for the fractured survivors of the war—Fitzgerald's "Crack-up" persona "in a single morning . . . would go through the emotions ascribable to Wellington at Waterloo" ("Crack-up" 71). (Diver, of course, is compared to Grant, waiting in Galena for his "intricate destiny.") And eventually, like Diver, the persona of the essays, finds his "nervous reflexes . . . giving way—too much anger and too many tears" ("Crack-up" 71).

These and other parallels between novel and essays, between protagonist and persona, record Fitzgerald's continuing inquiry into the decline of American idealism, the failure of Dick Diver's (and America's) inherited belief that "nothing could be superior to 'good instincts,' honor, courtesy, and courage." [12]

In *Tender Is the Night* the values of Dick Diver and his father, the values of an older America, are replaced by those embodied in the characters of Tommy Barban, Rosemary Hoyt, and the "new" Nicole. And Dick's inability to accommodate himself to the new order defines *his* "crack-up" at the end of the novel. The moral and historical schism between "old" and "new" America in the novel persists in the "Crack-up" essays. The persona of these essays sees his self-immolation as something "very distinctly not modern" ("Handle With Care" 81) and clearly sees his own crack-up not merely as a personal failure but as a trauma of culture.

Thus, in "Handle With Care," he identifies himself "with the objects of [his] horror and compassion" and finds his crack-up duplicated in "a dozen men of honor and industry since the war" (81). He speaks of "one famous contemporary" who "played with the idea of the Big Out for half a year" and of another "who spent months in an asylum unable to endure any contact with his fellow men," and he emphatically concludes, "of those who had given up and passed on I could list a score" ("Handle With Care" 81). In "Pasting It Together," the narrator speaks of "a deflation of all my values," and recounts how his "passionate belief in order" and a "feeling that craft and industry would have a place in any world . . . were swept away" (78). And this essay concludes with the image of the narrator "standing at twilight on a deserted range, with an empty rifle in my hands and the targets down. No problem set—simply a silence with only the sound of my own breathing" (77–78). In meaning, as well as in rhetoric and rhythm, this passage calls clearly to mind Fitzgerald's description of Dick Diver in 1925 at the pivotal point of *Tender Is the Night*, "listening to the buzz of the electric clock, listening to time." [13]

Fitzgerald carries the parallels between novel and essays yet further. He observes in "Handle With Care" that "the ones who had survived had made some sort of clean break" (81). Like Tommy Barban, Nicole, and Rosemary, they had made the kind of break with history that is "irretrievable because it makes the past cease to exist" (81). Most clearly for Fitzgerald, those who had survived the Boom and the Crash, seemingly unscathed, are the "villains" of the "Crack-up" essays, just as they are the "villains" of *Tender Is the Night*.

It is one of the plangent ironies of the essays that those "survivor-villains" are also the audience that Fitzgerald addresses—the readers of *Esquire*. James L. W. West III gives us a summary description of the magazine: "Expensively printed on glossy paper" and costing fifty cents in the 1930s (most magazines cost five or ten cents), carrying advertisements for "better brands of clothing, accessories, automobiles, and liquor," the magazine was aimed at the market of "well-to-do males"—survivors all, I suggest. [14] The dialogue between the persona and the readers of the "Crack-up" essays, therefore, is extremely vexed, for Fitzgerald is addressing an audience he believes can understand him, if at all, only with great difficulty.

This radical dislocation between author and audience generates a tonality of antagonism throughout the essays; however, the persona's antagonism toward those who have prospered while he has floundered is rooted not in personality but in Fitzgerald's ethical and historical assumptions. The persona-narrator openly admits in "Pasting It Together" that he would always "cherish an abiding distrust, an animosity, toward the leisure class" and that he has "never been able . . . to stop thinking that at one time a sort of *droit de seigneur* might have been exercised to give one of them my girl" (77), but what really haunts the Fitzgerald persona "during the long night" is the recognition that the novel is being replaced by the movie — "a mechanical and communal art that . . . was capable of reflecting only the tritest thought, the most obvious emotion" (78). For the persona of "Pasting It Together," and for Fitzgerald, of course — who was on his way to Hollywood in an attempt to extricate himself from debt — the crisis is artistic, cultural, even philosophical, for in opposition to the movies, the persona defines the novel in moral rather than aesthetic terms as "the strongest and supplest medium for conveying thought and emotion from one human being to another" (78). The Fitzgerald persona can "neither accept nor struggle against" the "more glittering, . . . grosser power" of the mass-produced, mass-consumed triviality of the movies, but his personal crisis is once again set within the context of the larger national crisis as he compares his own obsolescence to that of the small merchant who has been crippled by the chain stores (78).

Ultimately, Fitzgerald depicts a self and a nation that have lost, or rather surrendered, their belief in the personal virtues of "honor, courtesy, and courage" to that "exterior force, unbeatable" — the power of bottom-line economics, mass production and mass marketing, and the dedicated self-interest that necessarily accompanies them. In this context, "Pasting It Together" is the most depressing of the three "Crack-up" essays because it is so dominated by the persona-narrator's sense of despair, concluding with the confession that "there was not an 'I' any more" (79). In effect, Fitzgerald is saying that there are not *any* "I's" anymore; his list of the five men who have constituted his "synthetic" self is, implicitly and ironically, a list of men who themselves can be but partial selves. But the essay ends on a note of antagonism and defiance that points ahead to the essentially satirical tone of "Handle With Care": "If you've had enough, say so—" he challenges his *Esquire* readers, and then continues, "but not too loud, because I have the feeling that someone, I'm not sure who, is sound asleep—someone who could have helped me to keep my shop open. It wasn't Lenin, and it wasn't God" (79–80).

The sleeping "someone" is Fitzgerald the dispossessed but uncompromised writer, I suggest, and he awakes with a vengeance in "Handle With Care," Fitzgerald's irony-laden "Modest Proposal." Like the narrator of Swift's essay, the "heady villainous" speaker in the last "Crack-up" essay is a persona within a persona, Fitzgerald's biographical presence being wholly given over to the ironic and sardonic "self" who has now *adjusted* to the new world order and become one with the "beady-eyed men . . . on the commuting train from Great Neck" and "the smooth articles who said: 'I'm sorry but business is business'" (82). This ironic putative self, who is identified with the new order, and who no doubt subscribes to *Esquire,* is characterized by a smile, combining "the best qualities of a hotel manager, an experienced old social weasel, a headmaster on visitors' day, . . . a body-vender in her first rotogravure, a hopeful extra swept near the camera, . . . and of course the great beam of loving kindness common to all those from Washington to Beverly Hills who must exist by virtue of the contorted pan" (82–83). In this most devastating passage, Fitzgerald's polar synecdoche of "Washington" and "Beverly Hills" trenchantly, but compellingly, indicts the moral vacuum and meretricious culture of the whole of "new America."

The other characteristic of this new "well-adjusted" self is "the voice." Tutored by a lawyer, the ironic new self is learning to speak with "that polite acerbity that makes people feel that far from being welcome they are not even tolerated and are under continual and scathing analysis at every moment" (83). This new smile-voice-self of "Handle With Care" is, summarily, the direct antithesis to the young Fitzgerald who had dreamed of being "an entire man in the Goethe-Byron-Shaw tradition, with an opulent American touch" (84).

By presenting this extravagant persona in the last essay Fitzgerald dramatizes just how much America has given up and just how poor a bargain it has made. As the narrator says in the last paragraph of the essay, "there is a price to pay" (84)—and it is a high price indeed. Continuing the pose of the thoroughly adjusted and "uncrackable" modern American, the persona declares, "I do not any longer like the postman, nor the grocer, nor the editor, nor the cousin's husband, and he in turn will come to dislike me, so that life will never be very pleasant again, and the sign *Cave Canem* is hung permanently just above my door. I will try to be a correct animal though, and if you throw me a bone with enough meat on it I may even lick your hand" (84).

This closing passage of the essay has embarrassed admirers of Fitzgerald ever since the essay first appeared, but viewed properly as Fitzgerald's conclusive judgment upon the *assumed* persona of the essay, the statement serves as his final satirical broadside at the grasping, amoral, beady-eyed, smooth articles to whom he addressed the essays.

The "Crack-up" essays, then, reflect Fitzgerald's recognition that the materials of his early art had been snatched from him by historical events, and he anatomizes and defines with excruciating honesty the waning vitality of his own early vision of himself and of the nation he admired so intensely. But the essays also illuminate Fitzgerald's awareness of a new direction in his art in the 1930s. Fitzgerald's maturity in the 1930s produces an art that is critical, evaluative, and reflective — perhaps a more descriptive term is elegiac — recounting Babylons revisited, lost decades, crazy Sundays, and last tycoons. This art, defined and exemplified in the art of the "Crack-up" essays themselves, reveals not Fitzgerald's fragility of mind and imagination but a strength, a versatility, and a resilience that allow him "to hold two opposed ideas in the mind at the same time, and still retain the ability to function" — that allow him to give a most poignant statement of all his dreams in a most pervasive account of their loss.

NOTES

1. Turnbull, *Scott Fitzgerald*, 270; Piper, *F. Scott Fitzgerald*, 234, 238; Hindus, *F. Scott Fitzgerald*, 90–91; Way, *F. Scott Fitzgerald and the Art of Social Fiction*, 151; Sklar, *F. Scott Fitzgerald*, 309.

2. Piper, *F. Scott Fitzgerald*, 238; Bruccoli, *Some Sort of Epic Grandeur*, 405.

3. Wilson, *Crack-up*, 7. All subsequent page references to *The Crack-up* are to the 1945 edition and appear parenthetically in the text. It must be noted that in the first edition of *The Crack-up* in 1945, the essay titles "Pasting It Together" and "Handle With Care" (but not the texts of the essays) were transposed. The later paperback printing, used here, has the titles in the correct order. My thanks to Judith S. Baughman, University of South Carolina, for clarifying this matter.

4. On the impact of Wilson's publication of *The Crack-up*, see Troy, "Scott Fitzgerald": "Upon the appearance of *The Crack-Up*, a selection by Edmund Wilson of Fitzgerald's letters, notebooks and fugitive pieces, it was notable that all the emptiest and most venal elements in New York journalism united to crow amiably about his literary corpse to this same tune of insufficient production" (56).

5. Prigozy, "Fitzgerald's Short Stories and the Depression," 119; West, "Fitzgerald and *Esquire*," 164; Way, *F. Scott Fitzgerald and the Art of Social Fiction*, 150, 149.

Sharing Way's uneasiness about the "Crack-up" essays is Donaldson, "Crisis of Fitz-gerald's 'Crack-Up'": "much of 'The Crack-Up' reads like a rationalization of Fitz-gerald's breakdown, and the three articles represent more an apologia than a con-fession" (179). And Donaldson goes further in arguing that the essays are "not about nervous exhaustion, emotional bankruptcy, or even an alcoholic breakdown. The subject of 'The Crack-Up' is Fitzgerald's misanthropy, and the self-hatred be-hind it" (182).

6. Way, F. Scott Fitzgerald and the Art of Social Fiction, 151; Frye, Anatomy of Criti-cism, 307–12.

7. Egan, Patterns of Experience in Autobiography, 12, 14–23, passim.

8. Ibid., 169–78.

9. Le Vot, F. Scott Fitzgerald, 295.

10. Piper, F. Scott Fitzgerald, 237.

11. See my larger treatment of this theme in "Fitzgerald's 'Figured Curtain.'"

12. Fitzgerald, Tender Is the Night, 236.

13. Ibid., 223.

14. West, "Fitzgerald and Esquire," 151.

WORKS CITED

Bruccoli, Matthew J. Some Sort of Epic Grandeur: The Life of F. Scott Fitzgerald. New York: Harcourt Brace Jovanovich, 1981.

Donaldson, Scott. "The Crisis of Fitzgerald's 'Crack-Up.'" Twentieth Century Litera-ture 26 (1980): 171–88.

Egan, Susanna. Patterns of Experience in Autobiography. Chapel Hill: University of North Carolina Press, 1984.

Fitzgerald, F. Scott. Tender Is the Night. New York: Scribners, 1934.

Frye, Northrop. Anatomy of Criticism: Four Essays. Princeton, N.J.: Princeton Univer-sity Press, 1957.

Grenberg, Bruce L. "Fitzgerald's 'Figured Curtain': Personality and History in Tender Is the Night." Fitzgerald/Hemingway Annual 1979: 105–36.

Hindus, Milton F. F. Scott Fitzgerald: An Introduction and Interpretation. New York: Holt, Rinehart and Winston, 1968.

Le Vot, André. F. Scott Fitzgerald: A Biography. Tr. William Byron. Garden City, N.Y.: Doubleday, 1983.

Piper, Henry Dan. F. Scott Fitzgerald: A Critical Portrait. New York: Holt, Rinehart and Winston, 1965.

Prigozy, Ruth. "Fitzgerald's Short Stories and the Depression." In The Short Stories of F. Scott Fitzgerald: New Approaches in Criticism. Ed. Jackson R. Bryer. Madison: University of Wisconsin Press, 1982. 111–26.

Sklar, Robert. F. Scott Fitzgerald: The Last Laocoön. New York: Oxford University Press, 1967.

Troy, William. "Scott Fitzgerald: The Authority of Failure." *Accent* 6 (1945): 56–60.

Turnbull, Andrew. *Scott Fitzgerald.* New York: Scribners, 1962.

Way, Brian. *F. Scott Fitzgerald and the Art of Social Fiction.* London: Edward Arnold, 1980.

West, James L. W. III. "Fitzgerald and *Esquire.*" In *The Short Stories of F. Scott Fitzgerald: New Approaches in Criticism.* Ed. Jackson R. Bryer. Madison: University of Wisconsin Press, 1982. 149–66.

Wilson, Edmund, ed. *The Crack-up.* New York: New Directions, 1945.

Going Toward the Flame

Reading Allusions in the *Esquire* Stories

EDWARD J. GLEASON

The allusions in Fitzgerald's *Esquire* stories published between 1935 and 1940, as well as others published posthumously, create a subtext that deepens our understanding of Fitzgerald's personal and artistic *angst* during those final years when he felt—to borrow an image from "The Long Way Out" (September 1937)[1]—the walls of the oubliette closing in on him. The pattern of references reveals a story-beneath-the-stories of the multiple dilemmas that had surrounded the author in the final half decade of his life. Not very far below the surface of even these innocuous *Esquire* stories lies evidence of the psychological mire he found himself in as a result of Zelda's institutionalization, his marital infidelities, strained friendships, income shrinkage, and a depletion of creative self-confidence. Many of the stories' themes are clear indications of the darker turn his thinking had taken, but even where theme does not provide hard evidence of authorial distress, a solid case may be made for inferring Fitzgerald's spiritual midnight through the allusions that came to him, weighted with a significance he would not consciously have been aware of, at the moment of descriptive decision making.

Two stories, both of which are strikingly and atypically short on the kind of allusions to which I refer, but which expose themes crucial to my reading of the meaningful references that pepper most of his *Esquire* fiction are "Design in Plaster" (November 1939) and "On an Ocean Wave" (February 1941). They present stripped-bare models of the themes of loss, desperation, weariness, and guilt that permeated Fitzgerald's thinking in the late 1930s.

Of course to say that these two or any of the stories written during his last five years are "short" on self-exposing allusions is, in a sense, absurd. He was— more than at any other period in his life—writing himself into his material, giving vent to, in James L. W. West III's words, "the autobiographical and confessional impulse,"[2] which apparently was the only powering force left in him. The overarching, if sometimes implied, allusion, then, in all his late stories—including the Pat Hobby sequence, the vapid sketches, and the plot-seeking prenarratives (vapidity and aimlessness can be, after all, poignant autobiographical messages)—is the *à clef* presence of the author.

Notwithstanding, the intensity of the loss and desperation that emanates from "Design in Plaster" elevates this story over others in suggesting the lengths Fitzgerald would go to in order to wrest back his life and his art. Rigidity is the "design" feature of Martin's body cast, and it is a metaphor for types of human inertness as well—Martin's emotional paralysis certainly, and Fitzgerald's emotional and artistic calcification by extension. Martin is in the midst of some key losses. He has lost, if temporarily, the physical mobility he had always taken for granted. More crucially, he has lost his ability to love, and marital separation has been the consequence. Later in the hospital alone, he begins to see what his life has come to. Feeling sorry for himself, jealous that his wife might be entertaining a male friend, and fearful that being alone could become a permanent condition, he resolves to do something. So frantic is he to "go somewhere toward the flame"[3]—whatever that means for him now—that he disregards all common sense and hobbles out of the hospital toward the apartment of his wife, Mary. At least she provides him with *some* direction in an otherwise directionless life.

But his efforts to reconnect with her are as disastrous as they are wrongly motivated. His actions cause him additional physical injury and, interpreted by Mary as a control ploy, they provide her with justification for inviting the male friend into her bedroom in the story's closing scene. Fitzgerald may have tried to mute the urgency of the predicament by working into the sequence outside Mary's door the paradoxically comic image of the fallen, cast-bound Martin's agony, but the motif of panic propelled by a sense of lostness is firmly fixed and lamentably autobiographical. Effectively without mate or muse in the last years, an emotionally impaired Fitzgerald may be glimpsed through stories such as this one searching out *his* lost flame, whether that flame be love, creative inspiration, fame, or the general feeling of exhilaration he experienced in those early years.

In "On an Ocean Wave," it is difficult to believe that, his life in imminent danger, Dollard "could not bring himself to cry out"[4] for help—difficult, that is, until we consider how pervasive the real-life sense of weariness and guilt must have been for Fitzgerald in his Baltimore/Hollywood years. Fitzgerald was bone-weary from a pattern of perceived failures. Clearly he was blaming no one but himself for his inadequacies as husband, father, friend, employee, and author. The climactic sequence of "On an Ocean Wave" may be interpreted as an allegory of self-sacrifice. Pinned down to accepting responsibility for his behavior, wearied from the furtiveness of the liaisons with Gaston Scheer's wife, and almost glad to be soon rid of the whole sordid business, Dollard simply gives in to the hypocritical Scheer's verdict that he should die, apparently by being tossed out the cabin's porthole. Fitzgerald's own crisis of confidence is imprinted on both the harsh judgment Dollard passes on himself and his easy abandonment of the will to live. Fitzgerald doubted now more than ever his intellectual depth (Dollard is a professor, but the level of his intelligence is suspect because he teaches at a technical college rather than a university); he doubted, using the financial yardstick, his importance as a writer (Dollard—dollar); he worried that his depleted imagination would result in fiction not worth reading (Dollard—dullard). The doubting is a serious matter for late-career Fitzgerald, but the epic weariness that signals a loss of the will to go on is tragic.

Fitzgerald was indeed not very good at disguising his preoccupation with the themes of loss, desperation, weariness, and guilt. Even the stories in the *Esquire* series that attempt to deflect thematic weight by reprising some of the flighty characters and innocent discourse of his earliest short fiction have embedded in them—most discoverably in the allusions—traces of the author's miseries. Fitzgerald's conscience does not ease up on him, not even in "lighter" moments of compositional exertion when all that is required of him is to locate a topical reference or two to animate a piece of dialogue or color in a scene.

Song titles and song lyrics are prominent among the categories of allusions that expose Fitzgerald's psychological fraying.[5] The popular songs alluded to in "Three Acts of Music" (May 1936) are not mindless, knee-knocking flapper tunes but somber Youmans, Berlin, and Kern ballads of love—especially love lost—and loneliness. At one point the Yonkers nurse, a coprotagonist, remarks about Berlin, "[His] songs don't sound—."[6] The word left out is "happy," and the pattern created by Fitzgerald's multiple references to song titles and song lyrics indicates, with a sad, self-referential appositeness, the regressive path toward unhappiness the lives of the two lovers has taken. She, from a poor background, and he, an intern from wealth (and spineless, apparently, since he seems to care more about his social status than he does about her), are a study in lost romantic opportunity, a study sketched out largely through the lyrics of popular music. "Tea for Two," appearing early in the story, may on its surface seem benign, but the words come to the couple from a distance and are leaked to them from the orchestra source as "*Tea* . . . / . . . *two* / *Two* . . . / . . . *tea,*" an elliptical rendering suggesting an elliptical relationship. The woman's first words after the song's words register are, "We can never get married" (712) and the intern's, "Well, let's kill the idea." Her picking up on the lyrics and humming, "*And you* . . . / . . . *for me* / *And me* . . . / . . . *for you*" mocks the applicability of the song's sentiments to them. The last word she intones is, appropriately, "*Al* —/ *o-* / *o-* / *n-n* . . ." (712).

The pattern continues in section 2 of the story with references to Berlin's "All Alone," "Remember," "Always," "Blue Skies," and "How About Me." Outside an operating room some years later, the song he tunes in to on the radio (she has invited him to turn it on) is "Remember," whose lyrics conclude with "You promised that you'd forget me not / But you forgot to remember." Back together again after a separation—he to Vienna (with its implications not of waltzes but of psychoanalysis), she to a supervisory position in a large hospital—they make plans less, it seems, to focus on one another than to get a band to play "All Alone." Their testy dialogue in a supper club is punctuated by the ironic lyrics of "Always," which promise unending love, and "Blue Skies," which posits an ironic atmosphere of benignity within which every variety of happiness is assured under sun-suffused skies.

A lyrical approximation of their atrophied relationship occurs in section 3 when Fitzgerald makes reference to "Smoke Gets in Your Eyes" and "Lovely to Look At." Middle-aged in this scene, the couple are further than ever from marrying, and the songs that thread their sad conversation invoke superficial ("*Lovely* / *to look at* / *Romantic* / *to know*" [715][7]) and fractured ("*They* / *asked me how I* / *knew-ew-ew*— / *[That our love was through]*" [716]) relationships. The story concludes with a paragraph that allows the woman to contemplate—with a sublimated desperation and colossal regret— "the wide horizon of how she might have lived" (716). The romance of song lyrics having proved as useless as her beau, the only thing she has to fall back on is the routine of her job. Since she can't imagine what the happiness of the song makers would be like, she can at least, in good nurse fashion, "try to make [their wives] happy" (716) should any of them turn up at her hospital. Is it difficult to read into her subdued desperation and ultimate resignation the late-career crisis of the author, convinced that artistic genius had jilted him and sensing that he was merely going through the motions of putting words on a page?

World War I—specifically a training camp "on the safe side of the ocean"— is the backdrop for "'I Didn't Get Over'" (October 1936), a story whose focal figure was driven by a social inferiority complex to make rash command decisions that ultimately cost human lives and who is, twenty years later, still attempting to deal with the guilt brought on by his fatal foolishness. Hibbing, the teller of the story-within-the-story and another alter ego of Fitzgerald, initially cloaks his guilt by identifying his narrative's protagonist as a "Captain Brown,"[8] but in the closing scene, when the other alumni back on campus for a reunion have left the card game and he is alone with the frame story's narrator, Hibbing rather forthrightly offers the truth that "I was that captain" (176). In his editorial note in *Afternoon of an Author*, Arthur Mizener links Hibbing's desperate wish to belong socially, and his subsequent disappointment, to Fitzgerald's: "The motive for Hibbing's outrageous conduct was all the snubs Fitzgerald had endured in his life: he used to keep lists of them, and was often thrown off by them much as Hibbing was, though not with quite such disastrous consequences. . . . His feelings in such matters were a part of that social self-consciousness which he understood and was subdued by all his life" (169).

Hibbing's guilt—and Fitzgerald's by extension—is two-fold: guilt at not having been "over there" in France where the real action was, and guilt at not having been able to save the soldiers from drowning. Fitzgerald lived his life troubled by the fact that he had also sidestepped a European combat tour. And the "soldiers" his beleaguered psyche might have convinced him he had lost were his wife, his daughter, and perhaps his once artistically confident self. The multiple allusions to Leavenworth suggest that Fitzgerald was serving a kind of prison sentence for *his* lack of a sense of social place and for the social indiscretions he seemed always to be committing. The figure of Stonewall Jackson is raised in this story as well as in "Afternoon of an Author" (August 1936) where the narrator cites the last words Jackson was alleged to have uttered on his deathbed: "Let us cross over the river and rest under the shade of the trees."[9] If the Jackson allusion in "'I Didn't Get Over'" is far more innocent—it seems to be a throwaway image connected to Abe Danzer riding a horse—the earlier use of the reference indeed explains its ironic appearance in Hibbing's descriptive discourse: even in revealing one's guilt, one is never purged of its spirit-deadening effects. Top-heavily burdened with guilt, the successful passage of either Hibbing or Fitzgerald across purifying rivers and into the comforting shade of trees seems unlikely.

The theme of weariness saturates "Afternoon of an Author." In his headnote to the story in *Afternoon of an Author,* Mizener reminds us of the title's derivation in Debussy's "L'Après-midi d'un Faune" (177), a languorous piece that, if the story were a movie script, would make a suitable musical score. The April setting of the story is one Fitzgerald uses on several occasions in his *Esquire* and *Esquire*-type fiction (including "The Long Way Out" and "News of Paris — Fifteen Years Ago"), but the April here is not the month of hope and revitalization; it is instead Eliot's ironic April, derisive of the featured artist whose talent is spent. What follows is a checklist of Fitzgerald's sublimated tensions. The source of the story's author's physical malaise is not clear (although we suspect alcoholic degeneration from the evidence of a recent review that spoke of him as being "fond of night clubs" [181]), but he is only in his late thirties or early forties, lives with a daughter, and is almost totally without creative inspiration. He has brief surges of compositional energy, but little of value comes of them. The magazine story that he has been playing with has no plot to it, and "the characters who started so bravely day-before-yesterday" are now so anemic they aren't "qualified for a newspaper serial." The man panics and thinks only of egress: "Shenandoah Valley or . . . Norfolk" (178) immediately perhaps, but there are also references to Maryland, New Orleans, Hollywood, the French Riviera, and Athens.

The term A.W.O.L. (179) sifts into his consciousness. And, as if he could escape into the remote past and be among men of truly heroic dimension, he calls up Generals Jackson, Lee, Grant, and the Marquis de Lafayette. But these once heroic leaders are not recalled in a context of success and nobility: Jackson is dying, Grant is "desperate," Lee is "shriveling" (179), and Lafayette's statue is reduced to a platform upon which two young lovers, impervious to the icon's significance, play love games. The "Athenian railroad station" is described as "pale," the "*Venite Adoremus*" he hears is eight months out of season, and Fitzgerald's ancestral state's anthem, "Maryland, My Maryland," has as its context a governor's funeral (180).

Even his escape to the barbershop does him no good. There he remembers how a story he once wrote about another barber misfired and "caused some hard feelings" (181), and, after his appointment, dance music overheard from a cocktail room triggers a sequence of interrelated recollections. First, he recalls how infrequently he had danced in the last five years, next, the "fond of night clubs" review, and finally that same reviewer's ironic assessment of the author's artistic energies as "indefatigable": "Something in the sound of the word in his mind broke him momentarily and feeling tears of weakness behind his eyes he turned away" (181). He heads home "to the growing seclusion of his life" (182).[10] He hopes for a creative "reforestation," resolving to "get started on an idea in the two hours before dinner." But instead he lies down. It is very late afternoon, late for both fictional and real authors here, and the light of the "late sunshine" (182) is fading fast.

The allusions in "Author's House" (July 1936) form a pattern of unhealthy movement backwards or, to use Fitzgerald's house-tour image, of movement from basement to cupola that is anything but spiritually uplifting. Houses surveyed here, all belonging to society's notables, are symbolic of the lives and lifestyles of their occupants. The houses and lives of famous actresses (such as Joan Crawford, Virginia Bruce, or Claudette Colbert) are typified by the image of "the hostess done up from behind with a bib explaining how on God's earth to make a Hollywood soufflée or open a can of soup without removing the appendix in the same motion."[11] Perceived through the medium of magazine accounts, such houses are simply beautiful and such lives innocent and carefree. But quite the contrary is the house-cum-life of the story title's author who is being visited and interviewed by a magazine writer whose Smart Set–type of assignment is the sketch we read. Although the article writer claims that, in order not to "leave a somber effect at the end" (184), he will begin his tour/interview with the cellar, the "ascent" to the "attic of Victorian fiction" (188) at the end is in fact a somber and depressing event. He quotes the author as claiming to have left the past ("everything I've forgotten—all the complicated dark mixture of my youth and infancy that made me a fiction writer instead of a fireman or soldier" [184]) behind him in that "dark damp unmodernized" (184) cellar, but the attic's contents reveal another kind of detritus of the past that is no more useful to him than what he buried in the cellar.

The movement from basement to attic should suggest progress and vitality, yet the texture of the attic items proclaims moribundity. Although the author calls it "pleasant" (188), the time of day is, again in this story, "late afternoon" (188) and the message of the attic collection is death. As lifeless as Victorian fiction are the "children's school books" and the "college year books," the "scrap books . . . clipping books . . . photograph books . . . 'baby books'" and grandparental love-letters and "great envelopes full of unfiled items" (188). The "little" magazines the article-writer inventories are either no longer publishing or significantly altered by the late 1930s (the Dial is defunct by 1929, the Mercury by 1932; St. Nicholas, which Fitzgerald read as a youth, was fading fast and would be gone by 1940, as would L'Illustration, which would be discontinued in 1944). This attic "library" should be a comfortable place for an author, but it is not so for a failed, inept, or exhausted one. The atmosphere suggests that some authors' lives reduce to the cold objects of their past, to the "loot" of authorship, which is "what one has instead of a bank balance"

(188). A negative bank balance can indicate, in addition to the absence of the cash that supposedly confirms achievement, an overdrawn emotional account as well.

There is no mention of a family with whom the author shares, or shared, the house; in fact the only reference to love is to a "killed" (184) love about which the author says, "That [pile of earth in the corner] is where I buried my first childish love of myself, my belief that I would never die like others, and that I wasn't the son of my parents but a son of a king, a king who ruled the whole world" (185). Unfulfilled in his life, his art these days seems to be re-duced to devising nasty responses to letters of inquiry, evidenced by the cruel hoax he plays on the poor Michigan woman who believes she saw a clue to her lost brother's whereabouts in an old 1927 *Saturday Evening Post* story by the author. Her letter asking for assistance has been forwarded to him in cir-cumstances of virtual ignominy: the *Post's* mail room crew has made nota-tions on the envelope that refer to the author merely as "X" (as in "whasis-name") who wrote a story for the magazine back in 1927. After first toying cruelly with the woman's hopes, he dashes those hopes by creating two devi-ously misinforming letters to her (this is the only type of fiction he is now capable of generating) — a lie upon a lie about her brother — and sending her a conscience-salving five dollars. He says, "A writer's temperament is continu-ally making him do things he can never repair" (188).

The question Fitzgerald seems to be asking about himself is "My scruples as a writer about what I will allow into print having long since been compro-mised, is there anything I won't resort to with words on a page to affect some type of audience somewhere?" But the creative nadir for the author is more extreme still than his letter-hoax low point when we consider that the words written on the page of this article are not even his but an interpolation by the article writer. It is not in the most pleasant of atmospheres, then, that we move into the house's upper section. The cupola, the last stop on our tour, should, for most writers reviewing their achievements, be the symbolic high point, the epitome of their life and art, but the allusions, description, and dialogue in this case dictate otherwise. It was once an escape, warm and womblike, for the author as a young man; it still provides a wonderful panorama of the sur-rounding terrain, but vision for the author has departed, and he and the speaker go, appropriately, down. The reduction motif is climaxed by our re-calling that this article itself has no real life. It cannot appear where the author would most like to see it appear — in the Mencken/Nathan-edited *Smart Set* — because, as we are told early in the story, the magazine doesn't carry "stories about painters, musicians and authors" ("these classes . . . are not a subject for portraiture" [184]), and more especially because the magazine had ceased operations in 1930.

Matthew J. Bruccoli's introduction to "An Author's Mother" (September 1936), the third story of the "Author's" trilogy, calls it an "obituary story" and invites a comparison between the story's "halting old lady in a black silk dress" and Molly McQuillan Fitzgerald, the author's mother, who, coincidentally, died the month the story appeared.[12] Allusions in this story suggest what the author surmises his mother's assessment of her son's profession was. Her judgment is rigidly qualified. The only author in the middlewestern city of her birth was "regarded as a freak" (736); on the other hand, if her son "could have been an author like Longfellow, or [the psalm-writing poet sisters] Alice or Phoebe Cary" (736–37), then that would have been fine. The sentimental novelists Mrs. Humphrey Ward and Edna Ferber also fall within her parameters of acceptability. Her son's books, however, are "not vivid to her"; she was only proud of him "in a way," and she believes that her son's profession was by and large "risky and eccentric" (737). In her dying moments, her confusion of reality and wish links her prodigal son with the type of writer she would have been comfortable with: " — my son, Hamilton who wrote 'The Poems of Alice and Phoebe Cary — '" (739). Though Fitzgerald loved his mother, even his own imagination could not secure from her the approval he sought.

Zelda is painfully recollected in "The Long Way Out" (September 1937), a story whose narrator tries to be matter-of-fact in rendering the account of a "Mrs. King."[13] Fitzgerald gains double distance from this sensitive subject by having a doctor tell the woman's split-personality story to his narrator. But the reality the story masks is too forceful for detachment. In the introductory paragraph, when social conversation turns to talk of torture chambers, the narrator refers to his "tendency to claustrophobia" so pronounced that "a Pullman berth is a certain nightmare." He would rather not think about things that close him in, and when the doctor begins the Mrs. King story, the narrator calls it a "relief" (443). But the sad tale of the mother's temporary, then permanent, confinement to the sanatorium makes the real relief, the narrator quotes the doctor as saying, a return to discussions of dungeons. The doctor's words are "For God's sake let's talk about something else — let's go back to oubliettes" (447). The personal and professional tug-of-war of wills between Zelda and Scott is paralleled in one of the symptoms of Mrs. King's need for confinement: her "delusion" had "something to do with the Declaration of Independence" (443). There are clear echoes here of the tension arising from Zelda's long desire for an identity apart from her husband. The story implies the factor of fate — there was nothing that could be done about Mr. King's fatal automobile accident—but there is guilt in its autobiographical overtones: could Scott have done more in his lifetime to head off Zelda's institutionalization?

"On Your Own," written in 1931 as "Home to Maryland" but unpublished until 1979 in *Esquire*, is another "obituary story." As in "The Long Way Out," Fitzgerald effected an artistic distancing from another somber topic, the death of a father, by creating the persona of Evelyn Lovejoy (described in the *Esquire* introduction as "a 'party girl' from a fine Southern family"[14]) who is returning to Maryland from London on a cruise ship to attend her father's funeral. But the story, despite attempts to leaven its seriousness with allusions to the Marx Brothers, Gershwin, Chaplin, Mickey Mouse, and the songs "[Shuffle] Off to Buffalo" and "You're Driving Me Crazy," is a catharsis for Fitzgerald, a reckoning with and lament for his father who had died that year, forcing the author to make a similar ocean journey from Europe to Maryland. The "relationship" that supposedly centers the story is not very convincing and is, in fact, at times boorish and silly. When Evelyn moves toward George at the story's end, she is motivated not by love for him but by the realization that "her father was dead" and that "she was alone" (337). George seems more a stand-in for her loss than a legitimate love interest. She only wants to "crawl into his pocket and be safe forever" (338).

Fitzgerald introduces an Evelyn who is only mildly grieved, someone whose surname and shipboard behavior suggest that the trip home is more inconvenience and interruption than a mourning and healing mission. References to the liners *Europa* and *Homeric* seem to reinforce this insouciance. The *Europa* passes her insignificant unnamed "medium-sized German boat" (324) on its way back to Europe, the destination she would prefer ("in New York they'll forget I'm alive" [327]). Others of her troupe are returning to America on the *Homeric*, and it seems appropriate that she not be on board this vessel whose name conjures up classic journeys of great seriousness. But Fitzgerald does not allow her to persist in her frivolousness. Her character is rescued by the poignance of the churchyard scene in "Rocktown" (328; read Fitzgerald's Rockville) where the author invokes a mixture of real and fictional ancestral names among the tombstones. We do come to read into the manuscript Fitzgerald's own sense of loss, which was the beginning of a series of losses in the dreadful decade that was to follow. And it is that loss that permeates his story material here and that makes the emotion finally worth paying attention to—not the patter-heart of the love game, but the grieving for a lost parent.

In a substantial number of other stories as well, it is reasonable to deduce a referencing pattern that reads as a signal of Fitzgerald's inner turmoil. The nurse in "An Alcoholic Case" (February 1937), who tends to the terminally alcoholic cartoonist, introduces the story's central allusion, Margaret Mitch-ell's 1936 novel *Gone with the Wind*. The book's sales in the half year following its June publication were enormous, a fact certainly not lost on the struggling creative mind of the once popular Fitzgerald as it searched for the appropriate descriptive filigree to fill out this story about another desperate struggler. For the youthful and still idealistic nurse, *Gone with the Wind* is not about war and loss but about "things so lovely that had happened long ago."[15] It has less sentimental implications for the cartoonist, however, whom Bryant Mangum understands as "a fictional version of Fitzgerald as he saw himself in early 1937."[16] The cartoonist's Civil War is waged with another of Fitzgerald's own nemeses, the bottle. It is mortal combat for each, and each is close to being a casualty ("death was in that corner where he was looking" [442], observes the nurse at the story's end).

"In the Holidays" (December 1937) is set at New Year's, but the plot is anything but hopeful. McKenna, once an Ohio State college student, is in the hospital to set up a murder on the floor below. While biding his time he tries to force himself sexually upon a young nurse. "The Guest in Room Nineteen" (October 1937) alludes to Easter and (again) the month of April, but the story is the antithesis of a resurrection; death is the spectral presence that prowls the motel hallways. Fitzgerald's narrator in "Financing Finnegan" (January 1938), an author, is critical of the fickle Finnegan, also an author, who is constantly running up debts to his agents and publishers while promising them fiction that never seems to get produced. Finnegan's shortcomings, George Montiero argues convincingly, are the composite shortcomings of Fitzgerald and Hem-ingway that Fitzgerald wrote not very subtly into the character for purposes that are one part self-flagellation for irresponsible behaviors, the other part payback for perceived slights, especially Hemingway's cutting reference to Fitzgerald in "The Snows of Kilimanjaro."[17] Yet he is "a great writer,"[18] says Finnegan's publisher, as if trying to convince himself that it is so. The narrator expresses contempt for that "facile flow . . . which distinguished [Finnegan's] work" (448). The phrase "facile flow" derives from Fitzgerald's own "After-noon of an Author" and the "fatal facility" indictment made against that story's protagonist. In "Finnegan" the phrase has biauthorial application, but Fitz-gerald seems always in these years to be harshest against himself, and it was he more than Hemingway who was guilty of balked productivity and an un-healthy relationship with Maxwell Perkins and other editors and publishers to whom he owed money and/or manuscripts. The Finnegan story is filled as well with allusions to killers ("Dillinger" [448]—here authors seem to be killers of their own talent and possibly of the trust of others), physical restraint/ jails ("*habeas corpus*" [453]), and unnatural solitude ("brown study" [455]).

There is also a climax that is improbable in the story's context but that has rather poignant authorial reverberations. Notwithstanding one attribution of Finnegan's miraculous return from the dead to Hemingway's death-cheating escapes from accidents in Africa, the more affecting source is Fitzgerald's subtextual wish to be resuscitated as a writer.

"The Lost Decade" (December 1939) is about an artist's attempt to effect a creative comeback. The artist is an architect, and his return is from a ten-year bout with alcohol. The story, written very late in Fitzgerald's *Esquire* period, has tones that are understandably both wistful and futile. Trimble is no longer interested in the buildings he once designed, only in the structure of human activity—in other words, living—he has missed out on. He speaks of Cole Porter coming back to the States from Europe in 1928 to capture the new human rhythms. Trimble's departure down the city street elicits an exclamation of "Jesus" from the respectful young writer Orrison Brown who has been assigned to accompany the older man. Among the many interpretations of the significance of that exclamation is that Fitzgerald is romanticizing the fate of failed artists: "Jesus" is the benedictory homage ("orison," of course, means prayer) young writers ought to pay their senior counterparts, especially those like Trimble who, Christlike, have been resurrected from the grave of nonproductivity.

The posthumously published story "Three Hours Between Planes" (July 1941) is about the necessity of adjusting to the way time has of deflating our illusions, in this instance a middle-aged man's youthful infatuation with a young girl who is now married and whom he stops to visit. His dream is thwarted (she even mistakes him for someone else), and the story concludes with the gloomy epiphany, "the second half of life is a long process of getting rid of things"[19]—evidently most of the idealized expectations of youth. In the story, Fitzgerald continues to work at divesting himself of his dreams of happily-ever-after marriages (reference to a dead wife), a reconstituted Jazz Age lifestyle (reference to the anachronistic lyrics of the flapper-era tune "Ain't We Got Fun"), and the identification with fictional heroes (a reference to the impossibility of anyone living like a fictional character for even "five blinding minutes" [468]). And the *Esquire*-genre story "News of Paris—Fifteen Years Ago," probably written in 1940 but posthumously published elsewhere, is dotted with references to the old Paris scene. But Fitzgerald cannot succeed in making his "hero" Henry Dell seem like anything other than a bounder and a lecher. His April day's "play" is not rakish and clever; it is cruel, irresponsible, and, given his final thoughts about his young French ward, almost degenerate. The tonal effect is melancholic rather than either nostalgic or madcap. Fitzgerald's fictional return to the scene of old revelings is out of tune (he alludes to Debussy here but this time to Parisian auto horns screeching him out), and he knows it. Henry *is* "a contemptible drone"[20] who had better get back to "duty," to more respectable behavior. The story's clipped dialogue — "intense," Sergio Perosa says, "in its bare diction . . . as if in a film script"[21] — is an unavoidable reminder of Fitzgerald's generally fruitless Hollywood scriptwriting period, a period where his own behavior, like Henry's, was something less than respectable.

The narrative about Fitzgerald's crisis that the *Esquire* allusions uncover is both reinforced by and helpful in elucidating what is revealed about that same issue in *The Last Tycoon*. The *Tycoon* plot is thickly laden with sick, dysfunctional, and doomed characters (even Cecelia, we know from the fragments, is tubercular and tells her story from a sanatorium), and its referential underpinning is uniformly depressing. Two categories of allusions stand out here — popular songs and history's high achievers. As the songs of the *Esquire* stories typically point toward some form of subtextual anxiety, so do those of *Tycoon*, whether the pointing is more direct as in "Lost," "Gone," "Smoke Gets in Your Eyes," "I'm on a See-Saw," and "When Day is Done," or less, as in the sardonic potential "Blue Heaven," "Top Hat," "Cheek to Cheek," and "Little Girl, You've Had a Busy Day" have in the context of the Hollywood community and Fitzgerald's painful matriculation within it. And as references to famous people in the stories typically have a significance beyond their surface function, the same may be said of the notable names spread across the chapters of *Tycoon*. Figures called up, mostly from the past but from the author's present as well, include Lincoln, Andrew Jackson, Botticelli, Spengler, Edison, Cortez, Shakespeare, Euripides, Freud, Marx, and Eugene O'Neill. They are on the one hand colorful daubs from his descriptive palette; on the other, within the larger narrative of author-disclosing-himself, their presence invites the uncomfortable, self-answering question of how late-career Fitzgerald sees himself in relation to this pantheon of successes. Again, behind the seemingly innocent facade of these references, Fitzgerald is sending out a major distress signal. Allusion-reading in the *Esquire* stories may help define the author's crisis more sharply. Fitzgerald in those last years was working out a long, sad farewell, trying desperately to forestall the inevitable flood of losses. The allusions tell us a little more about the frustrations implicit in that futile endeavor.

NOTES

1. The month and year in parentheses following a story indicate the date of the story's appearance in *Esquire*.

2. West, "Fitzgerald and *Esquire*," 149–50. Alice Hall Petry says in this regard that Fitzgerald is "arguably the most dramatic example in American history of an author whose private life is reflected, consciously or otherwise, in virtually everything he wrote" (*Fitzgerald's Craft of Short Fiction*, 4). Concerning Fitzgerald's tendency toward self-revelation in the stories I will consider, John A. Higgins observes, "As for the minor, unfamiliar stories, their value in . . . biographical areas equals and in some respects exceeds that of the major stories" (*F. Scott Fitzgerald*, 186).

3. Fitzgerald, *Afternoon of an Author*, 193.

4. Fitzgerald, *Price Was High*, 781.

5. Malcolm Cowley's essay "Third Act and Epilogue" notes how hard Fitzgerald worked to capture in his prose "the color of every passing year, its distinctive slang, its dance steps, its songs" (64). Ruth Prigozy's article "'Poor Butterfly'" provides a comprehensive listing of Fitzgerald's references to popular songs in his fiction and nonfiction. She comments that Fitzgerald was, throughout his career, fully in command of the rhetorical technique of using song lyrics to enhance a mood, reveal a character trait, or underscore a theme. "As Fitzgerald developed artistically," she states, "his use of popular music would increasingly serve to reveal nuances of personality, plot, and idea" (55). And, I argue, the technique would—more and more in his last half-decade—be rooted in coded messages about himself as well.

6. Fitzgerald, *Price Was High*, 713. All subsequent page references to "Three Acts of Music" are to the 1979 edition and appear parenthetically in the text.

7. Matthew J. Bruccoli observes, in an editorial footnote in *The Price Was High* (715), that Fitzgerald misquotes the lyrics to this song.

8. Fitzgerald, *Afternoon of an Author*, 172. All subsequent references to "'I Didn't Get Over'" are to the 1957 edition and appear parenthetically in the text.

9. Ibid., 169. All subsequent references to "Afternoon of an Author" are to the 1957 edition and appear parenthetically in the text.

10. Petry notes: "F. Scott Fitzgerald literally had no home." It should not be a surprise, she says, that, having moved around so much throughout his life, he "seems to have had little understanding of what a home and family are really like" (*Fitzgerald's Craft of Short Fiction*, 90). Consequently, in his fiction homes are presented either in "sentimental or melodramatic terms," or "as sources of relentless misery" (91). Doubtless the effects of this lack of a domestic rooting—especially later in life when such a rooting can be a source of stability—aggravated Fitzgerald's psychological crises.

11. Fitzgerald, *Afternoon of an Author*, 183. All subsequent references to "Author's House" are to the 1957 edition and appear parenthetically in the text.

12. Fitzgerald, *Price Was High*, 736. All subsequent references to "An Author's Mother" are to the 1979 edition and appear parenthetically in the text.

13. Fitzgerald, *Stories*, 443. All subsequent references to "The Long Way Out" are to the 1951 edition and appear parenthetically in the text.

14. Fitzgerald, "On Your Own," 56. The story was reprinted in *The Price Was High*; all

subsequent references to "On Your Own" are to the *Price Was High* appearance and appear parenthetically in the text.

15. Fitzgerald, *Stories*, 436. All subsequent references to "An Alcoholic Case" are to the 1951 edition and appear parenthetically in the text.
16. Mangum, *Fortune Yet*, 156.
17. Montiero, "Two Sets of Books."
18. Fitzgerald, *Stories*, 449. All subsequent references to "Financing Finnegan" are to the 1951 edition and appear parenthetically in the text.
19. Ibid., 469. All subsequent references to "Three Hours Between Planes" are to the 1951 edition and appear parenthetically in the text.
20. Fitzgerald, *Afternoon of an Author*, 225.
21. Perosa, *Art of F. Scott Fitzgerald*, 146.

WORKS CITED

Cowley, Malcolm. "Third Act and Epilogue." In *F. Scott Fitzgerald: A Collection of Critical Essays*. Ed. Arthur Mizener. Englewood Cliffs, N.J.: Prentice-Hall, 1963. 64–69.

Fitzgerald, F. Scott. *Afternoon of an Author: A Selection of Uncollected Stories and Essays*. Ed. Arthur Mizener. New York: Scribners, 1957.

———. "On Your Own." *Esquire*, January 30, 1979, 55–67.

———. *The Price Was High: The Last Uncollected Stories of F. Scott Fitzgerald*. Ed. Matthew J. Bruccoli. New York: Harcourt Brace Jovanovich, 1979.

———. *The Stories of F. Scott Fitzgerald*. New York: Scribners, 1951.

Higgins, John A. *F. Scott Fitzgerald: A Study of the Stories*. Jamaica, N.Y.: St. John's University Press, 1971.

Mangum, Bryant. *A Fortune Yet: Money in the Art of F. Scott Fitzgerald's Stories*. New York: Garland, 1991.

Monteiro, George. "Two Sets of Books, One Balance Sheet: 'Financing Finnegan.'" In *The Short Stories of F. Scott Fitzgerald: New Approaches in Criticism*. Ed. Jackson R. Bryer. Madison: University of Wisconsin Press, 1982. 291–99.

Perosa, Sergio. *The Art of F. Scott Fitzgerald*. Tr. by Charles Matz and Sergio Perosa. Ann Arbor: University of Michigan Press, 1965.

Petry, Alice Hall. *Fitzgerald's Craft of Short Fiction: The Collected Stories—1921–1935*. Ann Arbor, Mich.: UMI Research Press, 1989.

Prigozy, Ruth. "'Poor Butterfly': F. Scott Fitzgerald and Popular Music." *Prospects* 2 (1976): 41–67.

West, James L. W., III. "Fitzgerald and *Esquire*." In *The Short Stories of F. Scott Fitzgerald: New Approaches in Criticism*. Ed. Jackson R. Bryer. Madison: University of Wisconsin Press, 1982. 149–66.

A Dark Ill-Lighted Place

Fitzgerald and Hemingway, Philippe Count of Darkness and Philip Counter-Espionage Agent

H. R. STONEBACK

It shall be the story of Ernest. . . .

Just as Stendahl's [sic] portrait of Byronic man made *Le Rouge et Noir* so couldn't *my* portrait of Ernest as Philippe make the real modern man.[1]

— F. Scott Fitzgerald

In this essay, with its tripartite division, I am concerned, first, to reassess the matter of Philippe, the most neglected fiction in the Fitzgerald canon; second, to open a new line of inquiry through consideration of the Catholic resonances and modalities of both the Philippe stories and the Fitzgerald-Hemingway relationship; and third, to propose the hitherto overlooked probability that Hemingway's most direct response to Fitzgerald's portrait of Philippe as Hemingway may be discerned in Hemingway's play *The Fifth Column.*

Very little critical attention has been given to the Philippe stories; the few observers who have discussed them generally agree that they are failures. Matthew J. Bruccoli places them "among the worst fiction Fitzgerald ever published"; for Janet Lewis, they are Fitzgerald's "least successful fictions," albeit "interesting failures"; for Kermit W. Moyer, they are "not very good" stories but they "deserve more attention"; for William R. Anderson, they have a "curious hybrid quality" that is irritating, and he agrees with what he sees as the conclusion of Fitzgerald scholarship that "the 'Darkness' series" is "difficult and embarrassing to encompass"; and for Scottie Fitzgerald Smith, they represent Fitzgerald's "most abysmal failure." [2]

More recently, Kim Moreland has cogently suggested that Fitzgerald's enduring engagement with the Philippe project "performed a psychological rather than aesthetic function," providing the author "with a necessary psychological escape" from his own time, "however deleterious its effect on his art." And Peter Hays, while concurring with earlier assessments of the weakness of the Philippe stories, perspicaciously notes the pattern of character growth and maturation, Philippe's "growing self-control and growing willingness to recognize the rights of those the ninth century would have regarded as inferiors: peasants and women." [3]

I agree with all of these conclusions; the Philippe stories are indeed murky, dismal failures under any rubric: conception, execution, rendered life, characterization, style, dialogue, form, technique, and so forth. Most commentators have noted the ludicrous dialogue, the awkward pastiche of hard-boiled lingo and southern sharecropper talk put into the mouths of the ninth-century French characters in these tales. It could be said that the dialogue sounds as if it had been written by a drunk with a tin ear who had read, probably on a bad hangover, a few pages of Faulkner and Hemingway. All in the same breath, Philippe says things like "Howdy" and "God save you!"; or "I'll be back you rats . . . I'll let daylight through you" (with a sword!). And Philippe addresses his ladies as "little baggage" or "little chicken." [4] The Faulkner-Hemingway dialogue stew *is* embarrassing, and there is no need to say more about it. Overall, these stories would be lucky to get a C-minus in a creative writing course. The question we should ask is this: how could Fitzgerald, after the triumphant stylistic achievements of *The Great Gatsby* and *Tender Is the Night*, fail so miserably in these late stories? There are many possible answers to this question, but the shortest answer is one word—Hemingway.

The long answer to this question is inextricably intertwined with the *only* reason these stories are of any real interest—Fitzgerald's design of these tales as "the story of Ernest," his preoccupation with these stories as "the portrait of Ernest as Philippe," which, Fitzgerald hoped, would somehow tell the story of "the real modern man." For this reason alone, because of the very intensity with which Fitzgerald centered his "darkness" stories, his tales of "chaos and leadership," in the character and person *and* fiction of Hemingway, we must attempt to come to terms, at last, with Philippe, Count of Darkness.

The Philippe-Hemingway matter has been treated most fully by Janet Lewis, but even her discussion falls short of dealing adequately with the manifold Fitzgerald-Hemingway connections evinced in the Philippe material. Perhaps the primary reason for this is the insufficient grasp of Hemingway that has been brought to Philippe's table — the insufficiency of the critics, not of Fitzgerald. As for Hemingway scholarship, the Philippe matter has not even been raised; indeed the vast majority of Hemingway scholars seem utterly unaware of the most extraordinary fact that one of Fitzgerald's last ambitious projects was to have been a historical romance, with Hemingway starring as a medieval knight.[5]

The first Philippe story, "In the Darkest Hour" (given the subtitle "A Poignant Romance of Chaos and Leadership" in its October 1934 *Redbook* appearance),[6] begins: "On a May afternoon in the Year of Our Lord 872 a young man rode a white Arabian horse down a steep slope into the Valley of the Loire. . . . He was lost" (513). Raised in Moorish Spain, he has returned to his birthplace in France to claim his estate and inheritance as Philippe, the Count of Villefranche. In Fitzgerald's "lost generation" paradigm, Philippe must struggle to bring order and light out of the darkness and chaos of his ravaged and pillaged France; he must "struggle for mastery." How is Philippe like Hemingway? Bruccoli, among others, thinks he is "not recognizably so": "Anyone who did not know that Philippe was modeled on Hemingway would not be likely to make the identification."[7] I disagree. Philippe clearly embodies certain general characteristics of Hemingway; as Lewis puts it, "Fitzgerald is obviously attempting to portray the pride, bravado, the reckless courage and the skill that he so much admired in Hemingway."[8] Yes, *obviously* — this, and much more. Philippe is "broad and strong," has a "firm" mouth, eyes that are "somewhat cruel" as well as "shrewd and bright" (513). He speaks directly, sometimes harshly. He asserts his authority and mastery, he acts decisively. He can be "taciturn and scornful" (518) but also sensitive and romantic. He is a "hard-boiled count" *and* a man devoted to the people. He is a tough guy *and* an idealist. He is brutal in combat *and* disciplined in his prayers. He may have trouble sleeping, but in the dark hours, he thinks "creatively" (522) and prays devoutly. In short, Philippe is an exact and unmistakable portrait of Hemingway. But to see this clearly, we must know our Hemingway — the man and his fictions — and know him well, at least as well as Fitzgerald knew him.

It will be useful here to catalog a number of echoes and resonances of Hemingway and his work, to sample some of the Hemingway inklings found in the Philippe stories. From "In the Darkest Hour" we learn about key formative factors in the identity of Philippe, factors that might be summed up in two words: France, Spain. In these tales so much concerned with darkness and dawn, with sleepless nights and sunrises, with lost-generation undertones, we also meet characters such as Jacques (who is "hard-boiled" and "intelligent"), and Letgarde, a dislocated victim of war who has gone off with an outsider named Robert the Frog. Jacques, Letgarde, and Robert the Frog—Jake, Brett, and Robert Cohn? As the first tale ends, we see Philippe, standing guard over his camp at night, refusing to sleep. "I keep the watch," he tells Letgarde, who suggests he should go to bed: "Let the others get tired. I keep the watch." This is essential Philippe, keeping watch in the darkness, and this is Fitzgerald's essential Hemingway, as the story's last line has it: "Embodying in himself alone the future of his race, he walked to and fro in the starry darkness" (529).

The second Philippe story, "The Count of Darkness," begins at dawn, with Philippe, "who had eventually fallen off to sleep," waking up quickly. Letgarde joins him. After some conversation, in which Philippe utters some rather silly Hemingwayisms (or Fitzgerald's laughable notion of Hemingwayisms) such as "What do you want, little chicken?," the sun also rises as the story struggles to get in motion. Philippe grabs Letgarde, pulls her up on his horse, telling her, "Don't let go, baby, and nothing can happen to you." But Fitzgerald's "nothing," his tenuous version of Hemingway's nada, is closing in around Letgarde. When Philippe leaves her alone, she hears the singing of a wandering "hobo"-troubadour, and she is fascinated by his song. "Barefoot girl," the tramp sings, "Feet like trout for streams, / Silver trout for streams, / Whiter than the whitest pebble in the stream bottom—." If, for some readers, these lines will resonate with Hemingway's iconic trout, and, for others, they will seem to echo the famous opening sentences of A Farewell to Arms (those white pebbles in the riverbed), then perhaps the sentimentality of Fitzgerald's handling of the Philippe-Letgarde romance, and her drowning in the Loire, will possess a reverberant intertextuality with the story of the love and loss of Catherine and Frederic in Hemingway's novel. And we might see the Loire as another Big Two-Hearted River, since Philippe must deal with the complaints of his people about "the unfruitfulness of fishing on the Loire." Philippe-Hemingway, of course, is equal to the task: He declares: "Let's dope up a way of getting fish out of this stream"—and he does. Fishing in the dark, using lights to "blind the fish," and spears, they get their fish. (An interesting sidelight is that while Fitzgerald was working on this story, Hemingway invited him down to Key West for a fishing trip. Fitzgerald did not go, perhaps—among other reasons—because he wanted to avoid being overwhelmed by Hemingway's presence, by his technical expertise and exactitude, his codified ritual-fishing excursions, all of which Fitzgerald may have feared as potential intrusion, invasion of his process of composing his Philippe-Hemingway narrative.)

Fishing in the dark, then, is an appropriate metaphor, an apt summary of "The Count of Darkness." The fishing scene ends when the drowned body of Letgarde drifts downstream. Philippe holds her in his arms, kneels beside her, takes her in his arms again, rocking her "to and fro" in a kind of inverted piscatorial pietà vignette that must be the most bathetic scene Fitzgerald ever composed. "Poor little lost doggy," Philippe laments. Then, rather like a slippery trout, "her body slid from him." He kneels beside her again, says one *Ave Maria*, and then, in the brilliant moonlight, he finds he can "say *nothing*." Again, he tries: "'*Ave Maria* —' he began—and it seemed as if the trees told him *nothing*" (emphasis added). In brief, the Hemingway convergences are figured as follows: in the darkness, in his clean, well-lighted place by the big two-hearted river, Philippe, in the comminatory presence of nada, says his farewell to arms. A thoroughly Hemingwayesque tough-tender exemplar, "choked with emotion," Philippe disciplines his feelings in front of his men and commands them to dig her grave. "I guess I must be pretty much of a tough," he thinks as the story—at last—approaches its conclusion.

The third Philippe tale, "The Kingdom in the Dark," which Fitzgerald or more probably the editors at *Redbook* characterized as a look at "despair-ridden France of the Ninth Century" and which demonstrates "that national chaos does not fail to bring forth a leader," is mainly concerned with Philippe's construction of his fort, his political struggles with the King, and above all with his acquisition of a new girl—Griselda (Zelda?), who rides into his domain on a "swell horse," fleeing from the King. The moral and spiritual pivot of the story turns on Philippe's loyalty, his fidelity to Griselda. The King asks repeatedly if Philippe has seen her; although Philippe is protecting her, hiding her, he gives his solemn oath on a rosary that he knows nothing about her. "He would," Fitzgerald writes, "risk the fires of hell rather than betray this girl." Deeply troubled by his false oath— "he would not sleep well again until he had confessed himself, and been absolved" —he finally gets to sleep, only to be awakened after midnight by the cries of "fire!" The King has ordered that Philippe's fort and home be burned to the ground. The story ends at dawn, with Philippe and Griselda watching the smoldering ruins. Philippe, still troubled by his false oath and the possibility that "maybe Almighty Providence doesn't believe [him] any more," nevertheless pronounces a ringing vow to rebuild his domain.

The final story, "Gods of Darkness," begins with Philippe and Griselda sunbathing and skinny-dipping (favorite Hemingway activities) in the Loire. Merchants approach the ford, which Philippe controls and from which he derives his income; Philippe immediately blows his "deer's horn" to summon his men to come to his assistance. They take their 10 percent cut of the goods the merchants are transporting; Griselda covets some lovely material, thinking of the fine gown and cape it would make. After the merchants go on their way, as Philippe and Griselda talk of marriage, she wonders why they should share the booty with Philippe's people: "Why do you have to cut it with these monkeys in the valley?" Philippe is outraged: "They're not monkeys; and if they are, then *I'm* one. And if you can't get over that kind of talk, then you're no fit wife for a chieftain. They're *us*. I'm *them* — it's hard to explain —." Here Fitzgerald attempts to deepen his portrait of Philippe-Hemingway, to include 1930s-correct proletarian sympathies, oneness with the people, and thus evokes the so-called awakening of Hemingway's social consciousness in the 1930s.

Still echoing Hemingway biography rather directly, Fitzgerald has Philippe and Griselda go to the neighboring monastery to discuss their forthcoming marriage.[9] The Abbot takes Philippe aside to speak of another urgent matter. He asks Philippe if he knows why the people are so loyal to him after such a short time, why his right-hand man, Jacques, was able to bring them over to Philippe's side. Philippe has no inkling. The Abbot tells him it is because Jacques is "an important man in a cult." Hearing this, the devout Philippe crosses himself and knocks on wood. "That's exactly what I . . . mean," the Abbot says. "Our people aren't really Christian. They cross themselves — and then touch wood! That's the cult." After more talk of this "secret society," the Abbot asks for Philippe's help in stamping out this "pagan worship." Philippe affirms his intention: "My people are going to worship the Christian God."

Shortly thereafter, a large military force under the Duke of Maine enters Philippe's territory. Things look bad, but the "secret society" comes to the rescue. "Secret lingo" and passwords are exchanged between Jacques and Griselda; we learn that Griselda is also a member of the dark cult, and as the confrontation with the enemy approaches its climax, Philippe realizes that the "power from below" is a potent force, that the "powerful underground league" ties "his men to the men of the Duke of Maine."

After Philippe, employing one of the secret code words, seizes the Duke of Maine as a hostage, a temporary truce is established. Philippe is awakened at midnight by Griselda, for his final initiation into what he calls "this hoodoo stuff." She leads him to a cave, the proper passwords are given, and they enter. In this "dim cathedral," in this "deep locker-room of the earth," Fitzgerald writes, "the weekly *Esbat* of the Witch Cult was about to take place." Philippe sees many of his own people as well as the retainers of his hostage-enemy, the Duke of Maine, taking part in the ceremonies. The local "priestess" of the Witch Cult, Becquette, presides over the ritual. She harbors a grudge against Philippe, and when she finally recognizes him in this "dim cathedral," she denounces him. Philippe reminds everyone that he has an important hostage; he proposes a deal with the Duke's men who are also cult members: if they let him go, he'll let the Duke go if they all agree to vacate his domain. The deal is made. But Becquette is still enraged, and since she is a "goddess," since she is "sacred," then "no mere military agreement would stand beside her word." She shouts to her followers: "We'll burn his heart in pig's fat at the Sabbat! Christian! Blasphemer! I say it! I, priestess and Oracle!" Now Griselda comes to the rescue, as we learn that she is a higher-ranking witch and priestess of the cult: "Fool! You're talking before the chief priestess of the Witches of Touraine! Here's the sign—and the proof!" She reveals the pendant-symbol that identifies her as the "true priestess," and the crisis ends.

In the final movement of the story, after they've emerged from the "deep locker-room" (an allusion to Hemingway's earthy athleticism), as they ride home (with the sun about to rise), Philippe, sounding very much like Fitzgerald's version of a Spanish-Republican-Hemingway-cum-Huck-Finn, makes a series of pronouncements: "I haven't got any conscience except for my county, and for those who live in it . . . All right—I'll use this cult—and maybe burn in hell forever after. . . . But maybe Almighty Providence will understand" (Fitzgerald's ellipses). "If these witches know better," Philippe asserts, "then I'll be one of *them!*" Then, in one of Fitzgerald's more unfortunate passages, awkwardly parodying Hemingway content and style, Philippe's mind ("worn down . . . relaxed") stops working so intensely; he thinks about Becquette, how he'd "like to take a punch" at that "baby": "The sorer she got, the more I liked her!"

Thus the Philippe stories end, with his troubled Catholic conscience struggling to accommodate a new vision of darkness: "Half a god—half a devil. I'll play all their games—I'm playing to win." And Philippe and Griselda bathe again "in the sun of St. Anthony's summer," feeling "grateful to any god": "For the moment they did not care which one." With these final words of the unfinished and unrealized Philippe chronicle, we are left in the shadows of the "dim cathedral," the "deep locker-room" of Hemingway's chthonic athleticism *and* his telluric muscular Christianity, which plays to win; we are left somewhere near the dark heart of the enigma that is both Fitzgerald's fascination with Hemingway as well as his massive failure to make art, to render story (*historia*) from that fascination.

> Feel awfully about Scott. I tried to write him once (wrote him several times)
> to cheer him up but he seems almost to take a pride in his shamelessness of
> defeat. . . . Maybe the Church would help him.[10]
> — Ernest Hemingway

Clearly, there are many resonances of Hemingway and his fiction in the four Philippe stories. But the most deeply submerged portion of Fitzgerald's iceberg, potentially his most profound and engaging though unrealized or dimly inscribed subtext, has to do with Hemingway as a Catholic. It is difficult to decode Fitzgerald's scarcely legible palimpsest, his fumbling chiaroscuro portrait of Hemingway-the-Catholic-Knight, but the attempt must be made. This line of inquiry into Philippe has never been opened, perhaps because very few observers take seriously the importance of Catholicism in the lives *and* works of both Fitzgerald and Hemingway. I suggest that what we have in the Philippe stories is the angle of vision of a lapsed "Cradle Catholic," with Fitzgerald as a priest manqué contemplating the darkness and light in the work and person of a rather devout Catholic convert, as Hemingway was during the period that Fitzgerald knew him. Not unrelated to this Catholic matrix, this nexus of thought and feeling, is Fitzgerald's grasp of what might be called Hemingway's medievalism.[11]

For my purposes here, it will suffice to locate my understanding of Fitzgerald's Catholic sensibility somewhere close to the views of Andrew Turnbull, who sees Fitzgerald's work as "deeply religious in its spiritual yearning," as a reflection of "the religious sensibility which never left him," and Joan M. Allen, who sees Fitzgerald as a priest manqué whose "Catholic habit of mind" lingered to the end.[12] As for Hemingway, he was much more than the "nominal" Catholic some biographers and most observers make him out to be. He was, in fact, a devout convert who was, as I have argued in considerable detail elsewhere, a practicing Catholic for much of his adult life, especially during the years of his most intense creativity, and during the period of his friendship with Fitzgerald.[13] Even though most Hemingway biographers and critics refuse to accept, to understand, or to take seriously the Hemingway who said that the "only way he could run his life decently was to accept the discipline of the Church,"[14] I believe Fitzgerald understood this about Hemingway and took it quite seriously. As Turnbull notes, Fitzgerald "respected, and perhaps envied, all honest believers," admired people who had "true Catholic zeal."[15] Fitzgerald's recognition of this quality in Hemingway is the point of departure for his characterization of Hemingway as Philippe. There is more than a little respect and envy, admiration and skepticism, in Fitzgerald's reading of Hemingway's Catholicism.

In the first story, "In the Darkest Hour," Philippe is presented as "a devout Christian" who, along with fighting and flirting, claiming the land and his girl, spends a good deal of time praying. As he brings order to his ancestral domain, his guiding principle is: "I'll do nothing without the approval of the Church" (519). This devout Count, this knight who keeps watch in the darkness, embodies the salvation and "the future of his race" (529). In "The Count of Darkness," we again see Philippe in prayer, but this time, choked with grief over the death of Letgarde, he cannot complete his Hail Marys, and he approaches the nada-prayers of the Dark Night of the Soul. Fitzgerald may not have known his San Juan de la Cruz (as well as Hemingway did), but he did know his Hemingway and he does echo "A Clean, Well-Lighted Place" in this passage. In addition, although Philippe is a tough guy and a warrior and an often harsh, imperious leader, he is also the kind of Catholic knight who reprimands one of his men when he crosses himself inappropriately: "Don't do that . . . You only do that for a woman when it's the Sacred Virgin." All of this, of course, is precisely the Hemingway mode and code of Catholic precision, ritual, and discipline.[16]

In the third story, "The Kingdom in the Dark," Philippe does not pray, does not negotiate with the local monastery, does not seek the blessing of the Abbot for action; yet the story is spiritually centered and it turns on the "false oath" Philippe takes on the rosary, and his sleepless anguish, his longing for confession and absolution. The title of the story — of all the stories, for that matter — points to the overall design, the master motif: the Dark Night of the Soul that Philippe must experience in order to refine and anneal his faith and zeal. (Of course, it is a given that in this badly flawed and unfinished chronicle, that is, the intended novel, the design is unrealized and the master motif is unresolved. This, however, does not provide the reader with absolution of the burden of reckoning with Fitzgerald's optative design, the spiritual biography of Philippe-Hemingway.)

In "Gods of Darkness," the final installment of Fitzgerald's unfinished soap opera, we see Philippe crossing himself and knocking on wood (a double sign that Hemingway often made and Fitzgerald probably witnessed). When Philippe does this, the Abbot of the monastery suggests that he is behaving like one of the superstitious peasant-cult members. (Biographers and friends of Hemingway frequently note that Hemingway was as superstitious as a medieval peasant.)[17] In any case, superstition notwithstanding, Philippe assures the

Abbot firmly that his people are going to be good Catholics. After this exchange with the Abbot, we follow Philippe to the Witch Cult ceremony in the cave, where he realizes the power of darkness and comes to some accommodation with the cultic force. It might be argued that Fitzgerald is here calling into question or gainsaying the Catholic identity of Philippe-Hemingway. Such a conclusion, however, is unwarranted; all that we really know is that Philippe has learned the power of darkness, that he is determined to *use* the cult to accomplish his goals.

We cannot know how Fitzgerald intended to develop his religious themes in subsequent chapters. We only know that in Philippe's "struggle for mastery" he must master the darkness; as the Count of Darkness he must make the darkness count in the final score, and he will play their games if he must, because he is "playing to win." Risky business, indeed, but not necessarily a denial or betrayal of his faith; in fact, Philippe's descent into the "dim cathedral" of the goddess is both a kind of Harrowing of Hell and a Dark Night of the Soul, which has the very property, the specific function, of strengthening and deepening faith. All of this, then, is the very stuff of Hemingway. As Archibald MacLeish put it, Hemingway was one of the most "spiritually powerful creatures I have ever known." [18] Fitzgerald felt this power, too, and I think he knew better than did MacLeish that the power was both spiritual and Catholic.

If the contemporary reader is troubled by such trifles as the fact that Philippe kills men in one paragraph, prays in the next, and vows to make his domain Catholic in the next, it is only necessary to be reminded that this is the Church Militant, the crusading Catholicism of the Middle Ages — precisely the Church that Hemingway loved and identified with most fully. Saint James or Santiago Matamoros or Saint-Jacques — pilgrim saint *and* slayer of infidels — occupied center stage in Hemingway's iconographic pageant, along with Roland. [19] Fitzgerald knew all this, and there was good reason for him to worry when he was working on Philippe and heard that Hemingway was working on a new book: "I hope to God it isn't the crusading story that he once had in mind, for I would hate like hell for my 9th century novel to have to compete with *that*." [20] It wasn't, but Fitzgerald had reason to be concerned, just as he had reason (and sufficient knowledge of Hemingway's brand of medievalism) to work into the fabric of the Philippe chronicle some of Hemingway's favorite motifs, such as the horn that Philippe blows to summon aid, its "mournful imperative note" a clear echo of Roland's horn that so haunted Hemingway's imagination. Or Philippe's scorn for the pacifist Abbot as he reminds the peace-loving cleric that there used to be "bishops who fought out front with battle-axes." This allusion to Bishop Turpin in *The Song of Roland* is an equally direct allusion to Hemingway's love of and frequent creative use of the great *Chanson*. And Philippe's right-hand man, Jacques, is an avatar of Hemingway's favorite saint, Santiago/Saint-Jacques. In addition, Philippe in his role as student of medieval fortifications precisely echoes Hemingway the careful student of military defenses and the walled cities of the Middle Ages.

In sum, even if such observers of Hemingway's life and work as Carlos Baker find it very "odd" and "surprising"[21] that Fitzgerald used Hemingway as his model for his medieval knight, it seems to me perfectly natural — I am tempted to say inevitable — that Fitzgerald spent a good part of his last decade brooding about a Catholic knight in medieval France, brooding about Hemingway as a knight frenchified and Francophilic (far more so than that leading shibboleth of Hemingway criticism — his supposed Hispanophilia — has allowed). Above all, it is perfectly apt that Fitzgerald spent his last years brooding about Hemingway as a Catholic knight in a twentieth-century Waste Land.

> Down through the valley of the Loire . . . Ernest amused himself by imagining that he was a medieval knight riding his horse along the riverbank. The notion stayed with him all the way south [to Spain].[22]
> — Carlos Baker

What was Hemingway's response to the Philippe stories? In Bruccoli's various brief accounts of the Philippe question, he merely notes that "Hemingway's reaction to the series is unknown"; or, as he put it in *Scott and Ernest*, where one would hope for a more detailed treatment than the one page devoted to this rich matter: "there is nothing to indicate that Hemingway recognized himself — if he ever read the stories" (125).[23] At this moment, I am unable to present *documentary* evidence that Hemingway knew the Philippe stories. Yet perhaps such evidence will be unearthed if this essay serves one of its purposes — to encourage more extensive investigation of the Philippe-Hemingway connection. Nor is there any reason to be distressed or dissuaded by the momentary lack of such hard evidence, for isn't it absurd to think that Hemingway, in spite of Fitzgerald's efforts to keep quiet his use of Hemingway as Philippe (see Fitzgerald's correspondence with Maxwell Perkins), would not have heard about it through his well-developed literary grapevine? Moreover, given what is clearly the mutual intensity of the Fitzgerald-Hemingway relationship, I suggest that it is axiomatic that they both read everything that the other published. And when Hemingway read the Philippe stories we can be certain that he recognized himself; we can count on it.

There is another kind of evidence of Hemingway's response to Philippe. In 1953, when he traveled south through France by car, as Baker reports, "Ernest amused himself by imagining that he was a medieval knight riding his horse" along the Loire. He continued his knightly musings all the way south from the valley of the Loire to Spain. When I asked Mary Hemingway about this trip, her answers were revealing:

> HRS: Did Ernest do this often—I mean, openly play the medieval knight?
> MH: Well . . . I wouldn't say often. [Laughter.] At least not publicly.
> HRS: Then it was the Loire Valley that triggered it on this trip?
> MH: Yes, I suppose so. We'd been up at Chartres, admiring the medieval knights in the stained glass and the sculpture. Then we drove through the Loire Valley. Maybe it was that awful Fitzgerald stuff about Ernest as a medieval knight that he was thinking about.
> HRS: The Philippe stories?
> MH: Was that the name Fitzgerald used? I'd forgotten.[24]

At the time of this "interview," I had little interest in the Philippe stories, so I did not pursue the matter. Clearly, Mary Hemingway knew about them, and Hemingway's role in them, and perhaps she had discussed them with him. At the very least, it is fascinating to have her suggestion that, nearly two decades after the appearance of Philippe, Hemingway might have been *playing* Philippe and thinking about Fitzgerald's characterization.

There is still another kind of evidence of Hemingway's response to Philippe. I propose that Philippe of Villefranche, Fitzgerald's Count of Darkness, is twinned with Philip of Madrid, Hemingway's counter-espionage agent in *The Fifth Column*. At first I resisted this notion, a rather startling intertextuality that has never before been noted or suggested, but I am now convinced that the final Fitzgerald-Hemingway dialogue occurs in these works, the most neglected of each writer. That is, I propose that *The Fifth Column* is, in part, a deliberate response to Fitzgerald's stories.

Consider the texts: darkness is setting and theme in both Fitzgerald and Hemingway; *The Fifth Column* begins in darkness, with Madrid under shellfire, with discussion of going to a cave for shelter, with the hotel electrician shouting, in an "almost prophetic voice," "*Camaradas, no hay luz!*"[25] The opening dialogue—"Have you seen Philip?" "Philip who?" "Our Philip" "Our Philip was . . . with that Moor" (4)—echoes playfully Fitzgerald's identification of Philippe as a rather mysterious character with Moorish connections. In act 1, scene 2, Hemingway establishes another aspect of Philip's character with the recounting of his antics in a bar, "blessing people" from a cuspidor (5). This, of course, does not represent, as some Hemingway critics would have it, Hemingway's rejection of the Church's rituals, but it does point to Philip's antic disposition, his cover for his true identity as secret agent, and it does resonate with Philippe's fear of blasphemous deeds (the "false oath," the dark ceremonies with the Witch Cult).

Hemingway's opening scenes establish his relationship with Dorothy Bridges. (Does her name reflect Philippe's ambition to *bridge* the Loire, and the metaphorical bridging of Christianity and the Witch Cult provided by Griselda?) Dorothy is a "big blonde," and her long hair, "blonde like a wheat field" (48), is just one of her features that closely resemble that other tall blonde, Griselda, whose long hair streams around her head "as if the two shocks of it were golden wings." Both Dorothy and Griselda covet fine things and nice clothing—Dorothy flaunts a fancy cape, Griselda wants a fancy cape—and their selfish desires in the midst of the deprivation of the people around them outrage both Philip and Philippe. Philippe scolds Griselda, declaring his oneness with the people—"They're *us*, I'm *them*"—and Philip lets Dorothy know that he is with the people now, that he's through with the idle rich and the Riviera and all that: "I've been to all those places and I've left them all behind" (98). In fact, the characterization of Dorothy may owe as much—or more—to Fitzgerald's Griselda as it does to Martha Gellhorn, who is generally seen as Hemingway's model for Dorothy.

Moreover, the matter of France and Spain figures importantly in both Fitzgerald and Hemingway. Philippe comes north from the luxury of Moorish Spain to reclaim his French homeland from chaos. Philip comes south from France, where he has spent much of his life in luxury, to struggle, to fight—in solidarity with peasants, "Moorish tarts," and others—to save Spain. Philippe fights the Northmen, Philip fights the Germans. Philippe takes a Duke hostage, Philip takes a German general hostage. Philippe is determined to fight as long as it takes to win his wars, and he will play whatever games necessary to win; Philip proclaims: "We're in for fifty years of undeclared wars and I've signed up for the duration" (95)—and he too will play the games of darkness and counter-espionage necessary to win. Of course, Philippe and Philip are both strong, tough men, firm in their discipline, imperious in command.

Philippe's last name is Villefranche, which may seem to echo indirectly in all of Philip's talk about the resorts of the Riviera. Philip's last name is Rawlings, which resonates with the rawness of Philippe as well as his bizarre lingo, so awkwardly deployed in Fitzgerald's curious dialogue. Philip Rawlings speaks curiously, too, in a strange pastiche of tough American and civilized English. Moreover, much is made, in the world of both Philip and Philippe, of "secret lingo," of passwords and code words and secret societies.

A good deal more could be said of echoes and resonances, but the heart of the matter is this: Philippe and Philip are both engaged in a "struggle for mastery," and for both the struggle is military and political, personal and spiritual. Both fight to redeem the time and bring order to a place in the name of the people. Both struggle in the darkness and are troubled by the deals they make with darkness—for Philippe, the Witch Cult, for Philip, the Stalinist cult. In these works, Fitzgerald and Hemingway engage, however irresolutely, the dark, ill-lighted places of the human spirit; both writers brood the Dark Night of the Soul, and the dark souls of their knights: Philippe, Count of Darkness, and Philip, Counter-espionage agent. If *The Fifth Column* is, in part, a response to Fitzgerald's Philippe, it is Hemingway's rather clumsy effort to show how Philippe-Philip must realize his knightly mission in the Waste Land of a war-torn modern world (just as Fitzgerald hoped that his "portrait of Ernest as Philippe" would make, define, the "real *modern* man"; emphasis added). Bruccoli and all previous commentators to the contrary, I think we do have Hemingway's response to Philippe.

If we further consider *The Fifth Column* as a response to the Philippe stories, we must bear in mind that Hemingway's play was written in December 1937 and published in October 1938. Only three of the Philippe stories had been printed by these dates; the last, "Gods of Darkness," was written and submitted to *Redbook* in December 1934 but was not published until 1941 because, as Bruccoli has it, "*Redbook* gave up on the series." [26] Still there is the possibility—for which I have not yet located hard evidence—that Hemingway saw a copy of the final Philippe manuscript in the intervening years. Moreover, given the fact that Fitzgerald extensively revised "Gods of Darkness" (can we determine exactly when he did so?), there are further compelling intertextual possibilities. I suggest that Fitzgerald recognized the Philip-Philippe resonances in *The Fifth Column*, and this recognition inspired him in the direction of revisions, expansion, and completion of the Philippe chronicle.

Consider, as evidence, the correspondence between Perkins and Fitzgerald from March 9 through December 30, 1938. On April 8, for example, Perkins writes Fitzgerald that he has received the manuscript of "*the play*," which he refers to only as "*Philip*." Perkins gives Fitzgerald a summary of the play's action, including quotation of two key passages, and concludes that "Philip" is "really splendid." He also notes that at the same time he received the

"Philip" manuscript he received a letter in which Hemingway "especially mentioned you."[27] Responding to this letter, Fitzgerald writes (April 23): "As to Ernest, I was fascinated by what you told me about the play, touched that he remembered me. . . . and fascinated, as always, by the man's Byronic intensity." Then, a few paragraphs later, he informs Perkins that he has "gone back to the idea of expanding the stories about Phillippe [sic]." The letters from this period contain ongoing references to Philip and Philippe. On December 24, after "Philip"/*The Fifth Column* is published, Fitzgerald writes a long letter detailing his plans regarding *Philippe:* 1) that it should be "entirely rewritten and pulled together into a 30,000 word novelette"; 2) that *Philippe* "is to some extent completed in the 4th story"; and 3) "I can find time for such a rewrite of *Phillipe* [sic] as I contemplate—I could finish it by the first of February."[28]

Thus the haunting Fitzgerald/Hemingway and Philippe/Philip intertextuality continues to unfold. Who can guess where it might have led had Fitzgerald lived to complete *Philippe*? We do know that a few years after Fitzgerald's death Hemingway created another character, a young man who loves France, whose story begins in the shadow of a medieval castle/walled city in France. In various manuscript stages his name is *Philip*; by the time *The Garden of Eden* was as finished as it would get, his name was David. And then, of course, there is Philip Haines, who might be regarded as another unfinished self-portrait by Hemingway. Could it be that Fitzgerald's portrait of Philippe-Hemingway, whatever else it accomplished, provided for Hemingway a long-standing coded name for his excessively autobiographical characters? Finally, it should be noted that if one central reason that the Philippe stories fail has to do with Fitzgerald's "fascination" with the personality of Hemingway and the attendant paucity of *created* character, the same rubric may be applied to *The Fifth Column.* The play fails miserably, it has been argued, because of Hemingway's "narcissism," as Carlos Baker puts it, because of the way Hemingway freighted Philip with "so many of his own personal traits, desires, and allusions."[29] Arguably, then, "Philip"/*The Fifth Column* fails due to redoubled "fascination": Hemingway's fascination with Fitzgerald's "fascination," with the portrait of Philippe-Hemingway, with the self-portrait of Philip inscribed on the Philippe palimpsest, and so forth, ad infinitum.

In conclusion, while I record here my agreement with critical judgments of the Philippe stories as Fitzgerald's *worst* published fiction, and *The Fifth Column* as Hemingway's *worst* published writing, it is nevertheless essential that we move beyond the rather flip philippics these works have elicited when, in passing, they have been noted at all. Philip and Philippe *are* fascinating failures; and if the fascination is, at last, merely personal, or largely biographical, still the entire matter of Philippe—especially as redefined here—does cast a rare, strange light on the Fitzgerald-Hemingway relationship. Perhaps it all adds up to a dark caveat, warning writers not to center their work on old friends, or on the fictions of old friends.

NOTES

1. Fitzgerald, *Notebooks*, 159.
2. Bruccoli, *Some Sort of Epic Grandeur*, 388; Lewis, "Fitzgerald's 'Philippe, Count of Darkness,'" 29; Moyer, "Fitzgerald's Two Unfinished Novels," 240; Anderson, "Fitzgerald After *Tender Is the Night*," 44–45; Smith, "Colonial Ancestors of Francis Scott Key Fitzgerald," 496.
3. Moreland, *Medievalist Impulse*, 133; Hays, "Philippe, 'Count of Darkness,'" 303. These two essays, which appeared after this essay was written, are useful contributions to the slowly growing body of commentary on the Philippe stories, although they do not engage the matters with which I am concerned here.
4. Given the necessity here of extensive quotation and summary of the Philippe stories—little-known texts that are rather difficult to access—I have chosen to dispense with internal citation of the three stories available only in *Redbook*, to avoid pointless documentation and unnecessary textual clutter.
5. Brief mention of Philippe occurs sporadically in Hemingway studies. Carlos Baker devotes one paragraph to Philippe in his 697-page biography (*Ernest Hemingway*, 273–74). However, there is no evidence that Hemingway critics or biographers have actually read the Philippe stories, let alone studied them for their significant Fitzgerald-Hemingway resonances. If the Fitzgerald-Hemingway relationship is as central to the lives and careers of both writers as we generally seem to believe, this neglect of Philippe is a most curious anomaly. The anomalous neglect verifiable by bibliographic survey is underscored by scholarly conversation: at dozens of Hemingway conferences I have asked scores of my Hemingway colleagues about Philippe. At most, four or five persons were vaguely aware of Philippe, though they had not read the stories.
6. "In the Darkest Hour" is the only one of the four to be collected; it appears in Fitzgerald, *Price Was High*, 512–29. All subsequent page references to "In the Darkest Hour" are to the 1979 edition and appear parenthetically in the text.
7. Bruccoli, *Some Sort of Epic Grandeur*, 387; Bruccoli, *Fitzgerald and Hemingway*, 181.
8. Lewis, "Fitzgerald's 'Philippe,'" 23.
9. Fitzgerald must have known that Hemingway—in order to marry his second wife, Pauline, in the Church—had to be interviewed by priests and seek the dispensation of the Archbishopric of Paris to permit Catholic marriage (see Stoneback, "In the Nominal Country of the Bogus," 123–24).

10. Baker, *Hemingway: Selected Letters*, 437–38.

11. For the most detailed discussion of Hemingway's Catholicism and the most extensive documentation of the facts of his conversion to and practice of his faith, see Stoneback, "In the Nominal Country of the Bogus." For detailed treatment of aspects of Hemingway's medievalism, see Stoneback, "From the rue Saint-Jacques."

12. Turnbull, *Scott Fitzgerald*, 270, 37; Allen, *Candles and Carnival Lights*, 122.

13. Stoneback, "In the Nominal Country of the Bogus," *passim.*

14. Baker, *Ernest Hemingway*, 333.

15. Turnbull, *Scott Fitzgerald*, 220.

16. Hemingway's concern with details of Catholic form is illustrated by an incident with Morley Callaghan that Fitzgerald probably heard about. Hemingway insisted on taking Callaghan to visit Chartres Cathedral and "was highly critical of Morley for . . . forgetting to genuflect before the high altar" (Baker, *Ernest Hemingway*, 204).

17. Jeffrey Meyers, even though he fails to grasp either the facts or the more subtle aspects of Hemingway's Catholicism, does note the unavoidable fact that Hemingway identified with Catholic ritual and custom, that it "satisfied the medieval superstition he nourished" (*Hemingway*, 186). See also Stoneback, "In the Nominal Country of the Bogus," 133–35 and *passim.* In addition, my extensive conversations and interviews with Hemingway family and friends—Mary Hemingway, Gregory Hemingway, Toby Bruce, George Herter, William Walton, and others—confirm what could be regarded as Hemingway's medieval peasant mode of superstitious fondness for the sign of the cross and the triple (trinitarian) knock on wood. William Walton, in the course of many conversations with me over the years, repeatedly referred to Hemingway as a "medieval peasant" when it came to his Catholicism, and Walton, of course, witnessed the "double sign" in point here. Santiago, in *The Old Man and the Sea*, is another case in point.

18. Baker, *Hemingway: Selected Letters*, xx.

19. See Stoneback, "From the Rue Saint-Jacques," *passim.*

20. Bruccoli, *Fitzgerald and Hemingway*, 180.

21. Baker, *Ernest Hemingway*, 273, 274.

22. Ibid., 511.

23. Fitzgerald, *Price Was High*, 512; Bruccoli, *Fitzgerald and Hemingway*, 181. Perhaps the reason Bruccoli thinks that there is not much in the portrait of Philippe that is recognizable as Hemingway is illuminated by this passage from Bruccoli's discussion of "The Crack-up": "The greatest hero Fitzgerald found was life-dominating Ernest Hemingway. The intensity of Fitzgerald's identification with Hemingway is hard to understand. . . . Fitzgerald saw Hemingway as someone who shared his values—which is puzzling at first. Fitzgerald was a great believer with a 'heightened sensitivity to the promises of life.' Hemingway confronted an antagonistic world in which there was *nothing to believe* except courage. . . . The Hemingway code provided a method for enduring in the *absence of traditional beliefs.* . . . the Hemingway hero copes . . . by substituting courage and discipline for the *lost beliefs*" (Bruc-

coli, *Scott and Ernest*, 157; emphasis added). While such views have long infected Hemingway criticism and biography, they must — given the overwhelming contrary evidence in Hemingway's life and work — be discarded. Fitzgerald knew (far better than most commentators on Hemingway know) how *devout*, how *Catholic* Hemingway was. For the purposes of this essay, it is clear that we cannot *get* Fitzgerald's portrait of Philippe-Hemingway, that devout medieval knight, unless we get the facts and subtleties of Hemingway's Catholicism straight.

24. I had numerous conversations with Mary Hemingway, primarily during the years 1976–82; none of these conversations were scholarly "interviews," thus there was never, strictly speaking, a *topic* to be pursued. It is worth stressing that Philippe was the furthest thing from my mind in the conversation quoted here; Mary Hemingway raised the Philippe question without any prodding. My notes on this conversation indicate that it took place in the winter of 1979.

25. Hemingway, *"The Fifth Column" and the First Forty-Nine Stories*, 13. All subsequent page references to *The Fifth Column* are to the 1938 edition and appear parenthetically in the text.

26. Fitzgerald, *Price Was High*, 512.

27. Kuehl and Bryer, *Dear Scott/Dear Max*, 243–44; emphasis added.

28. Ibid., 244–45, 251.

29. Baker, *Ernest Hemingway*, 385–86.

WORKS CITED

Allen, Joan M. *Candles and Carnival Lights: The Catholic Sensibility of F. Scott Fitzgerald*. New York: New York University Press, 1978.

Anderson, William R. "Fitzgerald After *Tender Is the Night*: A Literary Strategy for the 1930s." *Fitzgerald/Hemingway Annual* 1979: 39–63.

Baker, Carlos. *Ernest Hemingway: A Life Story*. New York: Scribners, 1969.

——, ed. *Ernest Hemingway: Selected Letters—1917–1961*. New York: Scribners, 1981.

——. *Hemingway: The Writer as Artist*. Princeton, N.J.: Princeton University Press, 1972.

Bruccoli, Matthew J. *Fitzgerald and Hemingway: A Dangerous Friendship*. New York: Carroll and Graf, 1994.

——. *Scott and Ernest: The Authority of Failure and the Authority of Success*. New York: Random House, 1978.

——. *Some Sort of Epic Grandeur: The Life of F. Scott Fitzgerald*. New York: Harcourt Brace Jovanovich, 1981.

Fitzgerald, F. Scott. "The Count of Darkness." *Redbook*, June 1935, 20–23, 68, 70, 72.

——. "Gods of Darkness." *Redbook*, November 1941, 30–33, 88–91.

——. "The Kingdom in the Dark." *Redbook*, August 1935, 58–62, 64, 66–68.

——. *The Notebooks of F. Scott Fitzgerald*. Ed. Matthew J. Bruccoli. New York: Harcourt Brace Jovanovich/Bruccoli Clark, 1978.

——. *The Price Was High: The Last Uncollected Stories of F. Scott Fitzgerald*. Ed. Matthew J. Bruccoli. New York: Harcourt Brace Jovanovich, 1979.

Hays, Peter L. "Philippe, 'Count of Darkness,' and F. Scott Fitzgerald, Feminist?" In *New Essays on F. Scott Fitzgerald's Neglected Stories*. Ed. Jackson R. Bryer. Columbia: University of Missouri Press, 1996. 291–304.

Hemingway, Ernest. *"The Fifth Column" and the First Forty-Nine Stories*. New York: P. F. Collier, 1938.

Kuehl, John, and Bryer, Jackson R., eds. *Dear Scott/Dear Max: The Fitzgerald/Perkins Correspondence*. New York: Scribners, 1971.

Lewis, Janet. "Fitzgerald's 'Philippe, Count of Darkness.'" *Fitzgerald/Hemingway Annual 1975*: 7–32.

Meyers, Jeffrey. *Hemingway: A Biography*. New York: Harper & Row, 1985.

Moreland, Kim. *The Medievalist Impulse in American Literature: Twain, Adams, Fitzgerald, and Hemingway*. Charlottesville: University Press of Virginia, 1996.

Moyer, Kermit W. "Fitzgerald's Two Unfinished Novels: The Count and the Tycoon in Spenglerian Perspective." *Contemporary Literature* 15 (1974): 238–56.

Smith, Scottie Fitzgerald. "The Colonial Ancestors of Francis Scott Key Fitzgerald." In *Some Sort of Epic Grandeur: The Life of F. Scott Fitzgerald*, by Matthew J. Bruccoli. New York: Harcourt Brace Jovanovich, 1981. 496–509.

Stoneback, H. R. "From the rue Saint-Jacques to the Pass of Roland to the 'Unfinished Church on the Edge of the Cliff.'" *Hemingway Review* 6, no. 1 (1986): 2–29.

——. "In the Nominal Country of the Bogus: Hemingway's Catholicism and the Biographies." In *Hemingway: Essays of Reassessment*. Ed. Frank Scafella. New York: Oxford University Press, 1991. 105–40.

Turnbull, Andrew. *Scott Fitzgerald*. New York: Scribners, 1962.

PART FOUR

Toward an American Tradition

Fitzgerald's Twain

EDWARD GILLIN

In *The Far Side of Paradise,* Arthur Mizener offered an insight that still merits attention: "At every stage of his career F. Scott Fitzgerald made a hero out of the most representative and brilliant man he knew." Before college Fitzgerald had found idols on football fields, in athletes with golden names like Sam White and Hobey Baker and Buzz Law. The roster eventually expanded to include such glittering additions as Ernest Hemingway, Gerald Murphy, and Irving Thalberg. And if Fitzgerald had his heroes, he also knew well the highest form of praise. "When I like men I want to be like them," Fitzgerald wrote in one of his notebooks. "I want to lose the outer qualities that give me my individuality and be like them. I don't want the man; I want to absorb into myself all the qualities that make him attractive."[1]

Van Wyck Brooks, who grew up and attended school with Fitzgerald's editor Maxwell Perkins, never knew of this confessed mimetic tendency in the writer Perkins helped to discover. When Brooks published *The Writer in America* thirteen years after Fitzgerald's death, ironically enough he chose F. Scott Fitzgerald as a perfect example of a talent who'd floundered in "perpetual adolescence" for want of a proper literary guide. "How many . . . American writers have grown up in a world that afforded no hint of a model for their emulation," Brooks asked, "so that in their youth they never saw a writer whom they would have 'cared to resemble' and scarcely heard of one in their country or their region?" F. Scott Fitzgerald, Hart Crane, and other modern American writers, "unsure of themselves and unsure of their tradition," were so many literary orphans, according to Brooks.[2]

Brooks's diagnosis of Fitzgerald's plight, at least, was both perceptive and dead wrong. A precocious writer such as Fitzgerald undoubtedly did require models to build his career upon; at times his life was a naked plea for guidance, support, and validation. But there was also, from the beginning of that professional career, a dimension of earnest purpose that Brooks never fathomed. Shortly after he left Princeton, the young Fitzgerald had announced to a bemused Edmund Wilson, "I want to be one of the greatest writers who have ever lived."[3] What might have startled Wilson further, considering his friend's propensity to "be like" those he admired and to "absorb" their qualities, is that the one writer F. Scott Fitzgerald wished to become had in fact already existed—a figure Van Wyck Brooks had played a part in creating.

As Robert Sklar has noted briefly, there were "uncanny similarities" between the young author and someone he was interested in during the early 1920s—Mark Twain. Both grew up in the provincial Midwest. Both were raised by strong mothers and weak fathers. They were pranksters and self-promoters. And Fitzgerald certainly evinced the same confusion of awe, envy, and resentment toward great wealth that characterized Twain's career.[4] But the number of such traits that F. Scott Fitzgerald developed *after* the time Mark Twain's legend first swam into his ken suggests a case "uncanny" beyond Sklar's sense of the term.

Existing records establish that Fitzgerald's study of Mark Twain was at least as thorough as his knowledge of those hitherto more "recognized" influences such as Tarkington, Wells, James, and Conrad. He was forcibly struck by Twain's short novel *The Mysterious Stranger*, for instance, which appeared posthumously in 1916. Although he himself owned the illustrated first edition, by 1921 he was rummaging through London bookstores to obtain a copy for friend Shane Leslie.[5] In 1923, he still proclaimed *The Mysterious Stranger* "a startling revelation" and one of the "ten best books" he had read.[6] When Perkins mailed Fitzgerald a copy of *The Ordeal of Mark Twain* in 1920, the editor noted that Brooks's study brought to mind "views which you had expressed frequently." In subsequent letters between the two, Fitzgerald would toss in knowing references to "Mark Twain's essays" and "Paine's biography"[7]—the latter a three-volume, 1,700-page examination of Twain that Fitzgerald, never known at Princeton for intellectual doggedness, assured Edmund Wilson was "excellent." (He wrote H. L. Mencken he was "revelling in" the same work.[8]) In letters, book reviews, and fiction of the period Fitzgerald referred to Twain a number of times. His personal library holdings contained a good number of

Twain's short works, in collections such as *Sketches New and Old* and *The Man That Corrupted Hadleyburg and Other Stories*.[9]

Occasionally he obtained a fancy volume such as a 1923 illustrated version of *The Prince and the Pauper*. Some of these books (most notably his copy of the Brooks study) are heavily underlined and annotated. *The Mysterious Stranger* has a fly-sheet listing of Twain works that have been pencil-checked; beneath this Fitzgerald inscribed two more titles, including *What Is Man?*, a collection of posthumous essays published in 1917. If such a checklist represents Fitzgerald's methodical survey of an earlier author, the investigation may have been reaching its nether ends by October 1921. At that time the young author, confessing himself "sick to my stomach" with modern fiction, begged Mencken where he might obtain a copy of Twain's obscure venture into pornography, *1601*.[10] A great deal of more accomplished, more significant, and even more provocative Mark Twain primary material was in print and widely available at the time Fitzgerald made the request: how much had he already exhausted?

Certainly he was by this time adept at dropping Twainian references with an air of casual assuredness. Book reviews by Fitzgerald in the early 1920s show him, here describing Twain as "a man of exceptional talents," there (apparently alluding to *Life on the Mississippi*) noting Twain's devotion to the piloting profession. Any aura of glibness behind such passing remarks is dispelled when they are set against a 1922 interview in which Fitzgerald accurately relates an anecdote involving Mark Twain and Bret Harte. The length and detail of his retelling demonstrate that the story's source — probably Paine's three-volume biography, where the events are described in detail[11] — was more than passingly familiar to the young author of *This Side of Paradise*. And over a dozen years later Fitzgerald, by then a member of the International Mark Twain Society, would dutifully verify a lifelong admiration by sending this organization a testimonial to *Huckleberry Finn*, "the first to look back at the Republic from the perspective of the West."[12] Over and over it becomes plain that Fitzgerald's library holdings are not to be compared to Jay Gatsby's gorgeous roomful of volumes with uncut pages. Fitzgerald clearly *read* his Twain books.

Nor was the early reading without impact. Even as Fitzgerald absorbed more and more titles, it seems that Mark Twain's literary performances were shaping his own. This is well established in a story such as "The Curious Case of Benjamin Button," for which Fitzgerald openly acknowledged a Twainian source.[13] But Twain's influence may also be detected in a piece such as "Dalrymple Goes Wrong." In this early story, Fitzgerald twits the wages-of-sin doctrine through the saga of Bryan Dalrymple, an unprincipled war veteran who cheats and lies his way not to the penitentiary but to a promising career in the state senate. The cynicism of the narrative follows a pattern that Twain had employed in such sketches as "Luck" (where a general's every blunder leads to some staggering military victory) and "The Story of a Bad Little Boy" (about the title character's unwarranted good fortune throughout life). The craven Dalrymple shows himself a hero when "he had had behind him the moral support of half a billion people" but becomes a "bandit" when pitted alone "against that same moral pressure."[14] *What Is Man?* had argued Twain's familiar views of determinism and conscience in closely corresponding rhetoric. Twain's philosophical question-and-answer dialogue demonstrates that an individual loves "the approval of his neighbors and the public" more than peace; hence, he notes, even a timid man can be driven to war. Similar concerns about conscience and selfishness permeate the concluding sections of *This Side of Paradise,* where Amory Blaine "interrogates" himself in a series of questions and answers about life that strongly resemble the catechismal format and the contents of Twain's book. When Amory discovers his own "selfishness" and intends to use the discovery to "bring poise and balance into my life,"[15] he precisely summarizes Twain's prescriptions for reconciling selfishness with the human need for self-approval.

Fitzgerald may have made equally adept use of Twain's lighter side. One Twain tale in a collection Fitzgerald owned, "The £1,000,000 Bank-Note," might have inspired such stories as "The Offshore Pirate" and "Myra Meets His Family," with their similar blends of hoax-tale and romance. But perhaps none of Fitzgerald's early writing reveals the influence of Mark Twain so much as his early travel pieces:

> God damn the continent of Europe. It is of merely antiquarian interest. Rome is only a few years behind Tyre and Babylon. . . . France made me sick. Its silly pose as the last thing the world has to save. I think it's a shame that England and America didn't let Germany conquer Europe. It's the only thing that would have saved the fleet of tottering old wrecks. My reactions were all philistine, anti-socialistic, provincial and racially snobbish. I believe at last in the white man's burden. We are as far above the modern Frenchman as he is above the Negro. Even in art! Italy has no one.[16]

The remarks come not from one of Twain's *Quaker City* notebooks but from a 1921 Fitzgerald letter. Fitzgerald's posture as "philistine" here reveals no expatriate-era internationalism, no cultured veneer of Princetonian cosmopolitanism. Rather it expresses a gruff jingoism akin to that of the American author who'd once hay-raked the Old World and its Old Masters, and who'd notoriously described humanity as a form of animal life between the angels and the French.

Not surprisingly, when Fitzgerald wrote to literary agent Harold Ober proposing to write a series of twelve travel articles, he named his ambitious model: "I swear they will be, in book form, the biggest thing of their kind since 'Innocence Abroad' [sic]."[17] Although Fitzgerald's travel book never fully developed, certain essays such as "The Cruise of the Rolling Junk" and "How to Live on Practically Nothing a Year" bear a decidedly Twainian stamp. The latter, for example, opens as the narrator flings a bogus fortune-teller from a skyscraper window—a broad touch of farcical violence right out of the southwestern humor tradition that inspired similar Twainian narrators to "assassinate" troublesome guides and beggars.

Fitzgerald also varies his narrative personae just as Twain did in his travel writings. One moment he plays the smug American "vandal" impatient with a Parisian waiter's incomprehensible language ("His French strikes me as very bad"); the next moment he is the naive "innocent" seeking information from a wary Briton. (Finding that "getting an answer from an Englishman is about as complicated as borrowing a match from the Secretary of State," he corners one wheelchair invalid who "jerked spasmodically" but proves "unable to leave his seat.") "All the celebrities of Europe have spent a season in Cannes," Fitzgerald tells us in his "How to" article. "Even the Man with the Iron Mask whiled away twelve years on an island off its shore."[18] Neither the places nor the irreverent attitudes toward them have changed much since Twain's travels. (It is noteworthy that the narrator of *The Innocents Abroad* had previously situated the Man in the Iron Mask as though he were a complacent tourist residing "for a season" on the Isle d'If.[19])

When Fitzgerald becomes a motorist, in "How to Live on Practically Nothing a Year," his rickety automobiles are as unimpressive as the ignoble steeds that bore Twain through the Far West and the Holy Land:

> Now when you run up to somewhere you have to have an automobile, so we bought the only new one in town next day. It had the power of six horses—the age of the horses was not stated—and it was so small that we loomed out of it like giants; so small that you could run it under the veranda for the night. It had no lock, no speedometer, no gauge, and its cost, including the parcel-post charge, was seven hundred and fifty dollars. We started for Cannes in it, and except for the warm exhaust when other cars drove over us, we found the trip comparatively cool.[20]

Twain admirers will appreciate not just the tall-tale tradition evoked in such a passage but also its deft manipulation of comic exaggeration and understatement. The techniques are comparable to those of the literary humorist who'd once deadpanned about crowded berth conditions on a Hawaiian coastal schooner, "One might swing a cat in it, perhaps, but not a long cat."[21]

In a *Smart Set* article appearing right between the issues that carried Fitzgerald's first professional fiction, the trusted Mencken had already saluted Twain as, "by long odds, the largest figure that ever reared itself out of the flat, damp prairie of American literature."[22] Another Fitzgerald confidant and mentor, Maxwell Perkins, was also a Clemens admirer. As already noted, he had sent his young author a copy of *The Ordeal of Mark Twain* in June 1920. This was barely two months after the publication of Fitzgerald's first novel and his marriage to Zelda Sayre. During one of the most productive and hectic years of his life, Fitzgerald was then seeing *Flappers and Philosophers* through its proofs. Nonetheless, he found time to read Brooks's volume almost immediately. In a week he was writing back to Perkins, "I can't tell you how much I liked 'The Ordeal of Mark Twain.' Its [*sic*] one of the most inspirational books I've read and has seemed to put the breath of life back in me. Just finished the best story I've done yet & my novel is going to be my life's masterpiece."[23] If *The Beautiful and Damned* proved less than that, the biographical criticism that Fitzgerald saluted as one of its inspirations may still merit attention.

Van Wyck Brooks had presented Twain as a satirist born gifted, on a par with Swift or Voltaire. But he charged that Twain's hunger for financial success and popular affection conspired with the mediocre standards prevailing in American culture. And so a native literary genius atrophied, according to *The Ordeal of Mark Twain*, ultimately expending itself in works packed with violent humor and crude philosophical gloom. Brooks's account is particularly hard on the institution of marriage. *The Ordeal* tends to shift a great deal of blame for Mark Twain's corruption onto the invalided shoulders of Olivia Langdon Clemens. Livy's genteel Elmira constituted, in Brooks's phrase, "an intricate system of privilege and convention" in which Twain had to "make good"—and the publication of his best-selling *Innocents Abroad* provided the key introduction. "His provisional acceptability in this new situation," Brooks noted acidly, "was due not to his genius but to the fact that he was able to make money by it." Furthermore, this initial acceptance locked Twain into a lavish lifestyle of partying and entertaining, eastern-fashion, "absolutely committed to a scale of living such as no mere literary man at the outset of his career could ever have lived up to."[24]

The admonition to future authors here is unmistakable. And it is entirely logical to assume that Fitzgerald might heed it. After all, he had secured the on-again, off-again engagement to Montgomery belle Zelda Sayre only after *This Side of Paradise* rescued him from the unpromising future ill-omened by his hardscrabble work as an advertising copywriter. Even as he read *The Ordeal of Mark Twain*, New York City after the Armistice was opening up to the young Fitzgeralds boundless opportunities for extravagance; as the author later wrote, "We felt like small children in a great bright unexplored barn." [25] Thus it is not unreasonable to fit *The Ordeal of Mark Twain* into systems such as those proposed by Robert E. Long and James E. Miller, whereby a reformed Fitzgerald goes out to seek higher models for his writing (Conrad, James) and purer models for his life. [26]

The facts, though, suggest that Fitzgerald did not immediately shun a sullied Mark Twain. He did much of the previously mentioned reading and made some of the favorable comments about Twain after his absorption in Van Wyck Brooks. In a 1922 book review of Charles Norris's novel *Brass*, Fitzgerald identified Mark Twain as "a man of exceptional talent"; another review labeled Booth Tarkington the "best humorist since Mark Twain." [27] Clearly, the appeal of Mark Twain as an author had not vanished as a result of Brooks's condemnation.

Nor does Fitzgerald appear to have been deterred from the spell cast by Twain's personality. Fitzgerald undoubtedly read *The Ordeal of Mark Twain* in earnest. As Sklar and Long have contended, the book should have had some chastening effect on the young author. But if Fitzgerald noticed Brooks's puritanical condemnation of the Clemenses' lavish lifestyle ("There were always guests; they were coming and going constantly" [28]), what Fitzgerald *did* at this time constitutes the well-known saga of riotous glamour and high living in Prohibition-era New York. From 1920 to 1922, in the midst of that wild spree, he published two novels and two collections of short fiction. All sold very well. By 1922 he was also working up an assault on Broadway, beginning "an awfully funny play that's going to make me rich forever." [29] The theatrical smash would be a pipe dream, of course, and Fitzgerald's biographers are left with the sheer spectacle of the financial waste in those frenzied years. Mizener can only express wonder at it all: "A man who intends to be a serious writer in the twentieth century knows that he will be lucky to average a quarter of Fitzgerald's income over a lifetime; and it is hard to believe anyone could be so subject to extravagance that he would have to sacrifice his whole career to it." [30]

Yet such financial waste was only a symptom of greater profligacy in Brooks's subject. The far graver charge leveled in *The Ordeal of Mark Twain* involved the waste of raw talent. To support that enormous, reckless lifestyle, Brooks had maintained, Twain demeaned himself by undertaking lucrative hackwork as a journalist and magazine sketch writer, employment which brought him popularity at the cost of artistic development. What is striking about this now-familiar critical diagnosis is the extent to which F. Scott Fitzgerald followed its pattern *subsequent* to his reading of *The Ordeal of Mark Twain*. In an analysis of Fitzgerald's literary career, Matthew J. Bruccoli attributes to Fitzgerald an "abysmal sense of literary public relations."[31] Bruccoli cannot explain such failure in light of what he considers the high goals Fitzgerald cherished for his work. As with the mystery Mizener mentions, this riddle may be solved by a daring proposal—namely, that Fitzgerald might have chosen the waste and excess of his early professional career (and deliberately advertised the fact of his profligacy) *in conscious imitation* of a literary idol.

Such a speculation certainly helps to explain the endless letters where the writer laments the painful frittering of talent on second-rate magazine pieces. (Fitzgerald, one discovers, was almost always the first critic to denigrate one of his own stories; frequently his is a comparatively rare negative voice.) It would also help account, in its way, for the author's frequent boasts of forthcoming royalties, and his complaints when book sales lagged. Fitzgerald's correspondence and meticulously kept ledgers insured a permanent record of the business side of his profession—the side Brooks implicitly urged true artists to disdain. Indeed, the pre-*Gatsby* period when Long and Miller (among others) wish to consider Fitzgerald a novice entering some Conradian or Jamesian order of high art unavoidably corresponds with his period of work on *The Vegetable*, the play explicitly designed to secure popularity and fortune for its author. How could a conscience-stricken reader of *The Ordeal of Mark Twain* come to this pass?

The first explanation of the paradox lies within Brooks's portrait itself. Many elements in the exaggerated indictment, while socially "correct" in the 1920s, would hardly alienate a young romantic like F. Scott Fitzgerald. For that Twain legend featured the stuff of romance: the young provincial who succeeds in the glamorous East; the lover's self-abnegation on behalf of a beautiful woman; the individual whose reckless overreaching somehow reifies the excesses of his era. By sternly representing Twain as an utterly failed artist, "the supreme victim of an epoch in American history,"[32] the critic clearly intended to rally the Young Generation against society's cruel deficiencies in culture and taste. But in the process Brooks had created a tragic hero. And it was this hero Fitzgerald seized on for his second novel.

The Beautiful and Damned is a magnum opus on waste, as its sardonic epigraph ("The victor belongs to the spoils") forecasts. Literary discussions in the novel hum with a current of Brooksian ideas, especially related to the prostitution of art. When Dick Caramel follows a promising first novel, *The Demon Lover*, with a string of popular successes, Anthony Patch cautions him against producing "trash." The literary warning has no effect. Much later in the novel, when Caramel's name has become "almost a byword of contempt," Patch will scan his friend's collected novels in his personal library— "'The Demon Lover,' true enough . . . but also seven others that were execrably awful, without sincerity or grace"—wedged into a bookshelf alongside works by Mark Twain.[33] This glance into the literary destiny of Richard Caramel was written in 1921, while *This Side of Paradise* was still enjoying healthy sales and reputation. However much a reader might incline to associate Caramel's career with his creator's, it was plainly too soon for Fitzgerald to have personally experienced anything like the wasted energies and overwhelming literary mistakes of his author-character. At the time Fitzgerald composed *The Beautiful and Damned* the most plausible model for Richard Caramel couldn't have been himself, in other words; but it very well could have been that "failed" writer he'd been reading about in Van Wyck Brooks's *The Ordeal of Mark Twain*. Fitzgerald does not appear to embrace the Brooks censures uncategorically—Twain's name, coupled with Dreiser's among "contemporary novelists" represented in the library, stands in ironic contrast with Dick Caramel's— but Fitzgerald obviously wished to engage Brooks's theme of the great strains that American society places on its talented sons. Caramel had earlier tried to justify his "downright cheap" stories as an attempt to "widen his audience": "Wasn't it true that men who had attained real permanence from Shakespeare to Mark Twain had appealed to the many as well as to the elect?"[34] Anthony Patch and Maury Noble can only nod their heads in sad disapproval; they presumably have a proper Brooksian sensitivity toward the tragic perils that underlie such reefs of thought.

But if *The Ordeal of Mark Twain* stimulated a youthful Fitzgerald's vision of a hero of grand failure, his more confident side found encouragement in Albert Bigelow Paine's flattering official biography. (It is helpful to remember that Fitzgerald read *Mark Twain, a Biography* after he'd finished Brooks's tendentious study—and then he'd enthusiastically recommended the three-volume work to Edmund Wilson and H. L. Mencken.) In Paine's account, Fitzgerald would have encountered some close parallels between Twain's youth and his own. Here was Twain the cruelly sensitive boy who wouldn't reach eight before a brother and sister died of childhood diseases, matching Fitzgerald's own terrible sense that the early deaths of two sisters had marked the psychic origins of his literary career. Fearful resonances exist, too, in the parents' tense marriages, in the maternal dominance of each family, in the mutual scrapes with poverty. Twain, like Fitzgerald, transformed his boyhood "imagination of disaster" into a creative spirit that led him from West to East, to marriage and fame. And Paine's biography is brightened by frequent depictions of the author's winning self-effacement, his enthusiasm for current projects, his kindness toward fellow artists—all attributes that Fitzgerald might have recognized in his own personality.

F. Scott Fitzgerald had a natural fondness for children, and he surely did not need to learn such feelings from the affectionate father and family man immortalized in the Paine biography. It is reasonable to believe, though, that Twain's playful storytelling and his willingness to participate in his daughters' amateur theatricals were facets of personality that heightened Fitzgerald's capacity for identifying with the author from an earlier generation. (At one point, Paine mentions Twain's ability to spin an enchanting tale for his daughters from a mere glance at a picture on the wall; one immediately recalls Fitzgerald's remarkable semiautobiographical narrative based on impromptu storytelling, "Outside the Cabinet-Maker's.") Fitzgerald evidently could charm his daughter with fairy tales; he'd also join her friends in putting together shows and creating games. Years later a grown-up Scottie Fitzgerald would recall being taught the entire chronological sequence of English kings and queens from one of the games her father invented. Intriguingly, Paine's biography had emphasized that the precise goal of the history games that Mark Twain designed for his young "playmates" was to teach the reigns of English monarchs in historical sequence.[35]

Paine describes how Twain fled to Europe for literary stimulation when the East Coast environment distracted him, and of course Fitzgerald would join a whole literary generation in reverse migration. But when Europe proved no ultimate sanctuary, the Fitzgerald family followed the Clemenses' pattern of restless relocation in this country and abroad. In neither case did marriage ever involve settling down. With weird appropriateness, one of the houses Fitzgerald moved into most expectantly—hoping to restore order to his family life while accomplishing serious literary work—was "Ellerslie" in Wilmington, Delaware. The author might have at the time vaguely recalled a story and a photograph in his treasured copy of the Paine biography. "Ellerslie" had been the name given to a play cottage that satisfied the Clemens children's "hunger for retreat" at Quarry Farm, the idyllic haven where Mark Twain drafted much of his greatest work.[36]

From the opening pages of *Mark Twain, a Biography*, with the first-volume depiction of John Marshall Clemens's money struggles, there is an intense preoccupation with financial success and failure. Twain's own Horatio Alger rise to the world of wealth exemplified by his Hartford mansion is exquisitely detailed, even as Paine notes the accumulating frequency of foolhardy speculations and business ventures. Then near the end of volume 2, disaster strikes. With the failure of his publishing house and his typesetter investment, Twain faces bankruptcy. The author confronts, in his waning years, the most grievous threat to a man's reputation — the peculiarly awful nineteenth-century disgrace of financial ruin. What follows is masterful storytelling. Despite a profound loathing for the lecture circuit — where the artist in Twain feels he must degrade himself to the level of "buffoon" — despite a killing schedule of engagements, the writer who had exposed the Gilded Age's lack of honor travels around the world to pay off his creditors "one hundred cents on the dollar." [37] His one-man financial crusade is an open secret. An entire planet that had grown to laugh at his jokes and then admire him for his social convictions now embraces him for his sterling character. Paine's narrative values Twain's other accomplishments, naturally: the literary achievements, the social crusading, the personal magnetism. But it is this emergence from debt that finally seems to assert the man's greatness. Where Brooks saw only tragic failure, Paine found triumphant heroism in the author's life.

To Fitzgerald this alternative vision offered its own compelling promise. For Paine's biographical portrait reverberates on the note that Twain had quite completely known "his people and his period," [38] becoming American literature's representative man. This celebration of the great *and* popular writer was easier to relish as a model than Brooks's tragic figure, certainly, since it offered the pleasant vision of having it all — reckless and extravagant youth, passion, genius, near madness, despair — plus the overwhelming personal triumph that Brooks had denied. Not surprisingly, Fitzgerald's description of the ideal literary man he'd hoped to become sounds like Paine's hybridized hero: "an entire man in the Goethe-Byron-Shaw tradition, with an opulent American touch, a sort of combination of J. P. Morgan, Topham Beauclerk and St. Francis of Assisi." [39]

Of course, the masterstroke of Twain's financial recovery proved difficult to match, and Fitzgerald must have chafed under his profound handicaps. Though securing Zelda's hand may have seemed similar to Mark Twain's courtship of Olivia Langdon in the common compulsion to prove some economic potential to "make good," the Langdons had definitely contributed far greater material benefit to the Clemens marriage than the Sayres had been able to provide the Fitzgeralds. Thus the younger author could never squander such a great fortune, because he would never possess one. Nonetheless, the Fitzgeralds could — and would — waste and spend, earn and waste again, every bit as profligately as anyone before them. Fitzgerald periodically announced his horror at the sudden "discovery" of terrible indebtedness throughout his career—in 1924-25, in 1929, in the mid-1930s, at the end of his life. After expressing suitable repentance each time, he'd immediately sit down to work his way out of the difficulty. The amount of indebtedness seemed to grow more and more disastrous each time, the challenge of recovery greater. But one of the cruelest ironies of the situation was the *loss* of esteem Fitzgerald sensed with each fresh endeavor, despite the increased burden of trying to climb out of debt while the depression dried up his fiction markets. When he poured his efforts into writing short stories for the magazines or scripts for Hollywood—potboiling that played the essential role in his career that journalism and lecturing played in Twain's—Fitzgerald must have wondered that his labor was met with contempt rather than respect even by his closest friends. He may have always cherished a hope that the brilliant triumph-from-the-ashes achieved by Paine's hero would climax his own career. Yet in the end came a final irony. Dying before the comeback, Fitzgerald's most typical epitaph would mirror that accorded the "tragic" hero of Brooks's analysis: the supreme victim of an epoch in American history.

Nevertheless, a sensitivity to the way the green light of the "two" Twains beckoned to Fitzgerald early in his career must keep this from becoming the final word. For if Fitzgerald could be criticized by contemporaries for his courtship of glitter and worship of dazzle—condemned by Brooks in unconscious repetition as another half-developed, perpetually adolescent author— he also gained significance from a profound involvement with his own time, the sort of identification Albert Paine had prized in his biographical subject. There is, after all, a powerful artistic truth behind the fact that each writer used his fiction near the start of his career to christen his respective era. Twain's Gilded Age remains as essential a part of the American story as Fitzgerald's Jazz Age.

Like so many moderns, Fitzgerald sometimes chafed at the writer's need for a public; yet he also understood the role of democracy in literature. "Art invariably grows out of a period when, in general, the artist admires his own nation and wants to win its approval," he wrote in one notebook. "This fact is not altered by the circumstance that his work may take the form of satire, for satire is the subtle flattery of a certain minority in a nation. The greatest grow out of these periods as the tall head of a crop."[40] Here, instead of posing as Brooks's ideal artist-revolutionary, Fitzgerald sounds a note that seems far truer to his career than any of the "models" for writers fashionable during his time. For Fitzgerald would become no Joycean exile but rather the quintessence of his generation. His career crystallized almost every phase of the American 1920s and 1930s: the jazzy exuberance that followed the Great War, the boom of the mid-1920s, the crushing blows of 1929, years of depression, and the grim resolve toward recovery. He was a sensitive student of history who appreciated his own role in defining the generation to which he belonged. And this — perhaps his most enduring legacy — may partially have stemmed from a desire to emulate the great American writer who had once represented, in his own turn, the boisterous Mississippi River frontier of the 1830s and 1840s, the sectional strife of Civil War, the subsequent excesses of American industrialism, and the unsettling emergence into a fearful new century.

The young Fitzgerald could not know how an identification with Mark Twain, how an almost mystical splitting and doubling of personality, would turn out, of course, when he acquired — probably soon after its 1917 publication — his copy of Twain's philosophical work *What Is Man?* This was a posthumous release, its author already dead seven years. What made Scott Fitzgerald's volume most remarkable, therefore, was its unique presentation inscription. "F. Scott Fitzgerald," the faded ink on its flyleaf read, "from Mark Twain F. S. Fitzgerald."[41] The writing is in Fitzgerald's own deliberate hand.

NOTES

1. Mizener, *Far Side of Paradise*, 99; Wilson, *Crack-up*, 329.
2. Brooks, *Writer in America*, 75–76, 83.
3. Wilson, "Thoughts on Being Bibliographed," 54.
4. Sklar, *F. Scott Fitzgerald*, 138.
5. Turnbull, *Letters*, 379.
6. Fitzgerald, "10 Best Books I Have Read," 67, 68.
7. Kuehl and Bryer, *Dear Scott/Dear Max*, 30, 46.
8. Wilson, *Crack-up*, 256; Bruccoli and Duggan, *Correspondence*, 88.
9. Kuehl, "Scott Fitzgerald," 190. The appendices to this study contain valuable information concerning the Twain-related holdings in Fitzgerald's personal library.
10. Bruccoli and Duggan, *Correspondence*, 88.
11. Bruccoli and Bryer, *F. Scott Fitzgerald in His Own Time*, 127; Fitzgerald, "Defeat of Art," 12; Bruccoli and Bryer, *F. Scott Fitzgerald in His Own Time*, 252–53; Paine, *Mark Twain*, 2:587–88.
12. Bruccoli and Bryer, *F. Scott Fitzgerald in His Own Time*, 176.
13. Fitzgerald, *Tales of the Jazz Age*, ix.
14. Fitzgerald, *Flappers and Philosophers*, 236.
15. Twain, *What Is Man? and Other Essays*, 54–55; Fitzgerald, *This Side of Paradise*, 280.
16. Turnbull, *Letters*, 326.
17. Bruccoli, *As Ever*, 76.

18. Fitzgerald, *Afternoon of an Author,* 101, 102, 107, 109.
19. Twain, *Innocents Abroad,* 104.
20. Fitzgerald, *Afternoon of an Author,* 108.
21. Twain, *Roughing It,* 444.
22. Budd, *Critical Essays on Mark Twain,* 43.
23. Kuehl and Bryer, *Dear Scott/Dear Max,* 31.
24. Brooks, *Ordeal of Mark Twain,* 109, 111.
25. Wilson, *Crack-up,* 28.
26. Long, *Achieving of "The Great Gatsby,"* 171–73; Miller, *Fictional Technique of F. Scott Fitzgerald,* 67–81.
27. Bruccoli and Bryer, *F. Scott Fitzgerald in His Own Time,* 127, 131.
28. Brooks, *Ordeal of Mark Twain,* 131.
29. Kuehl and Bryer, *Dear Scott/Dear Max,* 271n.
30. Mizener, *Far Side of Paradise,* 195.
31. Bruccoli, *Fitzgerald and Hemingway,* 134–35.
32. Brooks, *Ordeal of Mark Twain,* 267.
33. Fitzgerald, *Beautiful and Damned,* 188, 422.
34. Ibid., 422, 222.
35. Fitzgerald, *Six Tales of the Jazz Age and Other Stories,* 5–6; Paine, *Mark Twain,* 2: 751–52 and 3:1437–38.
36. Paine, *Mark Twain,* 2:825.
37. Ibid., 2:1007.
38. Ibid., 2:657.
39. Wilson, *Crack-up,* 84.
40. Ibid., 179.
41. Kuehl, "Scott Fitzgerald," 191.

WORKS CITED

Brooks, Van Wyck. *The Ordeal of Mark Twain.* New York: E. P. Dutton, 1920.
———. *The Writer in America.* New York: E. P. Dutton, 1953.
Bruccoli, Matthew J. *Fitzgerald and Hemingway: A Dangerous Friendship.* New York: Carroll & Graf, 1994.
Bruccoli, Matthew J., ed., with the assistance of Jennifer McCabe Atkinson. *As Ever, Scott Fitz—: Letters between F. Scott Fitzgerald and His Literary Agent Harold Ober—1919–1940.* Philadelphia: J. B. Lippincott, 1972.
Bruccoli, Matthew J., and Jackson R. Bryer, eds. *F. Scott Fitzgerald in His Own Time: A Miscellany.* Kent, Ohio: Kent State University Press, 1971.
Bruccoli, Matthew J., and Margaret M. Duggan, eds., with the assistance of Susan Walker. *Correspondence of F. Scott Fitzgerald.* New York: Random House, 1980.
Budd, Louis J., ed. *Critical Essays on Mark Twain, 1919–1980.* Boston: G. K. Hall, 1983.

Fitzgerald, F. Scott. *Afternoon of an Author: A Selection of Uncollected Stories and Essays*. Ed. Arthur Mizener. 1957. New York: Scribners, 1969.

———. *The Beautiful and Damned*. New York: Scribners, 1922.

———. "The Defeat of Art." *Fitzgerald/Hemingway Annual 1977*: 11–12.

———. *Flappers and Philosophers*. 1920. New York: Scribners, 1959.

———. *Six Tales of the Jazz Age and Other Stories*. New York: Scribners, 1960.

———. *Tales of the Jazz Age*. New York: Scribners, 1922.

———. "10 Best Books I Have Read." *Fitzgerald/Hemingway Annual 1972*: 67–68.

———. *This Side of Paradise*. New York: Scribners, 1920.

Kuehl, John. "Scott Fitzgerald: Romantic and Realist." Diss. Columbia University, 1958.

Kuehl, John, and Jackson R. Bryer, eds. *Dear Scott/Dear Max: The Fitzgerald-Perkins Correspondence*. New York: Scribners, 1971.

Long, Robert E. *The Achieving of "The Great Gatsby": F. Scott Fitzgerald, 1920–1925*. Lewisburg, Penn.: Bucknell University Press, 1979.

Miller, James E. *The Fictional Technique of F. Scott Fitzgerald*. The Hague: Martinus Nijhoff, 1957.

Mizener, Arthur. *The Far Side of Paradise*. Boston: Houghton Mifflin, 1951.

Paine, Albert Bigelow. *Mark Twain, A Biography: The Personal and Literary Life of Samuel Clemens*. 3 vols. New York: Harper, 1911.

Sklar, Robert. *F. Scott Fitzgerald: The Last Laocoön*. New York: Oxford University Press, 1967.

Turnbull, Andrew, ed. *The Letters of F. Scott Fitzgerald*. New York: Scribners, 1963.

Twain, Mark. *The Innocents Abroad, or, The New Pilgrims' Progress*. Hartford, Conn.: American Publishing Company, 1869.

———. *Roughing It. The Works of Mark Twain*. Vol. 2. Ed. Franklin R. Rogers and Paul Baender. Berkeley: University of California Press, 1972.

———. *What Is Man? and Other Essays*. New York: Harper, 1917.

Wilson, Edmund, ed. *The Crack-up*. New York: New Directions, 1945.

———. "Thoughts on Being Bibliographed." *Princeton University Library Chronicle 5*, no. 2 (1944): 51–61.

NOTES ON CONTRIBUTORS

DANA BRAND is associate professor and chair of the Department of English at Hofstra University. He is the author of *The Spectator and the City in Nineteenth-Century American Literature* and of articles on a variety of topics in American literature and film, most recently "Rear-View Mirror: The American City and the American Male in Alfred Hitchcock's 'Rear Window'" in *Hitchcock's America*.

JACKSON R. BRYER is professor of English at the University of Maryland. He is cofounder and president of the F. Scott Fitzgerald Society and author of *The Critical Reputation of F. Scott Fitzgerald*; editor of *F. Scott Fitzgerald: The Critical Reception, The Short Stories of F. Scott Fitzgerald: New Approaches in Criticism*, and *New Essays on F. Scott Fitzgerald's Neglected Stories*; and coeditor of *F. Scott Fitzgerald in His Own Time: A Miscellany, Dear Scott/Dear Max: The Fitzgerald-Perkins Correspondence, The Basil and Josephine Stories*, and *French Connections: Hemingway and Fitzgerald Abroad*.

CATHERINE B. BURROUGHS is visiting associate professor of English at Wells College and lecturer at Cornell University. Her publications include *Reading the Social Body* and *Closet Stages: Joanna Baillie and the Theater Theory of British Romantic Women Writers*. Her edited volume, entitled "Women in British Romantic Theatre: Drama, Performance, and Society, 1790–1840," is forthcoming from Cambridge University Press."

RICHARD ALLAN DAVISON is professor of English at the University of Delaware. He has published three books on Frank, Charles, and Kathleen Norris and more than sixty articles in such journals as *Modern Fiction Studies, Studies in Short Fiction, Modern Drama, Journal of Modern Literature, American Literary Realism, American Literature, Studies in American Fiction*, and *Hemingway Review*. He is coediting a book of interviews with contemporary American actors and actresses, "The Actor's Art," and writing a study of the New York theater in 1958.

STEVEN FRYE is professor of English at Antelope Valley College. He has published articles on Herman Melville, James Fenimore Cooper, William Gilmore Simms, and Charles Brockden Brown in such journals as *Leviathan, Kentucky Review, Southern Quarterly*, and *American Studies*. He has also published literary essays and book reviews in *Centennial Review, Modern Fiction Studies*, and *Western American Literature*.

GEORGE GARRETT is the author of eight novels, including his "Elizabethan Trilogy" (*Death of the Fox, The Succession*, and *Entered from the Sun*); seven books of short

269

fiction, including his collected stories, *An Evening's Performance*; eight volumes of poetry, most recently *Days of Our Lives Lie in Fragments: New and Old Poems, 1957–1997*; and five books of nonfiction, including a biography of James Jones. He has also written two published plays and three produced screenplays, translated plays by Plautus and Sophocles, and edited twenty-one books. He recently retired as Henry Hoyns Professor of Creative Writing at the University of Virginia.

EDWARD GILLIN is associate professor of English at the State University College of New York in Genesco. He is the author of numerous essays and book reviews on Fitzgerald and has also published articles on Herman Melville, Thomas Wolfe, Lillian Hellman, and several Irish playwrights. He is working on a book about Mark Twain and the American Civil War.

EDWARD J. GLEASON is associate professor and former chair of the Department of English at Saint Anselm College. In addition to his work on Fitzgerald, he is researching a biography of André Dubus.

BRUCE L. GRENBERG retired in 1995 as associate professor of English at the University of British Columbia. He is the author of *Some Other World to Find: Quest and Negation in the Works of Herman Melville*, and of essays in *Chaucer Review*, *Modern Fiction Studies*, *Fitzgerald/Hemingway Review*, and elsewhere.

JOHN KUEHL retired in 1988 as professor of English at New York University. He died on May 25, 1998. He was the author of *John Hawkes and the Craft of Conflict*, *Alternate Worlds: A Study of Postmodern Antirealistic American Fiction*, and *F. Scott Fitzgerald: A Study of the Short Fiction*; editor of *Write and Rewrite: A Study of the Creative Process* and *The Apprentice Fiction of F. Scott Fitzgerald: 1909–1917*; and coeditor of *Dear Scott/Dear Max: The Fitzgerald-Perkins Correspondence*, *The Basil and Josephine Stories*, and *In Recognition of William Gaddis*.

RICHARD LEHAN is professor of English and American literature at the University of California, Los Angeles. Among his publications are two books on Fitzgerald, *F. Scott Fitzgerald and the Craft of Fiction* and *"The Great Gatsby": The Limits of Wonder*, and, most recently, *The City in Literature: An Intellectual and Cultural History*.

ANDRÉ LE VOT taught for many years at the University of Paris III. He is the author of *F. Scott Fitzgerald: A Biography* and of many articles in such journals as *Esprit* and *Le Magazine Littéraire*.

ALAN MARGOLIES is professor emeritus of English at John Jay College of Criminal Justice, CUNY, and cofounder and vice-president of the F. Scott Fitzgerald Society. He is the editor of *F. Scott Fitzgerald's St. Paul Plays: 1911–1914* and of the Oxford World's Classics edition of *The Beautiful and Damned*, and associate editor of *F. Scott Fitzgerald: Manuscripts*. His articles have appeared in *Fitzgerald/Hemingway*

Annual, Twentieth Century Literature, Journal of Modern Literature, Resources for American Literary Study, Princeton University Library Chronicle, and *Papers of the Bibliographical Society of America.*

QUENTIN E. MARTIN has taught at Concordia University and Loyola University. He now lives and teaches in Brussels, Belgium. He has published essays on Hamlin Garland, Ernest Hemingway, and Fitzgerald, and is completing a book on the relationship between Garland's fiction and the Populist movement.

ROBERT A. MARTIN recently retired as professor of English at Michigan State University. He is the editor of *Arthur Miller's Theatre Essays, Arthur Miller: New Perspectives, The Writer's Craft,* and *Critical Essays on Tennessee Williams;* and the coeditor of *Rewriting the Good Fight: Critical Essays of the Spanish Civil War.* He is currently writing a study of Arthur Miller's life and plays.

RUTH PRIGOZY is professor of English and former chair of the Department of English at Hofstra University. She is cofounder and executive director of the F. Scott Fitzgerald Society. She has edited Fitzgerald's *This Side of Paradise* for the Enriched Classics series and *The Great Gatsby* for Oxford's World Classics, and has published articles on Fitzgerald, Salinger, the Hollywood Ten, and filmmakers Billy Wilder and Vittorio DeSica. She is currently editing "The Cambridge Companion to F. Scott Fitzgerald" and working on books on Billy Wilder and on Fitzgerald and American popular culture.

FRANCES KROLL RING worked for F. Scott Fitzgerald for the last twenty months of his life, an experience she has recounted in *Against the Current: As I Remember F. Scott Fitzgerald.* She taught magazine writing at the University of Southern California and held numerous editing jobs for journals, think tanks, and magazines. She is the editor of *A Western Harvest.*

BUDD SCHULBERG is the author of three novels, the first of which, *What Makes Sammy Run?,* won the National Critics Award, and the third of which, *The Disenchanted,* is his portrait of Fitzgerald. His screenplay for *On the Waterfront* won an Academy Award, and he received an Emmy for his television documentary, "The Angry Voices of Watts." His nonfiction books include *Moving Pictures: Memories of a Hollywood Prince* and *Sparring with Hemingway.*

CHARLES SCRIBNER III, an editor at Scribner, is the fifth generation of Charleses to work at the publishing house founded by his great-great-grandfather in 1846. There he oversees the works of such classic authors as Fitzgerald, Hemingway, and Wolfe. He received his Ph.D. in art history from Princeton University and is the author of *Rubens* and *Bernini,* among other publications in the field of Baroque art.

SCOTT F. STODDART is associate professor of English at Nova Southeastern University. He has written articles on Henry James, Stephen Sondheim, E. M. Forster, and

Stephen Crane; film adaptations of Fitzgerald and Wharton; and films by Martin Scorsese, Merchant and Ivory, and George Cukor. His book, *Prescriptive Lenses: The Gay Male Image in Hollywood Cinema*, is due out soon from University of Illinois Press.

H. R. STONEBACK is professor of English and director of graduate studies at the State University of New York at New Paltz. He is the author of *Cartographers of the Deus Loci, Singing the Springs & Other Poems, Hemingway's Paris: Our Paris?*, and more than a hundred published articles on American, British, Chinese, and French literature, more than thirty on Hemingway. Forthcoming work includes a critical glossary of *The Sun Also Rises* and a collection of essays on Hemingway.

BARBARA SYLVESTER is director of the University Writing Program at Western Washington University. She is currently preparing a critical study of Eudora Welty's fiction, identifying her modernist techniques, tracing the interconnections among her works, and articulating the patterns that reveal her developing, coherent thematic vision.

NANCY P. VAN ARSDALE is associate professor and former chair of the Department of English at East Stroudsburg University. Her research interests, besides Fitzgerald, include Edith Wharton, George Bernard Shaw, and professional communication. She was a 1995 Fulbright Scholar in Belgium and Luxembourg. Currently, she is coediting a volume of "Approaches to Teaching *The Great Gatsby*" for MLA.

MICHEL VIEL is professor of English at the University of Paris IV-Sorbonne. He has published several books on English linguistics, including *Initiation raisonnée á la phonétique de l'anglais (A Rational Introduction to English Phonetics)*, edited *Americans in Paris*, and translated *The Great Gatsby*. His articles and reviews have appeared in such journals as *Etudes anglaises, Bulletin de la Société de linguistique de Paris*, and *Historiographia Linguistica*.

INDEX

(all titles by Fitzgerald unless otherwise indicated)